Learn to
Program
with JavaScript™
2014 Edition

John Smiley

Smiley Publishing
Philadelphia

Smiley Publishing

PO Box 2062

Riverton, NJ 08077

U.S.A.

smileypublishing@johnsmiley.com

Learn to Program with JavaScript 2014 Edtion

ISBN: 978-1-61274-062-1

Other books by John Smiley:

How I taught Katy Perry (and others) to program in C++

How I taught Katy Perry (and others) to program in C#

How I taught Katy Perry (and others) to program in Java

How I taught Katy Perry (and others) to program in JavaScript

How I taught Katy Perry (and others) to program in Visual Basic 2010 Express

How I taught Katy Perry (and others) to program in Visual C# 2010 Express

Learn to Program with C#

Learn to Program with C++

Learn to Program with Java

Learn to Program with Java SE6

Learn to Program with JavaScript

Learn to Program with VB.Net 2010 Express

Learn to Program with Visual Basic 6

Learn to Program with Visual Basic 6 Examples

Learn to Program am with Visual Basic 6 Objects

Learn to Program with Visual Basic 6 Databases

Learn to Program with Visual Baisc 2010 Express

Learn to Program with Visual C# 2010 Express

My Climb To The Top (of the Bell Atlantic Tower)

The Complete Book of Stair Climbing 2012 Edition

This book is dedicated to my wife Linda

About the Author

John Smiley, a Microsoft Certified Professional (MCP) and Microsoft Certified Solutions Developer (MCSD) in Visual Basic, has been programming and teaching for more than 25 years. He is the President of John Smiley and Associates, a computer consulting firm serving clients both large and small in the Philadelphia Metropolitan area. John is an adjunct professor of Computer Science at Penn State University, Philadelphia University, and Holy Family College, and also teaches in a variety of Internet venues including SmartPlanet and ElementK.

In the heyday of the Dot-com revolution, John also made two television appearances on ZDTV's popular Screensavers television show.

On the writing front, John is the author of the immensely popular **Learn to Program with Visual Basic 6**, along with (chronologically) Learn to Program with Visual Basic 6 Examples, Learn to Program Databases with Visual Basic 6, Learn to Program Objects with Visual Basic 6, Learn to Program with Java, Learn to Program with VB.Net 2005 Express, Learn to Program with C# (using the .Net C# batch compiler), Learn to Program with Visual C# 2005 Express, Learn to Program with C++ (using the Borland batch compiler) and Learn to Program with JavaScript.

Future plans call for books on Visual Basic.Net 2008 Express, Visual C# 2008 Express, Visual Web Developer, Visual C++, and Python.

Feel free to visit John's Web Site at

http://www.johnsmiley.com

or contact him via email at johnsmiley@johnsmiley.com. He religiously answers all of his emails, although not necessarily instantaneously!

Contents

Acknowledgments

I want to thank first and foremost my wife Linda for her love and support.

This book is now the ninth I've written, and I can tell you it's easily been the most difficult.

I've written this book with no contract from any publisher---I'm told that computer book publishers don't believe there is a market for beginner books any longer. Ultimately, with no publisher in hand, and therefore no up front advance money, I had little financial incentive to finish this book, and have essentially spent a year writing it for free. This book truly has been a desire of love, and my belief that there are beginner programmers out there who will need and want it.

Having said that, I must thank those who still believe in the viability of my books.

Foremost among them is Lisa Wollin, of Microsoft. who emailed me over a year ago and told me that she would love to refer beginning JavaScript programmers to any book on JavaScript that I chose to write. Shortly after receiving her email, I decided to do exactly that. One year later, the book is finished.

Many thanks also go to the thousands of students I've taught over the years for your tireless dedication to learning the art and science of computer programming. Your great questions and demanding persistence in getting the most out of your learning experience truly inspired me, and has contributed greatly to my books. Many of you dragged yourself to class after a long hard day of work, or rose early on your Saturday day off to learn Visual Basic and the other programming languages I have taught. You have my greatest respect and admiration.

I also want to thank the many readers of my first eight books who took the time to write or email me about the books. Most of the time, the correspondence is incredibly glowing---I truly appreciate hearing from each of you, and I want you to know that I read and respond to each email I receive.

Thanks to the students of my Internet based Introduction to JavaScript class, who worked with the manuscript for this book, evaluating it, testing the code, and making suggestions for improvements, especially Tom Buening, Ron Hossler, Mark Nigogosyan, Rosa Pledger, and Rob Rivera. Special thanks to Sam Chiarella, Larry Fundell, Elaine Giles, and Tony Vescio for their many wonderful editing suggestions which have greatly improved the quality of the book.

I want to thank all the members of my family for their continued belief in and support of me over the years, in particular my mother, who continues to say several hundred novenas for the success of my books, and who has probably said just as many for this one I'm sure.

Finally, I want to acknowledge my father, who although not physically here to see this book, is surely flipping through the pages of it now. It's been over twenty five years since I last saw you---and your role in the writing of this and my others books can never be understated---you and mother have been a great inspiration and role model for me. I know that the God who made us all will someday permit us to be together again.

Organizations/Conventions Used in the Book

Each chapter of the book follows in a session in a make-believe college classroom. Read along and learn the material with the rest of the students.

Every chapter has example programs and practical exercises for you to complete. I encourage you to follow along with the example programs---and by all means complete the exercises in the book as well. If typing is not your strong suit, you can download both the completed examples and exercises via this link

http://www.johnsmiley.com/main/mybooks.htm

Care to take a quiz to test your knowledge? Follow this link and you can take a series of multiple choice quizzes drawn from the book

http://www.johnsmiley.com/tester/login.asp

Finally, if the book isn't enough for you to get going with JavaScript, consider joining me in an Internet-based JavaScript class. My introductory classes are held several times throughout the year---and I'll be teaching these classes for as long as I'm sojourning in this dimension. For more information, follow this link...

http://www.johnsmiley.com/main/training.htm

Chapter 1---Where Do I Begin?

"Where do I begin?" is a question I am frequently asked by my students, and this seems like a good question to tackle right at the beginning of this book. In this first chapter, we'll look at the development process of an actual working program through the eyes and ears of my university programming class and you will also be introduced to our 'class project'. By the end of the book, we'll have taken a real-life application through from the concept all the way to the finished product!

> **NOTE: Occasionally, my students get disillusioned when they hear that we won't be diving straight in and coding our application. However, when I remind them that programming is much the same as writing a report (or in other words, it is a two stage process of planning and then producing) they tend to settle down.**

Where Do We Begin

As part of answering the question, "Where do we begin?" this chapter looks at the Systems Development Life Cycle, which is a methodology that has been developed to ensure that systems are developed in a methodical, logical and step-by-step approach. We'll be looking at the Systems Development Life Cycle in quite a bit of detail, since the majority of this book will be spent in developing a real-world application. In this chapter we'll meet with a prospective client and conduct a preliminary interview with him. From that interview (and a subsequent one!) we'll develop a Requirements Statement, which provides details as to what the program should do. This Requirements Statement will form the basis of the application that we will develop throughout the rest of the book

> **NOTE: From this point on, you will follow me as I lead a group of my university students in an actual class on JavaScript. If I do my job right, you will be a part of the class, learning along with them as we complete a fifteen-week course about programming in JavaScript.**

Many books on computer programming have the reader, perhaps as early as the first chapter, code a program which 'cutely' displays a message box that says 'Hello World'. Then the author will point to the fact that within the first few minutes of reading their book, the reader has already written a working program. I'm not so naive as to believe that writing such a program makes you a programmer. Therefore, we'll opt for a slower approach. Simple programs, although great for the ego, are not the programs that are found in the real world. Real-world programs are written to meet someone's needs. These needs are frequently complex and difficult to verbalize. In this book, you and I will embark on a journey together that will see us complete the prototyping stage of a real-world project. I believe that this is the best way to learn programming.

In my university classes, I don't usually introduce the class project until several weeks into the semester. When I finally do introduce the class project, I give the students in my class a Requirements Statement. Since the class project is to develop a JavaScript application, with an event-driven paradigm (look that one up in the dictionary), I never tell my students exactly how the application should look, or how to program it. I tell them only what is required. In other words, I complete the hard part for them - gathering the user requirements.

Programming the Easy Way

When I first began to teach programming, some of my students would tell me that they just didn't know where to start when they first began to work on their programming assignments. They would start to program the application, then stop. Some of them would find themselves re-writing their code and re-designing their application several times. Then they would change it again. Face to face I could usually clear things up for them by giving them a gentle nudge or hint in the right direction. However, their work would show a definite lack of direction. Why the problem? They lacked a plan.

As soon as I realized this, I began to teach them more than just programming. I began to teach them the Systems Development Life Cycle (SDLC), the methodology I mentioned earlier. You see, people need blueprints or maps. They need something tangible, usually in writing, before they can begin a project. Just about all of my students agree that having a blueprint of some kind makes the development process that much easier.

Sometimes I'll meet former students of mine at the university, and I'll ask them how their other programming classes are coming along. Occasionally, they'll tell me that they're working on a great real-world assignment of some kind, but they just don't know where to begin. At that point, I'll remind them of what I told them in class - that they should begin with the design of the user interface, observe the default behavior of the design and then add code to fill in the gaps. That's not the problem, they tell me. The problem is that they don't know how to gather the user requirements for the system. They don't really know what the system should do.

Often the real problem is that the client isn't prepared to give the programmers a detailed enough Requirements Statement. In class the professor distributes a well-defined Requirements Statement but in the real world, programmers need to develop this themselves. Unfortunately, they may not know how to sit down with the prospective user of their system to determine what is required to satisfy the user's needs.

That skill, to listen to the user and determine their needs, is something that I now teach to some extent in all of my computer classes - whether they are programming courses, courses on Systems Analysis and Design, or Database Management.

Planning a Program is Like Planning a House

A friend of mine is a general contractor and home-builder. His job is similar to that of a programmer or system designer. He recently built an addition to a customer's house. He wouldn't think of beginning that work without first meeting with the owner of the house to determine their needs. He couldn't possibly presume to know what the owner wants or needs. The builder's role, in meeting with the owner, is largely to listen and then to advise.

My friend the home builder tells me that certain home owners may want a design that is architecturally unsound - either because their ideas and design are unsafe and would violate accepted building code regulations, or because they would violate local zoning regulations for their neighborhood. In some cases, he tells me, owners ask for features that he is certain they will later regret - and probably hold him responsible for. His role as an advisor demands that he inform the homeowner of these problems.

As soon as my friend believes that he understands what the owner wants, then he prepares a set of blueprints to be reviewed by the homeowner. Frequently the owner, after seeing his own vision on paper, will decide to change something, such as the location of a window or the size of a closet. The concrete characteristics of the blueprints make an agreement between the builder and owner easier to arrive at. The same can be said of a concrete plan for the writing of a program or the development of a system.

The big advantage of developing a plan on paper is that, while the project is still on paper, it's relatively painless to change it. Once the house has been assembled and bolted together, it becomes much more of a problem to change something.

The same is true of a computer program. Although it's not physically nailed or bolted together, once a programmer has started to write a program, changing it becomes very labor-intensive. It's much easier to change the design of a system prior to writing the first line of code.

In the world of software development, you would be surprised how many programmers begin work on an application without really having listened to the user. I know some programmers who get a call from a user, take some quick notes over the phone, and deliver an application without ever having met them! It could be that the user's requirements sound similar to something the programmer wrote last year, so the developer feels that will be good enough for the new client.

Other developers go a step further, and may actually meet with the client to discuss the user's needs. Nevertheless, sometimes the developer may not be a good listener, or just as likely, the user may communicate their needs poorly. The result may be that the user receives a program that doesn't come close to doing what they wanted it to do.

In this course, we'll develop a prototype for a real-world application called the Grades Calculation Project, and then take it through to the complete product. As we progress through the course together, we will work through one possible solution, but I want you to know that in JavaScript programming, the number of solutions are almost infinite. As I tell my students all the time, there are many ways to paint a picture. One of the things I love about teaching JavaScript is that I have never received the same solution to a project twice. Everyone brings his or her own unique qualities to the project.

I want you to feel free to take the Grade Calculation Project and make your solution different from mine. In fact, I encourage it, but you should stick close to the Requirements Statement that we are going to develop in this chapter.

We Receive a Call from our 'client'

During my Fall Semester Visual Basic class, I had been lucky enough to be contacted by a client, Joe Bullina, owner of the Bullina China Shop, who needed a fairly high tech computer program written to produce price quotation for the customers in his shop, and I had used the development of his program as the class project for my Visual Basic course.

JavaScript, by its very nature, is a bit more difficult to learn than Visual Basic, and although I knew I could ask the students in my JavaScript class to write the same program in JavaScript, I also knew that incorporating every feature found in the Visual Basic version of the China Shop program would be difficult to 'squeeze' into a one semester JavaScript course. Furthermore, I also knew that many of those same Visual Basic students would be present in the JavaScript class, and most likely they would be in the mood for a fresh 'challenge'--not a rehash of the China Shop program.

And so I was glad when one Monday morning, about a week before meeting with my JavaScript class for the first time, I received a phone call from Frank Olley, a fellow professor at the University, and Dean of the English Department. Frank and I knew each other well--in fact, at one time he had been a teacher of mine. Frank was wondering if I could write a program that he could use to calculate student grades

I asked Frank if he had considered using a spreadsheet program like Excel to do the calculations---his requirement sounded like a fine application for that.

He told me he had considered Excel--but he ultimately wanted the program to be able to run off of his University Web page---something Excel could not do.

Frank and I agreed to meet on Tuesday afternoon in his office.

We Meet with Our Client

I arrived at Frank Olley's office around 2 p.m. on a sunny Tuesday afternoon. Going into the Liberal Arts building, a large brick building, brought back pleasant memories of my college years. I hadn't been in the Liberal Arts building since I graduated some years back--the Computer Science building was now my haunt.

I found Frank's office, and was greeted by his secretary.

"Hi, I'm John Smiley, I'm here to meet Frank Olley."

"Just a minute Mr. Smiley, Mr. Olley is expecting you."

A few moments later, Frank came out of his office.

"Sorry to keep you waiting, John" Frank said, warmly extending his hand. "I was on the phone with Robin Aronstram and David Burton--I believe you know who they are."

Indeed I did---Robin Aronstram was the chairman of the Mathematics Department and David Burton was the chairman of the Science Department.

"I hope you don't mind if Robin and David attend our meeting," Frank continued, "I think they may want to 'piggyback' some requirements of their own on top of mine.

"Piggyback?" I asked.

"That's right, John," Frank replied. "I saw them both in the Faculty dining room today at lunch, and I mentioned to them that you were coming over to discuss writing a program to calculate student grades---they were wondering if you could include their requirements in the program also."

"I don't see why not," I said. Just then Robin and David arrived. During the course of the next twenty minutes or so the three of them laid out for me their unique requirements. There was a commonality in that each one required a program that could calculate the final grade for a student in their own department---English, Math and Science. On the other hand, each had their own requirements.

NOTE: This project, though 'real world' has been toned down a bit for learning purposes.

"The English Department," Frank Olley explained, "calculates the Final grade for a student taking an English course as 25% of their Midterm grade, 25% of their Final Examination grade, 30% for a semester long Research paper, and--because we expect our students to be able to speak in public and make oral presentations---20% for a half hour long Class presentation."

"The Science Department is similar," David chimed in, "except that we don't require a Class presentation. We calculate the grade for a student taking a Science course as 40% of their Midterm grade, 40% of their Final Examination grade, and 20% for a semester long Research paper."

Robin then explained that for a student taking a Math course, only a Midterm and Final Examination grade entered into the equation. "Each counts 50% toward their final grade," she said.

"Those requirements don't seem terribly complicated," I assured them. "Do you have any details in your mind as to what you want the program to look like?"

"Not really," Frank said. "I guess we were really hoping that you could take care of those details. Don't get us wrong. We know what we want the program to do, that is, calculate a student's grade. Beyond that, our biggest requirement is that the program be simple to use."

"Can you think of anything else?" I asked.

"Eventually, we'd like to have the program be accessible from the Web" David added . He hesitated for a moment and then added hopefully. "What do you think? The program doesn't sound too difficult, does it?"

Famous last words, I thought to myself. "No David, it doesn't," I said, "I could probably write this program in an hour or so...."

Robin noticed that my voice had trailed off.

"What's wrong?" she asked.

"Nothing's wrong," I said, "I was just thinking.."

I explained to Frank, Robin and David that on Saturday I would be meeting with my 'Introduction to Programming with JavaScript ' Spring Semester class for the first time. I then went on to explain to them that in my Fall Semester Visual Basic course, the class and I had developed a real-world application for a client in West Chester.

"Perhaps," I said, "this time around, we could have them work on your requirements as their class project."

Frank looked excited and nervous at the same time. "How would that work?" he asked.

"Well," I said, "each semester I give my JavaScript programming students a project to work on. JavaScript is a bit more complicated than Visual Basic, so although I was tempted to have them work on the same project as my fall semester Visual Basic students, I really thought that might be too much for a first JavaScript class. However, your project sounds ideal, and I think it will excite them. It's better than anything I could ever dream up, because it's real, with a real 'client'--you--- expecting real results. And your requirements, though they seem simple enough from a user point of view, have a few 'quirks' that will make it pretty challenging from a JavaScript programming perspective."

I looked at the group for a reaction. I saw a look of unease on David's face.

"I can take these requirements," I continued, "distribute them to my students on Saturday, and over the course of the semester, they can write the program for you. By the end of the semester, you'll have your program, and they'll have some real experience under their belts. Unless of course, you're in a huge hurry..."

"No," Frank said, "as long as they finish the program by the end of the Spring semester, we can use the program to calculate the grades in each of our departments. Of course, I'm guessing that the program your students write won't be as sophisticated as one that you would write. After all, your students are just beginners."

"Not at all, Frank" I said. "I'll be working with them every step of the way. You can expect a top-notch program, and I have no doubt that we can finish it on time for you to use in May."

I must have said the magic words; at this Frank smiled, extended his hand and said, "That sounds like a deal to me."

"There's just one more thing Frank," I said sheepishly.

"What's that John?" he asked.

"Would it be possible to 'pay' my students something for the development of the program?", I asked. "It doesn't have to be much---but paying them will permit them to legitimately cite this experience as paid professional experience."

"I'm sure there's something in the English Department budget to pay them," Frank said smiling. "How about the Math and Science departments?"

"That shouldn't be a problem," Robin said. "You mentioned that your Fall Semester Visual Basic class wrote a program for a local business. How much did you charge him?"

"He paid us $450," I said. "I was able to give each one of my students."

"Sounds like a bargain to me," David said, "I'm sure each of our departments will be able to kick in $150 for your students work---sounds like a great idea to me."

As I prepared to leave, I warned the group that what we had done this afternoon merely represented the first step, the tip of the iceberg, so to speak, in a six step process known as the Systems Development Life Cycle (SDLC). The first phase, the Preliminary Investigation, had begun and ended with our initial interview. Five phases of the SDLC remained.

As I walked to the door, Frank and I mutually agreed that I would deliver to him, in a week or so, a Requirements Statement drawn from the notes taken at today's meeting. I warned the group that when they read the Requirements Statement that I would send to them, the possibility existed that they would find some things that I had misinterpreted, and perhaps some things that they would be sure they had mentioned that wouldn't appear at all. I told him that the Requirements Statement would act as a starting point for their project. Until I received a confirmation from them confirming the Requirements, neither my student team nor I would proceed with the development of the program.

As I walked out the door of Frank's office, we all exchanged warm 'good byes'. Frank, David and Robin were all genuinely likable people, and I hoped this experience would be a rewarding one for them and the students in my class. I left Frank, Robin and David discussing an upcoming Freshman Social, and I headed off to teach a late afternoon class at the university.

The Systems Development Life Cycle (SDLC)

During my walk to my late afternoon class, I gave a lot of thought to Frank's program. The more I thought about it, the more I believed that having my students write the program was a great idea, and I was sure they would think so too. Working on a real-world application would be a great practical assignment for them. Even more so than something I made up, this project would give each of them a chance to become deeply involved in the various aspects of the SDLC. For instance:

- someone in the class would need to work on the user requirements

- someone else would be involved in a detailed analysis of the Grading program

- everyone would be involved in coding the program

- some students would work on installing the software

- some students would be involved in training and implementation

Four days later, on Saturday morning, I met my 'Introductory Programming with JavaScript' class for the first time.

As is my custom during my first class, I took roll, and asked each of the students to write a brief biography on a sheet of paper. Doing this gives me a chance to get to know them, without the pressure of having to open themselves up to a room full of strangers, although many of them will become good friends during the course of the class.

I only called out their first names as I like to personalize the class as much as possible. Usually, I have some duplicated first names, but this semester, that wasn't a problem.

"Valerie, Peter, Linda, Steve, Katherine Rose."

"If you don't mind, just call me Rose," she said.

"Rhonda, Joe, John."

"Jack, if you don't mind."

"Barbara, Kathy, Dave, Ward, Blaine, Kate, Mary, Chuck, Lou, Bob."

That makes eighteen students.

I began reading over their biographies. A few had some programming experience, using languages that were a bit dated. A number were looking to get into the exciting world of computer programming, either because they had an opportunity at work, or believed one would open up shortly. A couple of them were people looking to get into the work force after years away from it. One of the students, Chuck, was just fifteen, a local high school student.

Another student, Lou, was permanently disabled, and although he didn't look it, he wrote that his disability would probably end up restricting him to a wheelchair.

My classroom is about 40 feet by 20 feet and there are three rows of tables containing PCs. Each student has their own PC, and at the front of the room I have my own, cabled to a projector that enables me to display the contents of my video display.

My first lecture usually involves bringing the class up to a common level so that they feel comfortable with both the terminology and methodology of using a PC-based environment. This time, however, instead of waiting a few weeks before introducing the class project, I could hardly wait to tell them. In the first few minutes of class, I introduced the students to the Grade Calculation Project. Just about everyone in the class seemed genuinely excited at the prospect of developing a real-world application. They were even more excited after I offered to split the profits with them. For most of the class, this was their first programming course---and at its conclusion, they would all be paid as professionals, with a legitimate project to add to their resumes.

"You mean this course isn't going to be the usual 'read the textbook, and code the examples' course," Ward said.

"Exactly," I said, "we'll be developing a real world application, and getting paid for it!"

"How will we know what to do?" Rose asked nervously.

I explained that in today's class, we'd actually develop a Requirements Statement.

"A Requirements Statement," I said, "is just an agreement between the contractor (in this case us) and the customer (in this case Frank, Robin and David) that specifies in detail exactly what work will be performed, when it will be completed, and how much it will cost."

I continued by explaining that at this point, all we had were my notes from my initial interview with them. For the most part, this was just a quick sketch of the program. While we might very well have produced a quick sketch of the user interface in the following hour or so, we still did not know how to write a single line of code in JavaScript. There was still much to learn! Furthermore, while we could probably pretty easily come up with a sketch of what the program would look like, we still needed to concern ourselves with the processing rules (e.g., the calculated grades of the various student types) which Frank, Robin and David had given to me during our meeting.

TIP: Processing rules are known either as Business Rules or Work Rules.

"Can you give us an example of a business rule?" Peter asked.

"Sure Peter," I answered. "A good example would be a web-based ticket purchasing Web site, where customers are typically restricted from ordering large quantities of tickets. The Web site might have a business rule that prohibits the same customer from purchasing more than 4 tickets to the same event."

"That very thing happened to me just last week," Valerie said. "I tried to purchase an entire row of tickets to the upcoming Elton John concert, but the Web site restricted me to just 4."

I pointed out that I had agreed to drop off the Requirements Statement to Frank Olley sometime before we met for class next Saturday. I told my class that there was the possibility that the Requirements Statement would have some mistakes in it, and even some missing items. Frank might very well see something on the Requirements Statement that would cause him to think of something else he wants to the program to do. I cautioned them not to be too hasty at this point in the project. There was still a lot of planning left to do!

"Such hastiness," I said, "is exactly why the Systems Development Life Cycle was developed."

TIP: The SDLC was developed because many systems projects were developed which did not satisfy user requirements and the projects that did satisfy user requirements were being developed over budget or over time.

I saw some puzzled looks. I explained that the Systems Development Life Cycle (SDLC) is a methodology that was developed to ensure that systems are developed in a methodical, logical and step-by-step approach. There are six steps, known as phases, in the Systems Development Life Cycle:

Different companies may have different 'versions' of the SDLC. The point is that just about everyone who does program development can benefit from one form or other of a structured development process such as this one.

- The Preliminary Investigation Phase

- The Analysis Phase

- The Design Phase

- The Development Phase

- The Implementation Phase

- The Maintenance Phase

I continued by explaining that out of each phase of the SDLC, a tangible product, or deliverable, is produced. This deliverable may consist of a Requirements Statement, or it may be a letter informing the customer that the project cannot be completed within their time and financial constraints. An important component of the SDLC is that at each phase in the SDLC, a conscious decision is made to continue development of the project, or to drop it. In the past, projects developed without the guidance of the SDLC were continued well after 'common sense' dictated that it made no sense to proceed further.

"Many people say that the SDLC is just common sense," I said. "Let's examine the elements of the SDLC here. You can then judge for yourself."

Phase 1: The Preliminary Investigation

I told my class of my meeting with Frank, Robin and David, which essentially constituted the Preliminary Investigation Phase of the SDLC.

"This first phase of the SDLC," I said, "may begin with a phone call from a customer, a memorandum from a Vice President to the director of Systems Development, or a letter from a customer to discuss a perceived problem or deficiency, or to express a requirement for something new in an existing system. In the case of the Grades Calculation program, it was a desire on the part of Frank Olley to develop a 'program' to calculate grades of English students in his department---of course, you already know how it's quickly grown beyond that to include the Math and Science departments."

I continued by explaining that the purpose of the Preliminary Investigation is not to develop a system, but to verify that a problem or deficiency really exists, or to pass judgment on the new requirement.
The duration of the preliminary investigation is typically very short, usually not more than a day or two for a big project, and in the instance of the Grades Calculation Project, about an hour.

The end result, or deliverable, from the Preliminary Investigation phase is either a willingness to proceed further, or the decision to 'call it quits'. What influences the decision to abandon a potential project at this point? There are three factors, typically called constraints, which result in a go or no-go decision.

- Technical. The project can't be completed with the technology currently in existence. This constraint is typified by Leonardo Da Vinci's inability to build a helicopter even though he is credited with designing one in the 16th century. Technological constraints made the construction of the helicopter impossible.

- Time. The project can be completed, but not in time to satisfy the user's requirements. This is a frequent reason for the abandonment of the project after the Preliminary Investigation phase.

- Budgetary. The project can be completed, and completed on time to satisfy the user's requirements, but the cost is prohibitive.

"In the case of the Grade Calculation Project," I told my students, "Frank and I never came close to dropping the project. This is a project that all of us really wanted to pursue. And paying us something to do the programming is just icing on the cake!"

Needless to say, the students and I formally decided to take on the project, and proceed with the second phase of the SDLC.

Phase 2: Analysis Phase

The second phase of the SDLC, the Analysis phase, is sometimes called the Data Gathering phase.

NOTE: In this phase we study the problem, deficiency or new requirement in detail. Depending upon the size of the project being undertaken, this phase could be as short as the Preliminary Investigation, or it could take months.

I explained that what this meant for my class was potentially another trip to the Liberal Arts building to meet with Frank, Robin and David to gather more detailed requirements, or to seek clarification of information gathered during the Preliminary Investigation.

> **WARNING: As a developer, you might be inclined to believe that you know everything you need to know about the project from your preliminary investigation. However, you would be surprised to find out how much additional information you can glean if you spend just a little more time with the user.**

You might be inclined to skip portions of what the SDLC calls for, but it forces you to follow a standardized methodology for developing programs and systems. As we'll see shortly, skipping parts of the SDLC can be a big mistake, whereas adhering to it ensures that you give the project the greatest chance for success.

I told them that while some developers would make the case that we have gathered enough information in Phase 1 of the SDLC to begin programming, the SDLC dictates that Phase 2 should be completed before actual writing of the program begins.

"The biggest mistake we could make at this point would be to begin coding the program. Why is that? As we'll see shortly, we need to gather more information about the business from the 'owner'---in this case Frank, Robin and David. There are still some questions that have to be asked."

In discussing the SDLC with the class, I discovered that one of my students, Linda Schwartzer, had some Systems Analysis experience. Linda offered to contact Frank Olley, to set up an appointment to spend part of the day with the person who currently calculates the grades for the English department. This meeting would fulfill the data-gathering component of the Analysis Phase. In the short time I had spent with Linda, I sensed a great communicative ability about her, and so I felt very comfortable with Linda tackling the Analysis phase of the SDLC.

Typically, our first class meeting is abbreviated, and since we were basically frozen in time until we could complete Phase 2 of the SDLC, I dismissed the class for the day. Prior to Linda's meeting with Frank Olley, I emailed the following to him:

Hi Frank,

I want to thank you for taking the time to meet with me last Tuesday afternoon. As I discussed with you at that time, it is my desire to work with you in developing a program that can calculate student grades for the English, Math and Science departments.

The program will be developed as part of my Introduction to JavaScript computer class at the university. As such, your costs will be $450, payable upon final delivery of the program. In return, you agree to allow me to use your contract to provide my students with a valuable learning experience in developing a real-world application.

Sometime during the coming week, one of my students, Linda Schwartzer, will be contacting you to arrange to spend part meeting with the person who currently calculate grades in the English department. Although you may not see the necessity in this additional meeting, it will satisfy the next phase of the Systems Development Life Cycle I discussed with you at our meeting. Adhering strictly to the SDLC will result in the best possible program we can develop for you.

I'd like to take this opportunity to highlight the major points we discussed last week. We will develop a PC-based program, for you, with an eye toward web enabling it also. Here are the major functions that the developed program will perform:

1. This program will provide the user with a user-friendly interface for calculating a student's grade.

2. The user will be requested to designate the type of student--English, Math or Science---for which they wish to calculate a grade.

3. If the user indicates they wish to calculate the grade for an English student, the interface will prompt them for a Midterm examination grade, a Final examination grade, a Research Paper grade, and a Presentation grade. The final grade will be calculated as 25% of the Midterm examination grade, 25% of the Final examination grade, 30% of the Research Paper grade, and 20% of the Presentation grade.

4. If the user indicates they wish to calculate the grade for a Science student, the interface will prompt them for a Midterm examination grade, a Final examination grade, and a Research Paper grade. The final grade will be calculated as 40% of the Midterm examination grade, 40% of the Final examination grade, and 20% of the Research Paper grade.

5. If the user indicates they wish to calculate the grade for a Math student, the interface will prompt them for a Midterm examination grade, and a Final examination grade. The final grade will be calculated as 50% of the Midterm examination grade and 50% of the Final examination grade.

6. Once calculated, the grade will be displayed on the interface.

I think I've covered everything that we discussed last Tuesday. If I have missed anything, please let Linda know when she arrives in your office.

Regards,

John Smiley

This email, in essence, will become the Requirements Statement that we will formally develop shortly. The next day I received the following fax from Frank Olley:

Dear John

I reviewed your email, and everything looks fine.

One thing we forgot to mention last Tuesday is that the numeric grades need to be converted to 'letter' grades for report card purposes. Complicating matters is that the letter grade equivalents of all the departments are different. Here is a table explaining the breakdown.

DEPT	ENGLISH	MATH	SCIENCE
A	93 OR GREATER	90 OR GREATER	90 OR GREATER
B	85 TO 93	83 TO 90	80 TO 90
C	78 TO 85	76 TO 83	70 TO 80
D	70 TO 78	65 TO 76	60 TO 70
F	LESS THAN 70	LESS THAN 65	LESS THAN 60

Regards,

Frank Olley

Complicate the program? Sure, a bit. I was sure Linda would more than likely find other surprises as well. This new 'requirement' was about par for the course. I checked my notes, and Frank was correct---he never mentioned it. Of course, a good developer can anticipate requirements such as these. I just missed it.

Linda called me on Monday morning to tell me that she had arranged to meet with Frank Olley on Thursday morning. That Thursday evening Linda called to tell me that her observations of the English, Math and Science Department's current operations had gone well. Contrary to what I expected, she saw nothing in her observations of their day-to-day operation that contradicted the notes that I took during my preliminary investigation.

However, Linda reported that nothing out of the usual occurred. She did tell me that from her observations, it was obvious that the program would pay for itself in no time. All three departments had work-study students performing the calculations manually---and making lots of mistakes.

That Saturday, I again met with our class. After ensuring that I hadn't lost anyone in the intervening week (yes, everyone came back), we began to discuss the third phase of the SDLC---the Design phase.

Phase 3: Design Phase

"Phase 3 of the SDLC is the Design phase," I said.

I explained that design in the SDLC encompasses many different elements. Here is a list of the different components that are 'designed' in this phase:

- Input
- Output
- Processing
- File

"Typically," I said, "too little time is spent on the design phase. Programmers love to start programming." I continued by saying that you can hardly blame them, writing a program is exciting, and everyone wants to jump and in and start writing code right away. Unfortunately, jumping immediately into coding is a huge mistake.

"After all," I said, "you wouldn't start building a house without a blueprint, would you? You simply cannot and should not start programming without a good solid design."

> **NOTE: Even though at this point the class knew very little about JavaScript, they were already familiar with computer applications of one kind or other--either Microsoft Windows program, Macintosh programs, Linux programs or Web based programs (a knowledge of one of these is a requirement for the course). Designing and developing the 'look' of an application program is really independent of the tool that you'll use to program it.**

> **I should point out here that my role in the Design Phase was to act as a guide for my students. Frank Olley had told us what he wanted the program to do. Like any 'client', he described his program requirements in functional terms that he understood.**

> **My students were already familiar with computer applications, but at this point in our course, they were not JavaScript experts. However, knowing how to use a program was not sufficient for them to know how Frank Olley's requirements translated into the terms of a JavaScript program. Ultimately, it was my job to help them translate those requirements into JavaScript terms.**

I pointed out that critics of the SDLC agree that it can take months to complete a house, and making a mistake in the building of a house can be devastating; writing a JavaScript program, on the other hand, can be accomplished in a matter of hours, if not minutes. If there's a mistake, it can be corrected quickly.

Critics of the SDLC further argue that time constraints and deadlines can make taking the 'extra' time necessary to properly complete the Design Phase a luxury that many programmers can't afford.

"I answer that criticism in this way," I said, citing a familiar phrase that you have probably heard before. "It seems there is never time to do something right the first time, but there's always time to do it over."

The exceptional (and foolish) programmer can begin coding without a good design. Programmers who do so may find themselves going back to modify pieces of code they've already written as they move through the project. They may discover a technique halfway through the project that they wish they had incorporated in the beginning, and then go back and change code. Worse yet, they may find themselves with a program that 'runs' but doesn't really work, with the result that they must go back and start virtually from the beginning.

"With a good design," I said, "the likelihood of this nightmare happening will be reduced dramatically. The end result is a program that will behave in the way it was intended, and generally with a shorter overall program development time."

Armed with our notes from the Preliminary Investigation, Linda's notes from the Detailed Analysis, and Frank Olley's emails, my students and I began the Design Phase of the SDLC in earnest. By the end of the design phase, we hoped to have a formal Requirements Statement for the program, and perhaps even a rough sketch of what the user interface will look like.

I reminded everyone that the Requirements Statement would form the basis of our agreement with Frank, Robin and David. For some developers, the Requirements Statement becomes the formal contract to which both they and the customer agree, and sign.

Linda began the design phase by giving the class a summary of the three or four hours she spent in the English, Math and Science departments. Linda said that she felt comfortable in stating that nothing she had observed that day contradicted the view expressed in my notes, and in my email to Frank Olley.

Not everyone in the class had had the benefit of seeing my notes or the email, so I distributed to the class copies of my notes, my email to Frank Olley, and his reply email to me. I gave everyone a few minutes to review and digest the material.

We began to discuss the program requirements. I could see there was some hesitation as to where to begin, so I began the process with a question. "Let's begin by making a statement as to what we are trying to accomplish here," I said.

"We need to write a program to display the calculate final grade for a student in either the English, Math or Science departments," Dave said.

"Excellent," I said. Dave had hit the nail squarely on the head. The primary purpose of the program was to calculate a student's grade. To be sure, there would be more to the program than that, but from Frank Olley's point of view, all he needed the program to do was to display a student's grade.

"To clarify," Kate said, "we should probably state the student's 'letter grade' as opposed to the student's numeric grade."

"Good clarification Kate," I said, "Frank did add that in his email didn't he."

Frequently, new programmers are unable to come to grips as to where they should begin in the Design Phase. I suggested to my class that most programs are designed by first determining the output of the program. The reasoning behind starting with the output is that if you know what the output of the program should be, you can determine the input needed to produce that output pretty easily. Once you know both the output from, and the input to the program, you can then determine what processing or calculations that need to be performed to convert that input to output.

Output Design

I told my students that we were fortunate, in that the class's first project was one where the output requirements could be stated so simply: a grade calculation.

"Where will the grade calculation go?" I asked.

"To a printer?" Jack suggested. "On the computer screen," Rose countered.

"I agree with Rose," I said, "probably to the computer screen."

Some of the students seemed perplexed by my answer.

"Probably?" Dave asked.

I explained that Frank Olley and I had never formally agreed where the grade calculation would be displayed. The issue had never really come up.

"Let's be sure," I said, "to explicitly specify a display of the grade calculation in the Requirements Statement. Speaking of which…would anyone care to volunteer to begin to write up the specifications for it?"

Dave volunteered to begin writing our Requirements Statement, so he started up Microsoft Word and started typing away.

Rhonda made a suggestion for the color and font size for the program's calculated grade display, but Peter said that it was probably a bit premature to be talking about colors and font sizes at this point in our design. I agreed, and told them that I never include that amount of detail on a Requirements Statement.

"Is there any other output from the program?" I asked and several moments went by.

"I'd like to suggest that we display the date and time on the computer screen," Valerie suggested.

"Good idea," Mary said.

However, Linda disagreed, arguing that the display of the date and time was unnecessary considering the fact that the PC's at the university were all running Windows---and displayed the current time on the Windows TaskBar anyway.

"We could display the current date and time," I said, "but I'm inclined to agree with Linda---all of the PC's at the University that will run our program are Microsoft Windows based---and capable of displaying a date and time on their own. And while it's true that the beauty of the JavaScript programs we will learn how to write in this class are that they can run on virtually any operating system---and also within a Web page---I can't think of any environment in which the user can't be aware of the current date and time if they so desire."

The majority of the class agreed.

"Getting back to the display of the grade," Peter said, "do you think it would be a good idea to display the calculated numeric grade as well as the letter grade?"

"Yes, I think that's a great idea," Kathy added.

Taking a moment to summarize, I said, "I agree also. So we now have two output requirements---a grade calculation, where we display both the calculated numeric grade for the student, and the corresponding letter grade. I can't think of anything else from an output point of view, can you?"

"What about the individual components that make up the grade?" Rhonda asked. "Should we display those?"

"I think you'll see in a few moments Rhonda," I replied, "that the individual components that comprise the student's grade will be displayed in a 'window'."

"When you say window do you mean Microsoft Windows?" Joe asked.

"Not necessarily," I replied. "The term 'window' is a generic JavaScript term. Using JavaScript we can write programs for virtually any Internet Browser---and Internet Browsers run on a variety of Operating Systems. In this class we'll be using Microsoft Windows running Microsoft's Internet Explorer---but if we were using Linux based computers in this class we could write the same program for the Firefox or Mozilla Internet Browsers which run on Linux."

I waited to see if there were any questions--but there were none.

"I think we now have enough information to proceed to our next step," I said. "Does anyone know what that is?"

Barbara suggested that since we seemed to have the output requirements identified, we should move onto a discussion of processing.

"As I explained earlier, it will be easier for us if we discuss input into the program prior to discussing processing," I said. "It's just about impossible to determine processing requirements if we don't know our input requirements."

Input Design

"So does anyone have any suggestions as to what input requirements we need?" I asked the class.

Dave quickly rattled off several input requirements: a Midterm grade, a Final Examination grade, a Research Paper grade, and a Presentation grade.

"Excellent," I said. "of course, those requirements will vary depending upon the type of student that is being calculated."

"Is that another piece of Input?" Mary suggested, "the type of student whose grade is being calculated."

"Excellent observation Mary," I said. "Only for an English student will all four grades be required. A Science student's final grade is comprised of three component pieces---Midterm Final Examination and Research Paper, and a Math student's final grade is comprised of only two pieces---the Midterm and Final Examination grades."

"Anything else?" I asked.

"How will the input be entered into the program?" Kathy asked. "How will the user of the program let the program know what type of student they are entering?"

Designating the type of Student

Several students suggested that the user of the program could designate the type of student by entering the type using the computer's keyboard.

"My motto is to have the user do as little typing as possible," I said. "If we ask the user of the program to use the keyboard to enter the type of student into the program, we're going to have to insist that each user of the program type it consistently---that's something we can't count on. For instance, one user may type 'Math', another may type 'Mathematics', and still a third may type 'Calculus'."

"I see what you mean," Rhonda said. "But what's our alternative?"

I could see that some of the students were perplexed considering the alternatives to entering the type of student via the PC's keyboard---but you must remember that a number of them had come from the DOS world, and were accustomed to writing programs where there was a great deal of typing required of the user.

I explained that typically in a 'widows' based program, when there are a finite number of choices, it's best to display a list of choices for the user to choose from. Although JavaScript is capable of producing programs for operating systems besides Microsoft Windows, the class and I agreed that we would use our common knowledge of Microsoft Windows as a basis of our discussion for our JavaScript program that would be 'windows' oriented.

"Does anyone know of anything they've seen in Microsoft Windows that displays a list of alternatives for the user to choose from?" I asked. Mary said she recalled seeing a list of Font names and Font sizes to choose from on the Microsoft Word toolbar:

"That's a list of choices," she said. "Excellent, Mary," I said.

I said this list was actually a Windows ListBox object---and JavaScript was capable of producing a similar 'object'. Such a ListBox would be a good choice to use to display the available 'student types' in our program--alternatively, we could also use something known as a Radio Button to present the choices for student type to the user.

"Can anyone find an example of a Radio Button in Word?" I asked.

Ward said that he recalled seeing boxes on the Options submenu of the Tools menu that permitted him to specify 'settings' for saving documents in Word. I asked all of the students to take a look at this menu, and sure enough, there were several boxes, which the user can click with their mouse to select settings for saving documents in Word:

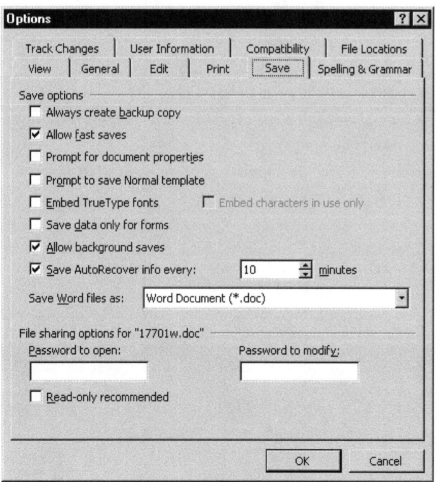

"Aren't those Check Boxes?" Dave asked. "I thought Radio Buttons were 'circles'?"

"You're right Dave," I answered, "these are Check Boxes--another type of interface object that is similar to a Radio Button. A Check Box is an object that can either be selected or not selected. Check Boxes enable the user to make a selection by clicking on the box with their mouse. The user can then de-select it by clicking on the Check Box again with their mouse."

"Why can't we use Check Boxes in our program?" Bob asked. "Can't we have one each to represent the English, Math and Science student?"

"We could use a Check Box to represent Student Types," I said, "but dong so presents a problem. As you'll see in a moment, only one Radio Button in a group of Radio Buttons can be selected at one time--and that's the behavior we want here. After all, a student can't be both an English student and a Math student at the same time. If the user of the program designates the student for whom they are calculating the grade to be an English student, we don't want the user to be able to select any other student type. Unfortunately, with a Check Box object, more than one Check Box can be selected at the same time."

"So with a Check Box object, more than one Student Type can be selected at the same time?" Rhonda asked. "We certainly don't want that."

"That's exactly right Rhonda," I said. "Check Boxes are fine for certain types of applications where more than one selection is permissible."

"Such as?" Chuck asked.

"For instance," I said, "if we were to write a program that asked the user to select their favorite sports---we could use Check Boxes to represent Baseball, Basketball, Football and Hockey. And a Check Box would be fine here--since it's perfectly reasonable for someone to have more than one favorite sport, and that's the way we phrased the question. But suppose we asked the user to specify their one and only, their absolute favorite sport---in this case a Radio Button would be the object to use to represent their four choices--since by it's very nature it prevents more than one selection from being made."

"You've used the term object several times?" Valerie said, "It's my understanding that JavaScript is an object-oriented programming language. Is that right?"

"That's right Valerie," I said. "In JavaScript, you'll see that when we designate a Radio Button to represent an item that the user can select, we're actually creating an instance of a Radio Button object from an already existing Radio Button template--called a class. This class has built in behavior--and in the case of a Radio Button object, it's that built in behavior that prevents more than one from being selected at the same time. We'll discuss Radio Button objects--as well as the other types of JavaScript objects---later on in the course."

"Can we see an example of a Radio Button object?" Joe asked.

"Sure thing," I said, "Check out the Print submenu of Word." I displayed it on the classroom project at the same time.

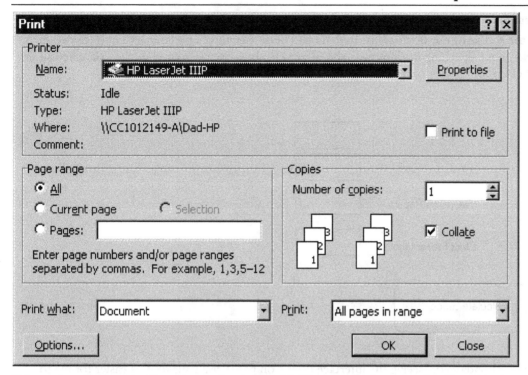

"Now take a look at the Page Range frame," I said. "For those of you not familiar with the term, a Frame is a section of a window---and as you can see, there are three Radio Buttons in the Page Range Frame. You'll notice that only one Radio Button within a Frame can be selected at one time."

"Sounds like a great object to use to represent the Student Type," Dave said.

"I agree," Peter said. "No typing required."

Just about everyone in the class---one student thought a Listbox was a better choice---agreed that using Radio Buttons to represent the Student Type was a good idea, so Dave added this to the Requirements Statement.

Designating the component grades

"OK," Ward said, "now that we had identified the Student Type, what happens--how do we get the user to enter the value for the component grades---Midterm examination, Final Examination, Research Paper and Presentation. We can't do that using any of the objects we've explorer so far, can we?"

"That's right Ward," I said, "we do need a way to permit the user to enter the component grades that make up the student's final grade. Does anyone see anything in Word that fits that bill?"

"How about the box next to the 'Pages' Radio Button in the Print Sub menu," Lou asked. "I just checked--and it permits the user to type something into it."

"That's excellent Lou," I agreed. "In Windows, that box is called a Text Box---JavaScript calls them TextBoxes. Regardless of what you call them, they are ideal for our application, since they permit the user to make an entry into them."

"Will we have four of them?" Rose asked. "One for each of the component grades?"

"Yes we will," I said. "Later on, you'll see that we can selectively hide some of the TextBoxes that are not appropriate for the Student Type the user selects."

"So you're saying if the user selects a Math Student Type, only two TextBoxes will be visible?" Valerie asked.

"That's right," I said, "and if the user selects a Science Student Type, three TextBoxes will be visible."

"This sounds like it's all going to be a lot of fun," Rhonda said, "I just wish I could envision what the interface will look like. Do we have to wait until we write the program to see what the interface will actually look like."

"Good question Rhonda," I said. "No we don't have to wait that long--there's no rule that says we can't sketch the User Interface using pencil and paper well before that."

The First Interface Design

As it turned out, during the course of our discussions, Barbara had been sketching a preliminary interface design. Upon hearing my remarks about sketching the interface, she offered to show the class what she had sketched so far, and I displayed it on the classroom projector.

"That looks great Barbara," Rhonda said, "seeing the interface design on paper really makes this easier for me to envision."

"I agree Rhonda," I said, "and you'll find that having a 'blueprint' like this will make programming the interface much easier later on."

I then asked Barbara if she would mind explaining the interface design to the rest of the class.

"Based on our discussion of Radio Buttons," she said, "I drew a Radio Button for each of the three Student types we have---English, Math and Science--each with an appropriate label. Pictured in the sketch is a TextBox for each of the four component grades, again appropriately labeled. As we discussed earlier, however, all four of the TextBoxes will not necessarily be visible---which of the four is visible will depend upon the Radio Button that the user selects."

"That's great Barbara," I said. "I noticed you also included a button captioned 'Calculate Grades.'"

"I thought it made sense," Barbara said, "to include a button that, when clicked, would trigger the calculation and display of the student's final grade."

"Do you have any ideas as to how and where we'll display the student's final grade?" Dave asked.

"I hadn't gotten that far," Barbara said, "I guess we could display the grade on the interface itself---or perhaps display a message. Can JavaScript display a message box?"

"Yes Barbara," I said, "JavaScript is capable of displaying a message box--although in JavaScript it's called an Alert Box."

"A message box can be quite an attention getter," Dave said. "I've seen some users entirely miss the display of information on the interface itself. Plus, with a message box, won't that continue to display until the user clicks on an OK button or something like that?"

"That's right Dave," I said, "a message box remains until the user clicks on an OK button."

"I vote for the message box," Rhonda said.

That seemed to be the majority opinion of the class---a message box it would be, although I emphasized that during the class, they could deviate from this design if they wished--by displaying the calculation in a JavaScript TextBox or TextArea object if they chose.

> **NOTE: We'll learn more about these objects in a later chapter.**

"What happens after the student's final grade is displayed in a message box?" Chuck asked. "I mean, should we automatically clear the TextBoxes to work on the next student."

"I was thinking the same thing," Kate said. "I suppose we could automatically clear the TextBoxes in preparation for the next student---but perhaps it would be better to have another button captioned 'Reset' which would unselect the Student type Radio Button currently selected, make all four TextBoxes visible, and at the same time clear them?"

"I like that idea a lot," Barbara said. So did everyone else, and so I asked Barbara to add a Reset button to the sketch. She did, and I then displayed the modified sketch of the user interface on the classroom projector.

⬭ English Student	Midterm:	☐
⬭ Math Student	Final:	☐
⬭ Science Student	Research Paper:	☐
	Class Presentation:	☐

| Calculate Grade | Reset |

I asked everyone to take a good, careful look at the interface.

"Remember what I told you earlier," I said, "now's the time to uncover anything that isn't quite right---changing the design on paper is a lot easier than changing the code after we've written it."

"I don't want to appear picky," Mary said, "but the sketch doesn't include a title bar for the Internet Browser window. Plus I presume that JavaScript windows have a control menu icon, plus the standard Minimize, Maximize, and Close buttons?"

"Mary's right," Barbara answered, "I didn't include any of those elements in the sketch. Should we be that detailed here?"

"It can't hurt," I said. "It's one less thing to forget when it comes time to actually write our code."

"I think I understand what the Minimized, Maximize and Close buttons are," Rhonda said, "those are the buttons on the right side of a window's Title bar--but what's a Control Menu Icon?"

"The Control Menu Icon," I said, "is the Icon on the left hand side of a window's Title bar--if you click on it, a submenu with menu items for Restore, Move, Size, Minimize, Maximize and Close will appear. We should probably include the Control Menu Icon on our sketch as well."

"What about menus," Steve asked. "Should we develop a menu for the Grade Calculation project?"

"That's a good question Steve," I said. "Creating menus in JavaScript is a bit of an advanced topic--and something we cover here at the university in our Advanced JavaScript class. For our purposes, this application doesn't 'cry out' for a menu since it's basically a program that performs a single function."

I noticed that Barbara had finished making the last changes to our interface on her sketch, and I took it from her and displayed it on the classroom projector.

☐   Grade Calculator   │ –□✕

○   English Student   Midterm: [   ]

○   Math Student   Final: [   ]

○   Science Student   Research Paper: [   ]

                         Class Presentation: [   ]

[Calculate Grade   ]   [Reset   ]

"That really is beginning to shape up," Ward said. "Did we forget anything?"

"I can't think of anything," I said, "but the great thing about doing the design on paper first is that if you do forget anything, it's a matter of making some changes to a sheet of paper--not to your program code."

"I have a question," Rhonda asked. "Are the captions that appear in the window objects themselves---or do they belong to the Radio Buttons and TextBoxes."

"That's an excellent question Rhonda," I said. "In other languages, such as Visual Basic and Java, the captions next to the Radio Buttons 'belong' to the Radio Button--however, in JavaScript they do not. We'll need to explicitly code some HTML in order to produce the caption next to the Radio Button--and the same applies to the captions next to our TextBoxes."

The Requirements Statement

We had been working pretty intensely, and in my opinion making some excellent progress, and so I suggested that we take a break. Before adjourning, I asked Dave, the student who was developing the Requirements Statement, to let us see what he had developed so far. I made copies of his work, and after break, handed these out to the rest of the class for discussion. Here is the copy of the Requirements Statement I gave to everyone.

REQUIREMENTS STATEMENT

Grade Calculation Program

GENERAL DESCRIPTION

The program will consist of an Interface on which there will be:

3 Radio Buttons, representing the three types of students for which grades can be calculated.

4 TextBoxes, appropriately labeled Midterm, Final, Research Paper, and Class Presentation, into which the user will enter the component grades necessary to calculate the student's final grade.

A button, captioned 'Calculate grade, which when clicked will display the student's Final numeric grade and letter grade in a message box.

A button, captioned 'Reset', which when clicked will clear the contents of the four TextBoxes.

OUTPUT FROM THE SYSTEM

The student's final numeric grade and letter grade in a message box

INPUT TO THE SYSTEM

The customer will specify:

The type of student whose grade is to be calculated

If an English student, the Midterm, Final examination, Research Paper and Class Presentation grades will be entered in the appropriate TextBox.

If a Math student, the Midterm and Final examination grades will be entered in the appropriate TextBox.

If a Science student, the Midterm, Final examination and Research Paper grades will be entered in the appropriate TextBox.

BUSINESS RULES

An English student's grade is calculated as 25% of the Midterm grade, 25% of the Final examination grade, 30% of the Research Paper grade and 20% of the Class Presentation grade.

A Math student's grade is calculated as 50% of the Midterm grade and 50% of the Final examination grade.

A Science student's grade is calculated as 40% of the Midterm grade, 40% of the Final examination grade, and 20% of the Research paper grade.

Each department has unique letter grade equivalents for the student's calculated final numeric average. Here is a table of the letter grade equivalents:

DEPARTMENT	ENGLISH	MATH	SCIENCE
A	93 OR GREATER	90 OR GREATER	90 OR GREATER
B	85 TO 93	83 TO 90	80 TO 90
C	78 TO 85	76 TO 83	70 TO 80
D	70 TO 78	65 TO 76	60 TO 70
F	LESS THAN 70	LESS THAN 65	LESS THAN 60

I explained to the class that the Requirements Statement could easily form the basis of a contract between the customer and the developer of the program. The Requirements Statement should list all of the major details of the program. You should take care not to paint yourself into any unnecessary programming corners by including any 'window dressing'. These can just get you into trouble later.

For instance, notice here that we didn't specify precisely where, on the interface, we would display the various JavaScript objects. Suppose, for instance, we had specified that both buttons are side by side at the bottom of the interface---but then decide later than we want to align them vertically instead. Theoretically, deviating from the Requirements Statement could be construed as a violation of contractual terms.

I asked for comments on the Requirements Statement and everyone seemed to think that it was just fine. However, several students turned their attention to the sketch of the user interface, and indicated that they believed there were still some problems with it.

Blaine suggested that our sketch didn't have identifying captions--specifically, he thought that we should have an identifying caption for the column of Radio Buttons and for the column of TextBoxes.

"That's not a bad idea Blaine," I said, and I asked Barbara if she would mind modifying her sketch. "We can insert add two JavaScript label objects to provide identifying captions. Anything else?" No one had anything else, and with that, we proclaimed the user interface designed---always subject to change of course at a later time if needed. I displayed the final sketch of the interface on the classroom projector. Barbara quickly made the changes to the sketch.

```
☐      Grade Calculator                                    ⌐ –□ X
```

STUDENT TYPES   **GRADES**

○   English Student   Midterm: [   ]

○   Math Student   Final: [   ]

○   Science Student   Research Paper: [   ]

                           Class Presentation: [   ]

(Calculate Grade)   (Reset)

Neither one of these changes were detailed enough to warrant mentioning them on the Requirements Statement, so Dave needed to make no changes to the Requirements Statement. Everyone agreed that the interface had come along quite nicely, but as they say, 'the proof is in the pudding.' It's only the customer's opinion that counts---and we'd have to see how Frank, Robin and David felt about it. With no more comments or suggestions on the user interface or the Requirements Statement, we set about completing the Design Phase of the SDLC by looking at Processing.

Processing Design

"Processing is the conversion of inputs to outputs, the conversion of Data to Information," I said. "At this point in the Design phase of the SDLC, we should have now identified all of the output from the program---a calculation of the student's grade---and all of the input necessary to produce that output--the component pieces of the grade."

I explained that just as a good novel will typically have several subplots; a JavaScript program is no exception. It contains several processing 'subplots' as well.

We have the main 'plot', that is the calculation of the student's grade, but we also have 'subplots' such as:

- Determining the type of student whose grade is being entered

- Selectively hiding and displaying the appropriate TextBoxes

- Ensuring that valid data---numbers between 0 and 100---are entered into the TextBoxes.

- Making the appropriate calculation.

- Displaying the calculated grade.

It's important to note that in Processing Design, we don't actually write the program. That's done later. In Processing Design, we specify the processes that need to be performed to convert input into output.

Looking at Processing in Detail

"Let's look at a simple example which isn't part of the Grade Calculation Project," I said, "that most of you are probably familiar with, the calculation of your paycheck."

I continued by saying that if you want to calculate your net pay, you need to perform several steps. Here are the steps or functions necessary to calculate your net pay:

1. Calculate gross pay

2. Calculate tax deductions

3. Calculate net pay

> **NOTE: Programming is done in the next phase of the SDLC, the Development Phase. Specifying how processing is to occur is not as important in this phase as specifying what is to occur. For instance, this sequence identifies the 'what' of processing, not the how. The 'how' is a part of the Development phase.**

These functions can be broken down even further. For instance, the calculation of your gross pay will vary depending upon whether you are a salaried employee or an hourly employee. If you are an hourly employee, your gross pay is equal to your hourly pay rate multiplied by the number of hours worked in the pay period. The specification of these functions is exactly what the designer must detail in the Processing Design phase of the SDLC.

When it comes to processing design, documenting the processing rules is crucial because translating processing rules into a narrative form can sometimes result in confusion or misinterpretation. Over the years, systems designers have used various 'tools' to aid them in documenting the design of their systems.

Some designers have used tools called flowcharts. Flowcharts use symbols to graphically document the system's processing rules. Here are the net pay processing rules we discussed earlier depicted using a flowchart. (My apologies to any accountants reading this; these calculations have been simplified for illustration purposes.)

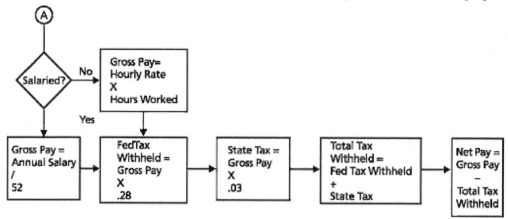

Other designers favor pseudo-code. Pseudo-code is an English-like language that describes in non-graphical form how a program should execute. Here are the same net pay processing rules depicted using pseudo-code:

Assumption: Pay is calculated on a weekly basis (52 pay periods per year).

Assumption: Salaried employee pay is Annual Salary divided by 52.

Assumption: Hourly employee pay is Hourly Rate multiplied by hours worked.

1. If employee is salaried, then go to Step 4

2. Employee is hourly, then calculate gross pay equal to hourly wage rate multiplied by hours worked in pay period

3. Go to Step 5

4. Employee is salaried, so calculate Gross Pay equal to Annual Salary divided by 52

5. Calculate Federal Tax withheld equal to Gross Pay multiplied by 0.28

6. Calculate State Tax withheld equal to Gross pay multiplied by 0.03

7. Calculate Total Tax withheld equal to Federal Tax withheld + State Tax withheld

8. Calculate Net Pay equal to Gross Pay less Total Tax withheld

> **NOTE: Both of these techniques found favor in the era of the Procedural Program.**
>
> **A Procedural Program is one that executes from top to bottom virtually without interruption. A procedural program ordains to the user exactly how they will interact with your program. For instance, in the Grade Calculation Project, the user will select a type of student, and then enter values for component grade pieces such as the Midterm or Final Examination grade.**
>
> **I frequently find students who have a strong programming background writing procedural programs. Procedural Programming (using languages like Basic, Fortran and COBOL) is like**

taking a ride on a tour bus, where all of the destination stops are pre-determined, and pre-ordered.

Windows programs are Event-Driven programs. Event-Driven programs (using languages such as Visual Basic, C++ and JavaScript) don't force the user to behave in a certain way, but rather react to the user.

An event-driven program does not attempt to 'dictate' to the user what they should do in the program, and when they should do it. Instead an event-driven program presents the user with a visual interface that permits them to interact with the program. This is more like choosing the rides at a carnival.

Once entry has been gained, the rides they go on and the order in which they ride them is entirely up to the user. An event-driven program must be able to work and respond to any eventuality.

"In my classes," I said, "I don't require the use of either flowcharting or pseudo-code. All that I ask from you is that you give careful thought to the processing that is necessary to solve the problem before beginning to code in JavaScript."

I could see some happy faces and I continued by saying that invariably, this means working out a solution on a piece of paper prior to coding it. Some students are more 'visual' than others, and they prefer to design their solution in graphical terms. Others are less 'visual' and their solutions look very much like the pseudo-code we saw earlier. The point is, without some written plan, the programming process can go awry.

I cited this example. Several years ago, I was teaching a class on another language called COBOL, and I gave my students the following programming problem:

> **Write a program to calculate the net wage of a laborer who works 40 hours at a pay rate of $5 per hour. Income tax at the rate of 20% of the gross pay will be deducted. What is the net pay?**

The correct answer is $160. Forty hours multiplied by $5 per hour results in a gross pay of $200. The income tax deduction is 20% of $200, which is $40. $200 less the $40 income tax deduction results in a net pay of $160.

A number of students calculated the net pay as $240. Instead of deducting the income tax deduction of $40 from the gross pay, they added it instead. When I questioned the methodology behind their incorrect answer, most of them told me they thought the problem had been so simple, that they hadn't bothered to work out the solution on a piece of paper ahead of time. They just started coding. Had they taken the time to work out the solution on paper first, they would have known what the answer should be and they wouldn't have submitted a program to me that calculated the results incorrectly.

"This is what I'm suggesting to you," I said. "Take the time to work out the solution on paper. You'll be happy that you did."

Back to the Grade Calculation Program

We continued by discussing processing design. I reminded my students that, in general, design is an iterative process. It's rare that the designer or programmer hits the nail perfectly on the head the first time. It's very possible that after going through processing design, you will discover that you are missing some crucial piece of input necessary to produce a piece of output. In this case, you would need to look at your input processing again. For instance, with the Grade Calculation program, we could have forgotten to ask the user to specify the type of student whose grade they wished to calculate--such an omission would have catastrophic consequences.

As a starting point in our processing discussion, we agreed to begin with our primary goal: To calculate a student's grade. We had already determined that in order to calculate a grade, we needed to know the type of student, and once we knew that, the individual grade components that made up the final grade.

We started with a hypothetical user entering a hypothetical student's information.

"Can anyone tell me," I asked "what the final grade for an English student would be if he or she scored an 88 on their midterm examination, a 90 on their final examination, an 85 on their Research paper, and a 75 on their Class presentation? Plus, can you tell me how you arrive at the result?"

"If I were solving this problem using pencil and paper," Ward said, "I would take the score for the student's midterm grade-88--and multiply it by .2, giving me a result of 22 which I would then set aside. I would then take the score for the final examination--90---and multiply it by .2, giving me a result of 22.5, which I would then set aside. I would then take the score for the student's Research paper---85---and multiply it by .3, giving me a result of 25.5, which I would then set aside. I would then take the score for the Class Presentation---75---and multiply it by .2, giving me a result of 15, which I would then set aside. Finally, I would take the four 'set aside; results---22, 22.5 25.5 and 15, and add them together to arrive at a sum of 85--which, if we refer to the Requirements Statement, equates to the letter 'B' for an English student."

"That's excellent Ward," I said. "

"I think we've got a problem here," Chuck said. "I went through the same process Ward just did--but I come up with a letter grade of 'C'."

Sure enough, we did have a problem. In looking over the Requirements Statement, it indicated that for an English Student, the numeric grade of 85 equated to both the letter 'B' and the letter 'C'.

"How did that happen?" Kate asked.

"Those are the numbers that Frank Olley supplied in his email," I said, "unfortunately, I missed catching this. Right now we a little problem---but I happen to know that Frank is in his office today---hopefully he can give us a quick solution to the problem."

I pulled out my cell phone (ah, the conveniences of modern living!) and gave Frank a quick call. Fortunately, he was still in his office. I explained that in his email to me outlining the numeric grade-letter equivalents, he had used the phrase '78 to 85' to describe the letter grade of 'C' for an English student---and then the phrase '85 to 93' to describe the letter grade of 'B'--what happens if the student scores a final numeric grade of '85' right on the nose.

I had to explain the problem once more for Frank--and then he apologized and explained that a numeric grade of '85' was the starting point for a 'B'---anything less than '85' was a C. I asked him if the same applied to the other categories--since we also had overlapping there. He said that it did, and based on our discussion, the class and I re-worked that table from the Requirements Statement to look like this...

DEPARTMENT	ENGLISH	MATH	SCIENCE
A	>= 93	>= 90	>= 90
B	< 93 AND >= 85	< 90 AND >= 83	< 90 AND >= 80
C	< 85 AND >= 78	< 83 AND >= 76	< 80 AND >= 70
D	< 78 AND >= 70	< 76 AND >= 65	< 70 AND >= 60
F	< 70	< 65	< 60

"That's better," I said, admiring my work.

"Maybe for you," Rhonda responded, "this reminds me of Algebra, and I think the table is a lot more difficult to read this way. Do we really have to express the rules for the letter grade computations this way? Those less than and greater than symbols always confused me."

"In the long run, we'll be better off," I said, "the way we've phrased the rules for forming the letter grades isn't much different from the JavaScript code we'll write. Plus, these are expressed in certain terms--unlike the previous version of the table which can the overlapping values."

"Have we missed anything with the grade calculation?" I asked. "Suppose," I added, "the user selects a student type of 'English' and enters value for a Midterm, a Final examination, and a Research paper--but fails to enter a value for the Class presentation--what should the program do?"

Everyone agreed that we needed to display some sort of error message if we didn't have all of the 'ingredients' necessary to arrive at a valid grade calculation. An error message is another form of output.

"I think we've already agreed on this," I said, "but how and when should the grade calculation take place?" I asked.

Mary suggested that we could trigger the grade calculation when the last component piece of the grade was entered.

"I think that would look pretty 'spiffy'," she said, "if we displayed an English student's grade right after the Class Presentation grade was entered into the TextBox--can we do that?"

"We can do that Mary," I said, "but you've got to be careful about anticipating the order in which the user of our program will interact with the objects in the window. Aren't you pre-supposing that the user will enter values into the various TextBoxes from top to bottom?"

Mary admitted that she was. I agreed. "You've got to be careful not to try to anticipate the order in which you think the user will interact with the objects in your pogrom," I said. "Midterm grade, Final Examination grade, Research Paper and Class Presentation---that's probably the order that you would make your selections. But that's not going to be the case with every user."

I explained that expecting users to perform actions in a particular order sounded very much like procedural programming. Like a trip to the Automated Teller Machine:

- insert card
- enter PIN number
- select withdrawal or deposit
- specify an amount
- deposit your cash or take your cash
- take your receipt
- take your card

I explained that Procedural Programming is something we want to avoid. Procedural programming often gives the user the feeling that they are being pushed or rushed---that they aren't really in control. When we write Windows programs, it's a great idea to give the user the impression that they are in control.

"That's why I suggested earlier the use of a button captioned 'Calculate Grade' to allow the user to tell the program when they are ready for a grade calculation," I said. "This way they won't get the impression that the program is waiting for them to do something."

The students thought about this for a moment, and agreed with the concept. We confirmed that we would place a button on the form captioned 'Calculate Grade'---and we further agreed that we would not perform a grade calculation until the user clicked on that button.

Now it seemed as though we were gaining momentum. As I mentioned earlier, during the course of processing design, we may uncover 'holes' in the input or output design---such as the 'overlapping' grade. That had been the case here. While it's certain that we would have eventually noticed these holes when we were coding the program, fixing these flaws while you are still in the design phase of the SDLC is much easier and cheaper than fixing them in the midst of programming the application.

In large projects particularly, portions of the project may be given to different programmers or even different teams of programmers for coding. It could be some time before flaws in the design are uncovered, in some cases weeks or even months. The longer it takes to discover these flaws, the more likely it is that some coding will have to be scrapped and re-done. A well thought out design phase can eliminate many problems down the line.

We'd plugged the hole in the Grade Calculation processing---now it remained to be seen if there were any other processing design issues.

"What about ending the program?" Steve asked. "Do we need to write code for that?"

I explained that we would need to write a few lines of JavaScript code to end the program--but that there was no need to formally state that in the Requirements statement. After a few moments of silence, it seemed that we were finished with the Design phase of the SDLC. Here is the **Final Requirements Statement** that the class approved:

REQUIREMENTS STATEMENT

Grade Calculation Program

GENERAL DESCRIPTION

The program will consist of an Interface on which there will be:

3 Radio Buttons, representing the three types of students for which grades can be calculated.

4 TextBoxes, appropriately labeled Midterm, Final, Research Paper, and Class Presentation, into which the user will enter the component grades necessary to calculate the student's final grade.

A button, captioned 'Calculate grade, which when clicked will display the student's Final numeric grade and letter grade in a message box.

A button, captioned 'Reset', which when clicked will clear the contents of the four TextBoxes.

OUTPUT FROM THE SYSTEM

The student's final numeric grade and letter grade in a message box

INPUT TO THE SYSTEM

The customer will specify:

The type of student whose grade is to be calculated

If an English student, the Midterm, Final examination, Research Paper and Class Presentation grades will be entered in the appropriate TextBox.

If a Math student, the Midterm and Final examination grades will be entered in the appropriate TextBox.

If a Science student, the Midterm, Final examination and Research Paper grades will be entered in the appropriate TextBox.

BUSINESS RULES

An English student's grade is calculated as 25% of the Midterm grade, 25% of the Final examination grade, 30% of the Research Paper grade and 20% of the Class Presentation grade.

A Math student's grade is calculated as 50% of the Midterm grade and 50% of the Final examination grade.

A Science student's grade is calculated as 40% of the Midterm grade, 40% of the Final examination grade, and 20% of the Research paper grade.

Each department has unique letter grade equivalents for the student's calculated final numeric average. Here is a table of the letter grade equivalents:

DEPARTMENT	ENGLISH	MATH	SCIENCE
A	>= 93	>= 90	>= 90
B	< 93 AND >= 85	< 90 AND >= 83	< 90 AND >= 80
C	< 85 AND >= 78	< 83 AND >= 76	< 80 AND >= 70
D	< 78 AND >= 70	< 76 AND >= 65	< 70 AND >= 60
F	< 70	< 65	< 60

I polled the class to see if everyone agreed with the Requirements Statement, and then revealed that we were now done with the Design Phase of the SDLC. I once again reminded everyone that the Design Phase of the SDLC tends to be an iterative process, and that we might find ourselves back here at some point. We then moved on to a discussion of the fourth phase of the SDLC--the Development Phase.

Phase 4: Development Phase

I told my class that we wouldn't spend a great deal of time discussing the Development Phase here since the rest of the course would be spent in developing the Grade Calculation Project, in which they would play an active role!

"The Development phase is," I said, "in many ways the most exciting time of the SDLC. During this phase, computer hardware is purchased, if necessary, and the software is developed. Yes, that means we actually start coding the program during the Development phase, and in this class, we'll be using JavaScript as our development tool."

I explained that during the Development Phase, we'd constantly examine and re-examine the Requirements Statement to ensure that we were following it to the letter, and I encourage all of them to do the same. I explained that any deviations (and there may be a surprise or two down the road) would have to be approved either by the project leader (me) or by our clients--Frank, Robin and David.

I also explained that our Development Phase would be split into two sections. First, we would develop a JavaScript Console Program that would perform the grade calculations that our final windows version would---with the difference being that the Console program wouldn't have a windows user interface.

"The Console program will allow us to prove that the logic behind the scenes of our program works," I said. "Once we've proven that, we'll spend the last few weeks of the class building the User Interface, and incorporating our already written logic into that version which will take on the appearance of a JavaScript Windows Program."

Everyone in the class seemed anxious to begin, but they promised me they would remain patient while I discussed the final two phases of the SDLC.

Phase 5: Implementation Phase

The Implementation Phase is the phase in the SDLC when the project reaches fruition. I explained to my students that after the Development phase of the SDLC is complete, we begin to actually implement the system. In a typical project, what this means is that any hardware that has been purchased will be delivered and installed in the client's location.

In the instance of our clients," I said, "they already had the equipment--during the Implementation phase, the JavaScript program that we write will be loaded onto their PC's."

Not surprisingly, everyone in the class agreed that they wanted to be there for that exciting day.

Barbara raised the issue of program testing. During the Implementation phase, both hardware and software is tested. We agreed that students in the class would perform most of the testing of the program, as we agreed that it would be unreasonable and unfair to expect our clients to test the software that we had developed in a 'live' situation. Naturally, our goal was that when the software was installed in the English, Math and Science departments, that the program should be bug (problem) free.

On the other hand, I cautioned them, almost invariably, the user will uncover problems that the developer has been unable to generate. I told them we would discuss handling these types of problems in more detail in our class on error handling.

"I've heard the term 'debugging used among the programmers at work," Valerie said. 'Is that something we'll be doing?"

"Most definitely Valerie," I said. "Debugging is a process in which we run the program, thoroughly test it, and systematically eliminate all of the errors that we can uncover. We'll be doing this prior to delivering the program to Frank, Robin and David."

I then explained that during the Implementation phase, we would also be training the users of the program-most likely work study students in the English, Math and Science departments---but perhaps Frank, Robin and David as well. Again, everyone in the class wanted to participate in user training. One of my students noted that she thought that there needed to be two levels of training performed:

Several students thought that it would be a good idea to have a student observing the users of the program during its first week of operation, in order to assist users in the operation of the system, and to ease any 'computer' anxiety that the users might be suffering. I thought this was a great idea, and also pointed out these observations would provide valuable feedback on the operation of the program from the most important people in the loop, the end users.

In fact, the mention of the word 'feedback' led quite naturally into a discussion of the final phase of the SDLC--- Audit (sometimes called Feedback) and Maintenance.

Phase 6: Audit and Maintenance Phase

Phase 6 of the SDLC is the Audit and Maintenance Phase. In this phase, someone, usually the client, but sometimes a third party such as an auditor, studies the implemented system to ensure that it actually fulfills the details of the Requirements Statement. The bottom line is that the system should have solved the problem or deficiency, or satisfied the desire that was identified in Phase 1 of the SDLC - the preliminary investigation.

More than a few programs and systems have been fully developed that, for one reason or another simply never met the original requirements. The Maintenance portion of this phase deals with any changes that need to be made to the system.

Changes are sometimes the result of the system not completely fulfilling its original requirements, but it could also be the result of customer satisfaction. Sometimes the customer is so happy with what they have got that they want more. Changes can also be forced upon the system because of governmental regulations, such as changing tax laws, while at other times changes come about due to alterations in the business rules of the customer.

As I mentioned in the previous section, we intended to have one or more members of the class in the English, Math and Science departments during the first week of system operation. That opportunity for the user to provide direct feedback to a member of the development team would more than satisfy the Audit portion of Phase 6.

In the future, we hoped that Frank, Robin and David would be so happy with the program that we had written for them, that he would think of even more challenging requirements to request of the class.

Where To From Here?

It had been a long and productive session for everyone. I told my students that in our next meeting we would start to discuss how a computer works, and we would actually begin to work with JavaScript.

Ward asked me how the progression of the project would work, that is, would we finish the project during our last class meeting, or would we be working on it a little bit each week? I said that I thought it was important that we develop the program incrementally. Each week we meet, we would attempt to finish some portion of the project. Developing the project in steps like this would hold everyone's interest, and give us a chance to catch any problems well before the last week of class.

Summary

The aim of this chapter was to tackle the question "Where do I begin?" We saw that the design of an application is best done systematically, with a definite plan of action. That way, you know that everything has been taken into account.

A good place to begin is with a requirements statement, which is a list of what the program has to be able to do. Usually, you get the information for this from whoever is asking you to write the program. It's a good idea to keep in continuous contact with this person, so that any changes they want can be tackled before it becomes too much of a problem.

A good systematic approach is embodied in the systems development life cycle (SDLC), which consists of six phases:

· The Preliminary Investigation: Considering the technical, time, and budgetary constraints and deciding on the viability of continuing development of the application.
· The Analysis Phase: Gathering the information needed to continue.
· The Design Phase: Creating a blueprint of the program's appearance and program structure without actually starting any programming.
· The Development Phase: Creating the application, including all interface and code.
· The Implementation Phase: Using and testing the program.
· The Maintenance Phase: Making refinements to the product to eliminate any problems or to cover new needs that have developed.

Using the SDLC method can make any problems you encounter in your design more obvious, making it easier for you to tackle them at a more favorable point in your design, rather than changing existing code.

Chapter 2--- Getting Comfortable With JavaScript

In this Chapter, you'll follow my JavaScript class as they take their first look at the JavaScript programming environment. The purpose of this Chapter is to give you an overview of how to create a JavaScript program using Windows Notepad and how to run it.

Getting Comfortable with JavaScript

I began our second class by getting straight to the point.

"In today's class," I said, 'we're going to concentrate on writing our first JavaScript program. I hesitate to call what we're going to be writing a 'program', since, as you'll see, JavaScript programs are relatively short. Thus the term 'script'. But there's no doubt, what we're doing is programming."

I then started Windows Notepad.

"Are you going to write this program using Notepad?" Ward asked. "Doesn't JavaScript have an Integrated Development Environment--an IDE--like some of the other programming languages you've taught us, such as Visual Basic?"

"Not specifically Ward," I said. "There are a number of IDE's and Editors that will permit us to write JavaScript, including Visual Studio 6 and Visual Studio.Net. However, the beauty of JavaScript is that all you need is a plain old editor to start writing your JavaScript program, and Windows Notepad will fit the bill perfectly."

> **NOTE: If you are using an Operating System other than Windows (such as Mac or Linux) you can use the Editors supplied with it as well. For Mac, that would be SimpleText.**

"Is there a Developer's Kit for JavaScript like there is for Java?" Rhonda asked?

"JavaScript is included within your Internet Browser," I said, "there's no need to download anything else to make your JavaScript programs 'work'."

> **NOTE: As of the writing of this book (June 2006), there are 5 major Internet Browsers in use. Internet Explorer has a market share of 65%, FireFox 25%, Mozilla 3.5%, Opera 2%, and Netscape 1%.**

"So we don't need to buy anything in order to write our JavaScripts?" Mary asked.

"That's right Mary," I answered, "we can write our JavaScripts using Windows Notepad and run them just by opening them within an Internet browser---in this class, we'll open them within Internet Explorer."

I waited to see if I was about to lose any of my students. No one got up in a panic to leave the classroom (you think I'm kidding but I've seen it happen!), and so I began again.

Writing Our First JavaScript program

"Unlike other programming languages, in which writing a program can be a long drawn out progress," I said, "Creating a JavaScript program is really just a two step process."

1. Create the Source File with a file name extension of .htm
2. Open and Run the program within your Internet Browser

"Let's take a look at that first step now," I said.

Create the Source File with a file name extension of .htm

"First, we use a Text Editor---Notepad is easiest in the Microsoft Windows environment---to create what is known as a Source File. In the case of JavaScript, at least in the beginning, our source file will be an HTM (also called HTML) document containing JavaScript code."

> **NOTE: Because JavaScript runs within an Internet Browser, the Source code for a JavaScript program can be included as part of an HTM Document---and initially, that's where we'll place our JavaScript code. However, in later chapters, you'll see that you can write JavaScript code and place it in a file containing nothing but JavaScript--and 'call' this code from an HTM Document. More to follow :)**

"Why is that?" Mary asked.

"We'll be using an Internet Browser to interpret and execute the JavaScript code we write," I answered, "and Internet Browsers work primarily with HTML documents. In fact, most of our work in JavaScript will be interacting with HTML Objects---but more on that later."

> **NOTE: Objects are an important element of JavaScript programming. Don't be afraid of the term--we'll examine this in later chapters.**

"I remember HTML," Rhonda chimed in. "I'm so glad I took that HTML class with you last summer. Do we need to be an expert at HTML in order to write JavaScript?"

"Absolutely not, Rhonda," I said. "A JavaScript programmer can get away with just a superficial knowledge of HTML---however, the more you know about HTML, the more powerful your JavaScripts can be."

I paused before continuing.

"Let's get back to that issue of the Source file. The Source file is really just an ordinary text file. As I indicated, in our early efforts, the Source file will contain some HTML code and some JavaScript code. After composing our Source file in Windows Notepad, we'll then save it to our computer's hard drive, giving it a name of our choice."

"What will be the File Extension for the Source file?" Blaine asked.

"HTML documents," I said, end with a period, followed by the letters 'htm'---this is called its file name extension. For instance, in a few minutes, we'll create a JavaScript Source File whose name is 'ILoveJavaScript.htm'..."

"I took a class on HTML last year," Bob interjected, "and the instructor had us save our HTML documents with the file extension .html. Is that wrong?"

"No Bob," I answered, "that's perfectly fine. You can name your HTML documents with either the .html or .htm extension. Most computer geeks, like me, prefer to type as little as possible--that's why I use .htm."

> **NOTE: HTML documents can be named with a file extension of .htm or .html--the choice is up to you. All Internet Browsers recognize both file name extensions. My personal preference is .htm.**

I paused to see if there were any questions before continuing.

"Using Notepad to write our first JavaScript program is a snap," I said. "Let's write a JavaScript program that will display the message, 'I love JavaScript!'..."

I then entered the following code into Notepad...

```
Untitled - Notepad
File  Edit  Format  View  Help
<html>
<body>
<script type="text/javascript">
document.write("I love JavaScript!")
</script>
</body>
</html>
```

"Before I discuss this code," I said, "let's save this source file first by selecting File-Save As from Notepad's Menu Bar...

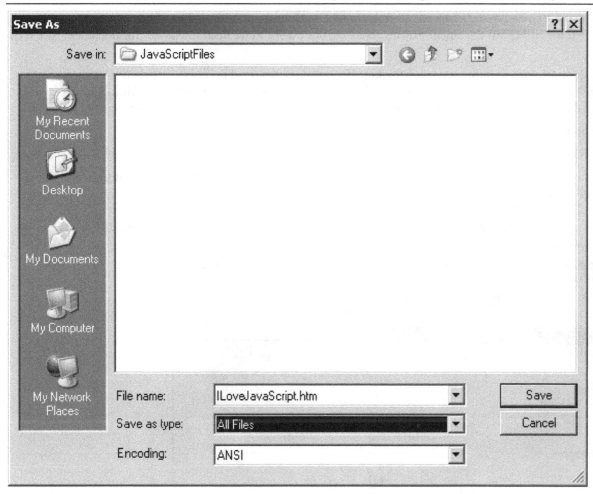

"I like to save all of my JavaScript source files in a folder called JavaScriptFiles," I said, "which is why I'm specifying 'JavaScriptFiles' in the 'Save in:' drop down Listbox. Notice how I have specified 'All Files' in the 'Save as type' Drop Down Listbox. After clicking on the Save button, you should notice that Notepad reflects the new file name…

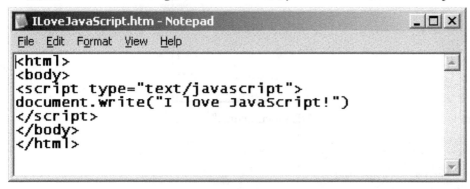

I gave some thought to explaining this code right now---but thought better of it. Better to *show* how it works before explaining *how* it works.

"We'll discuss the contents of this file in detail in just a few minutes," I said, "but for now, now that we have a good JavaScript source file, our next step is to…"

I was about to explain that our next step was to open the .htm document within an Internet browser, but Joe interrupted me.

"Compile it?" Joe asked.

"In other programming languages Joe," I said, "that might be true. However, JavaScript doesn't need to be compiled, it's interpreted by an Internet Browser, such as Internet Explorer. Our next step, believe it or not, is to simply open this document within Internet Explorer."

"Can we do that," Valerie asked. "Don't we need to type the URL into the Address Bar of Internet Explorer? But what's the URL for an HTML document that we create on our own? Do we need to upload this document to a Web Server?"

"Hold on Valerie," I said, admiring her quick thinking, "not so fast. Let's tackle your questions one at a time--but let's start backwards. First, there's no need to upload our HTML document to a Web Server. Although we certainly can (and will do that eventually), while testing our JavaScript programs, we can run them directly on our own PC."

"But what about the URL then?" Valerie persisted.

"What's a URL?" Peter asked. "I've never taken an HTML class."

Peter looked perplexed. "URL stands for Uniform Resource Locator, and it's just the Internet Address that you are probably used to typing into your Internet Browser in order to display a Web Page that is located on a Web Server somewhere on the World Wide Web. When we want to test JavaScript programs, as you've seen, we save the JavaScript in an HTML document. Once we've saved that document, all we need to do is select File-Open from the Internet Explorer Menu Bar..."

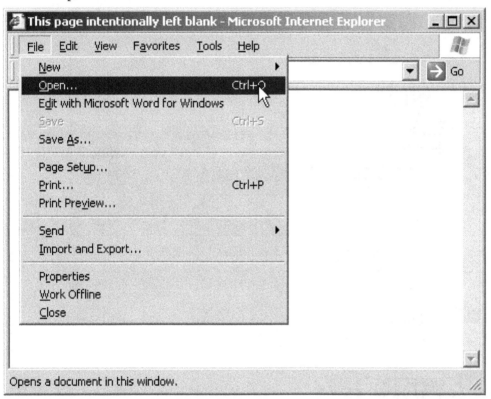

"...and tell Internet Explorer where to find, and open, our HTML Document...."

I clicked the OK button, and the following screenshot was displayed on our classroom projector...

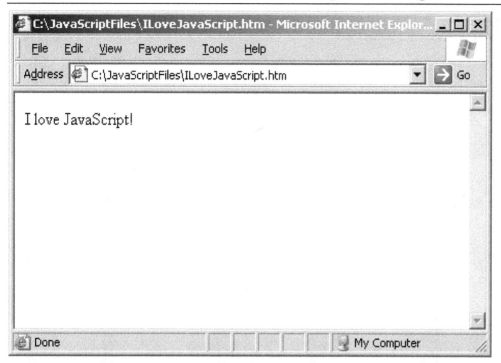

"What we've done here," I said, "is to write a program that displays 'I love JavaScript' on our Web Page. Notice the word 'Done' in the lower left hand corner of the Internet Explorer Window--to the right of the Internet Explorer icon. If there had been a syntax error with my JavaScript code, the Internet Explorer icon wouldn't display---an yellow exclamation point would be seen there."

NOTE: The official term for a Web Page is a Document. A Document is an HTML object. We'll learn more about the Document object, and other HTML objects, later on in the book.

"Oops,", I heard Rhonda say, "I just did what you did and received an error message. My Web page isn't displaying 'I love JavaScript'. What did I do wrong?"

I walked over to Rhonda's workstation. Sure enough, when I got there, her PC was indeed displaying an error message. Here's a screenshot of what I, and the rest of our class, saw.

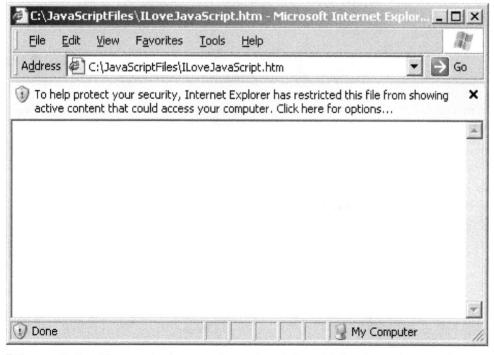

"I have a feeling I know what's wrong here Rhonda," I said, "and I don't think it's anything you did wrong. I suspect that our computer lab assistant has set up the security on your PC's Internet Explorer to prevent JavaScript programs from automatically executing. In fact, if we click on the error message, we should be presented with a choice that allows us to execute this JavaScript. Watch this..."

I then clicked on the 'Click here for options..." link, and the following screenshot was displayed on the classroom projector.

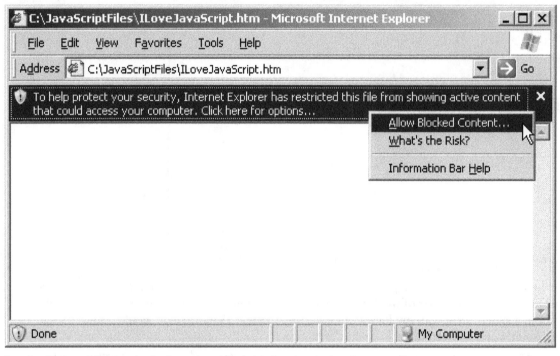

"Let's click on 'Allow Blocked Content'," I said, "and see what happens."

I did exactly that---clicked on 'Allow Blocked Content'---and the following Warning Message was displayed on Rhonda's monitor.

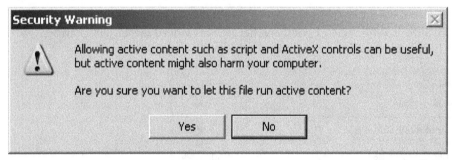

"All this is telling us," I said, "is that permitting Scripts and ActiveX controls to run on your PC can be dangerous. Script refers to JavaScripts---ActiveX Controls are something that you may remember we created way back in our Visual Basic Objects class."

"So if we click on the 'Yes' button," Jack said, "will we then see 'I love JavaScript' on Rhonda's monitor?"

"We should Jack," I said. I then clicked on the 'Yes' button, and the following screenshot was displayed on Rhonda's monitor. Through the magic of my computer lab, I was able to display the results on my classroom projector for all to see.

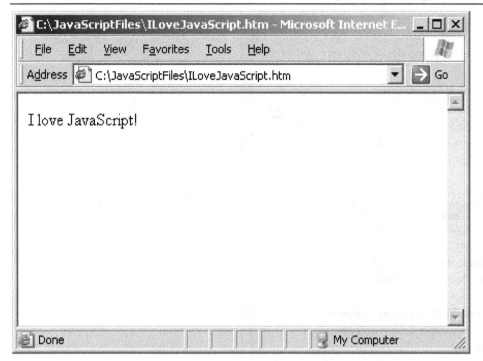

"It works," Rhonda said excitedly.

"Never a doubt," I said smiling.

"I just did the same thing," Kate said, "and received the same error message. Although I was eventually able to display the JavaScript result, this is going to be quite a pain in the neck if we need to go through that two-step process to display our programs. Is there a way to tell Internet Explorer not to 'block' our JavaScripts?"

"Good question Kate," I said. "Yes there is. If you select Tools-Options-Advanced from the Internet Explorer Menu Bar, and then scroll down to the Security Options, you will see a checkbox that says 'Allow active content to run in files on My Computer.' If we click the checkbox 'on', Internet Explorer will automatically run the JavaScript for us."

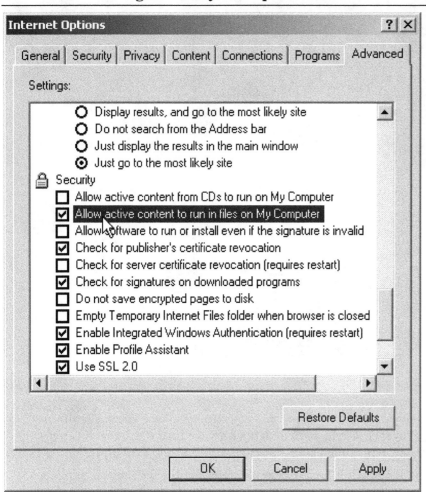

WARNING: Emails containing JavaScripts are a popular means of spreading viruses and other mayhem. If you receive an attachment with a file extension of .js, and this Security Option is selected, you may accidentally execute the JavaScript and its malicious content. Consider carefully whether you wish to permit active content to run on your computer without you being prompted.

"I realize that the problem wasn't with Rhonda's code," Steve said, "but suppose there was. Is there a way to see the code in our HTML document without going back into Notepad?"

"Yes there is Steve," I said, "if you select View-Source from the Internet Explore Menu Bar..."

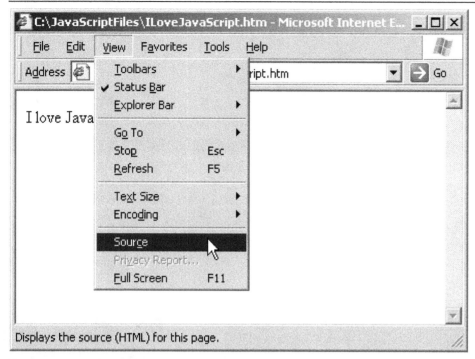

"Internet Explorer will open your source file in Microsoft Notepad."

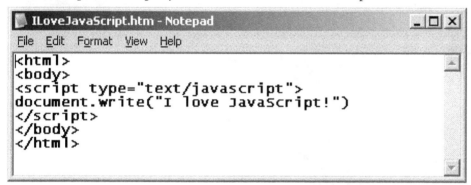

TIP: It's a good idea to leave your Source File open within Notepad while testing your JavaScript programs. That way, if something doesn't work the way you think it should, your Source File is still open for you to view.

"Ultimately," I said, "if you see the results you expect within your HTML Document window, that's good news. Any problems with your JavaScript Source file would either manifest themselves by NOT displaying the results you expect, or, if there's a syntax error in your JavaScript document, then you will see that Exclamation point I described earlier in the lower left hand corner of your Web Page."

To illustrate the point, I opened up my Source File using Notepad, and changed the word 'Document' to 'Docment'.

```
ILoveJavaScript.htm - Notepad
File  Edit  Format  View  Help
<html>
<body>
<script type="javascript">
docment.write("I love JavaScript!")
</script>
</body>
</html>
```

"I'm intentionally spelling the name of the 'Document' object incorrectly," I said. "I want to show you what happens if we now open this modified file in our Internet browser." I did so, and the following screenshot was displayed on the classroom projector.

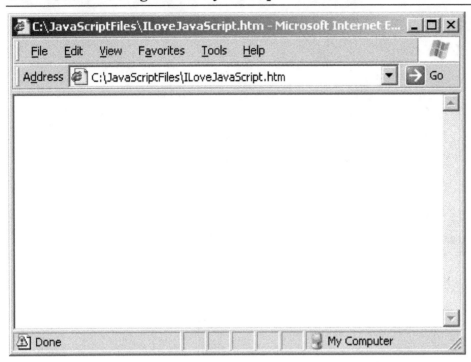

"I see what you mean," Dave said, "not only isn't 'I love JavaScript' displayed in the Web Document, but in the lower left hand corner of the window there's a yellow exclamation point."

"Absolutely correct Dave," I said, "and look what happens if we click on it." I did so, and this screenshot was displayed on the classroom projector.

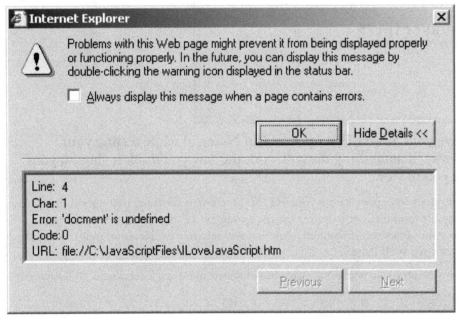

"Internet Explorer is trying to tell us what is wrong with our code," I said. "In this case, it's telling us that it doesn't recognize an object called 'Docment'. About all we can do now, is click the OK button, and then go back into Notepad and correct our Source file. Notice how the error message tells us the Line, and character position on the line that is causing Internet Explorer a problem. This can be a great help when trying to uncover the problem with one of our JavaScript programs."

I gave everyone in the class a chance to experiment a bit with our sample JavaScript program.

"I know in our C++ class," Joe said, "you were able to warn us in advance as to the common types of errors we were likely to make in C++---I know that really helped me a lot. Can you do something similar for us in this JavaScript class?"

"Many of the common errors that beginners make in C++," I said, "are due to inexperience working with the C++ compiler. JavaScript isn't compiled---an Internet Browser interprets it on the fly. For that reason, those nuisance type errors simply don't exist. As you'll see, most of the errors you make will simply be syntax errors."

"Are you going to explain this code?" Rose asked.

"You bet, " I answered,

I suggested that since we had been working for a while, now would be a great time to take a break, and fifteen minutes later, I began the discussion of our code by displaying it on the classroom projector.

Elements of a JavaScript program

I debated with myself as to whether I should begin my discussion of the code with a full-fledged entry into Object Oriented Programming--or whether I should simply explain what the code was doing, and then relate it to Object Oriented Programming.

Object Oriented Programming can be confusing to beginner students, but is something that JavaScript excels at. Finally, I decided to begin with a simple discussion of the code, and so I displayed it on the classroom projector.

```html
<html>
<body>
<script type="text/javascript">
   document.write("I love JavaScript!")
</script>
</body>
</html>
```

The HTML Tag

"Part of this discussion," I said, "will be a review for some of you, since I'll be explaining the elements of an HTML Document. Don't forget---for our beginning efforts at least---that JavaScript programs are embedded within HTML Documents."

"That's what the HTML Tag designates, is that right?" Dave asked.

"That's correct Dave," I said. "HTML makes use of what are known as tags---these are instructions to the Internet Browser on how the Web Page is to be formatted---tags appear within angle brackets, like these and in almost all cases, they appear in pairs, with the second tag, called an 'end tag' beginning with a backslash..."

```html
<html>
<body>
<script type="text/javascript">
document.write("I love JavaScript!")
</script>
</body>
</html>
```

"In an HTML document, the first tag will always be the <html> tag," I said. "This tag tells your Internet Browser that what it is 'reading' is an HTML document. The last tag in your HTML document will always be the </html> tag, or the ending HTML tag. This tells your Internet Browser that it has reached the end of the HTML document. Notice the 'sandwich' effect of these tags."

"I've seen some HTML source code where these tags are capitalized," Dave said, "Does it matter?"

"HTML is not case sensitive," I said, "and your Internet Browser doesn't care how you capitalize the tags that you use in your HTML Document. However, the World Wide Web Consortium, known as the W-3-C, which is the agency that oversees the development of the World Wide Web, recommends the use of lowercase tags in your HTML Documents."

"Why is that?" Mary asked.

"The next generation of HTML," I answered, "which is called XHTML, will be case sensitive, and lowercase tags will be required for it. So even though this class is not a class on HTML or XHTML, you will be required to write a little HTML in order to get your JavaScript programs to run---so it's a good idea to get into the habit of writing with lowercase tags right from the beginning."

The Head and Title Tags

"What comes next?" Rose asked.

"Following the HTML tags comes the Body Tag," I said, "although most Web Pages will also have Head and Title tags. As you might have guessed---since we didn't use them in our first program---the HEAD and TITLE tags are not required. However, if you want a custom Title Bar for your Web Page, you'll need a TITLE tag. and if you are going to have TITLE tags, you must have HEAD tags."

"Custom Title Bar?", I heard Chuck mumble.

"A TITLE tag provides a custom title for the Title Bar of the Window that displays our Web page," I said. "You may have noticed earlier that when we opened our sample Web page, the Title Bar displayed the file name and path of our HTML document. If we use a TITLE tag, we can display a custom Title Bar."

As a demonstration, I modified our Source Code file to include HEAD and TITLE tags...

```
<html>
<head>
<title>
I love JavaScript!
</title>
</head>
<body>
<script type="text/javascript">
document.write("I love JavaScript!")
</script>
</body>
</html>
```

"Notice," I said, "That the TITLE Tags are tags 'sandwiched' within the HEAD tag. Within the TITLE Tags appear the value, or Tag Attribute, for your Title Bar" I then opened up the modified Source File within Internet Explorer. The following screenshot was displayed on the classroom projector.

"Notice the custom Title Bar," I pointed out. "Previously, we had displayed the path and file name of our Source Code file. Now it reads, 'I love JavaScript!'.

"I like it," I heard Ward say. "Should we include one in our Source Code file?"

"It's up to you Ward," I said, "but for the demonstration programs in this class, I won't be including TITLE Tags. By accepting the default Title Bar, you'll see the Path and File name of the Source Code file I'm opening in Internet Explorer."

The Body Tag

"So what about that BODY tag?" Linda asked.

"I seem to recall," Rhonda interrupted, "in our HTML class, that whatever we wanted to display within our HTML Document we put within the BODY Tag.

"That's absolutely right Rhonda," I said. "However, this is a bit confusing in a JavaScript class. As we'll shortly see, we can use JavaScript to display text within our HTML document, or we can use plain old HTML to do it. Let me modify the Source Code we've already written to use HTML to display 'I love HTML' within our HTML document. Look at this HTML code..."

```
<html>
<head>
<title>
I love HTML
</title>
</head>
<body>
I love HTML
</body>
</html>
```

"Notice how I've removed the Script tag," I said. "which is the JavaScript part that we wrote earlier. Don't worry--- I'll be putting it back shortly. For now, take a look at what's between the BODY Tags---'I love HTML!'. If we open this Source File in Internet Explorer, that's exactly what will be displayed in the Body of the HTML Document." I then did so--and the following screenshot was displayed on the classroom projector.

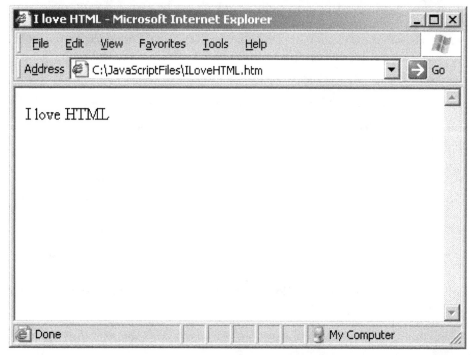

"Does everyone see?" I said, "This is the way most people display text in a Web Document--by including it within the BODY Tag."

"I understand what happened," Rhonda said, "but if we don't need to use JavaScript to display text within the body of an HTML document, what good is JavaScript?"

"JavaScript is much more powerful than plain old HTML," I answered. "because it can be used to create HTML Documents that are much more dynamic than ordinary HTML."

"What do you mean by dynamic?" Lou asked.

"For instance," I said, "the HTML code we see here will ALWAYS display 'I love HTML'. in our Web Document. Using JavaScript, we can vary the display of our HTML Document based on the time of day, the day of the week, or even the user's answer to a question we pose."

"That sounds great," Rhonda responded. "That sounds very much like what Visual Basic can do with a Windows Form."

"That's exactly the idea," I agreed. "Web Documents are very much like Windows Forms."

The Script Tag

"Let's get back to that SCRIPT Tag," I said, as I displayed our *original* code on the classroom projector.

```
<html>
<body>
<script type="text/javascript">
document.write("I love JavaScript!")
</script>
</body>
</html>
```

"Does everyone see the <script> and </script> tags," I said. "Just about everything that you see between those is our JavaScript program. With the exception of the type parameter, which just identifies the type of script as JavaScript, the rest is our program. In fact, in this code, all we have is a single line of JavaScript code, the execution of the **write()** method of the **document** object What we want to 'write' to the document object, our Web page, is enclosed within quotation marks within the parentheses following the write method..."

document.write("I love JavaScript!")

"I'm afraid you're losing me with this talk of objects and methods," Steve said.

"JavaScript is very much Object Oriented," I said, "and we'll discuss this in more detail as the class proceeds. Suffice to say, for now, that objects, such as the document object, possess methods, which can be executed to produce certain pre-defined results. In this case, executing the **write()** method of the **document** object displays the text that appears within the pair of parentheses and within the quotation marks, upon our Web Page. Ordinarily, there would be other instructions in our JavaScript program, but for our first program, I wanted to keep it simple."

"Are there other methods of the document object?" Mary asked.

"Oh yes Mary," I answered, "there are many more that we'll be examining as the class goes on."

"What can be 'written' to the Document?" Dave asked. "I know that in HTML, we could italicize or make text bold. Can we do that with the write() method?"

"Excellent question Dave," I said. "In theory, we can write any HTML formatting tag to our document--the way we would with an ordinary Web Page."

"I'm lost," Rhonda said sheepishly.

"Well, in an HTML document," I said, "we would use the HTML bold tags to make the phrase 'I love JavaScript!' bold on our Web Page, like this..."

I love JavaScript!

"To do the same thing in a JavaScript program," I continued, "we do the same thing--except we need to do so within the write() method of the document object, like this..."

```
<html>
<body>
<script type="text/javascript">
document.write("<b>I love JavaScript!</b>")
</script>
</body>
</html>
```

I then opened the Source file within Internet Explorer, and the following screen shot was displayed on the classroom projector.

"Ah, it's bold," Rhonda said. "I see now. Basically, you're just writing HTML to the Document object, but within the context of a JavaScript program."

"Exactly right Rhonda," I said. "Any HTML that we could code in an HTML document can be coded in a JavaScript program within the write() method of the Document object."

> **Never Fear: Don't be overwhelmed by the HTML that's been presented this far in the course. There isn't that much to it, and I think my explanation will help you understand. If you need more, feel free to pick up a copy of my HTML book, Learn to Program with HTML.**

"Getting back to that Type parameter of the SCRIPT Tag," Kathy said, "are there other Scripting languages besides JavaScript?"

"Yes, there are several Kathy," I said, "Although the two primary ones are VBScript, and the subject of this course, JavaScript."

I waited to see if there were any more questions before continuing.

HTML and JavaScript Comments

"Does JavaScript support comments the way other programming languages do?" Dave asked.

"Yes it does," I said. "Comments are a wonderful way to let the reader of your code know who wrote the code, when it was written, and what you are trying to do. However, this topic of comments can be tricky, particularly when you are writing JavaScript code within an HTML document as we are here."

"What do you mean?" Valerie asked, "when you say 'tricky'?".

"Tricky," I said, "from the point of view that you are writing both HTML and JavaScript in the same source file. And unfortunately, the comment syntax is different for HTML and for JavaScript."

"Which means that within the same source file you can have both HTML and JavaScript comments, each one following different rules?" Dave asked.

"You hit the nail on the head Dave," I said. "Personally, I prefer to create JavaScript source files and 'call' my JavaScript code from within my HTML documents. But this can be more complicated for a beginner to fathom. So, in the beginning of our studies anyway, we'll be mixing JavaScript and HTML together. And each one has distinct rules for comments. Let me show you can example of an HTML comment". I then displayed this Source file on the classroom projector.

```
<!-- This is a comment -->
<html>
```

```
<body>
<script type="text/javascript">
document.write("I love JavaScript!")
</script>
</body>
</html>
```

"As you can see," I said, "an HTML comment begins with a left angle bracket, followed by an exclamation point. The comment then follows, and the end of the comment is marked by a right angle bracket."

"What about the two dashes following the exclamation point, and the two dashes preceding the right angle bracket?" Valerie asked. "Are they required?"

"No, they're not required Valerie," I said, "although it's common to include them to make the comment stand out a bit more. We could also have written the code this way..."

```
<! This is a comment >
<html>
<body>
<script type="text/javascript">
document.write("I love JavaScript!")
</script>
</body>
</html>
```

"It does look a little sparse without those dashes," Peter said, "I see what you mean by the dashes making the comment stand out a bit."

"Can comments span more than one line?" Dave asked.

"Good question Dave," I said, "and yes, they can span more than one line, like this..."

```
<!--
Programmer: John Smiley
Date Written: January 21, 2014
-->
<html>
<body>
<script type="text/javascript">
document.write("I love JavaScript!")
</script>
</body>
</html>
```

"Can comments only appear in the beginning of our HTML document?" Rose asked.

"Comments can appear anywhere," I said, "It's a good idea to place comments wherever you think an explanatory comment is needed, like this..."

```
<!--
Programmer: John Smiley
Date Written: January 21, 2014
-->
<html>
<body>
<!-- Our first piece of JavaScript code -->
<script type="text/javascript">
document.write("I love JavaScript!")
</script>
</body>
</html>
```

"These are not JavaScript comments, is that right?" Mary asked.

"That's right Mary," I said, "these have all been examples of HTML comments. JavaScript comments will appear within our JavaScript code---and that's the code that appears within the SCRIPT tags. Typically, you tend to see comments in JavaScript code when the code appears in a file of its own--something we'll do later on in the class. But they can appear within the SCRIPT tag when we embed our JavaScript code within an HTML Document. Let me show you." I then displayed this code on the classroom projector.

```
<html>
<body>
<script type="text/javascript">
//This is a JavaScript comment included within the SCRIPT Tag
document.write("I love JavaScript!")
</script>
</body>
</html>
```

"JavaScript actually has two forms of comments," I said. "The first is a single line comment, and uses a double set of forward slashes as I've done here. The double slash can appear anywhere on a line--that is, in the front of the line as we've done here, or at the end, like this..."

```
<html>
<body>
<script type="text/javascript">
document.write("I love JavaScript!") //document.write displays text on a Web Page
</script>
</body>
</html>
```

"JavaScript also supports multi-line comments, just like HTML does," I said. "Take a look at this code..."

```
<html>
<body>
<script type="text/javascript">
/*
Programmer: John Smiley
Date Written: January 21, 2014
*/
document.write("I love JavaScript!")
</script>
</body>
</html>
```

"That's similar to the C++ comment, isn't it?" Valerie asked.

"Yes it is Valerie," I answered, "in fact, it's identical to the C++ style."

"I must say I'm a little confused," Rhonda said, "suppose we mess up the comments? What will happen?"

"Well, if you make a mistake with the format for the comment," I said, "Three things can happen, depending upon the type of comment. If you make a mistake with the HTML comment, most likely the comment--or what you thought was the comment---will appear on the Web Page---like this..."

I then displayed this code on the classroom projector.

```
!--
Programmer: John Smiley
Date Written: January 21, 2014
-->
<html>
<body>
<script type="text/javascript">
document.write("I love JavaScript!")
</script>
```

```
</body>
</html>
```

"It's not obvious," I said, "but I'm missing the left angle bracket that is required to begin a multi-line comment. If we open this document within Internet Explorer, here's what we'll see..."

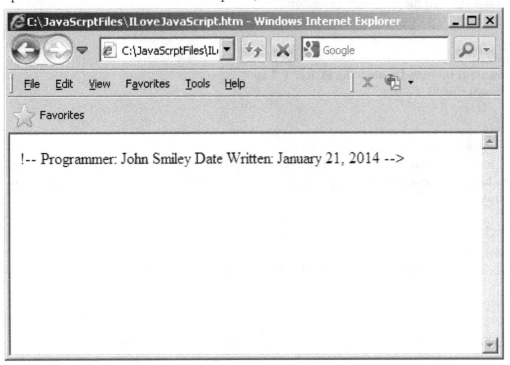

"Wow, that really created a mess," Rhonda said. "Suppose we make a mistake with a JavaScript comment?"

"Your Internet Browser," I said, "will attempt to interpret the comment as JavaScript. Most likely, you'll generate a JavaScript error..."

"And we'll wind up with that exclamation point in the lower left hand corner, right?" Kate asked.

"That's right Kate," I said. "Take a look at this code, where instead of a double forward slash for my intended comment, I have just one."

```
<html>
<body>
<script type="text/javascript">
document.write("I love JavaScript!") /document.write displays text on a Web Page
</script>
</body>
</html>
```

"If l open this document within Internet Explorer," I said, "here's what we'll see..."

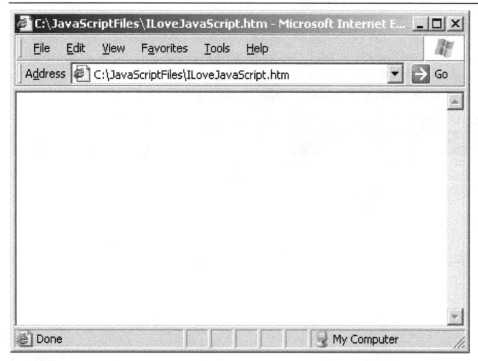

"I don't see the exclamation point icon in the lower left hand side of the window," Jack said.

"No," I agreed, "in this case, the badly formatted comment wasn't severe enough to cause a JavaScript error---on the other hand, it prevented the rest of our code from being properly executed---nothing was displayed on our Web Page."

"I think I may just stay away from comments," Rhonda said.

"Don't worry Rhonda," I said, "I'm sure you'll use them when appropriate---once you have the format down, you'll be fine."

"I know you said earlier that we would be doing exercises of our own for practice," Kathy said. "Will we be coding comments in the exercises that we do?"

"I've already noticed," I said, "that some of you are not the fastest typists in the world, so our exercises will not explicitly include comments---I'll leave the comments up to you to insert as you complete the exercises."

I waited to see if there were any other questions--but no one seemed to have anymore.

"What I'd like to do now," I said, "is to give you a chance to write, compile and run a JavaScript program of your own--with my assistance. As we'll do during the remainder of the course, I have a series of exercises for you to complete which will lead you through that process."

I then distributed this exercise for the class to complete.

Exercise 2-1 Coding your first JavaScript program---Grades.htm

In this exercise you'll write your first JavaScript program--which will form the basis of our class project. By the way, if typing these exercises bores you, feel free to follow this link to find the completed solutions for all of the exercises in the book. Just click on the JavaScript book, then follow the link entitled exercises ☺

http://www.johnsmiley.com/main/books.htm

1. Using Windows Explorer, create a folder on your hard drive called \JavaScriptFiles\Grades. This will be the 'home' of our class project, the Grades Calculation Project.

2. Use the editor of your choice (if you are using Windows, use Notepad) and enter the following code. For future compatibility with XHTML, be sure to spell your tags (the code in angle brackets <>) in lower case.

```
<html>
<body>
<script type="text/javascript">
   document.write("It's not much, but it's a start")
</script>
```

```
</body>
</html>
```

3. Save your source file as '**Grades.htm**' in the \JavaScriptFiles\Grades folder (select File-Save As from Notepad's Menu Bar). Be sure to save your source file with the file name extension 'htm'.

4. Use Internet Explorer to Open your Source File. You should see this screen shot

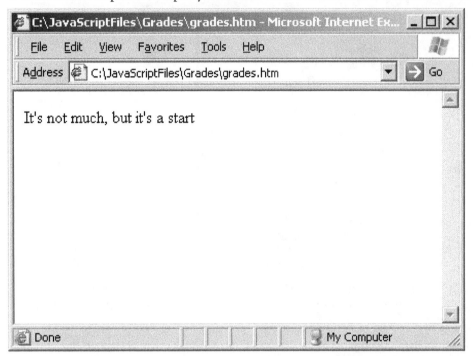

Aside from some people in the class who didn't seem very familiar with Notepad, this exercise seemed to go pretty smoothly. In just a few moments, everyone in the class had completed coding their first JavaScript program--the Grades program. This source file, although very simplistic, would eventually form the basis of the program we would give to Frank, Robin and Dave.

"Is this the program we'll be using to calculate grades for the English, Math and Science departments?" Mary asked.

"It looks like all this does is display a message to the Internet Explorer Document Window?"

"That's right Mary," I said. "Have you heard the expression that the journey of a thousand miles begins with the first step? This is the first step. From there, everything else will be built. And even though displaying this message isn't part of the user requirements, I want the program to do 'something' when you compile and run it--just to prove to you that there is some activity going on in there."

There were no questions about the actual coding of their first JavaScript program---it was almost identical to the sample we had been working on.

Just then I noticed Kate--she was obviously having a problem.

"Need help?" I asked her.

"I've been trying to correct this for the last ten minutes," she said. "Nothing is being displayed in my Internet Explorer Window. This isn't nearly as easy as Visual Basic, is it?"

"JavaScript requires a little more attention to detail," I said, noticing that she was right---nothing was being displayed in her Browser Window. "Let's select View-Source from the Internet Explorer Menu Bar and see what's going on.

> **NOTE: I could also have opened up the Grades.htm source file in Notepad to view Kate's source file. In fact, while running your JavaScript programs, there's no need to close Notepad prior to opening your Source File in your Internet Browser--just make sure you save the file before trying to open it. This way, if there's a problem, you can simply check the file in Notepad.**

"I see what the problem is," I said, "it's the same mistake I 'intentionally' made earlier. You spelled the HTML object 'document' incorrectly."

Kate smiled--then corrected the spelling.

"Nothing's changed," she said sadly.

"That's because Internet Explorer has to be told to re-read your Source File," I said.

She was about to close Internet Explorer and open another Internet Explorer window when I told her that she could either select View-Refresh from the Internet Explorer Menu Bar, or just press the [F5] Function key. Both actions tell Internet Explorer to refresh the 'page' from the Source. Kate did this, and the correct message was displayed in her Internet Browser.

"I know we haven't done all that much," Rhonda said, "but I feel pretty good about what we've done so far. My programming friends all told me how difficult JavaScript was--but so far, so good."

"JavaScript can be difficult," I said, "but as you know, here at the university, we have a reputation for doing a pretty good job with beginners. One step at a time, I always say, and the next logical step in next week's class will be to give you a JavaScript code overview to show you what the language can do."

It had been a very productive class---everyone now had the beginnings of the Grades Calculation program in place.

It had also been a pretty long class, and as I glanced up at the clock on the wall, I realized our class was over. I then dismissed class for the day.

Summary

In this chapter you were exposed to the 'nitty gritty' of the JavaScript environment. You saw that writing a program in JavaScript is pretty basic. You use an editor to create a JavaScript source file, and then open it within an Internet Browser.

In the next chapter, you'll be exposed to data

Chapter 3---Data

In a computer program, data is extremely important. As we saw in Chapter 1, data is brought in or 'input' into a computer program in order to be processed into meaningful output. In this chapter, we'll discuss the concept of data in a computer program. You'll learn about program variables, the different types of JavaScript Data Types, and the many operations that can be performed on that data.

Computer Data

"Data can be a very complex topic," I said, "but it's an extremely important one. Failure to understand data can lead to problems with your programs down the line. What you learn today may seem very theoretical to you, but it will be vital for your future-programming career. Even if you don't see an immediate application for it, look at the information you receive today as something that you can tuck into your programming back pocket for future use."

Variables

"In the JavaScript programs that we write," I said, "the data with which we work will come from three places---first, from the user, in the form of selections that they make usually from objects that we place on a window. Secondly, from external sources, such as a disk file or a database, or thirdly, sometimes internally in the form of variables."

"Variables?" Rhonda asked.

I continued by explaining that variables are placeholders in the computer's memory where we can temporarily store information. Values---numbers and characters, for example, are stored in variables while the program is running. As their name implies, the values of the variables can change at any time.

"I'm a little confused as to why we would create a variable in the first place," Barbara said. "Isn't all of the data that we need---especially in the program we're writing in this class--- entered by the user? Why do we need to store anything 'temporarily'?"

"That's a good question Barbara," I said. "and to a great degree, you're right. Most of the data that computer programs need is entered by the user, or comes from a disk file or database. However, there may be times when your program may need to create and use a variable in order to store the answer to a question that you have asked of the user, or the result of a calculation or, as we will see a little later on in today's class, to keep track of a counter--which is a variable that counts something.."

"You said that variables enable us to store information temporarily," Kate said. "I assume that means until our program ends? A variable can't last beyond the running of a program, can it?"

"That's true Kate," I said. "In JavaScript, variables are 'born' when the program (or script) in which they appear starts to execute, and 'die' when that program (or script) ends."

Our first variable

I asked everyone to consider a hypothetical program, which I hoped would illustrate the need for variables in a program.

"Let's write a JavaScript program," I said, "that declares two variables, assigns each one a value, and then displays the sum of the two variables in our Internet Browser. I should warn you that most of what you will see in this program you haven't learned yet--but you will today…"

I then displayed this program on the classroom projector…

```
<! Example3-1 -->
<html>
<body>
<script type="text/javascript">

var number1
var number2

number1 = 12
number2 = 23
```

```
document.write(number1 + number2)
</script>
</body>
</html>
```

Note: JavaScript variable names are case sensitive. A variable declared with the name number is considered to be different than a variable declared with the name Number. Be careful!

"I've included liberal amounts of white space in the program," I said. "White space just means empty lines in our source file---it makes the program easier to read." I then saved the program as '**Example3-1.htm**', and opened it up within Internet Explorer. The following screen shot was displayed on the classroom projector...

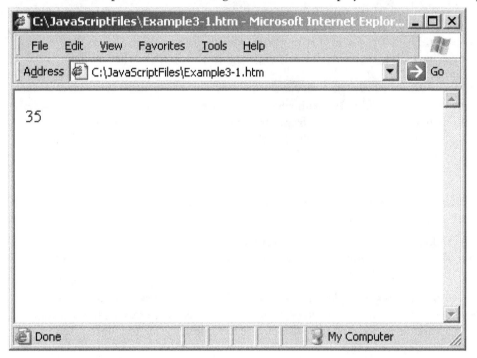

"That's cool," I heard Kate say. "35 is the sum of 12 and 23--the values of variables number1 and number2!"

"That's excellent Kate," I said,

I waited to see if everyone else in the class had a similar understanding.

"Let me explain what's going on here," I said. "Last week, we used the write() method of the document object to display a message in our Web Browser. That message was called, in computer programming terms, a literal constant. The only way to change the value of a literal constant is to change our source code. In this program, we're once again using the write() method to display something--but in this case, it's the value of the sum of two variables. In computer programming, a variable is something whose value can change while the program is running. Let's examine our source code now..."

Declaring a variable

"We begin the process by declaring the variable *number1* using this line of code..."

```
var number1
```

"and the variable **number2** using this code..."

```
var number2
```

"What is *var*?" Mary asked.

"var is the keyword used to let JavaScript know that we are declaring a variable," I said. "We follow it with the name of the variable---which can really be anything we want."

"Is the word 'var' required?" Ward asked. "I've dabbled a bit with JavaScript, and I'm not sure I've always seen it used."

"In actuality Ward," I said, "var is not required to declare a variable--but it's a good idea to use it. Using var makes reading our Javascript program, and understanding what it is doing, a lot easier."

Assigning a value to a variable

"What are those next two lines of code doing?" Joe asked.

"These two line of code are assigning the number 12 to the variable number1," I said. "and the number 23 to the variable number2. In JavaScript, the equal sign is called the Assignment Operator..."

```
number1 = 12
number2 = 23
```

I gave the class a minute to ponder this.

"What's going on inside those parentheses," Rhonda asked. "Last week, when we used this method, we had 'I love JavaScript!' inside the parentheses within quotation marks?"

"In this case Rhonda," I answered, "we are telling JavaScript to take the *VALUE* of the variables number1 and number2, add them together, and display them in our Internet Browser..."

```
document.write(number1 + number2)
```

"That makes sense," Blaine said, "although I must confess I'm still not totally clear on this concept of a variable."

"Let me go over this again," I said, "because it is important. I like to compare a variable to a Post Office Box. When you rent a Post Office Box, you are assigned a box number, and when mail for your box arrives, the postal clerk places your mail in your box according to the number you've been assigned. If you need to retrieve your mail, knowing your number, you can use your key to access it. Variables in JavaScript are very similar. When you declare a variable, you use this syntax...."

```
var number1
```

"...which tells JavaScript that you wish to declare an Integer type variable with the name number1. This is similar to going to the Post Office and renting a box. The great thing about JavaScript---and other programs as well---is that you can give the variable an easy-to-remember name that you can recognize later--you don't need to work with a hard-to-remember 'Post Office box' number. Thereafter, whenever you need to interact with the variable, you use its easy-to-remember name, as we did when we assigned a value to it using the JavaScript assignment statement..."

```
number1 = 12
```

"...and as we did when we used the variable's name in the write() method of the document object...."

```
document.write(number1 + number2)
```

"Do you need to assign a value to a variable after you've declared it?" Chuck asked. "In other words, do you have to initialize it?"

"Excellent question," I said. "Failing to provide a value to a variable you declare can result in some rather strange results. For instance, if we had forgotten to assign a value to the variable number2, like this..."

```
<! Example3-2 -->
<html>
<body>
<script type="text/javascript">

var number1
var number2

number1 = 12

document.write(number1 + number2)

</script>
</body>
</html>
```

"would result in this display in our browser..."

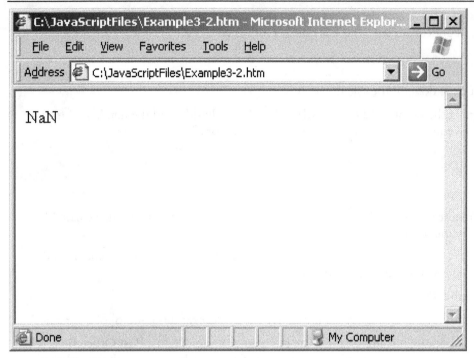

"NaN?" Kate asked. "What does that mean?"

"NaN stands for 'Not-A-Number." I answered. "JavaScript is telling us that our attempt to add the value of the variables number1 and number2 resulted in something that is not a true number.."

"And the reason for that is because number2 was not initialized with a value, is that right?" Valerie asked.

That's right Valerie," I agreed, "since number2 was declared as a variable, but never given a value, it really had no value. When we tried to add it to the value of variable1, we confused JavaScript, which then displayed 'NaN'."

> **NOTE: Assigning a value to a variable after you have declared it is called Initialization**

Declaration and Assignment combined

"I think some languages permit you to combine the declaration and assignment of a value to a variable," Dave said, "can you do that in JavaScript?"

"Yes you can combine them Dave," I answered. "Here's the same program using that technique…"

```
<! Example3-3 -- >
<html>
<body>
<script type="text/javascript">
var number1 = 12
var number2 = 23
document.write(number1 + number2)
</script>
</body>
</html>
```

"…in a language such as JavaScript that tends to be 'wordy'," I said, "programmers frequently look for ways to streamline their code---this is one way to do it…"

```
var number1 = 12
```

"In fact," I said, "if you want, you can declare more than one variable on the same line, by using a comma to separate them, like this…"

```
<! Example3-4 -- >
<html>
<body>
<script type="text/javascript">
```

```
var number1, number2
number1 = 12
number2 = 23
document.write(number1 + number2)
</script>
</body>
</html>
```

"...and to take it a step further, you can declare and initialize more than one variable on the same line of code, like this..."

```
<! Example3-5 -- >
<html>
<body>
<script type="text/javascript">
var number1 = 12, number2 = 23
document.write(number1 + number2)
</script>
</body>
</html>
```

"When I'm teaching," I said, "I like to make things as plain and obvious as possible, so I avoid 'condensing' my code like this in the classroom, but you will see it a lot in the programming world."

I paused to see if I had lost anyone--but everyone seemed OK.

"One more thing I'd like to show you," I said, "is how to make our output in the console a little more user friendly…"

I then displayed this code on the classroom projector…

```
<! Example3-6 -- >
<html>
<body>
<script type="text/javascript">
var number1 = 12
var number2 = 23
document.write("The answer is ")
document.write (number1 + number2)
</script>
</body>
</html>
```

I then saved the program as '**Example3-6.htm**', and opened it up within Internet Explorer. The following screen shot was displayed on the classroom projector…

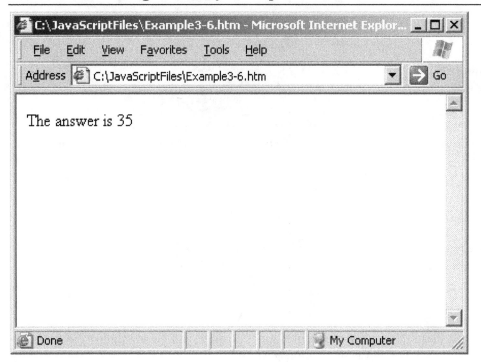

"This line of code," I said,

document.write("The answer is ")

"uses the write() method of the document object to display the phrase "The answer is" in our Internet Browser.

"Just curious," Rhonda said, "but I would have thought that the number 35 would be on a separate line from the phrase 'The answer is'. I've been experimenting with this myself---I don't seem to be able to get the number 35 on a new line."

"I see Rhonda," I said, "you thought that by executing document.write() again, the result would be on a separate line. In some programming languages, that might be true--but in JavaScript, this isn't the case. No matter how many distinct executions of the write() method of the document object you have, the display will remain on the same line. What you have to remember is that ultimately, your JavaScript is generating HTML code, and in order to 'force' your output to a new line, you need to embed the proper HTML tag within the argument you provide to the write() method of the document object."

"I remember tags," Kate said, "we discussed those in the first week of the class."

"So how do we do that?" Peter asked.

"We use the BR tag, like this," I said. I then displayed this code on the classroom projector. "Notice how the BR tag is in lower case, enclosed within angle brackets, and enclosed within quotation marks."

```
<! Example3-7 -- >
<html>
<body>
<script type="text/javascript">
var number1 = 12
var number2 = 23
document.write("The answer is <br>")
document.write (number1 + number2)
</script>
</body>
</html>
```

I then saved the program as '**Example3-7.htm**', and opened it up within Internet Explorer. The following screen shot was displayed on the classroom projector...

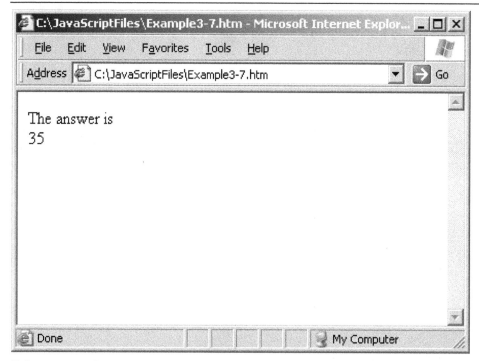

"The BR tag tells our Internet Browser to insert a line break in the display," I said. "In this case, the line break occurs between the phrase 'The answer is' and the number 35.

NOTE: Notice that the embedded tag lies within the quotation marks of the string supplied to the write() method of the document object

"What are the rules for naming a variable?" Jack asked.

"Variable names must begin with a letter or an underscore character," I said, "and can be of any length--although remember this. Variables with long names make coding more difficult, as invariably you'll need to refer to it again somewhere in your code. Make your variable names short but meaningful--I avoid single character variable names such as 'x'."

I paused a moment before continuing.

"Some JavaScript programmers," I said, "like to reduce the number of lines of code that they write---if we wish, we can streamline our code a little bit by using this syntax..."

```
<! Example3-8 -- >
<html>
<body>
<script type="text/javascript">
var number1 = 12
var number2 = 23
document.write("The answer is " + (number1 + number2))
</script>
</body>
</html>
```

I then saved the program as '**Example3-8.htm**', and opened it up within Internet Explorer. The following screen shot was displayed on the classroom projector...

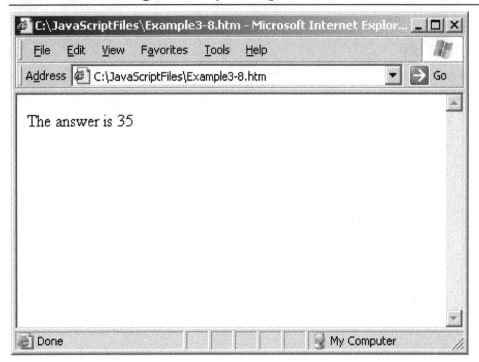

"As you can see, we achieved the same results," I said, "by using something known as CONCATENATION. Concatenation means to join--and in JavaScript, you use the CONCATENATION operator--the + sign---to join the sentence (also known as a string) 'The answer is ' to the result of the addition of the values of number1 and number2"

"I've worked with some languages," Dave said, "where concatenating a number--35---to a string would have caused the program to bomb---but that didn't happen here."

"What is Dave saying?" Mary asked.

"Dave is pointing out that the number 35 is not a String," I said. "We'll discuss Data Types in more detail later on in the class---but Dave is right, in some other languages concatenating a number to a string of characters would cause the program to bomb. JavaScript is doing us a favor here. If any part of the concatenation operation is a string, then all elements of the operation are treated as if they are Strings."

"I don't find the concept as confusing as the number of parentheses," Kate said, "how do you know how many and where to put them?"

"I admit, that can be confusing Kate," I answered. "One quick rule of thumb is that you must always have an EVEN number of parentheses, and you must have the same number of left parenthesis as right parenthesis. Aside from that, here are some other hints. The 'argument' to the write() method must be contained within parentheses, and because I wanted to concatenate the result of the addition operation of number1 and number2 to the end of the string, I placed that addition operation within parentheses also…."

document.write("The answer is " + (number1 + number2))

"…If I hadn't done that, and instead had written the code like this…"

```
<! Example3-9 -- >
<html>
<body>
<script type="text/javascript">
var number1 = 12
var number2 = 23
document.write("The answer is " + number1 + number2)
</script>
</body>
</html>
```

"…we would have gotten an entirely different result…"

I then saved the program as '**Example3-9.htm**', and opened it up within Internet Explorer. The following screen shot was displayed on the classroom projector...

"What happened?" Rhonda asked. "12 plus 23 isn't 1223--it's 35?"

"What happened here," I said, "is that we wound up concatenating the string 12 to the end of the string 'The answer is ' and then concatenating the string '23' to the end of that concatenated string--like this..."

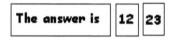

"All of which points up that a number and a String are two different animals!" Ward said. "So are you saying placing parentheses around the addition operation caused the addition to be performed first--and that sum--35--was then concatenated to the string 'The answer is '?"

"Exactly right Ward," I said.

"I hate to say this," Rhonda said, "but I just accidentally wrote some code in which I assigned a value to a variable, but forgot to first declare it---now I'm really confused."

"You've discovered, Rhonda" I said, "that JavaScript doesn't require you to declare a variable before using it. This is considered poor programming practice and can cause problems in your program. It's good programming practice to always declare your variables before using them."

> **Note: JavaScript variables do not need to be declared before using them. This is another example of why JavaScript is not considered a Strongly typed Programming Language. Good programming practice dictates that you always declare your variables prior to using them--- and be sure to use the var keyword.**

Variable Scope and Lifetime

"I think I understand what a variable is and what it's used for," Rhonda said. "But what do the programmers I work with mean when they talk about Variable scope and lifetime?"

"Scope and lifetime?" Chuck asked, adding emphasis to Rhonda's question.

"Scope," I said, "refers to what parts of your JavaScript program can 'see' the variable you've declared. I haven't mentioned this before, but some JavaScript programs that we write will consist of functions, which are modules of code within our program. So far, all of the variables that we've declared have been declared outside of any function--

-simply because we haven't coded any functions. Scope is a term that describes whether a variable declared in a function can be seen outside that function."

"So what's the answer?" Ward asked.

"I suspect," Dave chimed in, "that variables can be seen only in the function in which they are declared?"

"That's right Dave," I said, "Variables declared outside of a function---like the ones we've been working with today---can be seen anywhere within our program. However, variables declared within a function possess what is known as local scope, and can only be seen in the function in which they are declared. We'll learn more about these when we create functions of our own later on in the class."

"I'm a little confused," Rhonda said. "Is local scope a good thing or a bad thing?"

"The rule of thumb," I said, "is to give your variable as narrow a scope as necessary. Provided its value does not need to be accessible to code in other functions, local scope is a good thing. On the other hand, if you need to have the value of that variable accessible from another function in your program, then that's .."

"A bad thing!" Rhonda answered, finishing my sentence, and obviously understanding what I was getting at. "OK, I think I'm beginning to understand. Declaring variables requires a bit more thought than I believed…"

"If you wanted to make the value of that variable visible to other functions in your program," Steve said, "that's when you would declare it outside of any function."

> **NOTE: We'll learn more about Functions in an upcoming chapter---if this discussion of function variables doesn't make a lot of sense to you right now, don't worry too much about it.**

"What about lifetime?" Lou asked.

"Lifetime refers to how long a variable, once declared, lives," I said. "Again, as was the case with Scope, this will depend upon the type of variable that you declare. Variables declared in a function exist for as long as the function is executing--as soon as the function ends, the variable--and its value---goes away. Variables declared outside of any function--as the one's we've declared today are---exist for as long as our JavaScript program is executing."

Constants--Sorry, not in JavaScript Yet:(

"Does JavaScript support Constants?" Dave asked.

"Constant?" Linda asked, "that sounds like it should be the opposite of a variable."

"You're right Linda," I said, "in some programming languages, that's exactly what it is---a placeholder in the computer's memory, given an easy-to-remember name that holds a value just like a variable, but unlike a variable, its value, once initialized, can never be changed. Constants can be pretty useful---unfortunately, JavaScript doesn't support Constants---although it's possible a future version of JavaScript will. The word 'const' is a reserved word set aside for future use by the ECMA."

"ECMA?", Rhonda asked.

"Yes, Rhonda," I answered, "the ECMA is the board that governs the JavaScript language. Features of JavaScript---present and future---are listed there. Here's a link to their website."

http://www.ecma-international.org/publications/standards/Ecma-262.htm

No one had any more questions on Variables or Constants--and so it was time to move on.

JavaScript Data Types

"I noticed," Dave said, "that when you declared your variables earlier, you didn't specify a Data Type for the variable. I think in just about every programming language I've used, I needed to specify a Data Type at the time I declared my variable."

"Good question Dave," I said, "In JavaScript, no Data Type is specified when you declare a variable. JavaScript *dynamically* determines the Data Type of a variable based on its contents."

"In other words," Dave added, "the value you assign to the variable determines its Data Type?"

"That's right Dave," I said.

"What's a Data Type?" Mary asked.

"A Data Type is simply the 'kind' of data stored in a variable's memory location," I said. "Storage requirements for v are different based on the type of data stored in them. For instance, a number is stored in a different format than a letter or a series of letters."

"How many Data Types are there in JavaScript?" Rose asked.

"There are three basic Data Types," I said, "Numbers, Strings, and Boolean."

I paused before continuing.

"As I mentioned, and Dave clarified," I continued, "in JavaScript, the Data Type of your variable is determined by the value you assign to the variable. Unlike some other programming languages, no 'upfront' thought needs to be given at the time you declare your variable---but a review of the JavaScript Data Types is still important---particularly when you are assigning values to the variables you declare. Each JavaScript Data Type has unique memory requirements, along with capabilities and operations that you can perform on them---and you should be aware of these. Let's begin our discussion with the Numeric Data Type."

Numeric Data Types

I began to discuss the JavaScript Numeric Data Types. "JavaScript Numeric Data Types," I said, "store a number which will later be used in a mathematical calculation."

"Like we did when we declared number1 and number2 variables?" Blaine asked.

"That's right Blaine," I said. "In JavaScript, there are two categories of numeric Data Types---Integers, which are whole numbers, such as 1 or 2, and Floating Point numbers, which are numbers with a fractional part, such as 1.2 or 2.4. Regardless as to how JavaScript treats a number--whether Integer or Floating Point--the important point to realize is that we can use it in a mathematical calculation---which is what we did earlier when we added two numeric variables together to produce a sum."

"How large can our numbers be that we assign to a variable?," Ward asked.

"Quite large," I answered, "larger than anything I can envision you or I assigning to a variable. In JavaScript, numbers can have up to 308 digits---in other words, numbers can be as large as 9, followed by 307 additional digits."

"You're right," Ward answered, "I can't conceive of a number that large."

The String Data Type

"What about a telephone number or a social security number?" Kate asked. "Those both contain numbers--but are usually written with dashes in them. If we assign those to a variable, would JavaScript store them as a number?"

"And what about a Street address," Rhonda said, "that contains both a number and a street name."

"In both of those cases," I said, "The Data Type would be a String Data Type. Anytime you make an assignment to a variable with a value that is other than a number you wish to use in a mathematical way, the assignment must be made within quotation marks."

"I'm not sure I understand," Steve said.

"You might or might not have noticed this," I explained, "but all of the variable assignments that we've coded today have been made using this syntax.."

var number1 = 12

"Notice," I continued, "that the number 12 appears to the right of the equals sign. If we had assigned a name to this variable instead, the name would have to appear within quotation marks, like this..."

var name = "Steve"

"In a similar way," I said, "a street name would have to appear within quotation marks---even though part of it contains a number..."

var street = "22 Twain Drive"

"I see now," Rhonda said. "So numbers that we will be using for calculations don't need to be sandwiched within quotation marks---words, special symbols and numbers that really aren't for calculations need to be sandwiched within quotation marks."

"That's excellent Rhonda," I said, "I couldn't have said it better myself." Rhonda beamed.

"Suppose you assign a number using quotation marks?" Jack asked.

"That will cause JavaScript to treat the variable like a String," I said. "If we try to use it in a mathematical calculation, we'll wind up performing String Concatenation---just like we saw a little earlier. Let me show you. Notice how the variable number2 has been assigned a value of '23', within quotation marks..."

```
<! Example3-10 -- >
<html>
<body>
<script type="text/javascript">
var number1 = 12
var number2 = "23"
document.write("The answer is " + (number1 + number2))
</script>
</body>
</html>
```

I then saved the program as '**Example3-10.htm**', and opened it up within Internet Explorer. The following screen shot was displayed on the classroom projector...

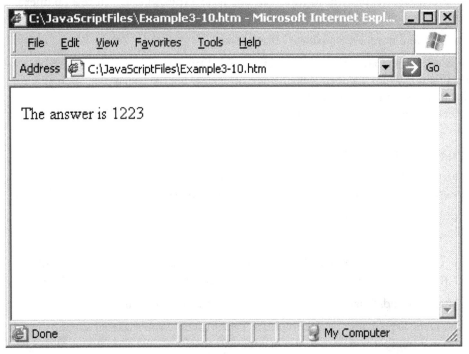

"As you can see," I said, "because we 'accidentally' assigned a String value to number2, when we 'added' the variables number1 and number2, we performed String Concatenation, not addition..."

"What happens if you try to make that name assignment without quotation marks," Jack asked?

"Let's see," I said. I then wrote the following code. "This is the correct version of the code, with my name enclosed within quotation marks."

```
<! Example3-11 -- >
<html>
<body>
<script type="text/javascript">
var name = "John Smiley"
document.write("My name is " + name)
</script>
</body>
</html>
```

I then saved the program as '**Example3-11.htm**', and opened it up within Internet Explorer. The following screen shot was displayed on the classroom projector...

Don't Forget: If typing these examples and exercises isn't something you want to do, feel free to follow this link to find and download the completed solutions for all of the examples and exercises in the book. Just click on the JavaScript book, then follow the link entitled exercises ☺

http://www.johnsmiley.com/main/books.htm

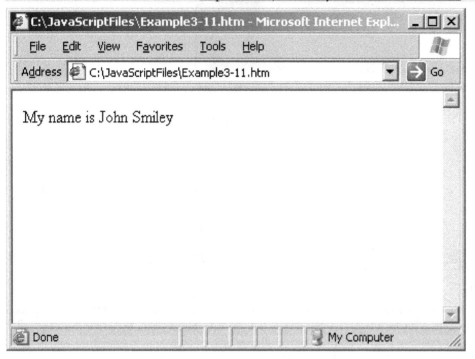

"That's the way it should work," I said. "Now let's follow Jack's suggestion and 'forget' to enclose my name within quotation marks." I then modified the code to look like this...

```
<! Example3-12 -- >
<html>
<body>
<script type="text/javascript">
var name = john smiley
document.write("My name is " + name)
</script>
</body>
</html>
```

I then saved the program as '**Example3-12.htm**', and opened it up within Internet Explorer. The following screen shot was displayed on the classroom projector...

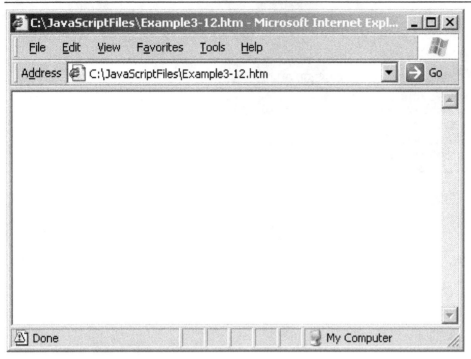

"Nothing happened," Rhonda said.

"It appears so," I said, "but take a look at the lower left hand corner of our browser window. JavaScript is telling us there's an error somewhere. Fortunately, I know what it is--but if we click on the yellow icon, the error message will be far from illustrative."

I then clicked on the yellow icon, and the following screenshot was displayed on the classroom projector.

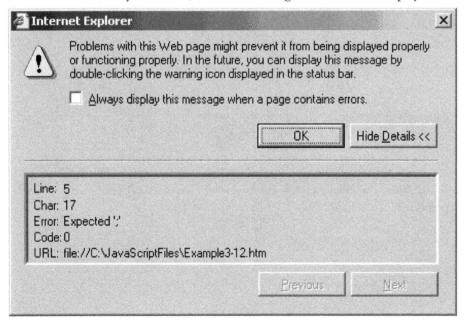

"JavaScript is telling us there is something wrong with Line 5," Dave said, "that's the line with the declaration and initialization of the variable name."

"Exactly Dave," I said, "in most instances, that's the most detail we'll get from a JavaScript error---a message telling us what line the error is on---and a character position. In this case, character position 17 specifies the letter 'S'."

The Boolean Data Type

No one had any more questions on the String Data Type, and so it was time to move onto the Boolean Data Type.

"Boolean Data Types," I said, "can have only two possible values---True or False."

NOTE: The Boolean Data Type is named after George Boole--a noted mathematician, whose

area of expertise was Boolean Algebra--mathematics that deals with Truth Tables.

I displayed this code on the classroom projector:

```
<! Example3-13 -- >
<html>
<body>
<script type="text/javascript">
var married = true
var retired = false
document.write("The value of married is " + married)
document.write("The value of retired is " + retired)
</script>
</body>
</html>
```

I then saved the program as '**Example3-13.htm**', and opened it up within Internet Explorer. The following screen shot was displayed on the classroom projector...

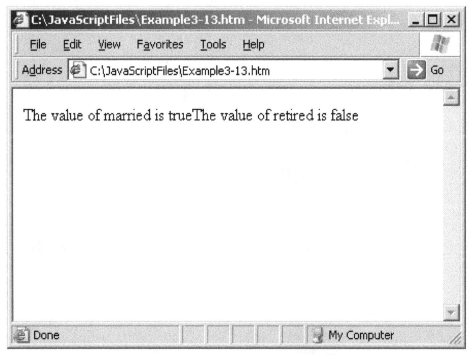

I explained that I had declared two Boolean variables, one called married and the other retired, and then assigned the values True and False to the respective variables.

"What we've done here," I said, "is to declare two Boolean variables—one to represent someone's marital status, and the other to represent their retirement status. The Boolean variable is ideal to use when the value of the variable can only be a True-False or a Yes-No outcome. Notice how the assignment of true or false to a Boolean variable is made without enclosing it within quotation marks or apostrophes--something that beginning students sometime do."

"Isn't something wrong with the display?" Kate said. "The two sentences have run together."

"Oops," I said, "I forgot to use the
 HTML tag I used earlier. Let's modify this program so that it's a little neater." I then modified the code to look like this...

```
<! Example3-14 -- >
<html>
<body>
<script type="text/javascript">
var married = true
var retired = false
document.write("The value of married is " + married)
document.write("<br>")
```

```
document.write("The value of retired is " + retired)
</script>
</body>
</html>
```

"Let's see the difference," I said, as I saved the program as '**Example3-14.htm**', and opened it up within Internet Explorer. The following screen shot was displayed on the classroom projector...

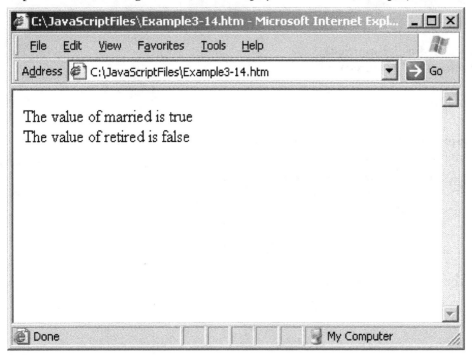

"That's better," Kate said, "that's a lot easier to read."

"Isn't there another tag <p> that we can use?" Dave asked.

"Yes there is Dave," I said. "The difference between the two tags is that <p> also inserts a blank line. Let me show you."

I then modified the program to look like this...

```
<! Example3-15 -- >
<html>
<body>
<script type="text/javascript">
var married = true
var retired = false
document.write("The value of married is " + married)
document.write("<p>")
document.write("The value of retired is " + retired)
</script>
</body>
</html>
```

...saved it as '**Example3-15.htm**', and opened it up within Internet Explorer. The following screen shot was displayed on the classroom projector...

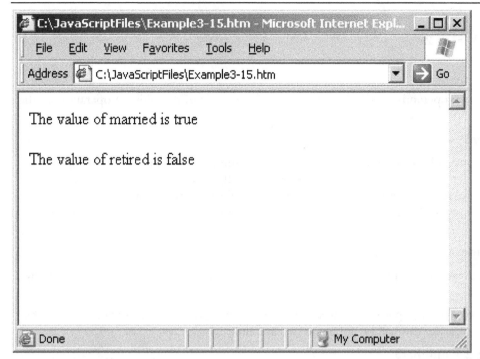

"See the difference?" I asked. "Both tags produce an easier-to-read display--but the <p> tag inserts a blank line between the two statements, and <br> doesn't."

> **NOTE: In order to be compatible with future HTML versions, type your HTML tags in lower case. Also, future versions of HTML will require both opening and closing tags. Right now, certain tags, such as <p> and <br> do not require a closing tag. Future versions of HTML will require a closing tag of </p> for the paragraph tag, and what is known as a 'self closing' tag for the break tag that will look like this
**

No one had any other questions about JavaScript Data Types, and so, after a quick break, we moved onto a discussion of Data operations.

Operations on Data

"Since you now know something about JavaScript's Data Types," I said, after the break, "now's the time to learn how to perform operations on that data. Let's start with Arithmetic Operations."

Arithmetic Operations

I explained that arithmetic operations are performed on numbers or on data stored in numeric variables.

"You can't perform arithmetic operations on any other kind of data," I said. "If you do, you'll either get a runtime error or your results will be wrong. Now let's look at the various arithmetic operations available in JavaScript."

I paused a moment before continuing.

"Before I begin," I said, "it's important to note that most operations are performed on operands. An operand is a fancy term for either the numeric constant--a number---or the variable that appear on either side of an operator. When an operation statement is executed, some result is generated. In JavaScript, You have several choices as to what to do with this result---you can choose to ignore it, or discard it. You can assign it to a variable, or you can use it in an expression of some kind, as we did earlier today when we displayed the result of an addition operation in the console by using it with the write() method of the document object. Here's a list of the JavaScript Arithmetic Operators…"

Operator	Meaning	Example	Result
+	Addition	11 + 22	33
-	Subtraction	22 - 11	11
*	Multiplication	5 * 6	30

| / | Division | 21 / 3 | 7 |
| % | Modulus | 12 % 5 | 2 |

The Addition Operator (+)

"The addition operation (+) adds two operands," I said, as I displayed this example of the addition operation on the classroom projector:

number3 = number1 + number2

"…In this example, we're taking the result of the addition of the variables number1 and number2, and assigning that value to the variable number3. Notice that I didn't say that the addition operation adds two numbers--that's not necessarily the case, as it wasn't here. In JavaScript, an Operand can be a number, a variable, or any expression that results in a number. Ultimately, as long as JavaScript can evaluate the expression as a number, the addition operation will work."

"What do you mean when you say evaluate?" Kate asked.

"When JavaScript evaluates an expression," I replied, "it examines the expression, substituting actual values for any variables or constants that it finds."

I took a moment to emphasize that JavaScript performs operations on only one pair of operands at one time. "That means that even a complex expression like this will be done one step at a time…"

number4 = number1 + number2 + number3

"…we'll learn more about complex expressions like this later," I promised.

"What's an Operand again?" Ward asked.

"An Operand is something to the left or right of the operator symbol," I said. "No matter how many operators appear in an expression, JavaScript performs an operation on just two operands at a time."

"That's a little surprising to me," Rhonda said. "Are you saying that no matter how fast my PC, it still performs arithmetic the way I was taught in school---one step at a time."

"That's right Rhonda," I said. "one operation at a time---although computers perform those operations at the speed of light!" I then displayed this earlier program--**Example3-6**---to my students once more…

```
<! Example3-6 -- >
<html>
<body>
<script type="text/javascript">
var number1 = 12
var number2 = 23
document.write("The answer is ")
document.write (number1 + number2)
</script>
</body>
</html>
```

"Remember this one?" I asked. "Here we're taking the result of the addition operation of number1 and number2 and using it as an expression with the write() method of the document object. The parentheses around the addition operation ensures that it is executed first, prior to its concatenation to the string 'The answer is '."

"In this example," Linda said, "you first assigned values to variables and then performed the addition operation on the value of the variables. Is it possible to perform the addition on numeric literals?"

"Yes you can," I said, as I displayed this code:

```
<! Example3-16 -- >
<html>
<body>
<script type="text/javascript">
document.write("The answer is ")
document.write (12 + 23)
```

```
</script>
</body>
</html>
```

I saved the program as '**Example3-16.htm**', and opened it up within Internet Explorer. Once again, the number 35 was displayed in the console.

"What are the numeric literals that Linda was talking about," Rhonda asked. "Are those the numbers in the write() method?"

"Exactly Rhonda," I replied. "Those are the numeric literals." I waited to see if there were any other questions before moving onto the Subtraction operator.

The Subtraction Operator (-)

"As you may have guessed," I said, "the subtraction operator (-) works by subtracting one operand from another and returning a result. In actuality, it subtracts the operand on the right side of the subtraction operator from the operand on the left. Look at this example:"

```
<! Example3-17 -- >
<html>
<body>
<script type="text/javascript">
var number1 = 44
var number2 = 33
var result = 0
result = number1 - number2
document.write("The answer is " + result)
</script>
</body>
</html>
```

I then saved the program as '**Example3-17.htm**', and opened it up within Internet Explorer. The following screen shot was displayed on the classroom projector…

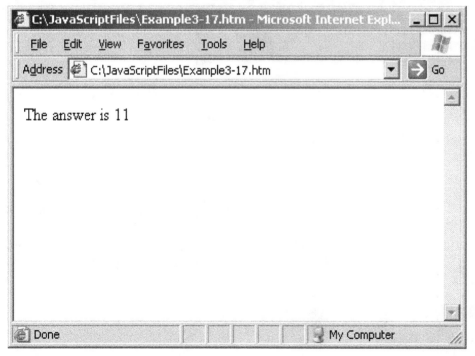

"As you can see," I said, "the value of the variable number2 was subtracted from the value of the variable number1 and the result was then…"

"You switched things up a bit here," Ward said.

"What do you mean," Rhonda asked Ward.

"Professor Smiley declared a 'extra' variable called result," he answered.

"That's exactly right Ward," I said, "I wanted to illustrate how you can assign the result of the subtraction operation to another variable---in this case, I called the variable 'result', be we could call it anything we want."

So far so good---no one had any questions about the Subtraction Operator.

The Multiplication Operator (*)

"Let's take a look at the Multiplication Operator," I said. "Like the Addition and Subtraction Operators, the multiplication operator (*) works with two operands, multiplying them together."

"Now this is a little different than what I used in school," Mary said. "In school, we used the letter 'X' to denote multiplication."

"I did as well," I said, "but the computer uses the asterisk as the multiplication operator instead---except for the symbol itself, everything works as you would expect:"

```
<! Example3-18 -- >
<html>
<body>
<script type="text/javascript">
var number1 = 4
var number2 = 3
var result = 0
result = number1 * number2
document.write("The answer is " + result)
</script>
</body>
</html>
```

I then saved the program as '**Example3-18.htm**', and opened it up within Internet Explorer. The following screen shot was displayed on the classroom projector...

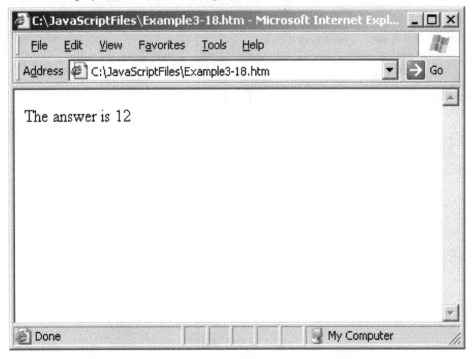

Again, no problems--time to move on to Division.

The Division Operator (/)

"The division (/) operator works by subtracting one operand from another and returning a result. It divides the operand on the left side of the division operator by the operand on the right. Look at this example:"

```
<! Example3-19 -- >
<html>
<body>
<script type="text/javascript">
var number1 = 5
var number2 = 2
var result = 0
result = number1 /number2
document.write("The answer is " + result)
</script>
</body>
</html>
```

I then saved the program as '**Example3-19.htm**', and opened it up within Internet Explorer. The following screen shot was displayed on the classroom projector...

Don't Forget: If typing these examples and exercises isn't something you want to do, feel free to follow this link to find and download the completed solutions for all of the examples and exercises in the book. Just click on the JavaScript book, then follow the link entitled exercises ☺

http://www.johnsmiley.com/main/books.htm

"Exactly what we would expect," I said. "Notice how the result is a Floating Point number--a number that has a fractional part."

"And we didn't need to do anything 'special' in terms of our variable declaration to make that happen?" Steve said.

"That's right Steve," I said, "Remember, in JavaScript, the Data Type of the variable is determined by the data that is stored in it. The result of 5 divided by 2 is a Floating Point number---so right now, that's the Data Type of the variable named 'result'.

I waited to see if there were any questions--but there weren't. Time now to move onto the more difficult Modulus Operator.

The Modulus Operator (%)

"The Modulus operator," I said, "deals with remainders. The result of the Modulus operation is the remainder of a division operation. For instance, 23 divided by 3 is 7, with a remainder of 2."

"So the result of 23 modulus 3 is 2?" Dave asked.

"That's right," I said. "It's that simple."

"What's the symbol for the Modulus operation?" Ward asked.

"It's the percent (%) sign," I said. "Let me give you an example of the Modulus Operation."

```
<! Example3-20 -- >
<html>
<body>
<script type="text/javascript">
var number1 = 23
var number2 = 3
var result = 0
result = number1 % number2
document.write("The answer is " + result)
</script>
</body>
</html>
```

I then saved the program as '**Example3-20.htm**', and opened it up within Internet Explorer. The following screen shot was displayed on the classroom projector...

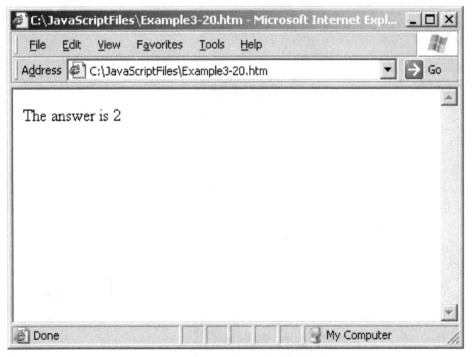

"As you can see," I said, "the Modulus operation has resulted in a the remainder of 2 being displayed in our Internet Browser."

"I think I'm OK with the mechanics of the Modulus operation," Rhonda said. "I just can't understand why you would ever want to use it. Can you give us an example?"

"The usefulness of the Modulus operation," I said, "is *not* as obvious as some of the other arithmetic operators. One of the more useful characteristics of a Modulus operation is that if the result of the Modulus operation is zero, you know that the first expression is evenly divisible by the second expression. Even better--if you 'mod' operand1 by 2, and the result is 0, that means that operand1 was an *even* number. If the result is 1, operand1 was an *odd* number."

I gave everyone a chance to think about this for a moment.

"So if you 'mod' a number by 2, there are only two possible results, 0 and 1?" Ward asked.

"That's right Ward," I said, "let me show you."

```
<! Example3-21 -- >
<html>
<body>
```

```
<script type="text/javascript">
var oddnumber1 = 3
var evennumber1 = 4
var oddnumber2 = 5
var evennumber2 = 6
var result = 0
result = oddnumber1 % 2
document.write("The answer is " + result + "<br>")
result = evennumber1 % 2
document.write("The answer is " + result + "<br>")
result = oddnumber2 % 2
document.write("The answer is " + result + "<br>")
result = evennumber2 % 2
document.write("The answer is " + result)
</script>
</body>
</html>
```

"What I'm doing here," I pointed out, "is declaring 4 variables--and assigning two of them even numbers, and two of them odd. Using the Modulus operator, we can determine if the number is even or odd by examining its result. 1 is an even number, and 0 is an odd number..."

I then saved the program as '**Example3-21.htm**', and opened it up within Internet Explorer. The following screen shot was displayed on the classroom projector...

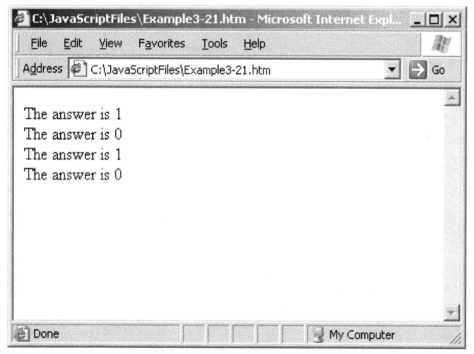

"As you can see," I said, "the result of the Modulus operation is either a 0 or a 1---0 indicates an even number and 1 indicates an odd number."

"It can't be that easy," Ward said. "I think I once had a programming assignment to do like this in a class I took several years ago, and as I recall, it was quite a bear to solve--the Modulus operator---I'll need to remember that one."

"Could we have used an If statement here to make this code a bit more elegant? Dave asked.

"We could have Dave," I said, "except we won't be talking about the If statement until next week. Remind me about it then and we'll use the Modulus operator along with an If statement."

I glanced at the clock on the wall---class was almost over.

"We have two more operators to discuss before break," I said, "the Increment Operator and the Decrement Operator."

The Increment Operator (++)

"One of the most common operations performed on a variable," I said, "is to increment it--that is to add 1 to its value. In other programming languages, this code would be used to do that…"

```
<! Example3-22 -- >
<html>
<body>
<script type="text/javascript">
var number1 = 5
number1 = number1 + 1
document.write("The answer is " + number1)
</script>
</body>
</html>
```

I then saved the program as '**Example3-22.htm**', and opened it up within Internet Explorer. The following screen shot was displayed on the classroom projector…

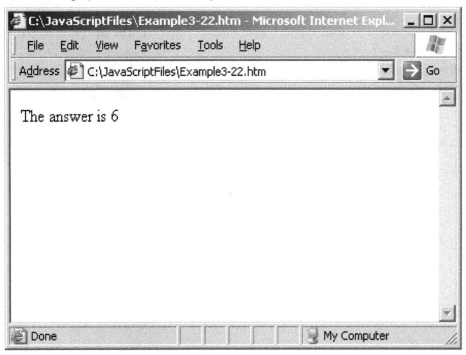

"How is that assignment statement read," Rhonda asked, "it's confusing me a little bit."

"The expression to the right of the equal sign is performed first," I said. "Read it this way---take the current value of the variable number1--which is 5---add 1 to it, giving a result of 6--and then assign that value to the variable number1. As a result, number1 was been incremented by 1."

"So that's how that's done," Blaine said. "But what about this Increment operator you mentioned?"

"The Increment operator is a shortcut method," I said. "Take a look at this…"

I then modified the code to look like this…

```
<! Example3-23 -- >
<html>
<body>
<script type="text/javascript">
var number1 = 5
number1++
document.write("The answer is " + number1)
```

```
</script>
</body>
</html>
```

"In JavaScript," I said, "the Increment operator is ++, which tells JavaScript to take the current value of the variable and add 1 to it..."

I then saved the program as '**Example3-23.htm**', and opened it up within Internet Explorer. The following screen shot was displayed on the classroom projector...

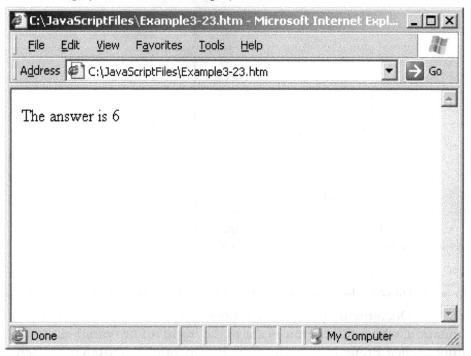

"The Increment Operator produces the same results," I said, "but saves us a few keystrokes--and probably results in less mistakes by programmers overall."

The Decrement Operator (--)

"What about the Decrement Operator?" Dave asked, "is that the opposite of the Increment Operator. Does it subtract one from the value of the variable."

"You're psychic Dave," I said, "that is exactly what it does. In JavaScript, the decrement operator is --. Take a look at this code..."

```
<! Example3-24 -- >
<html>
<body>
<script type="text/javascript">
var number1 = 5
number1--
document.write("The answer is " + number1)
</script>
</body>
</html>
```

I then saved the program as '**Example3-24.htm**', and opened it up within Internet Explorer. The following screen shot was displayed on the classroom projector...

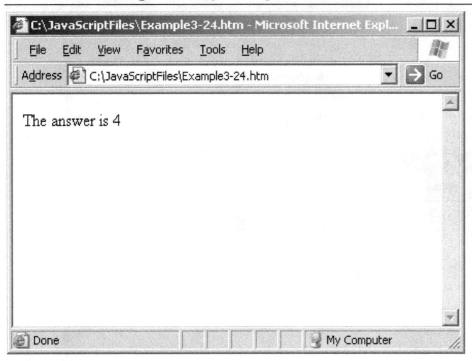

"As you can see," I said, "number1 was initialized with a value of 5---we subtracted 1 from it using the decrement operator, giving us a result of 4---again, this is just a shortcut to using this method..."

number1 = number1 - 1

No one seemed to have any problems with either the Increment or Decrement operators, and so I called for a break.

> **NOTE: Both the Increment and Decrement operators described here have been shown in what is known as Postfix notation, where the operators are to the 'right' of the variable. Both operators have another option, called Prefix Notation, where the operand is written to the left of the operator, like this...**
>
> **++x**
>
> **--y**
>
> **Both notations work identically in simple expressions, but in complex expressions, where many operations are being performed, the differences can be subtle, and for a beginner to the language to fully understand. For more on these operators, and Prefix Notation, check out this link**
>
> **http://www.webdevelopersnotes.com/tutorials/javascript/javascript_increment_decrement_operators.php3**

Order of Operations

"I mentioned earlier," I said, as we resumed after break, "that JavaScript, when it evaluates an expression containing more than one operation, performs each operation one at a time. The natural question then, is which operation JavaScript performs first."

"That's right," Jack said. "If there's an expression that contains more than one operation, how does it decide which operation to execute first?"

"I would think," Rose said, "that JavaScript would perform the operations left to right in the expression. That's how I would do it."

"That's probably what most people would think Rose," I said, "but that's not the way JavaScript does it. JavaScript follows a set of rules, known as the Order of Operations, which governs the order in which it performs these operations. A knowledge of the Order of Operations is crucial if you want your program to execute the way you intend."

I then displayed this code on the classroom projector and before running it, I asked everyone in the class to perform the calculation mentally themselves, and tell me the number they thought would be displayed in the console:

```
<! Example3-25 -- >
<html>
<body>
<script type="text/javascript">
document.write(3 + 6 + 9 / 3)
</script>
</body>
</html>
```

I asked for, and received, a number of different responses. A couple of students suggested the number 12 would be displayed; a few said 6 and a number of students said that the answer would depend on exactly when the division operation was performed. Not wishing to keep them in suspense any longer, I then saved the program as **'Example3-25.htm'**, and opened it up within Internet Explorer. The following screen shot was displayed on the classroom projector…

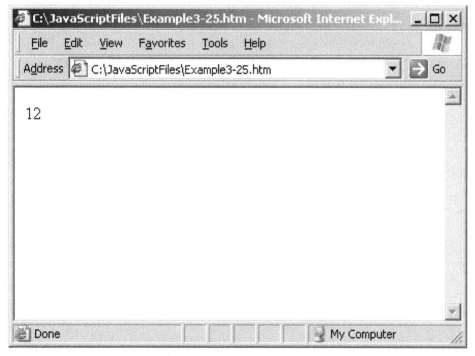

"It looks as though JavaScript performed the division first," Dave said.

"You're right, Dave," I said. "JavaScript evaluated the expression and broke it into three separate operations:"

1. 3 + 6
2. + 9
3. / 3

"Following the rules for the Order of Operations, JavaScript actually performed the *third* operation, division, first," I said. "The Order of Operations is determined by the following rules:"

1. Operations in parentheses () are performed first
2. Then any multiplication or division operations are performed, from left to right in the expression
3. Then any addition or subtraction operations are performed, from left to right in the expression

"What does all that mean?" Rhonda asked.

"Here's what happens," I said, "When JavaScript examines an expression, it first looks to see if there are any operations within parentheses. If it finds parentheses, it performs every operation within the parentheses first. Once all of the operations within parentheses are executed, JavaScript looks for operations involving multiplication or division, and performs them. If it finds more than one, it performs them from left to right."

"Finally, JavaScript then looks for operations involving addition or subtraction and performs them. Once again, it performs each one in turn starting at the left side of the expression and working its way to the right."

"Can you relate the Order of Operations to the code example you showed us?" Kathy asked.

"Sure," I said. "JavaScript first looked for parentheses in the expression. You've probably noticed that whenever we code the write() method of the document object, there's a pair of parentheses around the expression that we want to display in the console. Since the entire expression appeared within parentheses, it had no impact on the evaluation of the expression. JavaScript then looked for multiplication or division operators. It found just the single division operator, which it then performed first."

"So it actually performed the operation of 9 divided by 3 first," Valerie said. "No wonder the answer didn't agree with mine."

"After the division operation," I continued, "JavaScript looked for any addition or subtraction operators---it found two of them, and performed these operations left to right--3 plus 6 first, then the addition of that result--9---plus 3. I can show you how this all took place step by step---here are the results of the intermediate operations:"

1. **Step 1 : 3 + 6 + 9 / 3**
2. **Step 2 : 3 + 6 + 3**
3. **Step 3 : 9 + 3**
4. **Step 4 : 12**

I gave everyone a chance to take all of this in. "I hope this example shows you not only how JavaScript evaluates an expression containing mathematical operators, but how important it is to compose the expressions you code carefully. For instance," I said, "suppose we had intended to calculate the average of three numbers---3, 6 and 9--- with this piece of code. We know that to calculate an average, we would add 3 plus 6 plus 9 and then divide by 3. However, if we were to wager our jobs on getting the answer we wanted using this JavaScript code, we wouldn't have one very long!"

"You're right about that," Rose said, "but how could we code the expression to correctly compute the average of 3, 6 and 9?"

"One word," Jack suggested. "Parentheses."

That's right," I said, agreeing with Jack, as I modified the code, and displayed it on the classroom projector:

```
<! Example3-26 -- >
<html>
<body>
<script type="text/javascript">
document.write((3 + 6 + 9) / 3)
</script>
</body>
</html>
```

I then saved the program as '**Example3-26.htm**', and opened it up within Internet Explorer. The following screen shot was displayed on the classroom projector…

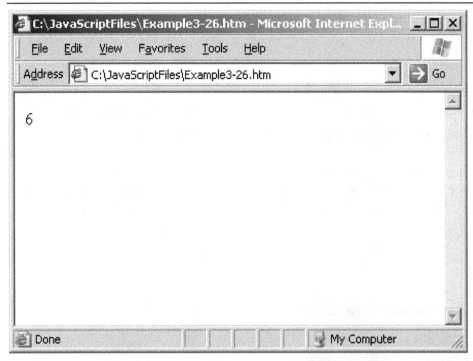

"That's better," I said, "This time, because we sandwiched the addition operations within a set of parentheses, JavaScript performed both addition operations prior to the division--exactly what we wanted to happen. Step by step, it looks like this:"

1. **Step 1 : (3 + 6 + 9) / 3**
2. **Step 2 : (9 + 9) /3**
3. **Step 3 : 18 / 3**
4. **Step 4 : 6**

"Please excuse my dear Aunt Sally," I heard Linda mutter silently.

"What was that Linda?" Rhonda asked. "Please excuse what?"

"**P**lease **E**xcuse **M**y **D**ear **A**unt **S**ally," Linda repeated. "I learned that in ninth grade Math class as a way to remember the Order of Operations. **P**arentheses-**E**xponentiation-**M**ultiplication-**D**ivision-**A**ddition-**S**ubtraction."

"I had forgotten all about that Linda," I said, "That expression does summarize the Order of Operations perfectly. Just one thing---JavaScript doesn't have an Exponentiation Operator."

"Also," Dave pointed out, "you didn't mention where the Modulus operator falls in the Order of Operations. I just did an experiment, and it appears to have precedence equal to the multiplication and division."

"That's right Dave," I said.

"Perhaps," Linda said, "we should modify our easy-to-remember phrase to read: **P**lease **E**xcuse **M**y **M**other's **D**ear **A**unt **S**ally---**P**arentheses-**E**xponentiation-**M**odulus-**M**ultiplication-**D**ivision-**A**ddition-**S**ubtraction."

"Sounds great to me Linda," Rhonda said, "I don't think I'll be able to forget it now!"

Comparison Operators

"I was talking to a programmer friend of mine," Ward said, "and she mentioned something called Comparison operators. Will we be covering those as well?"

"Yes, we will," I replied. "Just as arithmetic or mathematical operators perform and operation based on operands to the left and right of an operator and return a result, Comparison operators compare two expressions to the left and right of a comparison operator and return a result. In the case of a comparison operator, however, the result isn't a number---it's either a value of True or False. Here are the six comparison operators:"

Symbol	Explanation
==	Equal to
!=	Not equal to

<	Less than
<=	Less than or equal to
>	Greater than
>=	Greater than or equal to

"We'll only be discussing the most common comparison operator today: the equal to (==) operator," I said.

"Is that right?" Barbara asked. "Should that be two equal signs? Isn't the equal sign also used to assign a value to a variable?"

"You're right," I said. "The equal sign is used to assign a value to a variable in JavaScript--however, two equal signs are used for the comparison operator. We haven't yet learned about If statements---we'll do that next week--but in JavaScript, we could use this code to determine if the value of the variable *number1* was equal to 22…"

```
<! Example3-27 -- >
<html>
<body>
<script type="text/javascript">
var number1 = 22
if (number1 == 22) document.write("number1 is equal to 22")
</script>
</body>
</html>
```

"Notice that the assignment statement uses one equal sign…"

var number1 = 22

"…but within the If statement, we use the double equal sign (==) to compare the value of *number1* to the literal 22…"

"So the result of the If statement expression will either be True or False depending upon the current value of number1?" Dave said.

"That's exactly right Dave," I replied. "If the current value of *number1* is 22, the result of this comparison will be True.

As you'll see next week, when an If statement expression evaluates to True, the imperative statement following it--- in this case a statement to display a message in the Web Browser---is executed. "

I then saved the program as **'Example3-27.htm'**, and opened it up within Internet Explorer. The following screen shot was displayed on the classroom projector…

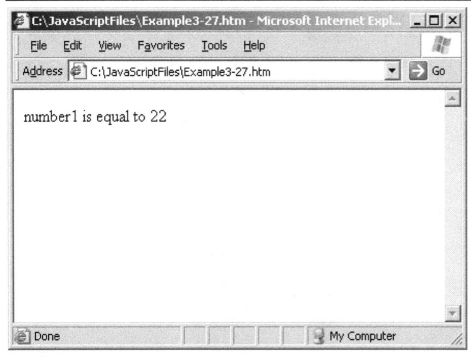

"Let's modify the program slightly," I said, "so that you can actually see the result of the comparison operation…"

```
<! Example3-28 -- >
<html>
<body>
<script type="text/javascript">
var number1 = 22
document.write(number1 == 22)
</script>
</body>
</html>
```

I then saved the program as '**Example3-28.htm**', and opened it up within Internet Explorer. The following screen shot was displayed on the classroom projector…

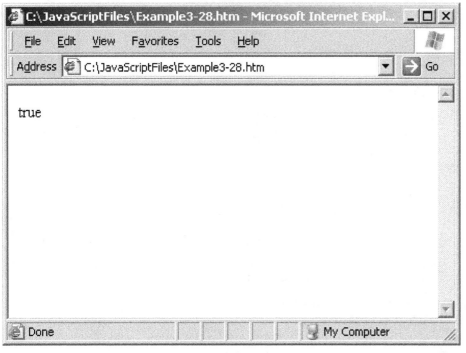

"That's cool," Kate said. "We really did display the result of the comparison operation, didn't we?"

"Yes we did Kate," I replied, "likewise, if the value of number1 is not equal to 22, the result of the comparison operation would be false. Like this…" I modified the code slightly….

```
<! Example3-29 -- >
<html>
<body>
<script type="text/javascript">
var number1 = 99
document.write(number1 == 22)
</script>
</body>
</html>
```

I then saved the program as '**Example3-29.htm**', and opened it up within Internet Explorer. The following screen shot was displayed on the classroom projector…

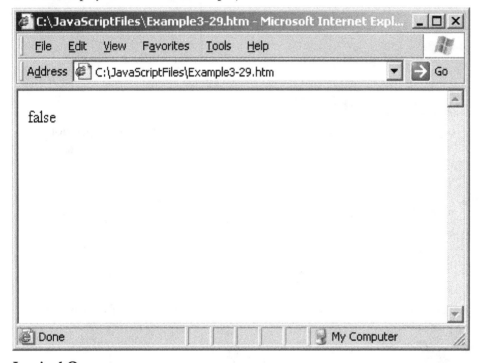

Logical Operators

"So far," I said, "we've examined Arithmetic operators and Comparison operators. Now it's time to look at a set of operators that sometimes cause beginner's hearts to skip a beat---Logical operators."

"Are those the And, Or and Not operators?" Blaine asked.

"That's right Blaine," I said. "In this JavaScript class, we'll be discussing three Logical operators: And, Or and Not. Just like Comparison operators, Logical operators return a True or False value as the result of performing an operation on two operands. I must warn you that Logical operations can be confusing for the beginner, primarily because of the necessity to understand the 'truth' or 'falseness' of their expressions. Let's take a look at these operators individually."

The And Operator (&&)

"An And operation," I said, "returns a True value if the expressions on *both* sides of the And operator evaluate to True."

"Can you give us a real-world example to make this easier to understand?" Ward asked.

"I think so, Ward" I said, as I thought a moment. "On Wednesday morning, your best friend Melissa telephones you and invites you to lunch on Friday. You'd love to go, but you have two problems that prevent you from saying 'yes' right away. First, you and your boss have not been on the best of terms lately, and you don't want to chance taking an extra long lunch on Friday--something which invariably happens when you go to lunch with Melissa. The only way you can envision going to lunch with your friend is if your boss happens to be out of the office on Friday."

"And the second problem," Barbara asked. "You said there were two problems."

"The second problem," I said, "is that you're short of cash and it's your turn to pick up the tab for lunch. Luckily though, Friday happens to be payday and cash won't be a problem---provided the direct deposit of your paycheck goes through early Friday morning, something that is 50-50 at best. You decide to call your friend on Friday at 11 AM to let her know for sure."

I could see that some of the students were wondering what my heart-felt example had to do with the And operator. I explained that we can express our dilemma in the form of two expressions joined with the And operator in this way.

"You can go to lunch with your friend Melissa if your boss is out of the office on Friday AND if the Direct Deposit of your paycheck gets into your bank account by 11 AM on Friday morning." I said.

"In other words, both expressions, the left-hand expression 'Boss out of office?' and the right-hand expression 'Money in Account?' must both be true for the AND operator to return a value of True.

Boss out of office AND Money in Account

"So what happens?" Rhonda asked.

"On Friday morning," I said, "you arrive at the office. You're saddened to hear that your boss has called in to say she has the flu and won't be in at all that day."

"So the left hand expression, Boss out of the office, is True," Dave said.

"That's right Dave," I said. "We're half way there. Our left hand expression evaluates to True. Now we have to wait on the Direct Deposit. The morning drags by as lunch time gets closer and closer. For the moment though, the AND operation is returning a False value, since the right-hand expression, Money in bank, is still returning a False value. Remember, the AND operation is True only if both the left-hand expression and right-hand expressions are True. Right now, only the left-hand expression, Boss out of Office, is True. Unfortunately, the last time you checked your balance, you find that your Direct Deposit still hasn't been made to your account, and $1.38 won't buy you and your friend Melissa much of a lunch."

"I wish we could see this graphically," Peter said.

"Actually Peter," I said, "we can express this dilemma in the form of something called a Truth Table---here it is."

Expression 1	AND	Expression 2	Result
True	AND	True	True
True	AND	False	False
False	AND	True	False
False	AND	False	False

"A Truth Table," I said, "shows you the four possible outcomes for the And operation. As you can see, there's only *one* way for an AND operation to return a True value, and that's if *both* Expression 1 (the left hand side) and Expression 2 (the right hand side) are True. On the other hand, there are *three* ways for the AND operation to return a value of False."

"I don't like those odds," Kate said laughing. "I don't think lunch looks too promising!"

"Can you re-write the True Table in terms of the boss and the money?" Rhonda said. "I think that might help me visualize this."

I took a moment to work up this revised table and then displayed it on the classroom projector. The current situation is highlighted in ITALICS:

Boss Out?	AND	Money in Bank?	Go to Lunch?
True	AND	True	True
True	AND	False	False
False	AND	True	False
False	AND	False	False

"That's better," Steve said. "This is beginning to make some sense to me now."

"Let's continue on with the story," I said. "As of 10:30, with no cash in the bank, lunch is a remote possibility. Just as you're about to call Melissa and tell her 'no', one last check of your bank balance shows that the Direct Deposit has made it, which means the right hand expression, Expression 2, is now True. Since both the left-hand and right-hand expressions evaluate to True, the entire AND operation is True, and you and Melissa can now go off to lunch."

Boss Out?	AND	Money in Bank?	Go to Lunch?
True	*AND*	*True*	*True*
True	AND	False	False
False	AND	True	False
False	AND	False	False

"What is the And Operator in JavaScript," Kate asked. "Is it the word 'And'?"

"Thanks Kate," I said, "I almost forgot---the JavaScript 'And' Operator is the double Ampersand (&&)."

"Can you give us an example of the use of the AND operation in JavaScript?" Dave asked.

I thought for a moment, then came up with this example…

```
<! Example3-30 -- >
<html>
<body>
<script type="text/javascript">
var name = "Smith"
var number = 99
if (name == "Smith" && number == 22)
   document.write("Both sides of the AND expression are True")
</script>
</body>
</html>
```

"Once again," I said, "let's use an If statement to evaluate the Truth or Falseness of the Logical expression we've coded, where we check to see if the value of the name variable is 'Smith' AND the value of the number variable is 22. If the expression evaluates to True, then we display an appropriate message in the console"

I then saved the program as '**Example3-30.htm**', and opened it up within Internet Explorer. The following screen shot was displayed on the classroom projector…

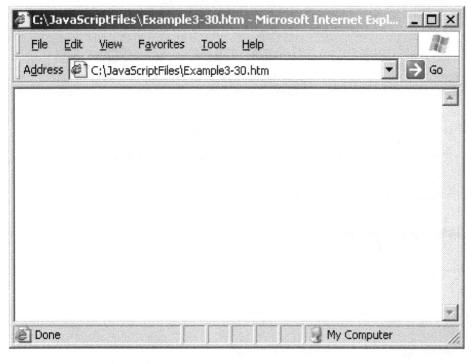

"Nothing happened," Rhonda said.

"You're right Rhonda," I said, "in that no message was displayed. In this expression, the left-hand side of the expression is True, since *name* is equal to Smith---but the right-hand side expression is False, because the value of *number* is 99, not 22. Therefore, the And Operation returns a value of False (consult the Truth Table to see this for yourself."

I then changed the code to assign the value 22 to the variable number...

```
<! Example3-31 -- >
<html>
<body>
<script type="text/javascript">
var name = "Smith"
var number = 22
if (name == "Smith" && number == 22)
   document.write("Both sides of the AND expression are True")
</script>
</body>
</html>
```

I then saved the program as '**Example3-31.htm**', and opened it up within Internet Explorer. The following screen shot was displayed on the classroom projector...

Don't Forget: If typing these examples and exercises isn't something you want to do, feel free to follow this link to find and download the completed solutions for all of the examples and exercises in the book. Just click on the JavaScript book, then follow the link entitled exercises ☺

http://www.johnsmiley.com/main/books.htm

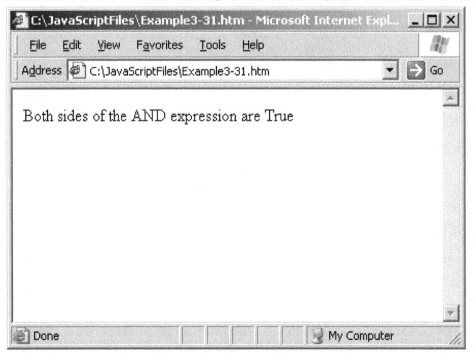

"Now the And operation returns a True value," I said, "because both the left hand and right-hand expressions are True---True And True equals True."

The Or Operator (| |)

"I think if you're comfortable with the And operation," I said, "you won't have too much trouble with the Or operation. An Or operation, just like the And operation, evaluates expressions to the left and right of the Or operator, returning a value of True or False. The differences are the rules for determining if the expression is True or False."

I displayed this Truth Table representing the Or operation on the projector:

Expression 1	OR	Expression 2	Result
True	OR	True	True
True	OR	False	True
False	OR	True	True
False	OR	False	False

"Notice," I said, "that with the Or operation, as was the case with the And Operation, we have four possibilities. In the case of the Or operator, however, three out of four results are True. In fact, with the Or operation, there is only one combination that returns a False values, and that's if both the left-hand and right-hand expressions are False."

"Can you give us another real world example to illustrate the Or operation?" Linda asked, "although I think it will be pretty hard for you to top that last one."

I thought for a moment. "OK," I said, "let's try this one. It's Friday morning. While dressing for work, you receive a phone call from the host of an early morning radio show that is running a contest. He tells you that if the month of your birthday ends in 'r' OR the last digit of your Social Security Number is 4, you'll be the lucky winner of $10,000!"

"Sounds great to me!" Ward said.

"Let me get this straight," Rhonda said. "All you need to do to win the $10,000 is to have one of those conditions be True--is that right?"

"That's right Rhonda," I said. "According to the rules of the contest, you'll win the $10,000 if either the left-hand expression is True---month of your birthday ends in the letter 'r'--or the right-hand expression is True---last digit of your Social Security Number ends in 4. Unlike our lunch date dilemma, where we needed both expressions to be True to go to lunch with our friend, with an Or operation only one side of the expression needs to be True. How do you like your odds now Kate?"

"I love them," she answered. "If that call were placed to me, I'd win the prize."

Kate wasn't alone---a quick poll of the class revealed that 4 out of the 18 students would win using the Or Operation. And guess what--if the contest had called for the AND operation, none of the students in the class would have won the cash!

I then displayed this truth table to reflect the radio contest. The three outcomes where the Or operation returns a True value are highlighted in ITALICS…

Birthday Month ends in 'r'	OR	Last Digit of Social Security is '4'?	Win $10,000?
True	OR	True	True
True	*OR*	*False*	*True*
False	*OR*	*True*	*True*
False	*OR*	*False*	*False*

I then took the **Example3-30** code example and modified it by changing the And operator to an Or---in JavaScript, the Or operator is this character (| |):

```
<! Example3-32 -- >
<html>
<body>
<script type="text/javascript">
var name = "Smith"
var number = 99
if (name == "Smith" || number == 22)
   document.write("One or both sides of the OR expression are True")
</script>
</body>
</html>
```

NOTE: The OR Operator is typed using this character | which is the character appearing on the same key as the backslash (\)--Beginners frequently mistake it for the exclamation point

I then saved the program as **'Example3-32.htm'**, and opened it up within Internet Explorer. The following screen shot was displayed on the classroom projector...

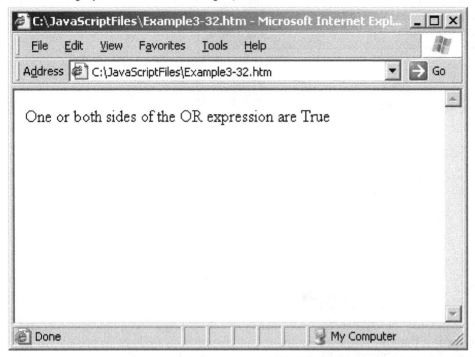

"Because one side of the expression is True--the left-hand side," I said, "True is returned from the Or Operation. If we were to change the value of Name from Smith to Smiley, both the left-hand and right-hand expressions would be false and the Or Operation would return a False value..."

I did exactly that, changing the code to look like this ...

```
<! Example3-33 -- >
<html>
<body>
<script type="text/javascript">
var name = "Smiley"
var number = 99
if (name == "Smith" || number == 22)
   document.write("One or both sides of the OR expression are True")
</script>
</body>
</html>
```

I then saved the program as **'Example3-33.htm'**, and opened it up within Internet Explorer. The following screen shot was displayed on the classroom projector...

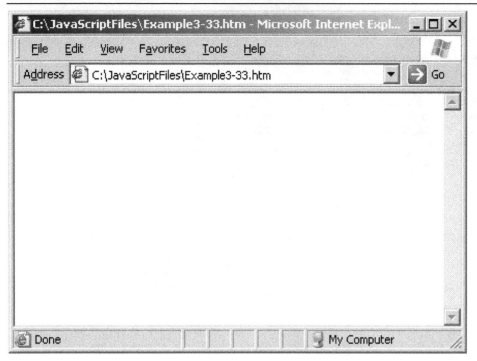

"Nothing is displayed in the Console because the OR expression evaluates to False," I said. "The only way that an Or Operation can return a False value is if both the left-hand and right-hand expressions evaluate to False. That's the case here---number, with a value of 99, is NOT 22, and name, with a value of Smiley, is definitely NOT Smith."

"I just entered some code on my own and received what appear to be incorrect results," Kathy said. "I'm receiving a message that one or both sides of the OR expression are True when in actuality, neither one is..."

I took a quick walk to Kathy's PC, and saw that she had written the following code...

```
<! Example3-34 -- >
<html>
<body>
<script type="text/javascript">
var name = "Smiley"
var number = 99
if (number == 22 ||33)
   document.write("One or both sides of the OR expression are True")
</script>
</body>
</html>
```

"See what I mean?" she asked. "The value of the variable number is 99, and I'm testing to see if it's either 22 or 33-- neither which is true. Yet if you open this code in Internet Explorer, it reports that one or both sides of the OR expression are True. I'm perplexed."

I copied Kathy's code, saved the program as '**Example3-34.htm**', and opened it up within Internet Explorer. The following screen shot was displayed on the classroom projector...

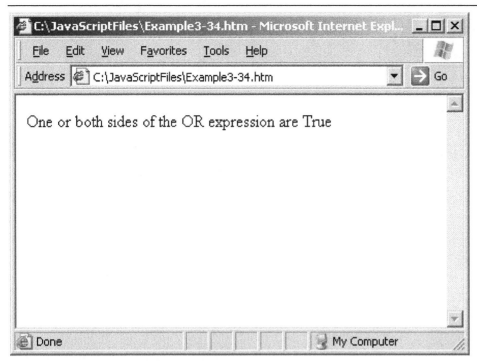

"What did I do wrong?" she asked.

"I know what you wanted to do," I said, "but you confused JavaScript. Your code was very much English-like, which is very tempting to do in JavaScript, but you see, you don't really have two expressions on either side of the Or operator. Your left-hand expression is 'number == 22' and your right-hand expression is just the number 99. Remember, each expression--left-hand and right-hand---must be able to be evaluated to a True or False value---your right hand expression can't be evaluated meaningfully to a True or False value, so in this case JavaScript assigned the right side expression a result of True."

"So how could I re-write this?" she asked.

"Like this," I said, "by repeating the variable name number in the right side expression."

I displayed the correct code on the classroom projector...

```
<! Example3-35 -- >
<html>
<body>
<script type="text/javascript">
var name = "Smiley"
var number = 99
if (number == 22 || number == 33)
   document.write("One or both sides of the OR expression are True")
</script>
</body>
</html>
```

I then saved the program as '**Example3-35.htm**', and opened it up within Internet Explorer. The following screen shot was displayed on the classroom projector...

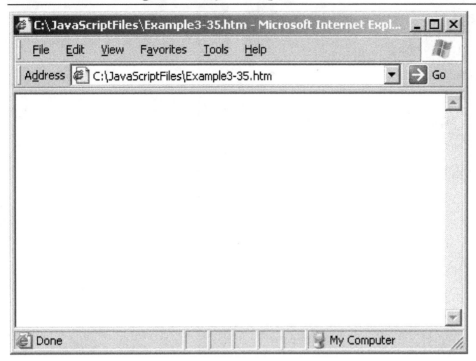

"See the difference," I said, "no statement is displayed in our Web Browser because both the left and right side expressions evaluate to False."

Wow, that was simple," Kathy said, "Why didn't I think of that?"

"You did what a lot of beginners do Kathy," I answered. "You wrote the code the way you would ask the question in conversation. Unfortunately, as English-like as JavaScript may appear to be, there are still some statements that can confuse it."

The Not Operator (!)

"We have one more logical operator to discuss today," I continued, "and it's the Not operator. As opposed to the other logical operators, which operate on two expressions, the Not operator is called a unary operator because it operates on just a single expression. The operator itself is the exclamation point (!)."

"What does the Not operator do?" Steve asked.

"The Not operator is used as a negation," I replied. "It evaluates an expression, takes the True or False result, and then returns the opposite value. So if an expression evaluates to True, the Not operator returns False. If the expression evaluates to False, the Not operator returns True."

"Why in the world would you want to do something like that?" Rhonda asked.

"The Not operator can simplify some types of program code," I said, "and make it easier to read and understand. Let me show you…"

I then displayed this code on the classroom projector.

```
<! Example3-36 -- >
<html>
<body>
<script type="text/javascript">
var number = 13
document.write(number == 13)
</script>
</body>
</html>
```

"Can anyone tell me what will happen when we run this code?" I asked. Dave suggested that the word True would be output in the console. .

"That's right," I said. "Since the value of number is 13, JavaScript will evaluate the expression number = 13 as True."

I then saved the program as '**Example3-36.htm**', and opened it up within Internet Explorer. The following screen shot was displayed on the classroom projector...

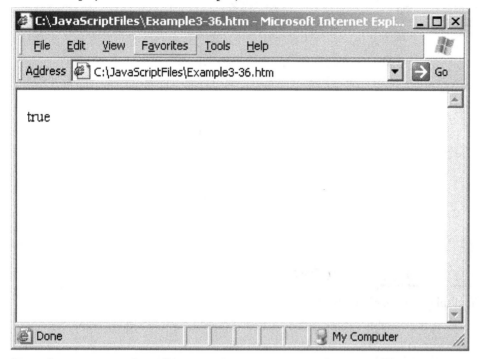

"Exactly as Dave predicted," I said. I then changed the code to look like this (notice the exclamation point in the line of code)

```
<! Example3-37 -- >
<html>
<body>
<script type="text/javascript">
var number = 13
document.write(!(number == 13))
</script>
</body>
</html>
```

"Now what will happen?" I asked. Dave answered that he thought the word *false* would appear in the console.

"Can you tell us why?" I replied.

"Because," he said, "the expression number == 13 will evaluate to True. Executing the Not operator on a True value gives us a False value."

"Excellent Dave," I said, "Bill Gates himself couldn't have stated it better."

I then saved the program as '**Example3-37.htm**', and opened it up within Internet Explorer. The following screen shot was displayed on the classroom projector...

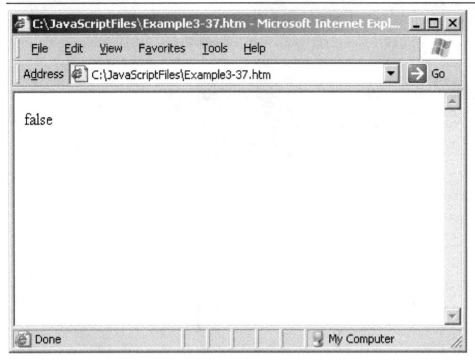

Dave was right; the word false was displayed in our Web Browser.

"Without the Not operator, to determine if a variable's value isn't a particular number would require some very hard to read and understand code, like this…"

```
document.write(number < 13 || number > 13)
```

"Is that all there is to the Not operator then?" Barbara asked.

"Basically, yes," I said. I paused before suggesting that we end the class by completing an   .

"In this exercise," I said, "you'll have a chance to continue working with the class project--Grades--which you created last week. We don't have a lot of changes to make to it--but we will enhance it with some variable declarations."

I then distributed this exercise for the class to complete.

Exercise 3-1 Add variables to the Grade Calculation program

In this exercise you'll find and load up the Grades JavaScript program you wrote last week--and then modify it to include variable declarations. For the sake of demonstration, you'll calculate the grade for an English student who has received a perfect score of 100 for each of the four individual component grade pieces.

1. Use the editor of your choice (if you are using Windows, use Notepad) and locate and load up the Grades.htm source file you created last week. It should be located in the \JavaScript\Grades folder.
2. Modify the code so that it looks like this...

```
<! Grades -- >
<html>
<body>
<script type="text/javascript">
var MIDTERM_PERCENTAGE = .25
var FINALEXAM_PERCENTAGE = .25
var RESEARCH_PERCENTAGE = .30
var PRESENTATION_PERCENTAGE = .20
var midterm = 100
var finalExamGrade = 100
var research = 100
var presentation = 100
var finalNumericGrade = 0
```

```
finalNumericGrade = (midterm * MIDTERM_PERCENTAGE) +
  (finalExamGrade * FINALEXAM_PERCENTAGE) +
  (research * RESEARCH_PERCENTAGE) +
  (presentation * PRESENTATION_PERCENTAGE)

document.write("Midterm grade is : " + midterm + "<br>")
document.write("Final Exam grade is :" + finalExamGrade + "<br>")
document.write("Research grade is :" + research + "<br>")
document.write("Presentation grade is :" + presentation + "<p>")
document.write("The final grade is: " + finalNumericGrade)
</script>
</body>
</html>
```

3. Save your source file as '**Grades.htm**' in the \JavaScriptFiles\Grades folder (select File-Save As from Notepad's Menu Bar). Be sure to save your source file with the file name extension 'htm'.

4. Use Internet Explorer to open your Source File. You should see output similar to this screen shot

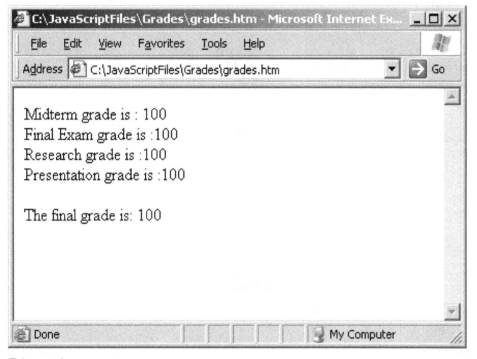

Discussion

JavaScript is a very sensitive language--and as such I didn't expect everything to go smoothly with this exercise. All in all, the exercise went well--although some students, particularly those who didn't follow the exercise precisely, had a number of problems.

For instance, it took Rhonda four or five tries before she wound up with a display of any kind. Most of her problems stemmed from not spelling her variable names the same way she declared them.

"I admit," Rhonda said smilingly, "I should have paid more attention to the syntax of the variable names. I guess I'm just not used to the case sensitivity of JavaScript."

Ward entirely missed the fact that some of our variables were CAPITALIZED.

"Why did you do that?" he asked.

"We learned earlier," I said, "that JavaScript doesn't support Constants---however, we can still convey the meaning, in our code, that the value of a variable is a constant one and shouldn't be changed once we declare and initialize it. That's why I named the 4 variables that define the relative percentages of an English student's grade with capital letters.

After about ten minutes, all of the class had finally completed their programs---and it was time to discuss what they had done.

"As you are beginning to realize by now," I said, "our JavaScript source files must always begin like this..."

```
<html>
<body>
<script type="text/javascript">
```

"…As I mentioned just a moment ago, I like to name variables whose values should not be changed with capital letters. Also, if the variable name is very long, I like to separate it with an underscore. That's why we named these variables like this…"

```
var MIDTERM_PERCENTAGE = .25
var FINALEXAM_PERCENTAGE = .25
var RESEARCH_PERCENTAGE = .30
var PRESENTATION_PERCENTAGE = .20
```

"…notice that we initialize these variables," I said. "I should tell you that as our project evolves, the code that you see in this JavaScript source file will be 'moved' to one or more support JavaScript files---in fact, this code will eventually be placed in a JavaScript source file called EnglishStudent.js--but more on that in a few weeks…."

"I was a little confused," Blaine said, "about your variable naming conventions. I think I would have begun the variable names with a capital letter."

"By convention," I said, "variable names begin with a lowercase letter. If a variable name consists of more than one word--as some of ours do, then the words are joined together, and each word after the first begins with an uppercase letter. That's why we named these variables like this

```
var midterm = 100
var finalExamGrade = 100
var research = 100
var presentation = 100
var finalNumericGrade = 0
```

"Why did we assign values of 100 to those four variables?" Kate asked, "but assign a value of 0 for finalNumericGrade?"

"In this program," I answered, "we were presupposing that our English student received perfect grades of 100 for their midterm, final examination, research project and class presentation, and so we assigned them values of 100. finalNumericGrade is the computed numeric grade for our English Student---we initialized it to 0 since our program will be calculating it. In later versions of this program, we'll prompt the user of our program for those component grade values."

I saw Kate nod her head and moved on.

I had thought that this next section of code would give the class problems, but it hadn't--although Mary did have a question.

```
finalNumericGrade = (midterm * MIDTERM_PERCENTAGE) +
    (finalExamGrade * FINALEXAM_PERCENTAGE) +
    (research * RESEARCH_PERCENTAGE) +
    (presentation * PRESENTATION_PERCENTAGE)
```

"I understand what you are doing in this next section of code," she said, "you're multiplying the component grade pieces by the applicable constant values."

"That's right Mary," I agreed. "Those five lines of code are really just a single JavaScript statement, performing a complex mathematical expression consisting of several operations."

"Did we really need those parentheses?" Dave asked. "Based on the Order of Operations, wouldn't the multiplication operations have been performed before the additions?"

"That's right Dave," I said, "we could have written the code like this, and the answer would still be correct…"

```
finalNumericGrade =
    midterm * MIDTERM_PERCENTAGE +
    finalExamGrade * FINALEXAM_PERCENTAGE +
    research * RESEARCH_PERCENTAGE +
    presentation * PRESENTATION_PERCENTAGE
```

"…but I'm a big believer in readability---I think the parentheses make the code easier to read for someone else---and leaves no doubt as to our intentions."

"I understood everything that was going on in this next section," Kate said, "except for the <p> on the next to last document.write() statement--what's going on with that? I remember that <br> is the tag that forces the output of document.write to the next line, but what does <p> do?"

```
document.write("Midterm grade is : " + midterm + "<br>")
document.write("Final Exam grade is :" + finalExamGrade + "<br>")
document.write("Research grade is :" + research + "<br>")
document.write("Presentation grade is :" + presentation + "<p>")
document.write("The final grade is: " + finalNumericGrade)
```

"You're right Kate," I said, "the <br> tag forces a new line. The <p> tag, also called the Paragraph tag, forces output to be displayed on a new line--after first skipping a line."

"So it's almost like a new paragraph?" Steve asked.

"You can think of it that way," I said.

"So that's where that blank line came from," Linda said, "I was wondering about that. Is formatting like this something that we'll concern ourselves with a great deal."

"Ultimately," I said, "we'll be developing a Graphical User Interface (GUI) using HTML forms which will make this a bit easier on us. But that's weeks away---for now, don't worry too much about it."

I glanced towards the clock on the classroom wall. We had actually gone a bit overtime. It had been a long, but very valuable one.

I then dismissed class for the day.

"Next week," I said, "we'll learn how to make our program a lot more intelligent through the use of Selection Structures."

Summary

This was quite an exhaustive look at the use of data in JavaScript. In this chapter, we learned about the importance of variables in JavaScript. We learned when, where and how to use variables, and about the different JavaScript variable types. In addition we discovered how we can use a variety of operations to manipulate the data contained in those variables.

Variables are defined in memory to hold data or information. Each variable has a Data Type that is determined by the value it holds.

JavaScript Data types can be categorized in three broad ways:
· Boolean: True or False values only
· Numeric: Numbers only, which can be Integer and Floating-Point Data Type.
· String: A set of characters, treated as text. Strings can hold numbers, but these are not numbers that you can perform arithmetic on.

Finally, we took a look at Arithmetic, Comparison and Logical operators. Operators act on expressions, and return a result. An example of a Arithmetic operator is the plus sign. We learned that multiple operators are treated in a defined order, called the Order of Operations: operations in parentheses are performed first, followed by multiplication and division, and finally addition and subtraction.

An example of a Comparison operator is the double equal sign. An example of a Logical operator is the AND operator, represented by the double ampersand (&&).

You should now be familiar, if not totally comfortable, with the ways we can manipulate data in JavaScript Programs. In our next chapter, we'll see how Selection Structures permit your program to make decisions.

Chapter 4---Selection Structures

In programming, one of the most important capabilities your program must possess is the ability to adapt to conditions that are encountered while the program is running. In this chapter, we'll continue to follow my JavaScript class as we examine Selection Structures, programming constructs that enable your program to adapt to those runtime conditions. Specifically, we'll learn about the If statement and the Switch statement. Along the way, we'll also get our first taste of writing a program that accepts input, and also writes to an output window.

Selection Structures

I arrived in the classroom a little later than usual, and found a little bit of a commotion.

"What's wrong?" I asked, noting that there was a group of students surrounding Rose and Jack.

"As you know," Jack said, "Rose and I are both engineers by trade and we work for the same company. For the last few months, we've been working on our company's biggest account---overseeing the construction of a new cruise ship in the United Kingdom. Construction is way ahead of schedule, and yesterday our supervisor told us that we're being called away to participate in the sea trials. So you see, this will probably be our last class!"

"I'm disappointed," Rose said, "because we had both hoped to finish the coding for the Grades Calculation Project before we left for the sea trials---but there's no way we'll be near to that point today."

I explained to both Rose and Jack that we would all be sorry not to have them present all the way through the project, but we hoped they would be able to return in time to see the final version of the Grades Calculation Project implemented in the English, Math and Science departments.

"But as far as the Grades Calculation Project," I said. "I have a surprise for you. By the end of today's class, we'll have coded a working prototype of the Grades Calculation Project---it's not quite what we'll be delivering to Frank Olley in a few weeks, but I think you'll be pleased with it---and pretty amazed at just how full featured it is."

As the obvious shock of my last statement subsided, I began our fourth class by telling everyone that during the next two weeks, we would be learning about the three types of programming 'structures' that form the building blocks of all computer programs.

"Structure?" Ward said. "That sounds like a house or a building."

"The building analogy is a good one Ward," I said. "We've already learned how the first step in developing a program is to develop a "blueprint" in the form of a Requirements Statement. Many years ago computer scientists discovered that any program can be written using a combination of three coding structures—much like a house can be constructed using a series of standard components. These three structures—the Sequence Structure, the Selection Structure and the Loop Structure---will form the basis of our discussion over the next few weeks."

"Will we be writing any code ourselves today?" Rhonda asked. "I know we wrote a bit of code last week--but I'm really getting anxious to get going."

"You'll have a chance to write a lot of code today," I answered. "Whenever possible, I try to have the exercises that we complete here in class ultimately lead to the completion of the Grades Calculation Project. However, from time to time we'll complete some exercises just for practice, and so that we don't confuse that work with the Grades Completion Project, if you want to save your practice exercises, you should save those in the Practice folder you created earlier in the class. Let's take a look at the JavaScript Sequence Structure now."

The Sequence Structure---Falling Rock

"As you'll see later on," I said, "both the Selection and Loop Structures require a special syntax to implement--but that's not the case with the Sequence Structure. Any code that we write is automatically part of a Sequence Structure. I like to analogize a Sequence Structure to the behavior of an falling rock."

"Falling Rock? What do you mean by that?" Steve said, obviously amused.

"Have you seen signs warning you of falling rock on the highway?" I said. "If you've ever seen rock fall, you know that once it gets rolling there's no stopping it. The same is true of JavaScript program code. For instance, let's look at the code we wrote last week that displays the final grade of an English student to the JavaScript Console..."

```
<! Grades -- >
<html>
<body>
<script type="text/javascript">
var MIDTERM_PERCENTAGE = .25
var FINALEXAM_PERCENTAGE = .25
var RESEARCH_PERCENTAGE = .30
var PRESENTATION_PERCENTAGE = .20
var midterm = 100
var finalExamGrade = 100
var research = 100
var presentation = 100
var finalNumericGrade = 0

finalNumericGrade = (midterm * MIDTERM_PERCENTAGE) +
  (finalExamGrade * FINALEXAM_PERCENTAGE) +
  (research * RESEARCH_PERCENTAGE) +
  (presentation * PRESENTATION_PERCENTAGE)

document.write("Midterm grade is : " + midterm + "<br>")
document.write("Final Exam grade is :" + finalExamGrade + "<br>")
document.write("Research grade is :" + research + "<br>")
document.write("Presentation grade is :" + presentation + "<p>")
document.write("The final grade is: " + finalNumericGrade)

</script>
</body>
</html>
```

"..this code is a perfect example of the Sequence Structure. Last we, we observed that the first line of code in our JavaScript program executes, followed by the second line of code, then the third and so forth, in SEQUENCE."

"Oh, I see where the term Sequence Structure comes from now," Valerie said. "You mean each line of code is executed, one after the other. But I guess I have to ask, what else could happen? Isn't every line of code evaluated by JavaScript?"

"Every line of code is evaluated by JavaScript," I said, "but not every line of code is necessarily executed once--some lines of code can be 'skipped' based on conditions found when the program is running. In other cases, lines of code may be executed more than once. That's where the JavaScript Selection and Loop Structures come into play. The Selection structure gives 'intelligence' to our program, in the form of decision-making capabilities, something the falling rock behavior of a Sequence Structure simply can't do. The Selection Structure allows us to SELECTIVELY execute lines of code based on conditions our program finds at run-time. Next week, we'll examine the Loop Structure that allows us to execute a line or lines of code REPETITIVELY."

I paused a moment before adding: "In order to illustrate the alternatives to the falling rock behavior of a Sequence Structure, I'd like you to complete a series of exercises based on a fictitious collection of seven restaurants in New York City. Pretend, for a few moments, that you have been hired by the owners of these seven restaurants to write a program to display their ads on a giant display screen in Times Square---in our case we're going to use our Internet Browser as our giant display screen. Here's our first exercise of the day, which will illustrate, I hope, the 'falling rock' behavior of JavaScript code.

I then distributed this exercise for the class to complete.

Exercise 4-1 Eat at Joe's – The Sequence Structure---Falling Rock behavior

In this exercise, you'll write a JavaScript program that displays information to the JavaScript console about the days of operation of seven restaurants in New York City. Pretend that the JavaScript Console is actually a giant display screen in New York City's Times Square….

1. Using Windows Explorer, create a folder on your hard drive called \JavaScriptFiles\Practice. This will be the 'home' of the JavaScript programs we create here in class that are not part of the Grades Calculation Class Project.
2. Use the editor of your choice (if you are using Windows, use Notepad) and enter the following code. Be EXTREMELY careful of the capitalization---JavaScript is very picky.

```
<! Practice4-1 -->
<html>
<body>
<script type="text/javascript">

document.write("Eat at Joe's<br>")
document.write("Eat at Tom's<br>")
document.write("Eat at Kevin's<br>")
document.write("Eat at Rich's<br>")
document.write("Eat at Rose's<br>")
document.write("Eat at Ken's<br>")
document.write("Eat at Melissa's")

</script>
</body>
</html>
```

3. Save your source file as '**Practice4-1.htm**' in the \JavaScriptFiles\Practice folder (select File-Save As from Notepad's Menu Bar). Be sure to save your source file with the file name extension 'htm'.
4. Use Internet Explorer to Open your Source File. You should see this screen shot.

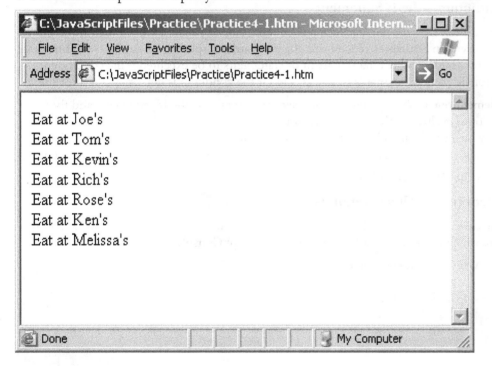

Discussion

Aside from some student's continued anxiety with writing code and opening it up using Internet Explorer, this exercise went extremely smoothly. Having warned them in the instructions for the exercise, my students were very careful with their capitalization--something that had tripped some of them up in the previous week's exercise. I gave everyone a chance to complete the exercise and then began to explain what we had done with this small program.

"This program seemed pretty straightforward," Rhonda said. "What were you trying to illustrate with it?"

"The Sequence Structure," I answered. "All of the code in our JavaScript program represents something known as a programming Sequence Structure. As I mentioned a little earlier, all that means is that the second line of code executes after the first line of code, the third line after the second line and so on."

"Falling rock behavior," Ward chimed in.

"Exactly right Ward," I said. "Does everyone remember how the write() method of the Document Object?"

"No problem," Valerie said. "The write() method displays output in our Browser Window, isn't that right?"

"That's right Valerie," I said.

There were no other questions about the exercise, and so I continued on.

"Having written this program for the owners of the seven restaurants," I said, "suppose that the owner of one of the restaurants, Joe's restaurant, takes a semi-retirement and decides to open his restaurant only on Sundays. Tom, proprietor of Tom's restaurant, hearing the news about Joe, thinks semi-retirement is a great idea, and decides to open his restaurant only on Mondays. Kevin follows suit and opens only on Tuesday. Soon the rest of the owners hear about this, figure that one day of work a week is a great idea, and the next thing we know Rich is open only on Wednesday, Rose only on Thursday, Ken only on Friday and Melissa only on Saturday. Hoping to save advertising costs in Times Square, each owner contacts us and informs us they want to advertise on our giant display screen only on the days that their restaurant is actually open. The question is: How can we handle this with our program?"

I gave everyone a moment or two to think about the problem.

"I suppose," Peter said, "we could write separate JavaScript programs for different days of the week---although if you tell me there isn't a better way than that, I may need to drop out of the class!"

"Peter is right," I said to the class, "we could write separate JavaScript programs for each day of the week---and he's also right in that there is a better way. We can make our program 'smart' enough to know what the date is, and based on that, the day of the week. Armed with that knowledge, we can then use the JavaScript Selection Structure to decide which restaurant advertisement to display on our giant display screen."

The JavaScript Selection Structure---the If Statement

"Selection structures," I continued, "can alter the default (falling rock) behavior of JavaScript code, but they are a little more complicated to write. Selection Structures require that the programmer specify one or more conditions to be evaluated---or tested---by the program, along with a statement or statements to be executed if the condition is determined to be True, and optionally, other statements to be executed if the condition is determined to be False.

In the next exercise, you'll implement one of the two JavaScript Selection Structures--the If statement--and the condition that you'll ask JavaScript to evaluate is the current day of the week. Based on Java's determination of the day of the week, decisions as to which restaurant advertising to display in the Console will be made. As you'll see, coding Selection Structures requires a little more 'up front' thought than merely coding a plain sequence structure."

I then distributed this exercise for the class to complete.

Exercise 4-2 The If Statement (or which restaurant is open today?)

In this exercise, we'll modify the code from Exercise 4-1 to determine the current date, the day of the week, and to use an If statement to determine which restaurant to advertise in the JavaScript Console.

1. Use Notepad (if you are using Windows) and enter the following code.

```
<! Practice4-2 -->
<html>
<body>
<script type="text/javascript">

var today=new Date()
var dayofweek = today.getDay()

if (dayofweek == 0)
   document.write("Eat at Joe's")
if (dayofweek == 1)
   document.write("Eat at Tom's")
if (dayofweek == 2)
   document.write("Eat at Kevin's")
if (dayofweek == 3)
   document.write("Eat at Rich's")
if (dayofweek == 4)
   document.write("Eat at Rose's")
if (dayofweek == 5)
   document.write("Eat at Ken's")
if (dayofweek == 6)
   document.write("Eat at Melissa's")
```

```
</script>
</body>
</html>
```

2. Save your source file as '**Practice4-2.htm**' in the \JavaScriptFiles\Practice folder (select File-Save As from Notepad's Menu Bar). Be sure to save your source file with the file name extension 'htm'.

3. Use Internet Explorer to Open your Source File. Depending upon the day of the week you do this exercise, you should see one of the restaurants advertised. *If today is Saturday*, you should see this screen shot.

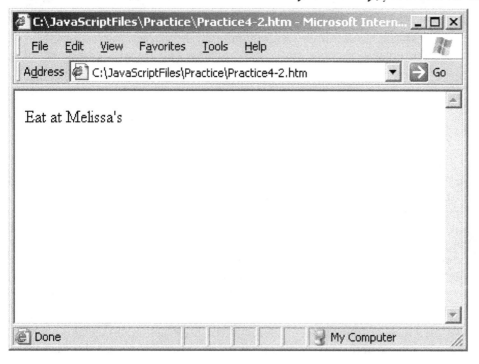

Discussion

Note: The computer week goes from Sunday (day 0) to Saturday (day 6)

I gave my students about ten minutes to complete the exercise. They seemed mesmerized with the ability of their program to behave intelligently. Although no one had any trouble completing the exercise, there were still a number of puzzled looks in the classroom.

"This is really cool," Steve said. "I had no idea you could do something like this with a programming language, although I must confess I don't think I understand half of the code we just wrote---starting with those first two lines of code."

"I was wondering that myself," Kathy said. "What are we doing with the date?"

"I suspected this variable declaration may have thrown some of you for a loop," I said.

var today=new Date()

"Is that what this is," Rhonda asked.

"That's right Rhonda," I answered, "*today* is a variable, but it's a special kind of variable called an Object variable. Instead of holding a number, or a string, it will hold a 'reference' to an object, in this case a Date object."

I waited to check for signs of confusion and saw plenty of it.

"So it's a Date Data Type?" Kate ventured.

"Date is not a Data Type in the sense that the Integer and String Data Types are," I said. "Date is an object---and this statement is declaring a variable of type Date."

"What does that mean?" Lou asked.

"Well," I replied, "when we declare a variable of a numeric type, we name and set aside some storage in the computer's memory to 'hold' data that numeric. When we declare a variable of a String type, we name and set aside some storage in the computer's memory to 'hold' data that is character based. When we declare a variable of type Date, we name and set aside some storage in the computer's memory to 'hold' data that is a Date object."

"Where's the variable name here?" Blaine asked. "I think I'm missing something somewhere."

"This statement," I said, "declares a Date variable called today---and then assigns the current date and time to the variable. Once the Date object is created, thereafter, we refer to the Date object by using the variable name today…"

var today=new Date()

"Date and time?" Mary asked.

"That's right Mary," I said, "a Date object, when created, is initialized with not only the current date but also the current time. That can come in very useful."

"I think that makes sense," Jack said, "I think it's just a matter of getting used to a variable referring to something other than a number or a character."

"It does take some getting used to," I said, "but remember, JavaScript is very much object-oriented. You'll be dealing with object variables like this quite often."

I waited for questions before continuing.

"Once the date and time is stored in the Date object--today--we can use some of the Date object's methods and attributes to our advantage. Here we are executing the getDay() method of the Date object---notice how we use the variable name today, not the word 'Date', to execute the method…"

var dayofweek = today.getDay()

"…the getDay() method of the Date object tells JavaScript to return a numeric value, between 0 and 6, that equates to the day of the week, where Sunday is 1, Monday is 2, through Saturday, which is 7. That return value is then assigned to the numeric variable 'dayofweek'. Since our class meets on Saturday, executing this method assigns the value 6 to the variable dayofweek."

I waited to see if anyone was confused--I wouldn't blame him or her if they were. A discussion of objects is a topic that, in other courses, I would ordinarily postpone until much later in the course---bit in JavaScript, it just can't be helped.

"It seems to me," Dave said, "that working with these built-in JavaScript objects can save the programmer a lot of effort and time. In other programming languages I've used, I've spent a bunch of time writing code to do what just this single line of JavaScript code just did."

"That's the idea of object-oriented programming," I said. "There are a number of JavaScript objects available for us to use that can make our programming lives easier."

"Getting back to the code," Rhonda interrupted, "now that the variable dayofweek has a number in it, what do we do with it?"

"That's where the next few lines of code come in," I said. "This line of code introduces us to our first JavaScript Selection Structure--the If Statement, which determines if the dayofweek variable is 0. The Date object considers 0 to be Sunday…"

if (dayofweek == 0)

"…A JavaScript If statement evaluates an expression to determine if it is True or False. In this case, the expression is 'dayofweek == 0'…"

"The expression that is evaluated as part of the If statement---does it have to be within parentheses?" Chuck asked.

"Good question Chuck," I said, "the answer is yes---the expression must be enclosed within parentheses--and it must be an expression that can evaluate to a True or False result"

"What happens if the expression evaluates to True?" Kate asked.

"If the expression evaluates to True," I said, "then any imperative statements following it are executed."

"What's an imperative statement?" Rhonda asked.

"Simply speaking," I said, "an imperative statement is a command. In this case, we coded just a single imperative statement to be executed if the day of week happens to be a Sunday…"

document.write("Eat at Joe's")

"…if you want to execute more than one imperative statement if the expression is true, you need to place each one within a block. In JavaScript, a block is coded that is placed within curly brackets, like this…"

```
if (dayofweek == 0) {
  document.write("Imperative Statement #1")
  document.write("Imperative Statement #1")
  document.write("Imperative Statement #1")
}
```

Note: A block is a group of statements between curly brackets { }

"…provided you understand how our first If statement works, the remainder of the If statements are pretty straight-forward. All we're doing is evaluating the value of the variable 'dayofweek' against the values 1,2,3,4,5 and 6 which represent Monday, Tuesday, Wednesday, Thursday, Friday and Saturday. Since we've covered all of our bases here-- one of these should evaluate to True, depending upon the current day of the week…"

```
if (dayofweek == 1)
  document.write("Eat at Tom's")
if (dayofweek == 2)
  document.write("Eat at Kevin's")
if (dayofweek == 3)
  document.write("Eat at Rich's")
if (dayofweek == 4)
  document.write("Eat at Rose's")
if (dayofweek == 5)
  document.write("Eat at Ken's")
```

"…and since our class meets on Saturdays, it's this expression that will evaluate to True, resulting in the advertisement for Melissa's restaurant being displayed in the JavaScript Console…"

```
if (dayofweek == 6)
  document.write("Eat at Melissa's")
```

"What happens if the expression should evaluate to False," Valerie asked. "Didn't you say earlier we could specify a statement, or statements, to execute if the expression is False?"

"Optionally, you can do that, yes," I answered, "using an Else clause of the If statement. We didn't do that in this case, instead opting to just have the next If statement executed."

"So if the If statement evaluates to False," Dave asked, "the Imperative statement or statements are 'skipped', and execution of the program picks up with the next line of code following them?"

"That's excellent Dave," I said. "I couldn't have said it better myself."

"I feel pretty good about If statements," Lou said, "is that all there is to them?"

"We still have some more to learn about them Lou," I replied. "There's still the Else clause to consider, plus there's another Selection Structure called the Switch statement we need to learn about. However, I thought this portion of the class would be a great time to give you an introduction to the world of JavaScript Popup Boxes."

JavaScript Popup Boxes

"Did you say Popup Boxes?" Blaine asked.

"That's right Blaine," I replied. "In JavaScript, a Popup Box is a special kind of window that we can display on top of our regular Browser window. A Popup Box tends to get the attention of the user a bit more emphatically than using the Browser window itself. In JavaScript, there are three kinds of Popup Boxes---the Alert Popup Box, the Confirm Popup Box, and the Prompt Popup Box. We'll be using all three in this class--although in today's class, we'll only be using two---Alert and Prompt."

The Alert Popup Box

I could sense that the class was getting a bit excited as I continued.

"Here's the code from our first program," I said, as I displayed it on the classroom projector.

```
<html>
<body>
<script type="text/javascript">

document.write("I love JavaScript!")

</script>
</body>
</html>
```

"…when we run this program, the phrase 'I Love JavaScript' is displayed in our Internet Browser. In order to make a message to the user 'stand out' even more, we can display this same message in a separate window or a message box of some kind---so let's convert this program to do exactly that."

I then displayed this code on the classroom projector

```
<! Example4-1 -->
<html>
<body>
<script type="text/javascript">

alert("I love JavaScript")

</script>
</body>
</html>
```

I then saved the program as **'Example4-1.htm'**, and opened it up within Internet Explorer. The following screen shot was displayed on the classroom projector…

"I love this," Ward said, "finally, output to something other than the Internet Browser Window."

"And all it took was that 'Alert' statement?" Peter asked.

"That's right Peter," I answered, "the 'Alert' statement tells our Internet Browser to display 'I love JavaScript' in a separate window---in this case, in what is known as an Alert window."

"Is that the significance of the exclamation point?" Valerie asked, "to alert the user to something."

"Absolutely right Valerie," I said, "use the Alert statement when you really want to get the user's attention."

"And all the user can really do is click on the OK button?" Blaine asked.

"That's right," I said, "he or she has no choice but to click on the OK button to continue the rest of our program--whatever that may be. As you'll see later on in the course, we can use the Confirm Popup Box to give the user two choices--OK and Cancel--but that's for another day."

"I was wondering," Linda said, "is there a way to 'end' the program after displaying this alert window? After the alert Popup box is displayed, if we click on the OK button, all we have is an empty Browser window."

"Good question Linda," I said, "and the answer is yes--but it's a question with two answers. At this point, our JavaScript program really has ended---we've reached the last line in our script. There are occasions--and we'll see that a little later on--where we want to prematurely end the execution of our JavaScript code, and just have the empty Browser window that we see here. We can do that with the exit statement, like this…"

```
<! Example4-2 -->
<html>
<body>
<script type="text/javascript">
```

```
alert("I love JavaScript")
exit

</script>
</body>
</html>
```

"As soon as JavaScript sees the 'exit' statement," I said, "execution of all subsequent lines of JavaScript code are bypassed. Of course, in this instance, there are no more lines of code--but we'll use the exit statement extensively later on in the class when we learn about If statements."

"You said my question had two answers," Linda said. "What's the second one?"

"Unlike the exit statement," I said, "which leaves the Browser window open, we can also close the Browser window, which is a more obvious and extreme way of ending the program. To do that, we code the close() method of the window object, like this..."

I then displayed this modified code on the classroom projector

```
<! Example4-3 -->
<html>
<body>
<script type="text/javascript">

alert("I love JavaScript")
window.close()

</script>
</body>
</html>
```

I then saved the program as **'Example4-3.htm'**, and opened it up within Internet Explorer. After the Alert Popup Box was displayed, I clicked on the OK button and the following screen shot was displayed on the classroom projector...

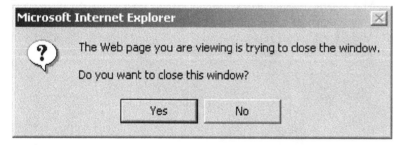

"What's going on?" Rhonda asked.

"Internet Explorer is telling us that a program is trying to close our Internet Browser window," I said, "in this case, that's exactly what Linda wants to do, so let's click on the OK button and watch it close."

I did exactly that--and the Internet Explorer Browser window closed.

"You have to ask yourself it this is really the behavior you want at that point in your program," I said, "For instance, if you use the Alert Popup box to display an error message to your user, do you really want the program to end like this?"

"Probably not," Linda said, "if you immediately end the program by closing the user's Browser, you don't give them a chance to correct their error."

"That's right," I agreed. "On the other hand, if the user has indicated they have no more work for your program to do, then it makes sense to close the Browser window. The bottom line--use the close() method of the Window object judiciously."

I could sense that my students were really excited to test the Alert Popup Box on their own---and so I distributed this exercise for the class to complete.

Exercise 4-3 The Restaurant program--another version

In this exercise, we'll modify the code from Exercise 4-2 to display the restaurant advertisements in a JavaScript Popup box instead of within the Browser Window.

1. Use Notepad (if you are using Windows) and enter the following code.

```
<! Practice4-3 -->
<html>
<body>
<script type="text/javascript">

var today=new Date()
var dayofweek = today.getDay()

if (dayofweek == 0)
    alert("Eat at Joe's")
if (dayofweek == 1)
    alert("Eat at Tom's")
if (dayofweek == 2)
    alert("Eat at Kevin's")
if (dayofweek == 3)
    alert("Eat at Rich's")
if (dayofweek == 4)
    alert("Eat at Rose's")
if (dayofweek == 5)
    alert("Eat at Ken's")
if (dayofweek == 6)
    alert("Eat at Melissa's")

</script>
</body>
</html>
```

2. Save your source file as **'Practice4-3.htm'** in the \JavaScriptFiles\Practice folder (select File-Save As from Notepad's Menu Bar). Be sure to save your source file with the file name extension 'htm'.

3. Use Internet Explorer to Open your Source File. You should see a restaurant advertisement output in an Alert Popup Box similar to this screenshot.

Discussion

As I mentioned, every one in the class seemed genuinely excited to get going with a Popup window of their own. Despite their excitement, no one had any major problems completing the exercise---although as always, there were the occasional typos.

"All we've done with this program" I said, "is output the display of the restaurant advertisements in a Popup Alert box instead of the Internet Browser window. Does anyone have any questions?"

No one had any questions about the exercise and because of the great progress we were making, before our first break I decided to cover the topic of accepting input into our program from the user by using the Prompt Popup Box.

The Prompt Popup Box

"Up to this point," I said, "we have not yet written a program that accepts data from outside of the program while it's running. In the programming world, the ability to accept user input or external data while the program is running is a common need, and there are many ways to accomplish this. For instance, a program can open and read data from a file on the user's PC or network; it can also open and read data from a database, which is a more sophisticated form of a data file. It can also accept data directly from the user..."

"Do you mean our program can ask the user a question, and then do something with their answer?" Rhonda asked.

"Yes Rhonda, " I said, "that's exactly what I'm getting at."

I thought for a moment and then wrote and displayed this program on the classroom projector.

```
<! Example4-4 -->
<html>
<body>
<script type="text/javascript">

var response = ""

response = prompt("What is your favorite programming language?")
document.write ("You have great taste. " + response + " is a great language")

</script>
</body>
</html>
```

I then saved the program as '**Example4-4.htm**', and opened it up within Internet Explorer. The following screen shot was displayed on the classroom projector...

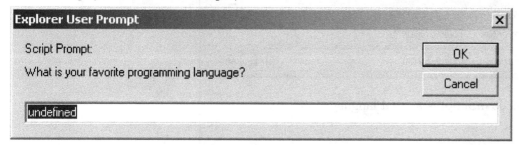

"It's not obvious," I said, "but the program is prompting us to name our favorite programming language. That's done via the Javascript Prompt function that you see in the program. By default, the Prompt function displays a Text Box into which the user can make an entry, along with two buttons---an OK button and a Cancel button."

"I see that," Kate said, "but why is the word 'undefined' in the Text Box?"

"Good question Kate," I said, "I hadn't noticed that until you mentioned it. I forgot that the Prompt function permits us to designate a default value to appear in the Text Box. When I didn't supply one, the word 'undefined' appeared instead. I can fix that like this..."

I then modified the program to look like this

```
<! Example4-5 -->
<html>
<body>
<script type="text/javascript">

var response = ""

response = prompt("What is your favorite programming language?","")
document.write ("You have great taste. " + response + " is a great language")

</script>
</body>
</html>
```

"Notice," I said, "that I've included a second 'argument' to the Prompt function---it follows the first argument. Since I don't want to sway the user's choice of a programming language in any way, I've decided to set a null, or empty, default value---I could just as easily have specified 'JavaScript' for the default, in which case the word 'JavaScript' would appear in the Text Box, and all the user would need to do is click on the OK button. As it is, now the Text Box will be empty, and the user will need to make an entry of their own."

I then saved the modified program as **"Example4-5.htm"** and opened it up within Internet Explorer. The following screen shot was displayed on the classroom projector...

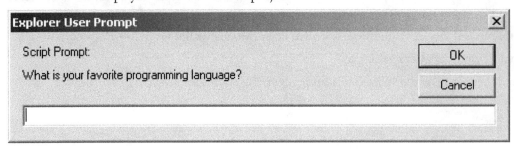

"That's better," I heard Kate say.

I then typed my favorite programming language---JavaScript---into the Prompt Text Box, and clicked on the OK button (I also could have pressed the ENTER key).

The following screenshot was displayed on the classroom projector...

Don't Forget: If typing these examples and exercises isn't something you want to do, feel free to follow this link to find and download the completed solutions for all of the examples and exercises in the book. Just click on the JavaScript book, then follow the link entitled exercises ☺

http://www.johnsmiley.com/main/books.htm

"That's great," I heard Ward say. "Internet Explorer is displaying, in its window, the value we entered into the Prompt Text Box."

'That's exactly right Ward," I said. "This is the first program we've written which has accepted input from the user."

"Can you explain this just a little bit," Rhonda asked, "I'm a little confused. What is response again?"

"Response," I answered, "is a variable that we declare to hold the contents of the user's response..."

var response = ""

"...If we want the user to give us an answer, we mustn't forget to ask the question, and we use the Prompt Function to do that. The Prompt function returns a value---in this case the value that the user enters into the Text Box. Notice how the return value is then assigned directly to the response variable..."

response = prompt("What is your favorite programming language?","")

"And the empty set of parentheses specifies a default value, is that right?" Dave asked.

"Absolutely correct," I said, "If we wanted to supply a real default value, all we need to do is include it as the second argument, like this..."

response = prompt("What is your favorite programming language?","JavaScript")

I waited to see if I had lost anyone.

"Finally," I said, "since we have the user's answer in the response variable, we can use it to confirm the user's great taste in a programming language, using the plus(+) operator to concatenate the value of the response variable to the string 'You have great taste'"

document.write ("You have great taste. " + response + " is a great language")

"I'm amazed that I actually understand what's going on here," Valerie said.

"What happens if we forget to assign the return value of the prompt method to the response variable?" Linda asked.

"Another good question," I said. "If we do that, the user's choice of a programming language will be lost, and we'll display the uninitialized value of the response variable in the browser window. By the way, that's a fairly common beginner type error to make. We'll be taking a closer look at that error in a few minutes."

I told my students that I'd like to give them a chance to experiment just a bit with the JavaScript Prompt method, and so I distributed this exercise for them to complete.

Exercise 4-4 Experimenting with the JavaScript Prompt() and Alert() methods

In this exercise, we'll write code to display a JavaScript Prompt, and to display the entry the user makes into a JavaScript Alert Popup Box. We'll discover several limitations of the Prompt Popup Box---whatever value we enter into the Text Box portion of the Prompt Box will be displayed in the JavaScript Alert Box--and if we enter nothing into the Text Box, or immediately click on the Cancel button, we'll receive some unsatisfactory results.

1. Use Notepad (if you are using Windows) and enter the following code.

```
<! Practice4-4 -->
<html>
<body>
<script type="text/javascript">

var response = ""

response = prompt("What is your first name?","")

alert("It's nice to meet you, " + response)

</script>
</body>
</html>
```

2. Save your source file as '**Practice4-4.htm**' in the \JavaScriptFiles\Practice folder (select File-Save As from Notepad's Menu Bar). Be sure to save your source file with the file name extension 'htm'.
3. Use Internet Explorer to Open your Source File. Enter your name in the Prompt Box and click on the OK button. Your name should then be displayed in a JavaScript Alert Box.
4. Execute your program again by clicking on your Internet Browser's refresh button. Instead of typing your name into the Text Box, this time immediately click on the OK button of the Prompt Popup Box. What does JavaScript display in the Alert Popup Box? **HINT**: When I did this I saw "It's nice to meet you, "
5. Execute your program once more by clicking on your Internet Browser's refresh button. Enter your name into the Text Box, but then click on the Cancel button. What does JavaScript display in the Alert Popup Box? **HINT**: When I did this I saw "It's nice to meet you, null"

Discussion

No one had any real problems completing the exercise---by now my students were getting pretty confident in their coding a simple JavaScript program---and I must say, they were having a great time doing it. I ran the program myself, entered my name, and a message box reading "It's nice to meet you, John" was displayed on the classroom projector.

"Did everyone have a chance to observe?" I said, "what happens when you made no entry into the Text Box, or if you make an entry into the Text Box, but then click on the Cancel button?"

I then ran the program, entered *nothing* into the Text Box, and clicked on the OK button. The following screen shot was displayed on the classroom projector...

"JavaScript is confused," I said, "and so it's displaying what it believes to be my name--- an empty string. If we run the program again, this time entering my name but then clicking on the Cancel button, we'll get a slightly different result."

I did exactly that and the following screenshot was displayed on the classroom projector.

"Null?" Rhonda asked.

"That's right," I said. "When we enter a value into the Text Box and then click on the OK button, the value entered into the Textbox is then assigned to the variable response. When we click on the Cancel button, however, the value assigned to the variable response is the special JavaScript value 'null'. In programming, null has a special significance---it literally means nothing, and the developers of the JavaScript Prompt function decided to return a null value if the user clicks on the Cancel button. This is simply a signal to the program using the Prompt function that the user has clicked on the Cancel button. Hopefully, you can see that null is not the same as an empty string."

> **Note: In programming, null has a special significance---it literally means nothing.**

"What can we do about this?" Linda asked. "Isn't there a way to determine if the user has not entered anything into the Textbox, or has just hit the Cancel button?"

The If...Else Statement

"If we want to ensure that the user enters something into the Textbox," I said, "then this code has a few deficiencies. The code is just blindly executing the write() method of the document object---regardless of what value is stored in the response variable."

"I guess the question is," Kate said, 'what do we want to do if the user enters nothing into the Text Box and then clicks on the OK button, or just clicks on the Cancel button."

"I would think if the user clicks on the Cancel button," Dave said, "their intent is pretty clear--they don't wish to enter their name, and we probably should just end the program. But clicking on the OK button without entering any value in the Text Box to me sounds like a mistake on their part--I would think we should ask them to enter their name again."

"I think you're right on both counts, Dave," I said. "Ending the program if the user clicks on the Cancel button is no big deal--you'll see that we can use an If statement to do that. Your last suggestion for when the user makes no entry and clicks on the OK button--asking them the question once again--is a bit more complicated, and is something we'll learn how to do next week when we discuss the JavaScript Loop structure. Today, we'll see that we can use an If statement to determine if the user has clicked on the Cancel button and then display a warning message to them. In fact, having to do so will give us a chance to work with the Else clause of the If statement I mentioned a little earlier."

"The Else clause?" Mary asked.

"That's right Mary," I said. "With the If statements we've seen so far, we've specified only the imperative statements to execute if the expression evaluates to True. Using the Else clause, we can specify one or more imperative statements to execute if the expression evaluates to False. Before we tackle the issue of checking for an empty Text Box or to see if the user has clicked on the Cancel button, let me show you a program that uses a simple If...Else statement..."

I then displayed this program on the classroom projector.

```
<! Example4-6 -->
<html>
<body>
<script type="text/javascript">

var response = ""

response = prompt("What is your favorite programming language?","JavaScript")

if (response == "JavaScript") {
  document.write("You have great taste. JavaScript is a great language")
}
else {
  document.write("It's not as good as JavaScript but " + response + " is also a great language")
}

</script>
</body>
</html>
```

I then saved the program as "**Example4-6.htm**" and opened it up within Internet Explorer. The program asked me what my favorite programming language was---I answered JavaScript (that option already appeared in the Text Box since I designated it as the default argument in the Prompt function), and was congratulated on my good taste.

"We used an If Statement to determine if the user entered 'Java'," I said. "Since the If Statement found what it was looking for…"

```
if (response == "JavaScript") {
```

"…it executed this imperative statement …"

```
document.write("You have great taste. JavaScript is a great language")
```

|"I have a question," Mary said. "Why did we use the default argument in the Prompt function this time--we didn't do that previously?"

"Good question Mary," I answered. "Notice the capitalization of the word 'JavaScript' in our If statement. We're looking for the word JavaScript spelled with a capital J and a capital S. Some users may spell it that way, but others may spell it with a capital J only--still others may spell it in all lower case. By providing a default of JavaScript, we reduce the possibility that the user will type the word JavaScript with a capitalization that we're not expecting."

"So JavaScript is case sensitive?" Blaine asked.

"Most definitely," I said, "capitalization counts. The word JavaScript spelled in all capitals is not considered the same as the word JavaScript spelled in all lowercase. But don't worry---later on in the course, next week in fact--we'll learn that there's a very easy way to deal with the many different ways that the user can spell the same word."

"I see we used the Else clause here," Kate said. "Do I understand that the statement following the word Else will be executed if the user enters anything other than 'JavaScript' into the Prompt Popup Box?"

"That's right Kate," I answered. "if the evaluation of this expression results in a False condition, then the statement or statements following the word 'Else' are executed…"

```
else {
   document.write("It's not as good as JavaScript but " + response + " is also a great language")
}
```

"Why are there braces sandwiching the imperative statements for the true and false conditions?" Valerie asked.

"Great observation Valerie," Ward said smiling, "I hadn't noticed that. What are you trying to sneak in there Professor Smiley?"

"I'm sorry," I said, "I meant to point that out. In theory, if you want to execute more than one imperative statement if the If statement evaluates to false, or more than one imperative statement if the If statement evaluates to false, you need to include the multiple imperative statements within a JavaScript block--and that's what the pair of braces is designating. In the case of this program, we only have one statement to execute, but if we had several, they would need to be sandwiched within braces. I like to use braces anyway---I think it makes the program more readable."

I waited a few moments before continuing. "Let's run this program again, and answer the question with another programming language."

I did exactly that--this time providing an answer of C++ as my language of choice. When I did, the following screenshot was displayed…

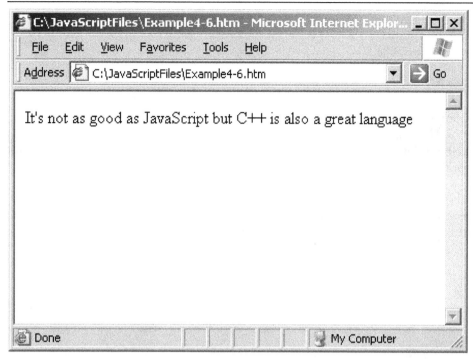

"The display of this message to the user was handled by the Else clause of the If statement," I said. "I should also mention that it's possible to code an If statement as the imperative statement that follows the Else clause."

"Wow, that sounds confusing," Rhonda said. "Why would we want to do that?"

"That allows us to handle situations where we have multiple conditions to test for," I answered. "For instance, if we wanted to display unique messages for a variety of answers that the user might provide to us."

No one had any questions about the If statement or the Else clause, and so I suggested that we turn our attention to using an If statement to handle the problems from exercise 4-4 where the user enters 'nothing' into the Text Box and then clicks on the OK Button, or simply clicks on the Cancel button.

Exercise 4-5 Using an If statement to check for an Empty Prompt Popup Box

In this exercise, we'll modify the code from Exercise 4-4, so that if the user makes no entry in the Text Box, or clicks on the Cancel button, we display an appropriate message.

1. Use Notepad (if you are using Windows) and enter the following code.

```
<! Practice4-5 -->
<html>
<body>
<script type="text/javascript">

var response = ""

response = prompt("What is your first name?","")

if (response == null) {
  alert("You clicked on the Cancel button")
}
else
if (response == "") {
  alert("You must make an entry in the Text Box")
}
else {
  alert("It's nice to meet you, " + response)
}

</script>
</body>
</html>
```

2. Save your source file as **'Practice4-5.htm'** in the \JavaScriptFiles\Practice folder (select File-Save As from Notepad's Menu Bar). Be sure to save your source file with the file name extension 'htm'.

3. Use Internet Explorer to Open your Source File. You should see a Prompt Box, asking you to enter your first name.

4. Enter your first name into the Text Box and click on the OK button. Your first name should then be displayed in the Alert Box.

5. Execute your program again by clicking on your Internet Browser's refresh button, and this time immediately click on the OK button of the Prompt Box. What does JavaScript display in the Alert Box?

6. Execute your program once more by clicking on your Internet Browser's refresh button. Enter your name into the Text Box, but then click on the Cancel button. What does JavaScript display in the Alert Box?

Discussion

"Because of the If statements we've added to our code," I said, "this program now exhibits quite a bit of intelligence. If the user clicks on the Cancel button, our program detects that by checking the value of the variable response against the keyword 'null'..."

```
if (response == null) {
    alert("You clicked on the Cancel button")
}
```

I ran the program myself, and immediately clicked on the Cancel button---the following screenshot was displayed on the classroom projector

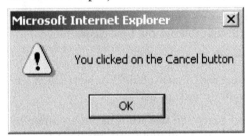

"Likewise," I continued, "if the user clicks the OK button without making an entry in the Text Box, we can detect that by using this code to determine if the value of the variable response is equal to the empty string..."

```
else
    if (response == "") {
        alert("You must make an entry in the Text Box")
}
```

I ran the program again, immediately clicked on the OK button and the following screenshot was displayed.

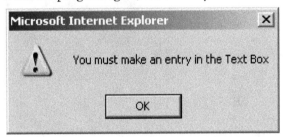

"I'm still not absolutely sure about the If statement syntax," Joe said. "Can you show us another example?"

After thinking for a few moments, I said, "To make this all a little more understandable for everyone, let me use Pseudocode to illustrate an Else statement intended to display the number of years until an employee is eligible for retirement."

I saw some puzzled looks.

"Pseudo-what?" Mary said, smiling.

"I think I mentioned Pseudocode earlier in the course," I said. "Pseudocode is a method that programmers use to express complex problems. Instead of coding the problem in a particular language, Pseudocode let's us concentrate on expressing the problem in an English-like way. Then, when we have it worked out to our satisfaction, we can translate the Pseudocode into whatever language we happen to be working work. Remember, what you see here isn't JavaScript code--so don't try to type it into a code window!"

NOTE: Pseudocode is a way of expressing a complex problem in an English-like way, prior to coding it up in an actual programming language.

I then displayed this Pseudocode on the classroom projector:

There is an employee working for a company. According to the rules of company…

```
If the employee's age is 62 or greater
   he/she must be retired
Else If the employee's age is 61
   he/she has 1 year until retirement
Else If the employee's age is 60
   he/she has 2 years until retirement
Else If the employee's age is 59
   he/she has 3 years until retirement
Else
   he/she has a really long time to go
```

I then suggested that we try implementing this Pseudocode in JavaScript, but I warned everyone that our code would be a bit unwieldy.

"Using a series of Else If statements can be pretty cumbersome," I said. "After we write the code for this exercise, in Exercise 4-7 we'll look at an alternative Selection Structure called the Switch Statement which many times can be used to streamline If…Else statements.."

Exercise 4-6 The If…Else…If Statement

In this exercise, we'll create a program to determine how long an employee has until he or she can retire.

1. Use Notepad (if you are using Windows) and enter the following code.

```html
<! Practice4-6 -->
<html>
<body>
<script type="text/javascript">

var response = ""

response = prompt("What is your age?","")

if (response == null) {
  alert("You clicked on the Cancel button")
}
else
if (response == "") {
  alert("You must make an entry in the Text Box")
}
else
if (parseInt(response) > 61) {
  alert(response + " - You must be retired")
}
else
if (parseInt(response) == 61) {
  alert(response + " - You have 1 year until retirement")
}
else
if (parseInt(response) == 60) {
  alert(response + " - You have 2 years until retirement")
}
else
if (parseInt(response) == 59) {
```

```
  alert(response + " - You have 3 years until retirement")
}
else {
  alert(response + " - You have a long time until retirement")
}
</script>
</body>
</html>
```

2. Save your source file as **'Practice4-6.htm'** in the \JavaScriptFiles\Practice folder (select File-Save As from Notepad's Menu Bar). Be sure to save your source file with the file name extension 'htm'.

3. Use Internet Explorer to Open your Source File. You should see a Prompt Popup Box asking you to enter your age.'

4. Execute your program multiple times, entering 62, 61, 60, 59 and 40 into the Text Box and click on the OK Button after each entry. Observe the various messages that are displayed in the JavaScript Alert Boxes.

Discussion

There was probably more code in this exercise than in any of the others we had done so far, and several of my students became confused and lost their places. Fifteen minutes later, though, I was happy to see that everyone in the class had successfully completed the exercise.

"I don't think we've ever written that much code," Rhonda said, "but I think it's pretty straight-forward--at least I think I understand most of what's going on."

"I think you're right, Rhonda" I replied. "we haven't written this much code before. When you write code that tests for a variety of conditions like we did here, your code can really 'balloon' in size---but sometimes that's something that just can't be helped. The code you've written for this exercise, though lengthy, is still pretty manageable--- suppose we had a requirement to display a different message for every age between 1 and 100?"

"That would really balloon the code," Mary said. "Will the Switch statement you alluded to earlier help cut down on the number of lines of code we have to write to test for multiple conditions?"

"It can," I said, "but before we discuss the Switch statement, I'd like to explain this code first--which by my count contains a total of six Else statements."

I displayed the first line of code on the classroom projector:

```
var response = ""
```

"You've seen this code before," I said. "What we're doing here is declaring a variable to 'hold' the value of the user's response which he or she will then type into the Textbox portion of the Prompt Popup Box. This statement then uses the Prompt method to ask the user to tell us their age, and then assigns the user's answer to the response variable...."

```
response = prompt("What is your age?","")
```

"These next few lines of code check to see if the user has clicked on the Cancel button," I said. "In a real-world program, at this point we would end the program---for now, while we're still getting comfortable with JavaScript, we'll display a message instead..."

```
if (response == null) {
  alert("You clicked on the Cancel button")
}
```

"...this section of code checks to see if the user has clicked on the OK button without first entering a value into the Text Box. If they have, we warn them that they need to make an entry..."

```
else
if (response == "") {
  alert("You must make an entry in the Text Box")
}
```

"I noticed," Rhonda said, "that in both of the above cases, as soon as the message is displayed to the user, the program ends--that is, in order to repeat the process, we need to click on the Refresh button of our Internet

Browser. At least for the case where the user clicks on the OK button without making an entry, shouldn't they be given the opportunity to type something into the Text Box without having to run the program all over again."

"You're right Rhonda," I said, "there is a way to do that---and that's something we'll learn how to do next week when we take up the topic of JavaScript Loop structures."

"What's going on with this next line of code?" Ward asked. "What is *parseInt*?"

"Good question Ward," I said, "parseInt is a JavaScript function that 'converts' a String Data Type to a Numeric Data Type."

Ward (and the other students) seemed thoroughly confused.

"Why do we need to do that?" Valerie asked.

"I may or may not have mentioned this," I said, "but the return value of the Prompt method--that is, the value that is typed by the user into the Text Box of the Prompt Popup Box is a String. Strings are handled differently than numbers in numeric comparison operations. Our code needs to work with the user's response as a number, so that we can perform numeric comparison operations against them. In order to do that, we first need to 'convert' the String value in the response variable to a Numeric Data Type, and we do that by executing the JavaScript parseInt function. Once that conversion is performed, we can determine if the value the user has entered is greater than 61…"

```
else
if (parseInt(response) > 61) {
```

"…using the greater than Comparison operator. We learned last week that Comparison operations return a True or a False value, and in this case, if the number entered into the Text Box is greater than 61, a True value is returned from this operation, and we then display the user's age, concatenated with the string '- You must be retired' in a message box."

```
alert(response + " - You must be retired")
```

"What would have happen if we don't 'convert' the String value in the response variable to a number?" Kate asked.

"We'll get," I answered. "what is known in the programming world as unpredictable results. In other words, wrong answers."

"What if the user's age is not greater than 61?" Kate asked. "This is where I became confused."

"If the user's age is NOT greater than 61," I said, "the Comparison operation returns a False value, and because of the Else statement, our code executes the imperative statement following the word 'Else'---of course, it turns out that the imperative statement is another If statement that is then evaluated by JavaScript…"

"Can we go back to that line of code again where we display the message?" Chuck said. "Why do we have a plus operator there?"

I explained that this line of code uses the concatenation operator, the plus sign (+)

```
alert(response + " - You must be retired")
```

"…to join the string ' - You must be retired' with the value of the 'response' variable. Therefore, if the number 73 has been entered into the Text Box, the Alert Popup box displays the following message: 73 - You must be retired

"That's clever," Steve said. "So we're actually using the value of the variable 'response' in the message--not a numeric literal."

"That's right Steve," I said. "Using the value the user has entered in the message, by using the value of the variable 'response', gives us a much more flexible and descriptive message. In this way, no matter what age the user enters into the Text Box, that age is then displayed in the Alert Popup Box."

I waited to see if there were any questions before continuing.

"In a similar way," I said, "we can use this code to determine if the value the user has entered into the Text Box is exactly equal to 61…"

```
else
if (parseInt(response) == 61) {
   alert(response + " - You have 1 year until retirement")
}
```

"…if it is, we then execute the imperative statement to display an appropriate message. If the entry in the Text Box is not equal to 61, we execute the imperative statement of the Else clause, itself another If statement, to determine if the user's age is 60…"

```
else
if (parseInt(response) == 60) {
   alert(response + " - You have 2 years until retirement")
}
```

"I'm OK with this," Linda said. "This is basically the same code we used to determine if the user's age is 61. If it is, we display a slightly different message…"

"That's right," I agreed, "and this code works in the same way, checking to see if the user's age is 59:"

```
else
if (parseInt(response) == 59) {
   alert(response + " - You have 3 years until retirement")
}
```

"Now can you imagine," I said, "if we needed to write individual lines of code for every age from 59 on down to 1. Fortunately, we can take care of all of those possibilities with this single Else statement:"

```
else {
   alert(response + " - You have a long time until retirement")
}
```

"By using the Else statement here," I said, "we tell JavaScript that all of the remaining ages fit into one category and to display a generic message indicating that the user has a long time until retirement."

I waited to see if there were any questions. To my surprise, everyone in the class seemed pretty comfortable with the If statement--now it was time to discuss another Selection Structure--the Switch Statement.

The Switch Statement

"The more alternatives we have in an If…Else…If statement," I said, "the harder the program is to write, read and modify, and the more likely it is that we'll make a mistake when we code it. I'd like to introduce you to another JavaScript Selection Structure called the Switch statement. Here's the code for a program that asks the user to enter a number, between 1 and 3, into the Text Box of a Prompt Popup Box."

I then displayed this code on the classroom projector:

```
<! Example4-7 -->
<html>
<body>
<script type="text/javascript">

var response = ""

response = prompt("Pick a number between 1 and 3","")

if (response == null) {
   alert("You clicked on the Cancel button")
   exit
}
if (response == "") {
   alert("You must make an entry in the Text Box")
   exit
}
switch(parseInt(response)) {
   case 1:
      alert("You entered the number 1")
      break
   case 2:
      alert("You entered the number 2")
      break
```

```
  case 3:
    alert("You entered the number 3")
    break
  default:
    alert("Oops, you entered a number not in the range 1 to 3")
    break
}
```

```
</script>
```

"Let me explain what I've done here," I said. "As has become our custom in any program that presents a Prompt Popup Box to the user, the first thing we do is declare our response variable…"

```
var response = ""
```

" and then prompt the user to enter a number between 1 and 3…"

```
response = prompt("Pick a number between 1 and 3","")
```

"…As we did in our previous exercise, we test the response variable for a null value to determine if the user has clicked the Cancel button…"

```
if (response == null) {
```

"…this time, instead of merely displaying a message to the user, we specify two imperative statements to be executed if the condition evaluates as True---displaying an Alert Box and ending the program by executing the Close() method of the Window object--- by 'sandwiching' both of the imperative statements within curly braces…"

```
alert("You clicked on the Cancel button")
exit
}
```

"There's that exit statement," Valerie said. "So when that's encountered, the rest of our JavaScript program is bypassed?"

"That's right Valerie," I replied.

"Why is it," Chuck said, "that we went the 'extra yard' this time by ending the program in addition to displaying the message to the user--that's new, isn't it?"

"We need to end the execution of the rest of our JavaScript code at that point because of the 'falling rock' behavior of our code," I said. "If all we did was display a message to the user, the rest of our JavaScript code would continue to execute, and within the Switch statement, we would wind up evaluating the value of the response variable using the parseInt function. In this case, since the value of the response variable does not contain a number, it makes no sense to go further. We can just end the JavaScript execution right here---and allow the user to click the Refresh button on their browser to start the program again."

I waited a moment before continuing.

"We then follow the test for the click of the Cancel button by checking to see if the user clicked on the OK button, but failed to make an entry into the Prompt Popup Box…"

```
if (response == "") {
```

"…if they have, we execute two imperative statements---a message to the user and the Close() method of the Window object…"

```
  alert("You must make an entry in the Text Box")
  exit
}
```

"…with those two tests out of the way, we now know that the user entered 'something' into the textbox. Of course, we're expecting a number between 1 and 3, but users don't always do what we expect them to. I should also tell you at this point that if the user enters something other than a number into the Prompt Popup Box--the letter 'a' for instance---we'll display a message that the number entered is not within the range 1 through 3. There are ways to check for a non-numeric entry in the Prompt Popup Box, but at this point in the course, it's a little beyond us. For now, let's concentrate on understanding the Switch statement which we execute with this line of code…"

```
switch(parseInt(response)) {
```

"The Switch statement," I said, "begins with the word Switch. The entirety of the Switch statement is enclosed within a pair of curly braces. The test expression can be a variable, but in actuality it can be anything that evaluates to a number or string Data Type."

"So that's why we were able to use the parseInt function within the test expression here," Dave said, "since it returns a Numeric Data Type."

"That's right Dave," I answered. "According to the rules for the Switch statement, the test expression must return a numeric or String Data Type."

I paused a moment.

"Now here comes the tricky part," I continued. "The result of the test expression is then evaluated, in turn, by each one of the successive case statements. If the result of the test expression matches the first case statement, then the imperative statement or statements following that case statement are executed. If the result does not match, then the next Case statement is matched to the test expression result. Once again, if the test expression matches the case statement, the imperative statement or statements following that case statement are executed. If the result does not match, then each successive Case statement is tested. You can code an optional Default case, which if present, is executed if NONE of the Case statements match the test expression. Here's our first Case statement looking to see if the test expression evaluates to the number 1. Notice, by the way, the spelling of the word 'Case'--it's in lower case--- if you spell it any other way, your program won't run at all. You won't receive an error--but 'nothing' will happen. Secondly, notice also that the line containing the Case statement ends with a colon…"

```
case 1:
```

"…once again, if the Case statement finds that the test expression is equal to 1, then the two imperative statements following the Case statement are executed. In this example, what that means is that we display a message to user, and then execute the Break statement…"

"What does the Break statement do?" Lou asked.

"The Break statement," I said, "tells JavaScript to skip the remaining Case statements, and to resume program execution with the next line of code following the end of the Switch statement."

"You mean the line of code after the ending curly brace?" Rose asked.

"That's right Rose," I replied. "In this code, we execute the Break statement after a Case statement matches the test expression--and that's because of a peculiarity with the Switch statement in JavaScript. In JavaScript, when a Case statement matches the test expression, ALL of the remaining imperative statements in each one of the Case statements is executed---regardless of whether the individual Case statements match the test expression. In most cases, you don't want that code to execute---and the only way to prevent it is to execute the Break statement…"

```
alert("You entered the number 1")
break
```

Dave had a question: "So you mean without the Break statements, if the user answers 1 at the prompt, we'll receive messages indicating that the user entered 1, followed by a message that the user entered 2, and finally a message that the user entered 3?"

"That's absolutely right Dave," I said. Dave, ever the excellent student, was coding the example himself just this way as I spoke. He nodded affirmatively.

> **NOTE: Within a Case statement, there's no need to 'sandwich' multiple statements within curly braces**

"…now, it's just a matter of evaluating the remainder of the Case statements…"

```
case 2:
    alert("You entered the number 2")
    break
case 3:
    alert("You entered the number 3")
    break
```

"The default Case," I said, "as I mentioned, is executed if NONE of the other Case statements matches the test expression…"

```
default:
   alert("Oops, you entered a number not in the range 1 to 3")
   break
```

"…this curly brace marks the end of the Switch statement."

```
}
```

"The Switch statement seems pretty powerful," Barbara said. "Are there any limitations to it?"

"Just one that I can think of," I said. "Case statements in JavaScript, unlike some other languages, must be an equality. For instance, you CAN'T specify a Case statement that looks like this…"

```
Case > 5 // NOT A VALID SYNTAX
```

or

```
Case 1 to 5 // NOT A VALID SYNTAX
```

There were no other questions. I thought it would be a good idea to let everyone take a turn at coding their own Switch statement before taking a break, and so I handed out this exercise for the class to complete.

Exercise 4-7 The Switch Statement

In this exercise, we'll work with the program from Exercise 4-6, modifying it to use a Switch statement instead of a series of If…Else statements.

1. Use Notepad (if you are using Windows) and enter the following code.

```
<! Practice4-7 -->
<html>
<body>
<script type="text/javascript">
var response = ""
response = prompt("What is your age?","")
if (response == null) {
  alert("You clicked on the Cancel button")
  exit
}
if (response == "") {
  alert("You must make an entry in the Text Box")
  exit
}
if (parseInt(response) > 61) {
  alert(response + " - You must be retired")
  exit
}
switch(parseInt(response)) {
  case 61:
    alert(response + " - You must be retired")
    break
  case 60:
    alert(response + " - You have 1 year until retirement")
    break
  case 59:
    alert(response + " - You have 2 years until retirement")
    break
  default:
    alert(response + " - You have a long time until retirement")
}
```

```
</script>
</body>
</html>
```

2. Save your source file as '**Practice4-7.htm**' in the \JavaScriptFiles\Practice folder (select File-Save As from Notepad's Menu Bar). Be sure to save your source file with the file name extension 'htm'.

3. Use Internet Explorer to Open your Source File. You should be prompted to enter your age.

4. Execute your program multiple times (by hitting the Refresh button on your Internet Browser), entering 62, 61, 60, 59 and 40 into the Prompt Popup Box and click on the OK Button after each entry. Observe the various messages that are displayed.

Discussion

No one seemed to have any great problems completing the exercise--although there were some students who spelled 'case' in other than lower case letters.

"Don't forget about the spelling of the word 'case'," I said, "and also remember to include your Break statements. Remember, the Break statement prevents ALL of the code in the Switch Structure from being executed."

"I can vouch for that," Rhonda said. "I forgot to include it and all of the code in the other Case statements really did execute---seeing is believing!"

"I really enjoyed this exercise, and I'm glad we took the time to do it" Ward said. "This exercise really helped solidify the concept of the Switch statement in my mind--it's just a shame that we couldn't have expressed every condition we were looking for in the form of a Case statement. I guess there was no way out of having one or two If statements."

"That's right Ward," I said. "Because we are restricted to expressing our Case statements in terms of an equality, we needed to check for an age greater than 61 using an If statement…"

```
if (parseInt(response) > 61) {
   alert(response + " - You must be retired")
   exit
}
```

"Did we forget to check for an age less than 59?" Rhonda asked.

"We did check for it---by using the Default Case statement," I said.

```
default:
   alert(response + " - You have a long time until retirement")
   break
```

"How so?" Rhonda asked.

"Since we had already checked for an age greater than 61, and for ages exactly equal to 61, 60 and 59, if we got to the point of executing the code in the Default Case statement, that would mean that the age entered into the Prompt Popup Box was less than 59."

"I see," Rhonda said. "I was a little confused because we didn't explicitly code what we were looking for---I see the Default Case statement is aptly named."

"We could have coded another If statement to be a little more explicit," I said

```
if (parseInt(response) < 59) {
   alert(response + " - You have a long time until retirement")
   exit
}
```

"...but I really wanted to give everyone a chance to work with the Default Case statement."

The classroom was pretty quiet---everyone seemed to be OK with the Switch statement. I asked if there were any questions. There were none, and so I told them to take a well-earned break.

"When we return from break," I said, "we'll use the Selection Structures we learned today to enhance the Grades Calculation Project---I think you'll be very pleased with what we're about to do with the project."

Continuing with the Grades Calculation Project

"We now know enough about JavaScript," I said, resuming after a fifteen minute break , "to add some intelligence to our Grades Calculation Project which we began working on last week. Last week we added code to the project to calculate the grade for a 'mythical' English student whose midterm, final examination, research and presentation grades were all perfect scores of 100. We displayed the student's perfect final grade of 100 in the Browser Window."

"We 'hard coded' the component grade pieces in the program code itself," Blaine said.

"That's right Blaine," I said. "Last week we didn't have the JavaScript skills to allow our program to accept input from a user--and so we had no choice but to 'hard code' the component grade scores. After what we've learned today about the Prompt Popup Box, and JavaScript Selection Structures, we'll be able to ask the user what type of student they wish to calculate, and to conditionally accept the component grade scores from the user based on that student type."

"Wow, do you mean we'll be able to calculate the grade for an actual student today?" Ward asked.

"That's right," I replied.

"That's exciting," Rhonda said. "but if I'm not mistaken, based on what you're saying we'll be doing with the project today, doesn't that mean that we've finished it?"

"That's an interesting point you raise, Rhonda," I said. "and strictly speaking, you're correct. By the end of today's class, we will have a working JavaScript program that basically fulfills the Requirements Statement we developed several weeks ago. What will we be doing for the remainder of the class, you may be wondering? 'We'll spend the remainder of the class learning even more about JavaScript, and enhancing the Grades Calculation project with our new knowledge."

I then distributed this exercise for the class to complete.

Exercise 4-8 Enhance the Grades Calculation Project

In this exercise, you'll modify the Grades Calculation Project you last worked on last week in Exercise 3-1 by giving it the ability to accept input from the user, and to calculate grades (both numeric and letter grades) for an English, Math or Science Student.

1. Use the editor of your choice (if you are using Windows, use Notepad) and locate and load up the Grades.htm source file you created last week. It should be located in the \JavaScript\Grades folder.
2. Modify the code so that it looks like this...

```
<! Grades -- >
<html>
<body>
<script type="text/javascript">

var ENGLISH_MIDTERM_PERCENTAGE = .25
var ENGLISH_FINALEXAM_PERCENTAGE = .25
var ENGLISH_RESEARCH_PERCENTAGE = .30
var ENGLISH_PRESENTATION_PERCENTAGE = .20
var MATH_MIDTERM_PERCENTAGE = .50
var MATH_FINALEXAM_PERCENTAGE = .50
var SCIENCE_MIDTERM_PERCENTAGE = .40
var SCIENCE_FINALEXAM_PERCENTAGE = .40
var SCIENCE_RESEARCH_PERCENTAGE = .20
var midterm = 0
var finalExamGrade = 0
var research = 0
var presentation = 0
var finalNumericGrade = 0
var finalLetterGrade = ""
var response=""

// What type of student are we calculating?
response = prompt("Enter student type (1=English, 2=Math, 3=Science)","")
if (response == null) {
```

```
    alert("You clicked on the Cancel button")
    exit
}
if (response == "") {
    alert("You must make an entry in the Text Box")
    exit
}
if (parseInt(response) < 1 || parseInt( response) > 3) {
    alert(response + " - is not a valid student type")
    exit
}
// Student type is valid, now let's calculate the grade
switch(parseInt(response)) {
// Case 1 is an English Student
    case 1:
        midterm = parseInt(prompt("Enter the Midterm Grade",""))
        finalExamGrade = parseInt(prompt("Enter the Final Examination Grade","" ))
        research = parseInt(prompt("Enter the Research Grade",""))
        presentation = parseInt(prompt("Enter the Presentation Grade",""))
        finalNumericGrade =
            (midterm * ENGLISH_MIDTERM_PERCENTAGE) +
            (finalExamGrade * ENGLISH_FINALEXAM_PERCENTAGE) +
            (research * ENGLISH_RESEARCH_PERCENTAGE) +
            (presentation * ENGLISH_PRESENTATION_PERCENTAGE)
        if (finalNumericGrade >= 93)
            finalLetterGrade = "A"
        else
        if ((finalNumericGrade >= 85) & (finalNumericGrade < 93))
            finalLetterGrade = "B"
        else
        if ((finalNumericGrade >= 78) & (finalNumericGrade < 85))
            finalLetterGrade = "C"
        else
        if ((finalNumericGrade >= 70) & (finalNumericGrade < 78))
            finalLetterGrade = "D"
        else
        if (finalNumericGrade < 70)
        finalLetterGrade = "F"
        alert("*** ENGLISH STUDENT ***\n\n" +
            "Midterm grade is: " + midterm + "\n" +
            "Final Exam is: " + finalExamGrade + "\n" +
            "Research grade is: " + research + "\n" +
            "Presentation grade is: " + presentation + "\n\n" +
            "Final Numeric Grade is: " + finalNumericGrade + "\n" +
            "Final Letter Grade is: " + finalLetterGrade)
        break
// Case 2 is a Math Student
    case 2:
        midterm = parseInt(prompt("Enter the Midterm Grade","" ))
        finalExamGrade = parseInt(prompt("Enter the Final Examination Grade",""))
        finalNumericGrade =
        (midterm * MATH_MIDTERM_PERCENTAGE) +
        (finalExamGrade * MATH_FINALEXAM_PERCENTAGE)
        if (finalNumericGrade >= 90)
```

```
        finalLetterGrade = "A"
      else
      if ((finalNumericGrade >= 83) & (finalNumericGrade < 90))
        finalLetterGrade = "B"
      else
      if ((finalNumericGrade >= 76) & (finalNumericGrade < 83))
        finalLetterGrade = "C"
        else
      if ((finalNumericGrade >= 65) & (finalNumericGrade < 76))
        finalLetterGrade = "D"
      else
      if (finalNumericGrade < 65)
        finalLetterGrade = "F"
        alert("*** MATH STUDENT ***\n\n" +
          "Midterm grade is: " + midterm + "\n" +
          "Final Exam is: " + finalExamGrade + "\n\n" +
          "Final Numeric Grade is: " + finalNumericGrade + "\n" +
          "Final Letter Grade is: " + finalLetterGrade)
        break
// Case 3 is a Science Student
  case 3:
    midterm = parseInt(prompt("Enter the Midterm Grade",""))
    finalExamGrade = parseInt(prompt("Enter the Final Examination Grade",""))
    research = parseInt(prompt("Enter the Research Grade",""))
    finalNumericGrade =
      (midterm * SCIENCE_MIDTERM_PERCENTAGE) +
      (finalExamGrade * SCIENCE_FINALEXAM_PERCENTAGE) +
      (research * SCIENCE_RESEARCH_PERCENTAGE)
    if (finalNumericGrade >= 90)
      finalLetterGrade = "A"
    else
    if ((finalNumericGrade >= 80) & (finalNumericGrade < 90))
      finalLetterGrade = "B"
    else
    if ((finalNumericGrade >= 70) & (finalNumericGrade < 80))
      finalLetterGrade = "C"
    else
    if ((finalNumericGrade >= 60) & (finalNumericGrade < 70))
      finalLetterGrade = "D"
    else
    if (finalNumericGrade < 60)
      finalLetterGrade = "F"
      alert("*** SCIENCE STUDENT ***\n\n" +
        "Midterm grade is: " + midterm + "\n" +
        "Final Exam is: " + finalExamGrade + "\n" +
        "Research grade is: " + research + "\n\n" +
        "Final Numeric Grade is: " + finalNumericGrade + "\n" +
        "Final Letter Grade is: " + finalLetterGrade)
      break
  default:
    alert(response + " - is not a valid student type")
}
</script>
</body>
</html>
```

3. Save your source file as **'Grades.htm'** in the \JavaScriptFiles\Grades folder (select File-Save As from Notepad's Menu Bar). Be sure to save your source file with the file name extension 'htm'.

4. Use Windows Explorer to Open your Source File.

5. Execute your program and test it thoroughly. See what happens if you immediately click on the Cancel button. See what happens if you click on the OK button without entering a Student Type into the Prompt Popup Box.

6. Indicate that you wish to calculate the grade for an English Student. Enter 70 for the midterm, 80 for the final examination, 90 for the research grade and 100 for the presentation. A final numeric grade of 84.5 should be displayed--with a letter grade of 'C'.

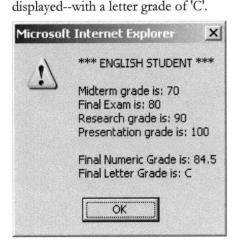

7. Click on your Browser's Refresh Button. Indicate that you wish to calculate the grade for a Math student. Enter 70 for the midterm and 80 for the final examination. A final numeric grade of 75 should be displayed--with a letter grade of 'D'.

8. Click on your Browser's Refresh Button. Indicate that you wish to calculate the grade for a Science student. Enter 70 for the midterm, 80 for the final examination. and 90 for the research grade. A final numeric grade of 78 should be displayed--with a letter grade of 'C'.

Discussion

"This exercise was a lot of fun," Rhonda said, "but although I was able to complete it, I must confess I'm not absolutely sure about everything that going on here."

"I suspect you're not the only who feels that way, Rhonda" I said. "There's a bunch of code in this exercise. Let's take a look at it now. Some of these variables---Constants really----appeared in the previous version of the program--and some are new to this version. Last week, we were only concerned with calculating the grade for an English student. In this version of the program, we're calculating Math and Science students also, and so we need to declare and initialize variables for those student types also. As you know, variables whose values shouldn't change during the running of the program are Constants in my book, and name them in upper case. We assign values to this group of variables equating to the relative percentage of the component grade for each one of the three student types we'll be calculating..."

```
var ENGLISH_MIDTERM_PERCENTAGE = .25
var ENGLISH_FINALEXAM_PERCENTAGE = .25
var ENGLISH_RESEARCH_PERCENTAGE = .30
var ENGLISH_PRESENTATION_PERCENTAGE = .20
var MATH_MIDTERM_PERCENTAGE = .50
var MATH_FINALEXAM_PERCENTAGE = .50
var SCIENCE_MIDTERM_PERCENTAGE = .40
var SCIENCE_FINALEXAM_PERCENTAGE = .40
var SCIENCE_RESEARCH_PERCENTAGE = .20
```

I paused a moment before continuing. "We declared these same variables in previous version of the program," I said, "but this time we're initializing their values to 0..."

```
var midterm = 0
var finalExamGrade = 0
var research = 0
```

```
var presentation = 0
var finalNumericGrade = 0
```

"...finalLetterGrade is a new String variable for this version of the program. We'll use it to 'hold' the student's calculated letter grade. Notice how we initialize it to an 'empty' string..."

```
var finalLetterGrade = ""
```

"...response should be a familiar variable to you now. We'll use it to store any responses we get from the user via the Prompt Popup Box..."

```
var response=""
```

"...this line of code is just a comment---as our programs get larger, use of comments is a good idea..."

```
// What type of student are we calculating?
```

"...at this point, with all of our Constants and variables declared, it's time to ask the user what type of student they will be calculating a grade for. This is a crucial piece of information for our program, and quite honestly, we're making things a little easier on ourselves by prompting the user to give us a number equating to the student type---1 for an English student, 2 for a Math student, and 3 for a Science student..."

```
response = prompt("Enter student type (1=English, 2=Math, 3=Science)","")
```

"I was wondering why you did that," Peter said.

"We could have asked the user to type in the actual student type as a String," I said, "but that can be tricky."

"How so?" Kate asked.

"There are two problems," I answered. "First, you really want to avoid having the user type in anything into your program. Keystrokes lead to typing errors, and typing errors cause program problems. Later on in the class you'll see that we'll avoid this whenever possible by having the user interact with Graphical User Interface components like Checkboxes, Radio Buttons, etc. If the user must type--and sometimes it's unavoidable---then reduce their typing to a minimum, which is what we're doing here by having them enter a single number--1, 2 or 3---instead of actually typing out English, Math or Science."

"You said there are two problems," Blaine said, "what's the second?"

"A second problem would be this," I said. "Even if the user managed to type in English, Math or Science properly---capitalization is an issue as well. For instance, some users might spell their entry in all UPPER CASE, some in LOWER CASE, and some in a combination in between."

"I hadn't thought of that," Linda commented.

"Did you know there are 128 different ways to spell the word 'Science' if you count the various combinations of upper and lower case letters?" I asked. "In theory then, we would need 128 different If statements for each student type--that's why we're prompting for a number instead of a String---although I must tell you that when we learn a little bit more about the String object, we'll find there's an easy way around this. For now, though, it's best if we prompt the user for the number 1, 2 or 3."

No one had any major objections to my rationale, and so I continued. "These next few lines of code we've dealt with all day long---here we're checking to see if the user has clicked on the Cancel button. If they have, we display a message and end the program by executing the exit method..."

```
if (response == null) {
  alert("You clicked on the Cancel button")
  exit
}
```

"...next we check to see if the user has clicked on the OK button without entering anything into the Text Box. Most likely this is a mistake, and if they have, we display a message to the user and end the program by executing the exit() method of the System object..."

```
if (response == "") {
  alert("You must make an entry in the Text Box")
  exit
}
```

"It really would be great," Ward said, "if instead of just ending the program here we could 'redisplay' the Prompt Popup Box."

"I totally agree Ward," I said, "and that's something we'll be able to do after next week's class when we learn about the JavaScript Loop Structure. For now though, we just gracefully end the program in either of these two cases. At this point in the program, if the Cancel button hasn't been clicked, and if the Text Box of the Prompt Popup Box has 'something' in it, we know that the user has made an entry into the Prompt Popup Box--now it's time to determine what's in it. As I mentioned earlier, if the user makes an entry into the Prompt Popup Box that is not a Number, the program will give us some strange results. It will be a few weeks before we learn how to handle that problem---for now, let's assume that the user has entered a valid number into the Prompt Popup Box. We need to determine if it's outside the range of valid numbers we're looking for. In other words, if it's less than 1 OR greater than 3, it's not 1, 2 or 3. Last week, we learned about the JavaScript OR(|) Operator, and coupled with an If statement, this line of code allows us to determine if the number entered is outside the range of numbers we're looking for..."

```
if (parseInt(response) < 1 || parseInt( response) > 3) {
   alert(response + " - is not a valid student type")
   exit
}
```

"...if the number entered into the Prompt Popup Box is either less than 1 OR greater than 3 (the < operator means less than and the > operator means greater than), we display a message to the user indicating that they have entered an invalid student type, and end the program."

"Now we're in business,?" Kathy said. "If the number entered isn't less than 1, and it's also not greater than 3, then it must be 1, 2 or 3..."

"You hit the nail right on the head Kathy," I said. "We now know that the number in the Text Box is either a 1, 2 or 3, and that allows us to use a Switch statement to deal with each one of those cases--each of which equate to a different student type..."

```
switch(parseInt(response)) {
```

"...Case 1 is the English Student. Within the Case statement, we use multiple Prompt() methods to prompt the user for the four component pieces that comprise the English student's final grade---Midterm, Final Exam Grade, Research and Presentation grades..."

```
// Case 1 is an English Student
   case 1:
      midterm = parseInt(prompt("Enter the Midterm Grade",""))
      finalExamGrade = parseInt(prompt("Enter the Final Examination Grade","" ))
      research = parseInt(prompt("Enter the Research Grade",""))
      presentation = parseInt(prompt("Enter the Presentation Grade",""))
```

I waited to see if there were any questions before continuing.

'This next sequence of code calculates the final numeric grade for an English student," I said. "Here we multiply the value entered by the user for each component piece of the grade by the appropriate Constant and then sum them to arrive at the final grade..."

```
finalNumericGrade =
   (midterm * ENGLISH_MIDTERM_PERCENTAGE) +
   (finalExamGrade * ENGLISH_FINALEXAM_PERCENTAGE) +
   (research * ENGLISH_RESEARCH_PERCENTAGE) +
   (presentation * ENGLISH_PRESENTATION_PERCENTAGE)
```

"...once we have the final numeric grade calculated, we use a series of If...Else statements to calculate the final letter grade. This code is pretty tedious, but relatively straightforward..."

```
if (finalNumericGrade >= 93)
   finalLetterGrade = "A"
else
if ((finalNumericGrade >= 85) & (finalNumericGrade < 93))
   finalLetterGrade = "B"
else
```

```
if ((finalNumericGrade >= 78) & (finalNumericGrade < 85))
  finalLetterGrade = "C"
else
if ((finalNumericGrade >= 70) & (finalNumericGrade < 78))
  finalLetterGrade = "D"
else
if (finalNumericGrade < 70)
  finalLetterGrade = "F"
```

"...now that we have the final numeric grade and the final letter grade calculated, it's time to display the results in an Alert box. This also is pretty straightforward. First, we display the type of student for whom we have calculated a grade..."

```
alert("*** ENGLISH STUDENT ***\n\n" +
```

"I'm not sure I've seen that \n syntax before," Rhonda said. "What' are those backslash+n characters for?"

"\n is called an escape sequence," I answered. "When JavaScript sees this combination of characters, it knows it's receiving some special formatting instructions, and instead of displaying that combination of characters in the Alert Box, JavaScript takes whatever characters follow this escape sequence, and places them on a new line in the Alert Box. That's why all lines of code, despite the fact that they are concatenated to the ones above them, don't run together on a single line in the Alert box---they appear on separate lines..."

```
"Midterm grade is: " + midterm + "\n" +
"Final Exam is: " + finalExamGrade + "\n" +
"Research grade is: " + research + "\n" +
"Presentation grade is: " + presentation + "\n\n" +
"Final Numeric Grade is: " + finalNumericGrade + "\n" +
"Final Letter Grade is: " + finalLetterGrade)
```

"I see," Rhonda said, "so that's how that happened."

"Notice how at this point the last line of code in this Case statement we execute is the Break statement," I said, "because we don't want the code in each of the other Case statements to execute. Remember, in Java, when a Case statement matches the test expression, not only do the imperative statements for that Case statement execute, so do the statements for every Case statement in the entire Switch statement. The only way to stop that behavior is to execute the Break statement, which then 'skips' execution of the program to the next line of code following the end of the Switch structure..."

```
break
```

"Here's the Case statement for the Math student," I continued. "It's similar to the English student, the obvious difference being that Math students do not have a Research or Presentation grade component, and of course, their component percentages are different..."

```
// Case 2 is a Math Student
  case 2:
    midterm = parseInt(prompt("Enter the Midterm Grade","" ))
    finalExamGrade = parseInt(prompt("Enter the Final Examination Grade",""))
    finalNumericGrade =
    (midterm * MATH_MIDTERM_PERCENTAGE) +
    (finalExamGrade * MATH_FINALEXAM_PERCENTAGE)
    if (finalNumericGrade >= 90)
      finalLetterGrade = "A"
    else
    if ((finalNumericGrade >= 83) & (finalNumericGrade < 90))
      finalLetterGrade = "B"
    else
    if ((finalNumericGrade >= 76) & (finalNumericGrade < 83))
      finalLetterGrade = "C"
      else
    if ((finalNumericGrade >= 65) & (finalNumericGrade < 76))
      finalLetterGrade = "D"
```

```
    else
    if (finalNumericGrade < 65)
      finalLetterGrade = "F"
      alert("*** MATH STUDENT ***\n\n" +
        "Midterm grade is: " + midterm + "\n" +
        "Final Exam is: " + finalExamGrade + "\n\n" +
        "Final Numeric Grade is: " + finalNumericGrade + "\n" +
        "Final Letter Grade is: " + finalLetterGrade)
      break
```

"Here's the Case statement for the Science Student…"

```
// Case 3 is a Science Student
  case 3:
    midterm = parseInt(prompt("Enter the Midterm Grade",""))
    finalExamGrade = parseInt(prompt("Enter the Final Examination Grade",""))
    research = parseInt(prompt("Enter the Research Grade",""))
    finalNumericGrade =
      (midterm * SCIENCE_MIDTERM_PERCENTAGE) +
      (finalExamGrade * SCIENCE_FINALEXAM_PERCENTAGE) +
      (research * SCIENCE_RESEARCH_PERCENTAGE)
    if (finalNumericGrade >= 90)
      finalLetterGrade = "A"
    else
    if ((finalNumericGrade >= 80) & (finalNumericGrade < 90))
      finalLetterGrade = "B"
    else
    if ((finalNumericGrade >= 70) & (finalNumericGrade < 80))
      finalLetterGrade = "C"
    else
    if ((finalNumericGrade >= 60) & (finalNumericGrade < 70))
      finalLetterGrade = "D"
    else
    if (finalNumericGrade < 60)
      finalLetterGrade = "F"
      alert("*** SCIENCE STUDENT ***\n\n" +
        "Midterm grade is: " + midterm + "\n" +
        "Final Exam is: " + finalExamGrade + "\n" +
        "Research grade is: " + research + "\n\n" +
        "Final Numeric Grade is: " + finalNumericGrade + "\n" +
        "Final Letter Grade is: " + finalLetterGrade)
      break
```

"…and finally, here's the code for the Default case---in theory, this code should probably never execute, but it's a good idea to include it anyway…"

```
default:
  alert(response + " - is not a valid student type")
```

"…this curly brace marks the end of the Switch statement…"

```
}
```

"Great fun," Ward said, "this is starting to be a lot of fun."

"I just realized," Dave said, "that we don't have any validation for the component grade values that the user enters. Is that a problem?"

"In theory, we would have the same problem with the input of those values as we do with the input of the Student type--that is, if the user enters a non-integer value into the Prompt Popup Box, the program will display some interesting results---but again, this is something we'll take care of in a few weeks when we develop our Graphical User Interface."

Dave and the rest of the class seemed content to wait until then to resolve the issue. I waited for questions, but there were none. I had expected my students to be pretty worn out at this point, but instead they were playfully experimenting with a program they seemed genuinely proud of. I dismissed class for the day, telling everyone that next week we would learn about the JavaScript Loop structures.

Summary

In this chapter, we examined Selection Structures and how they are used to vary the way a program behaves based on conditions found at run-time. We saw that there are several types of Selection Structures in JavaScript---two varieties of the If statement and the Switch statement.

Remember the falling rock? We've seen how we can use Selection structures to change this behavior, starting with the plain If…statement. If a condition evaluates to True, then the imperative statement or statements following the If statement are executed. The If…statement can be expanded to include alternative instructions for a False condition as well, using the Else keyword, and even further with a set of Else...If keywords.

After a number of "else's", your code will begin to look cumbersome. At this point, it's more elegant to use the Switch statement, although it does have some limitations.

We've also come to a significant point in our project – the working prototype of the Grades Calculation Project. This is a very important stage in the development process, because all the key working parts of the program are now in place. From this point onwards, we'll be adding functionality and code to turn our prototype into a professional-level program JavaScript program.

Chapter 5---Loops

In this chapter, we'll discuss the various types of Loop Structures available in JavaScript. As you'll see, Loop processing can give your programs tremendous power.

Why Loops?

"Last week I mentioned the term 'loops' quite often," I said, as I began our fifth class. "In today's class, we'll examine the Loop Structures available in JavaScript in some detail."

I continued by explaining that a loop allows the programmer to repeatedly execute sections of code without having to type those lines of code over and over again in the source code.

"The ability to have parts of your program repeatedly execute," I said, "can give it enormous power to do many types of operations that would otherwise be impossible."

"Can you give us an example?" Mary asked.

"Sure Mary," I said, "For instance, a common programming problem is one in which you need to read records from an external disk file into your program. Reading a single record from a disk file isn't difficult---the 'trick' in reading records from an external disk file (or a database) is that you do not know ahead of time how many records the program will need to read."

"What do you mean?" Peter asked.

"For instance," I replied, "a file may contain 10 records--or it may contain 5 billion. The point is, when you write your program source file, you don't know how many times to execute the line of code that is used to read a record from a file. This is where the JavaScript Loop Structure comes in handy--with just a few lines of code, it's possible to write code to read every record in a file---regardless of whether there are 10 records or 5 billion records."

"Are there different types of loops in JavaScript?" Dave asked. "I know there are in other languages such as C or Visual Basic."

"Yes there are Dave," I said, "JavaScript has several different types of loop structures, and we'll examine all of them today. One type of loop, called the For Loop, is designed to execute a section of code--called the body of the loop--a definite number of times, and for that reason I call the For Loop a 'definite' type of loop. Other JavaScript Loop structures are less definite in nature, which means that the number of times the body of the loop is executed is less definite. These types of loops, and how many times their loop bodies are executed, are dependent upon the evaluation of a test condition at run time. Let's go back to that example of reading an external disk file again. If we need to read all of the records from the disk file into our program, we do not know ahead of time how many records are in that file---in fact, the file could even be empty! This type of programming problem requires the use of an 'indefinite' type of loop, of which there are two in JavaScript---the While Loop and the Do-While Loop."

I suggested that we begin our examination of JavaScript loops with the For Loop.

The For Loop

I displayed the syntax for the For Loop on my classroom projector...

For (initialization; termination; increment)
statement or statements with statements appearing in a block

"This syntax," I said, "is the 'official' syntax for the For Loop, but I think for the time being, you may prefer this translation, which I think is a little easier for beginners to deal with…"

For (start at this value; keep looping as long as this expression is true; increment or decrement the value)
statement or statements with statements appearing in a block

"I always say a picture is worth a thousand words. Here's the way the code for a JavaScript For Loop would look like in a program designed to display the numbers from 1 to 10 in the Browser Window," I said, as I displayed this code on the classroom projector.

```
<! Example5-1 -->
<html>
```

```
<body>
<script type="text/javascript">

for (counter = 1;counter< 11;counter++)
  document.write(counter + "<br>")

</script>
</body>
</html>
```

"The For Loop," I continued, "begins with the keyword *for*, in lower case, followed by three arguments which appear in parentheses. A semicolon separates each argument. I think you're pretty familiar with arguments by now—arguments affect or determine the behavior of a JavaScript statement or function. In the case of the For Loop, these three arguments---initialization, termination and increment---determine the duration of the loop as you'll see in a just a few moments. In our example program, our first argument…"

for (counter = 1;counter< 11;counter++)

"…declare the variable 'counter' as a numeric Data Type and then assigns a value of 1 to it."

"I'm a little confused by that first argument," Rhonda said. "Is there anything magical about it? Or is it just an ordinary variable declaration?"

"It's really just an ordinary variable declaration," I said. "What makes it seem out of the ordinary is that the variable is declared and initialized as part of the For statement. This variable---sometimes called the Loop Control Variable---is just an ordinary variable. You can name the Loop Control variable anything you want. Typically, JavaScript programmers don't bother to name their Loop Control variables with very meaningful names, preferring instead to name them with single letter names such as i, j or k. Myself, I prefer to give my Loop Control variables a more meaningful name, and so I've named ours 'counter."

"So both the declaration and assignment of the Loop Control variable are done as part of that first argument?" Ward asked.

"That's right Ward," I replied. "Now on to the second argument, called the termination argument, which is actually a test expression, much like the one we saw last week with the If statement. In a For Loop, as long as the test expression evaluates and returns a True, the body of the loop, that is the statement or statements following the 'For' line are executed…."

for (counter = 1;counter< 11;counter++)

"…In this case, we're telling JavaScript to continue to execute the statements within the body of the loop for as long as the value of the Loop Control variable--counter—is less than 11. It's important to understand that in a For Loop, the body of the loop will NOT be executed, not even once, until the test expression is first evaluated. So long as the test expression returns a True value, the body of the loop is executed. If the test expression evaluates to a False value, the next statement following the body of the loop is executed."

"Let me make sure I follow," Barbara said. "The value of counter was initialized to 1--and we're telling JavaScript to execute the body of the loop as long as counter is less than 11."

"That's right Barbara," I answered.

"So what's to keep that from happening forever," she replied. "If counter starts out as 1, and the loop will execute as long as counter is less than 11, something needs to make the value of counter 11 or greater in order for the loop to stop--is that right?"

"That's excellent Barbara," I said, "that's exactly right. If we don't do anything to increment the value of counter, it will remain 1, and this loop will execute forever."

"Is that where the term 'Endless Loop' comes from," Valerie said. "I've heard some of the programmers at work use that term."

"That's right Valerie," I said, "that's exactly what that means—an 'Endless Loop' is a loop that continues to execute, usually because the programmer forgets to take steps to ensure that it will eventually stop."

"How will this loop ever stop then?" Rhonda asked.

"That's where the third argument--the increment argument---comes into play," I said.

for (counter = 1;counter< 11;counter++)

"The third argument, the increment argument" I continued, "tells JavaScript what to do to the Loop Control variable---which usually means we add 1 to it--but as you'll see later, we can add to or subtract from it anything we wish. In our example program, we use the JavaScript Increment Operator (++) to add 1 to the value of counter each time the test expression is evaluated."

"Based on what you're telling us then," Peter asked, "does that mean this loop will execute 10 times?" .

"Excellent Peter, that's exactly what it means!" I said.

I then saved the program as '**Example5-1.htm**" and opened it up within Internet Explorer. The following screenshot was displayed on the classroom projector.

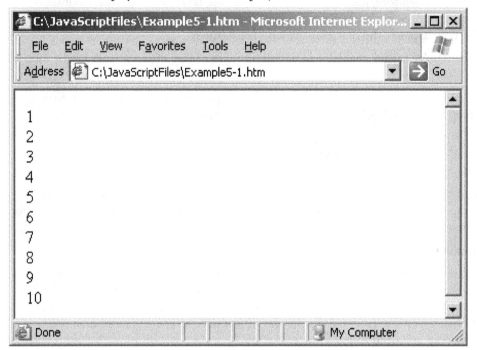

"Hey, that's pretty amazing," Kate said, "considering the fact that we displayed 10 numbers in the Browser Window with so little code."

"See what I mean about the power of loops," I said. "They can give a program enormous power."

"I'm still a little confused about what's happening here," Rhonda said, "I wish we could see this in slow motion."

"Maybe this will help," I said, as I displayed this table on the classroom projector.

Step	Value of counter	counter < 11	Body of Loop Executed?	document.write (Number displayed in Browser Window)	New value of counter after counter++
1	1	True	Yes	1	2
2	2	True	Yes	2	3
3	3	True	Yes	3	4
4	4	True	Yes	4	5
5	5	True	Yes	5	6
6	6	True	Yes	6	7
7	7	True	Yes	7	8
8	8	True	Yes	8	9
9	9	True	Yes	9	10
10	10	True	Yes	10	11
11	11	False	No		

"Step 1 shows you the value for the counter variable as the loop begins to execute," I said. "When the For line is executed for the first time, counter is declared and initialized to 1. After that, the test expression is evaluated for the first time. Since the value of counter is less than 11 (1 < 11), the body of the loop is executed, resulting in the number 1 being displayed in the Browser Window. Next, and it's important to understand the sequence, the value of counter is incremented using the JavaScript Increment operator (++)."

"So the incrementation of counter actually takes place after the body of the loop is executed?" Dave asked.

"That's right Dave," I replied. "That fools everyone the first time they see it. Now, in Step 2, the current value of counter---which is 2--is compared to 11. 2 is less than 11, which results in the test expression returning a True value, and so the body of the loop is executed. Therefore, the value 2 is displayed in the JavaScript Console. Counter is incremented by 1, giving it a new value of 3. Some beginners mistakenly believe that counter is initialized to 1 all over again--but as you can see, that only happens the first time the loop is executed."

"Just to make sure I understand what you've saying, the value of counter is incremented after the body of the loop is executed?" Linda asked.

"That's right," I said, "I know that takes some time getting used to---the test expression is evaluated, if it returns a True value, then the body of the loop is executed, followed by the increment or decrement of the Loop Control variable."

"I think I understand everything that's going on," Blaine said, "but what about when you get to Steps 10 and 11 of the table--that's when the loop ends, right?"

"In Step 10," I replied, "the value of the variable counter is 10. Since 10 is less than 11, the test expression once again evaluates to True, therefore the body of the loop--the display of the current value of the variable counter in the Browser Window---is executed. Then the value of counter is incremented by 1, giving it a value of 11."

"Doesn't the loop just 'end' at this point?" Joe asked.

"Not quite Joe," I answered. "Even though the value of counter has been incremented to 11, the test expression must formally be evaluated once more. At that point, the test expression returns a value of False, since 11 is NOT less than 11--it's equal to it. Once the test expression returns a False value, the loop is exited, meaning the line of code following the For statement or statements is executed. By the way, if you need to execute more than one statement as part of the body of the loop, you need to use a block, like this."

```
<! Example5-2 -->
<html>
<body>
<script type="text/javascript">

for (counter = 1;counter< 11;counter++) {
   document.write(counter + "<br>")
   document.write("for loop counter")
}

</script>
</body>
</html>
```

"My personal preference," I added, "is to use the block style--even if I'm only executing a single line of code within the body of the loop."

Variations on the For Loop Theme

I pointed out that our For Loop was a pretty 'vanilla' version of what the For Loop can do.

"What do you mean by vanilla?" Bob asked.

"By vanilla," I said, "I mean that in this example we specified all three arguments for the For Loop. Believe it or not, all three arguments are NOT required, and not including them can produce some behavior that interesting to say the least. Not providing all three arguments is not something I would recommend, but JavaScript does permit you to omit any one of the three arguments--or all three if you want to. For instance, you can code a For Loop that looks like this…"

I then displayed this code on the classroom projector.

for (; ;)

"What will this do?" Rhonda asked.

"This For statement would result in an endless loop," I said.

"An endless loop" Ward said. "Why would you want to do this?"

"Most likely you wouldn't," I said. "but there are occasions in the programming world where you would want to create an endless loop---and then use the Break statement to 'break out' of it. The point is, with all three arguments of the For statement being optional, it's really easy to do something like this--either because you think it's a good idea or because you accidentally code it that way. The example I showed you earlier is the prototypical example of the For Loop--but there are many other ways to code a For Loop. Some programmers, for instance, choose to increment their Loop Control variable within the body of the loop itself--leaving the third argument---the increment argument--empty like this…"

for (counter = 1;counter< 11;)

"…again, this isn't something I would recommend, but you may see some programmers do this. Still other programmers choose to leave the first argument--the initialization argument---empty like this…"

for (;counter< 11;counter++)

"…this is something you can do provided you initialize the Loop Control variable elsewhere in your program."

"Again, I presume that's something you don't recommend?" Bob asked.

"That's right Bob," I agreed, "I recommend coding all three arguments in the For Loop unless you can think of a very persuasive reason for not doing so--and in the beginning stages of your JavaScript programming career, I don't think you'll think of any."

"Assuming we do code all three arguments for the For Loop," Dave said, "are there any other variations possible with the For Loop."

"That's a great question Dave," I answered. "It's possible to vary all three arguments in such a way as to produce some very interesting results. For instance, if instead of incrementing your Loop Control variable you decrement it, the value of the Loop Control variable will decrease---and you can actually make your loop go 'backward'. And speaking of the Loop Control variable--it doesn't have to start out as 1--- it can be any value, in fact, it doesn't even have to be a positive number."

I explained that it's possible to simulate real-world situations more accurately if you get a little creative with the argument of a For Loop.

"Last week we examined some mythical restaurants in New York City," I said. "Today, let's deal with a mythical Manhattan hotel you own in which the floors of the hotel are numbered from 2 to 20. Let's further pretend that the hotel has three elevators. Elevator #1 stops at all the floors of the hotel, Elevator #2 stops only at the even numbered floors and Elevator #3 stops only at the odd numbered floors. Now suppose that we want to write a JavaScript program that displays, in the Browser Window, the floor numbers at which Elevator #1 stops. Here's an exercise to do exactly that using the JavaScript For Loop."

Exercise 5-1 Your first For Loop

In this exercise, you'll code a For Loop to display the floors at which Elevator #1 stops.

1. Use Notepad (if you are using Windows) and enter the following code.

```
<! Practice5-1 -->
<html>
<body>
<script type="text/javascript">
document.write("Elevator #1 stops at these floors...<br>")

for (counter = 2;counter< 21;counter++) {
    document.write (counter + "<br>")
}
```

```
</script>
</body>
</html
```

2. Save your source file as '**Practice5-1.htm**' in the \JavaScriptFiles\Practice folder (select File-Save As from Notepad's Menu Bar). Be sure to save your source file with the file name extension 'htm'.

3. Use Internet Explorer to Open your Source File. You should see the following output in the Browser Window.

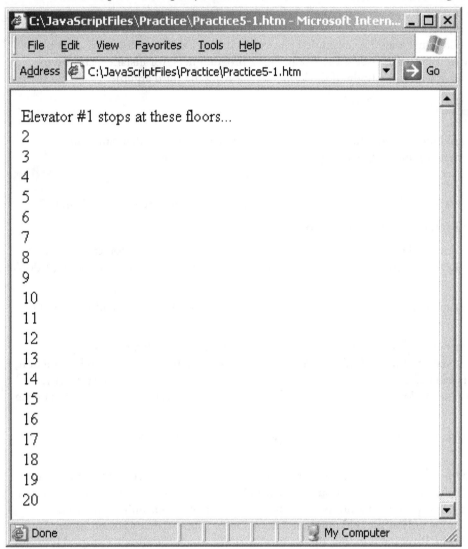

Discussion

Only one person had trouble completing the exercise---they accidentally included this line of code

**document.write("Elevator #1 stops at these floors...
")**

inside of the body of the For loop. As a result, 'Elevator #1 stops at these floors..." was displayed 19 times.

"Heading like this," I said, "need to be displayed only once--therefore, they should appear 'outside' the body of the loop."

"Where's the first floor of the hotel?" Kathy asked. "Why did the display start with the number 2?"

"Remember, the floors are numbered from 2 to 20," Mary said. "that's why the Loop Control variable was initialized to 2."

"That's right Kathy," I replied. "This was a good exercise to get your feet wet with the For Loop. Now let's get to work on a more challenging problem, Elevator #2---that's the elevator that stops only at the even numbered floors of the hotel. Do you have any ideas on how we should code a For Loop to display only the even numbered floors of the hotel?"

After a minute or two, Dave suggested that we code a For Loop, initializing our Loop Control variable to 2, using a test condition in which we compare the value of the variable to less than 21, and most importantly, that we increment the value of the Loop Control variable by 2---instead of 1.

"Excellent job Dave," I said, as I distributed this exercise for the class to complete.

Exercise 5-2 Modifying the For Loop to Handle Even numbered Floors

In this exercise, you'll code a For Loop to display the even numbered floors of the hotel at which Elevator #2 stops.

1. Use Notepad (if you are using Windows) and enter the following code.

```
<! Practice5-2 -->
<html>
<body>
<script type="text/javascript">
document.write("Elevator #2 stops at these floors...<br>")

for (counter = 2;counter< 21;counter=counter+2) {
   document.write (counter + "<br>")
}
</script>
</body>
</html>
```

2. Save your source file as '**Practice5-2.htm**' in the \JavaScriptFiles\Practice folder (select File-Save As from Notepad's Menu Bar). Be sure to save your source file with the file name extension 'htm'.
3. Use Internet Explorer to Open your Source File. You should see the following output in the Browser Window.

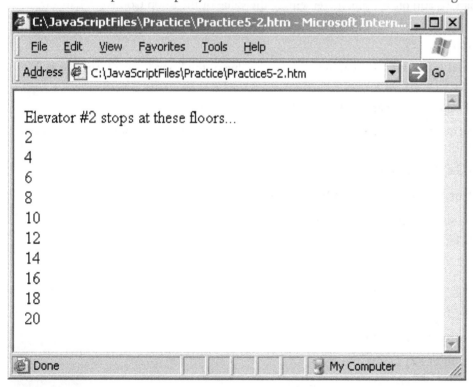

Discussion

"That was very clever, Dave," Rhonda said, obviously impressed. "I don't think I would have thought of incrementing the Loop Control variable by 2."

"Solving programming problems like this requires some imagination," I told Rhonda. "The more programs you write, the easier it will be to envision little 'tricks' like this to solve these types of problems."

"I noticed," Linda said, "that we incremented the value of our Loop Control variable 'counter' by taking the value of counter and adding 2 to it. It sure would be great if there was an increment operator to add 2 to a variable the way the (++) operator adds 1?"

"Actually Linda, there is," I replied. "Instead of using this code to increment the value of the counter variable by 2…"

```
counter=counter+2
```

"…we can use this code instead, which is a variation of the increment operator (++) we learn about a few weeks ago. The Addition Assignment (+=) Operator is used to increment the value of a variable by the number which follows it--in this case, +=2 adds 2 to a variable…"

```
counter+=2
```

"Cool," Chuck said. "Can you increment the variable by any number that way---and is there a way to subtract numbers as well?"

"You're right on both counts Chuck," I said, "This syntax can be used to add 3 to the variable counter.."

```
counter+=3
```

"…and this syntax will subtract 3 from the variable counter…"

```
counter-=3
```

"I've been thinking about Elevator #3," Lou said, "the one that stops only at odd numbered floors in the hotel? I know what you said about using your imagination to solve this problem--but so far, I haven't been able to get it to work. How should we code that loop?"

Linda suggested that a For Loop with a Loop Control variable initialized to 3, a test condition in which we compare the value of the variable to less than 21, and once again, incrementing the value of the Loop Control variable by 2 would be the way to go.

```
for (counter = 3;counter< 21;counter+=2)
```

"Of course," Lou lamented, "that was my mistake--I kept initializing the value of the Loop Control variable to 2 instead of 3."

"Shouldn't the initial value of the Loop Control variable be 1?" Rhonda asked.

"Don't forget Rhonda," I said, "the hotel has no first floor--the first odd numbered floor is 3---initializing the Loop Control variable to 3 takes care of that.."

I then distributed this exercise for the class to complete.

Exercise 5-3 Modifying the For Loop to Handle Odd Floors

In this exercise, you'll code a For Loop to display the odd numbered floors at which Elevator #3 stops.

1. Use Notepad (if you are using Windows) and enter the following code.

```
<! Practice5-3 -->
<html>
<body>
<script type="text/javascript">
document.write("Elevator #3 stops at these floors...<br>")
for (counter = 3;counter< 21;counter+=2) {
   document.write (counter + "<br>")
}
</script>
</body>
</html>
```

2. Save your source file as '**Practice5-3.htm**' in the \JavaScriptFiles\Practice folder (select File-Save As from Notepad's Menu Bar). Be sure to save your source file with the file name extension 'htm'.
3. Use Internet Explorer to Open your Source File. You should see the following output in the Browser Window.

Discussion

By this point, no seemed to be having any problems with our 'elevator' exercises.

"This is great fun," Joe said. "I didn't know you could do this kind of thing in a program. I can't wait to apply JavaScript loops to something practical."

"You'll get a chance to work with loop in the Grades Calculation project," I said. "But we still have some more work to do before we get to that point."

I continued by saying that all three of the For Loop's arguments (initialization, termination, and increment) could be expressed not only as numerical literals (that is numbers), as we had in the previous exercises, but also as variables. I then distributed this exercise to demonstrate my point.

Exercise 5-4 Modifying the For Loop to Work with Constants

In this exercise, you'll code a For Loop to display the floors at which Elevator #1 stops--but instead of using numeric literals for the Initialization, Termination and Increment arguments, you'll use a combination of variables.

1. Use Notepad (if you are using Windows) and enter the following code.

```
<! Practice5-4 -->
<html>
<body>
<script type="text/javascript">

var TOP_FLOOR = 20

document.write("Elevator #1 stops at these floors...<br>")

for (floor = 2;floor < TOP_FLOOR+1;floor++) {
  document.write (floor + "<br>")
}

</script>
</body>
</html>
```

2. Save your source file as '**Practice5-4.htm**' in the \JavaScriptFiles\Practice folder (select File-Save As from Notepad's Menu Bar). Be sure to save your source file with the file name extension 'htm'.
3. Use Internet Explorer to Open your Source File. You should see the following output in the Browser Window.

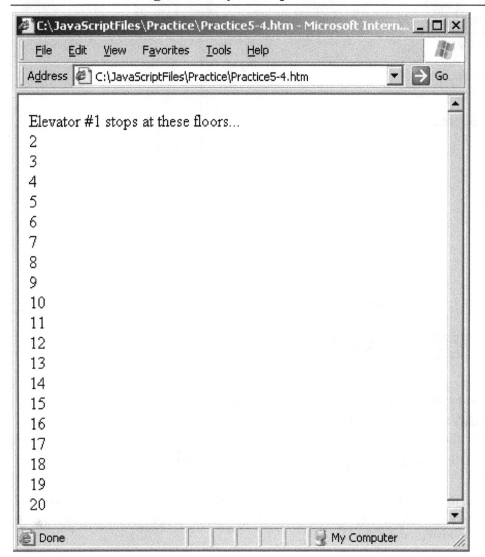

Discussion

"Does everyone see what we're doing here?" I asked.

"It looks like we've done two new things here," Linda said. "First, we used a more meaningful name for the Loop Control variable--floor---and we also declared a variable called TOP_FLOOR to use as part of the test expression in the termination argument of the For Loop."

"That's an excellent analysis Linda," I said. "Using a variable like this doesn't impact the behavior of the loop--but it does make your code a lot more readable."

I waited to see if there were any questions.

"Now let's suppose." I said, "that as an added challenge, we want to display the floors of our hotel backwards?"

"Wow, is that possible?" Steve asked.

"It can be done with a For Loop," I said, "but I have to warn you, we will have to be careful."

I then distributed this exercise for the class to complete.

Exercise 5-5 Displaying the Floors Backwards--but there's a problem

In this exercise, you'll code a For Loop to display the floors of the hotel--backwards. But beware---this code has a bug in it and won't behave properly.

1. Use Notepad (if you are using Windows) and enter the following code.

```
<! Practice5-5 -->
<html>
```

```
<body>
<script type="text/javascript">

document.write("Floors in the hotel, listed backwards are...<br>")

for (counter = 20;counter < 20;counter++) {
  document.write (counter + "<br>")
}

</script>
</body>
</html>
```

2. Save your source file as '**Practice5-5.htm**' in the \JavaScriptFiles\Practice folder (select File-Save As from Notepad's Menu Bar). Be sure to save your source file with the file name extension 'htm'.

3. Use Internet Explorer to Open your Source File. You should see the following output in the Browser Window.

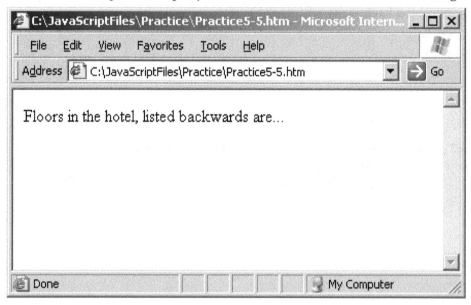

Discussion

"*Nothing* happened," Rhonda said. "No floor numbers were displayed--did the loop execute?"

Rhonda was correct. Nothing--except for the heading---was displayed in the Browser Window.

"Can anyone tell me what happened?" I asked.

No one had an immediate solution to what had, or hadn't, happened---but then Barbara spoke up.

"I think I know what the problem is," she said. "I know we intended to have the loop go 'backwards', but in the termination argument---the test expression immediately evaluates to False--that's why the body of the loop never executes."

"What's that Barbara?" Rhonda asked.

"Take a look at the initial value of our Loop Control variable," Barbara continued. "It starts at 20, because that's the top floor of our hotel and since we want to display the floors backward, that's where we want to start. But then the test expression asks whether the value of the counter variable is greater than 20. This is where the problem lies. As long as the test expression returns a True value, the body of the loop will execute---but the value of counter is 20, and obviously 20 is not greater than 20. Therefore, the test expression immediately evaluates to False, and the loop terminates."

"Excellent Barbara," I said. "That's exactly what happened. What we have here is a problem in the way I--and beginner programmers---sometimes code their loops."

"I would have thought," Ward said, "that JavaScript would have executed the body of the loop at least once."

"Not with a For Loop Ward," I answered. "although we'll see in just a few moments that there are some types of JavaScript loops where that is the case---that is, the body of the loop is executed at least once. With a For Loop, the test expression is always evaluated prior to the body of the loop executing."

"So how can we make this loop count backwards?" Rhonda asked. "What do we need to change?

"We need to correct our test expression," I said, "to make the loop count backwards."

I then distributed this exercise for the class to complete.

Exercise 5-6 Displaying the Floors Backwards Error! Bookmark not defined. **Correctly**

In this exercise, you'll correct the code from Exercise 5-5, so that the floors of our hotel are correctly displayed backwards.

1. Use Notepad (if you are using Windows) and enter the following code.

```
<! Practice5-6 -->
<html>
<body>
<script type="text/javascript">
document.write("Floors in the hotel, listed backwards are...<br>")

for (counter = 20;counter > 1;counter--) {
   document.write (counter + "<br>")
}

</script>
</body>
</html>
```

2. Save your source file as **'Practice5-6.htm'** in the \JavaScriptFiles\Practice folder (select File-Save As from Notepad's Menu Bar). Be sure to save your source file with the file name extension 'htm'.

3. Use Internet Explorer to Open your Source File. You should see the following output in the Browser Window.

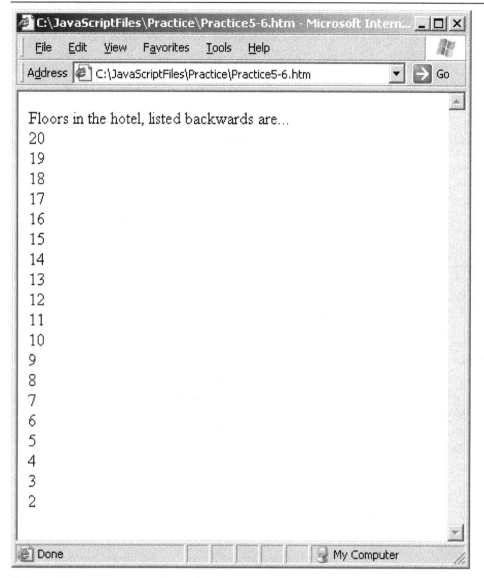

Floors in the hotel, listed backwards are...
20
19
18
17
16
15
14
13
12
11
10
9
8
7
6
5
4
3
2

Discussion

"That's better," Mary said. "Now the floors are displayed backwards."

"To make the loop count 'backwards'," I said, "you need to specify a test expression that evaluates the value of the Loop Control variable against the lower limit of the loop. That's what we did here."

There were no more questions, and so I suggested we take a break.

"When we return from break," I said, "we'll examine the indefinite kinds of JavaScript loops I've mentioned--the While Loop family."

While Loops

Resuming after break, I began a discussion of what I call the JavaScript indefinite loops, the family of While Loops.

"Compared to the For Loop," I said, "beginners to JavaScript find the While Loop a bit confusing at first, perhaps because there are actually two variations of it--the While Loop and the Do-While Loop. But you'll see that the only real difference in the behavior of the two variations is that, like the For Loop, the body of the While Loop is NOT guaranteed to execute even once, but with the Do-While Loop, the body of the loop is executed AT LEAST ONCE. We'll examine both types of While Loops during the last half of today's class."

"What are the differences between the While Loop and the For Loop," Steve asked, "and what are the similarities?"

"Just like the For Loop," I said, "the While Loop structure permits the programmer to repetitively execute a section of code. But as you'll see, when a While Loop ends is not nearly as 'definite' as it is for the For Loop."

"How so?" Mary asked.

"With the For Loop," I continued, "you saw that we designate a definite end point in the way in which we specify our termination argument. With a While Loop, there is no built-in Loop Control variable as there is with the For Loop--instead you need to specify an expression in the While statement that is very much like the test expression specified in the For Loop. What makes the While loop a bit trickier is that the expression is not written to test the Loop Control variable---instead the test expression is written to evaluate something else. Unfortunately, when first learning, quite a few beginners mis-code the test expression in a While Loop, resulting in something we mentioned earlier---an endless or infinite loop."

"What kinds of test conditions can you specify as the expression in the While Loop?" Ward asked.

"You can specify any condition that evaluates to a True or False value," I said, "just like the test expression we saw in the first For Loop we coded today."

"Can we see an example of the While Loop," Mary said.

The While Loop

"Sure thing Mary," I said, "let's take a look at the While Loop first, that's the type of While Loop in which the test expression is evaluated prior to the body of the loop executing even once."
I then displayed the syntax for the While Loop on the classroom projector:

```
while (expression) {
   statement or statements
```

"You're right," Joe said, "this does look a little confusing to me."

"Let's take it a step at a time," I said. "and I'm sure you'll be OK with this. The For Loop begins with the word 'while', followed by a test expression, which as I indicated earlier, is much like the test expression in an If statement. Unlike the For Loop, there isn't an initialization of a Loop Control variable at the top of the loop structure--just this single test expression. There's also no termination argument. As long as the test expression evaluates to True, the body of the loop will be executed. Therefore, it's up to the programmer to ensure that eventually the test expression evaluates to False--and that needs to be done using code within the loop itself--something we'll see in just a few moments. As was the case with the For Loop, the test expression is evaluated before the body of the loop is executed---this means that the body of the While loop is not guaranteed to execute even one time--if the text expression immediately evaluates to False, the loop structure is exited. As you'll see in a few moments, there's a variation of this loop in which the body of the loop is always executed at least once."

"Wouldn't you want every loop you code to execute at least once?" Rhonda asked.

"Not necessarily," I answered. "For instance, suppose you are using a loop to read records from a disk file, and you include the instructions to read the records within the body of the loop. If the file is empty---which can happen---you wouldn't want to execute the body of the loop even once--if you did, you would attempt to read a record from an empty file, which would generate an error."

"OK," Rhonda answered, "that makes sense to me."

At this point, there were no other questions, and I suggested that we complete an exercise to give everyone a chance to work with the While Loop---once again displaying the floors of our hotel.

Exercise 5-7 Use the While Loop to display the floors of our hotel

In this exercise, you'll code a While Loop to display the floors of our hotel in the Browser Window.

1. Use Notepad (if you are using Windows) and enter the following code.

```
<! Practice5-7 -->
<html>
<body>
<script type="text/javascript">

var counter = 2

document.write("The floors in the hotel are...<br>")

while (counter < 21) {
   document.write (counter + "<br>")
```

```
  counter++
}
</script>
</body>
</html>
```

2. Save your source file as **'Practice5-7.htm'** in the \JavaScriptFiles\Practice folder (select File-Save As from Notepad's Menu Bar). Be sure to save your source file with the file name extension 'htm'.

3. Use Internet Explorer to Open your Source File. You should see the following output in the Browser Window.

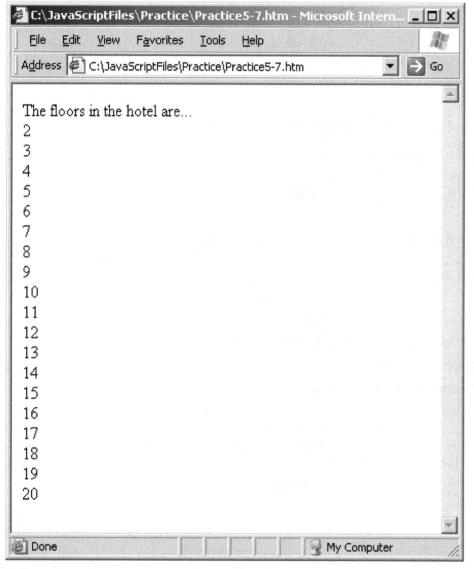

Discussion

"As you can see," I said, "we've successfully displayed the floors of our hotel--this time using a While Loop to do the job instead of a For Loop. I think once you get used to the format, you'll find that working with the While Loop--specifically coding the test expression--is somewhat intuitive. Remember, though, we need to do a little more work with the While Loop than with the For Loop. For instance, since there is no initialization argument, that means we needed to take care of that ourselves, before the loop structure is encountered, with this line of code..."

```
var counter = 2
```

"...then comes the While Loop, and it's test expression, in which we tell JavaScript to execute the body of the loop while the value of counter is less than 22..."

```
while (counter < 21) {
```

"...and to display the value of counter in the Browser Window..."

```
document.write (counter + "<br>")
```

"...As I mentioned earlier, because the While Loop does not have an increment argument of its own, it's imperative that we take care of incrementing the variable we are using to determine the duration of the loop--we do that with this code..."

```
counter++
```

"The variable counter," Blaine said, "reminds me of the Loop Control variable from the For Loop."

"You're right about that, Blaine" I said. "With the While Loop, there is no formal Loop Control variable as there is in a For Loop---in effect, we have to create our own...."

"How important is it to increment the value of counter inside of the loop?" Kathy asked.

"Vitally important," I said. "Beginners typically make two kinds of mistakes with the While Loop. Either they initialize the value of a variable they're using in their test expression inside the body of loop, or they increment the value of that variable outside the loop."

"What's wrong with that?" Rhonda asked.

"In our case, if we were to initialize the value of counter within the body of the loop," I said, 'each time the body of the loop is executed, the value of counter is reset to 2. That's not good in that the value of counter never gets to the point where the loop can terminate. And if we were to increment the value of counter outside the body of the loop, the value of counter would always be 2. As a result, the test expression (counter < 21) is always True, and the loop never terminates. In both cases, we wind up with an endless loop."

Joe had a question.

"Why didn't the number 21 display in the Browser Window?" he asked. "Why did it stop at 20."

"Because," I said, "our expression told JavaScript to execute the body of the loop 'while' counter is less than 21. As soon as counter is equal to 21, the test expression returns a False value, and the loop immediately terminates."

"You had said earlier that While Loops are more of an indefinite nature of loops," Linda said. "but this loop seemed pretty definite to me. Can you give us a better example of that?"

"I sure can," I said. "How about a loop that runs until the user tells it to stop?"

I then distributed this exercise for the class to complete.

Exercise 5-8 An Indefinite Version of the While Loop

In this exercise, you'll create a While loop structure that displays numbers in the Browser Window. However, the numbers will only be displayed for as long as the user chooses to continue to display them. A few words of warning here---in order to cut down on the number of lines of code we need to write, in this exercise we are not checking to see if the user clicks on the Cancel button in the Prompt Popup Box!

1. Use Notepad (if you are using Windows) and enter the following code.

```
<! Practice5-8 -->
<html>
<body>
<script type="text/javascript">

var counter = 1
var response = ""

response = prompt("Should I start counting?","Yes")
response = response.toUpperCase()

while (response == "YES") {
  document.write (counter + "<br>")
  counter++
  response = prompt("Should I Continue?","Yes")
  response = response.toUpperCase()
}
alert("Thanks for counting with me!")
```

```
</script>
</body>
</html>
```

2. Save your source file as **'Practice5-8.htm'** in the \JavaScriptFiles\Practice folder (select File-Save As from Notepad's Menu Bar). Be sure to save your source file with the file name extension 'htm'.

3. Use Internet Explorer to Open your Source File.

4. The program will ask you if you wish to start counting. Because we specified 'Yes' as the default for the Prompt Popup Box, 'Yes' is already in the Text Box.

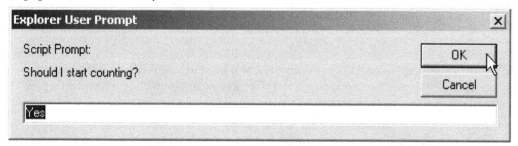

5. Now click on the OK button. The number 1 should appear in the Browser Window.

Don't Forget: If typing these examples and exercises isn't something you want to do, feel free to follow this link to find and download the completed solutions for all of the examples and exercises in the book. Just click on the JavaScript book, then follow the link entitled exercises ☺

http://www.johnsmiley.com/main/books.htm

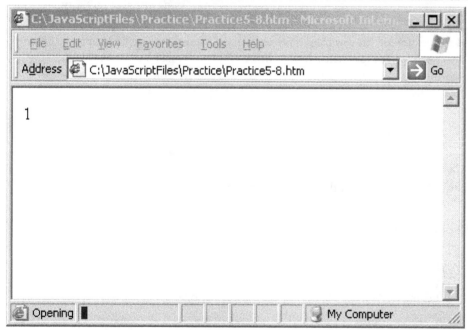

6. After the number 1 is displayed in the Browser Window, the program will then ask you if you wish to continue counting. Answer 'Yes' once again by clicking on the OK button.

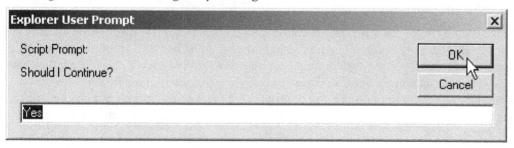

7. The number 2 will then be displayed in the Browser Window, and once again you'll be asked if you wish to continue counting. Numbers will continue to be displayed in the Browser Window for as long as you answer 'Yes'.

8. Answer 'No' to the prompt to continue counting. A thank you message will be displayed in a JavaScript Alert box and the program will end:

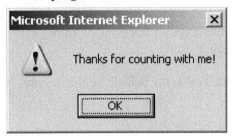

Discussion

There was a fair amount of confusion and problems with this exercise, and it took us about fifteen minutes to get through it. The exercise was tedious to type--and not everyone in the class was as attentive to the capitalization of the word 'YES' in their JavaScript source code as they needed to be.

"This code is a good example of the indefinite capabilities of the While Loop," I explained. "How long this loop executes is entirely up to the user, and determined at run time--not when the program is being coded. When we wrote this program, we had no idea how many numbers the user would want displayed in the Browser Window. The While Loop gives us a way for the loop to run indefinitely--but still with a way to end it. That's the beauty of the While Loop---in this case, as soon as the test expression evaluates to False, the loop ends."

I continued by saying that, as we had done in Exercise 5-7, the first thing we did here was to declare the variables we would use in the program.

"Remember," I said, "I can't emphasize this enough---with a While Loop there is no built-in Loop Control variable, so in order for the loop to eventually end, we need to declare a variable of our own which will then be used in a test expression to see if the loop should be terminated. In our previous exercise, we used the value of counter to determine if the loop should end--this program is a bit different in that we will let the user's response to question determine when the loop ends. That's the function of the variable response here, a variable whose value will be determined by the user. The variable counter, as it was in Exercise 5-7, is the 'number' we will display in the Browser Window--and we initialize it to 1..."

```
var counter = 1
var response = ""
```

"Now it's time," I said, "to use the Prompt function to display a message to the user, asking them if they wish to start counting. The user's response will then be stored in the variable response. Notice how we specify the default value for the Text Box as the word 'Yes'..."

```
response = prompt("Should I start counting?","Yes")
```

"...this next line of code is very significant..."

```
response = response.toUpperCase()
```

"I was going to ask you about that," Linda said. "What is the toUpperCase() function?"

"toUpperCase() is a JavaScript function," I said, "and it's designed to take a string value and 'convert' it to all Upper Case characters. In this case, the value of the response variable---that is, the user's answer---is replaced by that same answer, in all Upper Case characters. For instance, the string j-o-h-n would be converted to J-O-H-N."

"Why are we doing this?" Kate asked.

"In short," I said, "because we want to make our test expression manageable. In this way, no matter how the user spells the word 'YES'---all lower case, all upper case, or something in between, ultimately their response is converted to the word 'YES' in all Upper Case letters--and that will make determining if they answered 'YES' or something else much easier. Of course, by specifying a default value of 'Yes', we've made things a lot easier on the user---most likely, if they want to start counting, or continue counting, they'll simply click on the OK button. But you never know with users---they may type something into the Text Box on their own. This way, we can handle any variation on the way they capitalize the word 'YES'."

"I guess I'm missing something here," Chuck said, "but how does converting the user's response to upper case make the comparison easier?"

"Did you realize," I answered, "that the user can type the word 'YES' into the Text Box in eight different ways."

"What do you mean eight different ways?" asked Barbara.

"Each letter of the word 'YES' can be entered by the user in either upper or lower case," I explained. "And while it's nice to believe that the user would enter 'YES' in all Caps if we asked them, in reality, some users mix and match case as they're entering values into a Text Box. Let's take a moment to come up with all the possible combinations of the word 'YES' and you'll see that there are eight different ways of writing it…"

YES	yES
YEs	yEs
YeS	yeS
Yes	yes

"Now if we converting the user's response to all upper case characters," I said, "that means we only need to perform the comparison in our text expression to the word 'YES' in all capital letters. The alternative would be to write code using a series of Or operations that would look like this…"

```
while (
  (response == "YES") || (response == "YEs") ||
  (response == "YeS") || (response == "Yes") ||
  (response == "yES") || (response == "yEs") ||
  (response == "yeS") || (response == "yes")) {
```

"I see what you mean now," Ward said. "That makes sense, and even more sense if the user entered a word with 13 characters."

"That's right Ward," I said. "A word with 13 letters can be entered 8,192 different ways by the user--that's a comparison I wouldn't want to make using the Or Operator. Let's get back to that first line of the While loop, in which we tell JavaScript to execute the body of the loop provided the variable response is equal to the upper case value 'YES'…"

```
while (response == "YES") {
```

"Oh, so that's the benefit of having converted the user's response to upper case," Rhonda said. "The light bulb just went on!"

"Is this the type of loop in which the body is NOT necessarily executed once?" Blaine asked.

"That's right Blaine," I said. "Because the test expression in a While Loop is evaluated 'at the top' of the loop structure, the body of the loop will be executed only if the test expression evaluates to True--something that can only happen if the user answers 'Yes' to the question 'Should I start counting?' Provided the user answers 'YES' (or any of the eight varieties of 'YES', this next line of code will display the value of the counter variable in the Browser Window…"

```
document.write (counter + "<br>")
```

"and then this line of code will increment the value of counter…"

```
counter++
```

"…incrementing the value of counter is important, but it's not as important as it was in Exercise 5-7, since it's no longer the value of counter that determines if and when the loop ends. The responsibility for ending the loop is the response the user gives us to the question 'Should I continue', which is stored in the response variable. That's the key to the loop eventually ending. Notice how we also must 'upper case' the user's response to this question also…"

```
response = prompt("Should I Continue?","Yes")
response = response.toUpperCase()
```

"So the loop will continue until the user answers 'No'?" Ward asked.

"Not exactly, Ward" I said. "The loop will continue as long as the user enters 'Yes' or any of its eight variations into the Text Box. That means the loop will end if the user enters anything else into the Text Box, or until they click on the Cancel button---something which I mentioned earlier we are not checking for in this exercise. And so, if the user enters anything other than 'Yes' into the Text Box, the loop will end, and we then display this message to the user thanking them for counting with us and end the program."

```
alert("Thanks for counting with me!")
```

Prior to moving on, I repeated my earlier assertion that one of the biggest mistakes beginners make with the While Loop is to forget to include code within the body of the loop that enables the loop to end.

"Because the test condition we set up is to compare the value of the response variable to 'YES'," I said, "if we forgot to give the user the opportunity to change the value of that variable, we would wind up with an endless loop condition."

Do-While Loop

No one had any questions about the While Loop, and so it was time to move onto a discussion of the Do-While Loop. I displayed the syntax for the Do-While Loop on the classroom projector:

```
do {
   statement(s)
} while (expression)
```

"This variation of the While Loop is called the Do-While Loop," I said, "because the first line of the loop structure begins with the single word 'Do', and the last line of the loop contains the While statement. Everything else in between is considered the body of the loop."

"How is this Do-While loop different than the While Loop we just worked with?" Mary asked.

"Unlike the While Loop," I answered, "in which the body of the loop is NOT guaranteed to execute even once, with the Do While loop, the body of the loop will execute at least one time."

"Is it the location of the word 'While' that causes that behavior," Linda asked. "I notice that the test expression is located after the body of the loop."

"Great deduction Linda," I said. "In the While Loop structure we examined, because the word 'While' appeared as the first line of the loop structure, the test expression was evaluated prior to the body of the loop executing. With the Do-While loop, because the test expression appears as the last line of the loop structure, that means that the body of the loop is guaranteed to execute at least once."

No one had any other questions, and so I suggested that we complete an exercise in which we implemented the functionality from Exercise 5-8 using a Do-While loop instead.

Exercise 5-9 The Do-While Loop

In this exercise, you'll create a Do-While loop structure that displays numbers in the Browser Window. However, the numbers will only be displayed for as long as the user chooses to continue to display them. A few words of warning here---in order to cut down on the number of lines of code we need to write, in this exercise we are not checking to see if the user clicks on the Cancel button in the Prompt Popup Box!

1. Use Notepad (if you are using Windows) and enter the following code.

```
<! Practice5-9 -->
<html>
<body>
<script type="text/javascript">

var counter = 1
var response = ""

response = prompt("Should I start counting?","Yes")
response = response.toUpperCase()

do {
   document.write (counter + "<br>")
   counter++
   response = prompt("Should I Continue?","Yes")
   response = response.toUpperCase()
} while (response == "YES")

alert("Thanks for counting with me!")
```

```
</script>
</body>
</html>
```

2. Save your source file as '**Practice5-9.htm**' in the \JavaScriptFiles\Practice folder (select File-Save As from Notepad's Menu Bar). Be sure to save your source file with the file name extension 'htm'.

3. The program will ask you if you wish to start counting. Because we specified 'Yes' as the default for the Prompt Popup Box, 'Yes' is already in the Text Box. Click on the OK button. As was the case with Exercise 5-8, the number 1 should appear in the Browser Window.

4. After the number 1 is displayed in the Browser Window, the program will then ask you if you wish to continue counting. Answer 'Yes' once again by clicking on the OK button. The number 2 will then be displayed in the Browser Window, followed by the same question. Numbers will continue to be displayed in the Browser Window for as long as you answer 'Yes'

5. Answer 'No' A goodbye message will be displayed and the program will end.

Discussion

No one had any major problems completing the exercise.

"It looks like this program is behaving the same way as the program from Exercise 5-8," Rhonda said.

"You're right Rhonda," I said. "We've proven that we can implement the same functionality using a Do-While loop as we did when we coded the program using a While Loop."

"So what's the difference," Joe asked.

"The difference in the behavior," I said, "won't become apparent unless the user answers 'No' to the first question asked of them, 'Do you want to start counting?' If the user were to answer 'No' in response to this question in the Exercise 5-8 version of the program, the body of the loop will NEVER execute. That's not the case in the Exercise 5-9 version of the program. Because the test expression is at the 'bottom' of the Do-While structure, the body of the loop will execute once. Let me show you what I mean."

I then ran the code from Exercise 5-8, and answered 'No' to the question asking me if I wanted to start counting. The program immediately ended without displaying any numbers in the Browser Window.

"That's what I would expect," Ward said.

"Now let's see what happens," I said, "when we run the code from Exercise 5-9."

I then ran the code from Exercise 5-9, and answered 'No' to the question asking me if I wanted to start counting. Despite my answer of 'no', the program displayed the number 1 in the Browser Window anyway.

Don't Forget: If typing these examples and exercises isn't something you want to do, feel free to follow this link to find and download the completed solutions for all of the examples and exercises in the book. Just click on the JavaScript book, then follow the link entitled exercises ☺

http://www.johnsmiley.com/main/books.htm

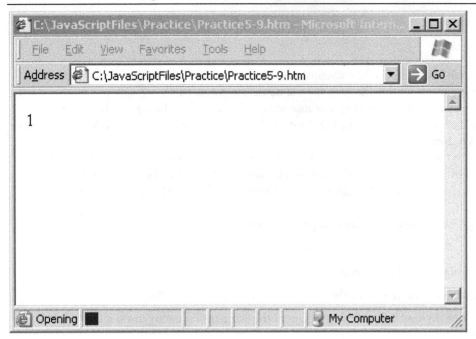

"I see the difference now," Rhonda said. "The program ignored our answer."

"It's not so much that the program ignored our answer," I answered, "but that it didn't check our answer until the body of the loop had executed once. In Exercise 5-8, the answer was evaluated at the beginning of the loop. Since the test condition evaluated immediately to False, the body of the loop was never executed. In Exercise 5-9, the test condition was evaluated after the body of the loop had already executed and displayed the number 1 in the Browser Window."

I asked if there were any questions about the While family of loops. There were none, and so I asked everyone to take a break.

"When we return from break," I said, "we'll be working on a modification to the Grades Calculation project to include loop processing."

Adding a Loop to the Grades Calculation Project

When my students returned from break, a couple of them immediately asked what we would be doing with the Grades Calculation project that involved a loop.

"Right now," I said, "as the project stands, it properly calculates the grade for an English, Math or Science Student-- but it only performs one calculation before ending."

"That's right," Blaine said, "one grade calculation and the program ends. By using loop processing, will we be able the make the program perform multiple calculations before ending?"

"You hit the nail right on the head, Blaine" I said.

"How will we do that?" Chuck asked.

"What we'll do," I said, "is 'sandwich' the code that performs the grade calculation within a loop structure so that we can calculate the grades for many students instead of just one. Can anyone suggest the kind of loop we should use to do that?"

"I suppose we could use a For Loop," Rhonda suggested, "but from what we've learned today, a For Loop is the best choice when we know for certain the number of times we want the body of the loop to execute. That wouldn't be the case here--since it's each time the program runs, there's likely to be a different number of grades to be calculated. I guess for that reason, the While Loop is the way to go."

"Great thinking Rhonda," I said, "and I agree, a While Loop makes sense to you. Now another question---should we use the While Loop or the Do-While variety? "

"I would vote for the While Loop," Valerie answered. "I think we should evaluate the test expression we code at the 'top' of the loop structure---not at the end of it."

"I agree Valerie," I said. "Although it's not likely that the user will run the program, and then have no grades at all to calculate, it is possible. I think it's 'safer' to ask the user if he or she has grades to calculate, and if so, then execute the body of the loop to calculate grades."

I saw some confusion in the eyes of my students, but I knew this would be cleared up when they started to code the modifications to the Grades Calculation project. I then distributed this exercise for the class to complete.

Exercise 5-10 Add a loop to the Grades Calculation Project

In this exercise, you'll modify the Grades Calculation Project you last worked on last week in Exercise 4-8 by giving it the ability to calculate more than one student's grade before ending.

1. Using Notepad (if you are using Windows) locate and open the Grades.htm source file you worked on last week. (It should be in the \JavaScriptFiles\Grades folder)
2. Modify your code so that it looks like this.

```
<! Grades -- >
<html>
<body>
<script type="text/javascript">

var ENGLISH_MIDTERM_PERCENTAGE = .25
var ENGLISH_FINALEXAM_PERCENTAGE = .25
var ENGLISH_RESEARCH_PERCENTAGE = .30
var ENGLISH_PRESENTATION_PERCENTAGE = .20
var MATH_MIDTERM_PERCENTAGE = .50
var MATH_FINALEXAM_PERCENTAGE = .50
var SCIENCE_MIDTERM_PERCENTAGE = .40
var SCIENCE_FINALEXAM_PERCENTAGE = .40
var SCIENCE_RESEARCH_PERCENTAGE = .20
var midterm = 0
var finalExamGrade = 0
var research = 0
var presentation = 0
var finalNumericGrade = 0
var finalLetterGrade = ""
var response = ""
var moreGradesToCalculate = ""

moreGradesToCalculate = prompt("Do you want to calculate a grade?","Yes")
moreGradesToCalculate = moreGradesToCalculate.toUpperCase()

while (moreGradesToCalculate == "YES") {

  // What type of student are we calculating?
  response = prompt("Enter student type (1=English, 2=Math, 3=Science)","")
  if (response == null) {
    alert("You clicked on the Cancel button")
    exit
  }

  if (response == "") {
    alert("You must make an entry in the Text Box")
    exit
  }

  if (parseInt(response) < 1 || parseInt( response) > 3) {
    alert(response + " - is not a valid student type")
    exit
  }

  // Student type is valid, now let's calculate the grade

  switch(parseInt(response)) {
```

```javascript
// Case 1 is an English Student
case 1:
  midterm = parseInt(prompt("Enter the Midterm Grade",""))
  finalExamGrade = parseInt(prompt("Enter the Final Examination Grade","" ))
  research = parseInt(prompt("Enter the Research Grade",""))
  presentation = parseInt(prompt("Enter the Presentation Grade",""))
  finalNumericGrade =
    (midterm * ENGLISH_MIDTERM_PERCENTAGE) +
    (finalExamGrade * ENGLISH_FINALEXAM_PERCENTAGE) +
    (research * ENGLISH_RESEARCH_PERCENTAGE) +
    (presentation * ENGLISH_PRESENTATION_PERCENTAGE)
  if (finalNumericGrade >= 93)
    finalLetterGrade = "A"
  else
  if ((finalNumericGrade >= 85) & (finalNumericGrade < 93))
    finalLetterGrade = "B"
  else
  if ((finalNumericGrade >= 78) & (finalNumericGrade < 85))
    finalLetterGrade = "C"
  else
  if ((finalNumericGrade >= 70) & (finalNumericGrade < 78))
    finalLetterGrade = "D"
  else
  if (finalNumericGrade < 70)
    finalLetterGrade = "F"
    alert("*** ENGLISH STUDENT ***\n\n" +
      "Midterm grade is: " + midterm + "\n" +
      "Final Exam is: " + finalExamGrade + "\n" +
      "Research grade is: " + research + "\n" +
      "Presentation grade is: " + presentation + "\n\n" +
      "Final Numeric Grade is: " + finalNumericGrade + "\n" +
      "Final Letter Grade is: " + finalLetterGrade)
  break

// Case 2 is a Math Student
case 2:
  midterm = parseInt(prompt("Enter the Midterm Grade","" ))
  finalExamGrade = parseInt(prompt("Enter the Final Examination Grade",""))
  finalNumericGrade =
    (midterm * MATH_MIDTERM_PERCENTAGE) +
    (finalExamGrade * MATH_FINALEXAM_PERCENTAGE)
  if (finalNumericGrade >= 90)
    finalLetterGrade = "A"
  else
  if ((finalNumericGrade >= 83) & (finalNumericGrade < 90))
    finalLetterGrade = "B"
  else
  if ((finalNumericGrade >= 76) & (finalNumericGrade < 83))
    finalLetterGrade = "C"
  else
  if ((finalNumericGrade >= 65) & (finalNumericGrade < 76))
    finalLetterGrade = "D"
  else
  if (finalNumericGrade < 65)
    finalLetterGrade = "F"
  alert("*** MATH STUDENT ***\n\n" +
    "Midterm grade is: " + midterm + "\n" +
```

```
      "Final Exam is: " + finalExamGrade + "\n\n" +
      "Final Numeric Grade is: " + finalNumericGrade + "\n" +
      "Final Letter Grade is: " + finalLetterGrade)
    break

  // Case 3 is a Science Student
  case 3:
    midterm = parseInt(prompt("Enter the Midterm Grade",""))
    finalExamGrade = parseInt(prompt("Enter the Final Examination Grade",""))
    research = parseInt(prompt("Enter the Research Grade",""))
    finalNumericGrade =
      (midterm * SCIENCE_MIDTERM_PERCENTAGE) +
      (finalExamGrade * SCIENCE_FINALEXAM_PERCENTAGE) +
      (research * SCIENCE_RESEARCH_PERCENTAGE)
    if (finalNumericGrade >= 90)
      finalLetterGrade = "A"
    else
    if ((finalNumericGrade >= 80) & (finalNumericGrade < 90))
      finalLetterGrade = "B"
    else
    if ((finalNumericGrade >= 70) & (finalNumericGrade < 80))
      finalLetterGrade = "C"
    else
    if ((finalNumericGrade >= 60) & (finalNumericGrade < 70))
      finalLetterGrade = "D"
    else
    if (finalNumericGrade < 60)
      finalLetterGrade = "F"
    alert("*** SCIENCE STUDENT ***\n\n" +
      "Midterm grade is: " + midterm + "\n" +
      "Final Exam is: " + finalExamGrade + "\n" +
      "Research grade is: " + research + "\n\n" +
      "Final Numeric Grade is: " + finalNumericGrade + "\n" +
      "Final Letter Grade is: " + finalLetterGrade)
    break
  default:
    alert(response + " - is not a valid student type")
}
moreGradesToCalculate = prompt("Do you have another grade to calculate?","Yes")
moreGradesToCalculate = moreGradesToCalculate.toUpperCase()
}
alert("Thanks for using the Grades Calculation program!")

</script>
</body>
</html>
```

3. Save your source file as '**Grades.htm**' in the \JavaScriptFiles\Grades folder (select File-Save As from Notepad's Menu Bar). Be sure to save your source file with the file name extension 'htm'.

4. Use Internet Explorer to Open your Source File.

5. Execute your program and test it thoroughly. We need to verify that the 'looping' behavior of the program is working correctly. After you start up your program, it should ask you if you have a grade to calculate. The Text Box of the Prompt Popup Box is already set to 'Yes'---so just click the OK button to answer Yes.

6. Calculate the grade for an English student. Enter 70 for the midterm, 80 for the final examination, 90 for the research grade and 100 for the presentation. A final numeric grade of 84.5 should be displayed--with a letter grade of 'C'.

7. After the Alert Box is displayed with the calculated grade, the program should ask you if you have more grades to calculate.

8. Answer yes by clicking on the OK button, and then calculate the grade for a Math student. Enter 70 for the midterm and 80 for the final examination. A final numeric grade of 75 should be displayed--with a letter grade of 'D'.
9. After the Alert Box is displayed with the calculated grade, the program should ask you if you have more grades to calculate.
10. Answer yes by clicking on the OK button, and then calculate the grade for a Science student. Enter 70 for the midterm, 80 for the final examination. and 90 for the research grade. A final numeric grade of 78 should be displayed--with a letter grade of 'C'. After the Alert Box is displayed with the calculate grade, the program should ask you if you have more grades to calculate.
11. Answer No (you'll need to type this into the Text Box)--you should be thanked for using the program, and then the program should end.

Discussion

Making the modifications to the code in the Grades class required careful attention to detail---but in the end, everyone was able to complete the exercise without a great deal of trouble.

"I have to say I'm really impressed with the practical use for this loop," Ward said.

"Me too," Rhonda said. "In a way, this program kind of reminds me of an Automated Teller Machine that, once you are done withdrawing your money, asks you if you have any more transactions to complete before giving you your card back."

"Can you go over the code?" Mary asked. "I think I understand what's going on here, but I want to be absolutely sure."

"I'd be glad to do that Mary," I said. "We made just a few enhancements to the code from last week's version of the Grades Calculation program, the major one being to 'sandwich', in a While Loop, the code that actually does the calculations. Prior to that, we needed to declare a variable to store the value of the user's answer to the question we are going to pose--does he or she have a grade to calculate. Because we already had a variable in the program called response which we use to accept the individual grade component values from the user, we declared a new variable called moreGradesToCalculatel for this purpose..."

var moreGradesToCalculate

"...having declared that variable to hold the user's response to our question, it's now time ask the question..."

moreGradesToCalculate = prompt("Do you want to calculate a grade?","Yes")

"...again, we 'uppercase' the user's response and store it right back in the moreGradesToCalculate variable..."

moreGradesToCalculate = moreGradesToCalculate.toUpperCase()

"Now here's the critical line of code," I said, "It's where we set up the While loop structure, using the user's response in the test expression..."

while (moreGradesToCalculate == "YES") {

"...if the user has answered 'Yes' to the question as to whether they have a grade to calculate, the value of moreGradesToCalculate is 'Yes', and we then execute the body of the loop---which is the code which we wrote last week to calculate the student's final numeric and letter grades."

"So really, not all that much has changed with this code," Joe said.

"That's right Joe," I said. "the really difficult code to calculate the grade was written last week--all we've done by placing it in the body of the loop is give our program the ability to calculate more than one student. We do that by asking the user this question..."

moreGradesToCalculate = prompt("Do you have another grade to calculate?","Yes")
moreGradesToCalculate = moreGradesToCalculate.toUpperCase()
}

"If the user answers anything other than 'Yes' or its many varieties," I said, "our test expression will evaluate to False, and the loop will terminate, followed by this code which thanks the user for using our program..."

alert("Thanks for using the Grades Calculation program!")

"...If the user answers 'yes', the body of the loop will execute once more, permitting a second student's grade to be calculated."

Ward expressed some concern over the growing length, and complexity, of the code in the Grades Calculation project.

"The code just keeps growing and growing," he said. "I realize there isn't much we can do about its length---however, it's getting so complex that I'm having a harder and harder time following it."

"I agree," Rhonda said, "but as I said last week, aren't we just about done with this project. I think we've fulfilled all of the requirements for the project, haven't we/"

"I think we have Rhonda," I replied, "from a functional point of view, there really isn't much that we'll be adding to the project. The remainder of the course we will spend in streamlining and fine tuning the program, and taking advantage of the some of the object-oriented characteristics of the JavaScript programming language. I think in doing so we'll be addressing Ward's concerns about the growing complexity of the code--although you'll see the overall number of lines of code in the project won't decrease. Object-oriented programs have a way of simplifying the complex nature of code. And we'll start doing that next week when we create some functions and methods of our own--which should make our program a little easier to follow."

It had been a long class. I could see that everyone was feeling proud of the product they were producing week by week. In addition, I could also see that they were pretty worn out; it had been an intense session. I then dismissed class for the day.

Summary

In this chapter, we discussed how loop processing can make our programming lives a lot easier, and make our programs extremely powerful. There are several types of loop statements.

Here's a reminder of some of the different loop structures we discussed:

· For Loops: these loops execute a definite number of times. The number of times that the loop runs is determined by the Start, End and Step parameters set in the 'For' line of the Loop Control.
· While loops: these loops execute an indefinite number of times, determined by a test condition. The While loop continues to run while a specified condition is True. In a While loop, the test expression is evaluated prior to the body of the loop executing even one time--therefore, in a While Loop, there is the possibility that the code in the body of the loop will not execute even one time.
· Do-While Loops: Like the While loop, the Do-While loop executes an indefinite number of times, determined by a test condition. The Do-While loop continues to run while the test expression evaluates to True. In a Do-While loop, the test expression is evaluated after the body of the loop executes--therefore, in a Do-While loop, the body of the loop is always executed at least one time.

We have also modified the Grades Calculation project so that it calculates more than one student's grade.

In the next chapter, we'll take a closer look at creating classes that simulate real-world objects.

Chapter 6---Creating Your Own Functions

In this chapter, we'll discuss how to make our programs more readable and efficient by creating our own functions. As we'll see during the course of the chapter, functions are pieces of code that perform a single task, and promote a concept called modularity.

Modular programs are easier to maintain and understand

"Starting today," I said, as I began our sixth class, "and continuing for the next three weeks or so, we'll be examining ways in which we can use some of JavaScript's Object Oriented features to make programs that are more readable, more efficient, and easier to maintain. Even more importantly, as you'll discover as you continue on with your JavaScript programming career, Object Oriented programming languages--and JavaScript is one of them---promote the concept of something called 'software reuse'--which means that a piece of code, once written, should not be tossed away or re-written for another program, but incorporated into 'classes' for use in another program. In other words, the same piece of code can then be used in multiple programs. We'll look at that in more detail next week when we see how we can create classes of our own. In today's class, we take the first step along the path of software reuse when we learn how to write functions of our own. We've already used JavaScript functions throughout the class--for instance, the write() function of the Document object and the parseInt() function. Today we'll learn how to create functions of our own that reside in the same file as the code that will execute the function. Eventually, we'll learn how to create functions that reside in separate files and which can then be executed or called from other files."

"If I'm correct," Blaine said, "I don't believe we've written any functions of our own yet, is that right?"

"That's right, Blaine," I answered. "all of the code that we've written so far has resided in the same 'area' or section of our JavaScript file. As our programs have gotten more complex, the number of lines of code in this area has grown and grown."

"Is that bad?" Kate asked, "I mean is there a limit to the number of lines of code that can go into this area?"

"There's no limit to the number of lines of code that can be placed in the main area of the program," I said, "However, the more lines of code in a single area of the program, the more difficult the program is to follow, understand, and to maintain."

"What do you mean by maintain?" Rhonda asked. "Is that like car maintenance?"

"Maintaining a program," I answered, "means changing or modifying the program. Programs need to be maintained for a number of different reasons. Some programs need to be modified because of a change in the business environment for which the program is written. Other programs need to be modified due to new governmental regulations. Other programs need to be modified because of requests from users. Regardless of the reason, you can be almost certain that any program you write eventually will need to be modified--if not by you, then by someone else. And even if all that needs to be changed is a single line of code, it that line of code happens to appear in an area of section of your JavaScript program that contains hundreds or thousands of other lines of code, whoever needs to find that line of code is going to have a heck of a time--unless the program was written in a modular fashion."

"Modular?" Lou asked.

"We'll see a little later on Lou," I said, "that modular programs are programs that are written in distinct, logical units."

"Do programs need to be changed all that often that we need to worry about this?" Blaine asked.

"Most programs that are written for commercial purposes will at one time or other need to be changed." I answered. "In fact, it's been estimated that the programming staff in a large corporation may spend up to 85% of its time modifying the code in already existing programs."

"That's incredible," Chuck said, "So making programs easier to read and maintain is important."

"Absolutely," I said. "In fact, it's pretty likely that the program we're writing for Frank Olley will need to be changed at some point. If the English, Math or Science Departments change the formula for the way a student's final grade is calculated, we'll need to change the Grades Calculation program."

"I see why programs need to be changed," Valerie said, "but how can creating functions of our own make that process easier?"

"So far," I answered, "in all of the code you've written for this class, I've pretty much told you exactly what line or lines of code to write, and where you needed to place them. In the real-world, however, this won't be the case. You're more likely to be asked, by a supervisor or project leader, to make a functional change to a program. In other words, you'll be told what change to make in terms like 'change the Federal Tax Withholding rate from 18% to 22%'. It will be up to you to find the appropriate JavaScript class file, locate the line or lines of code in the class that performs that calculation, decide upon the necessary changes and then apply them. From experience, I can tell you if all of the code in your program is located within one single area of your JavaScript file, finding and making changes to that code can be pretty tough."

"And this is where having more than one function in a JavaScript file will come in handy?" Rhonda asked. "I'm afraid I just don't see why."

"I think I can help," Dave said. "I work in a department that gets a tremendous amount of mail. We have a super efficient secretary, Millie, who by the time I sit down in my cubicle each morning, has separated everyone's mail and placed it on the individual's desk. On those days when Millie isn't in, the place is chaos. Anyone who is expecting an important piece of correspondence must sift through a huge pile of mail---eventually they find the piece they're looking for, but it's a painstaking job, and sometimes they accidentally pull out a piece of mail belonging to someone else."

"So that huge pile of mail, Dave," Rhonda said, "is like one big JavaScript file?"

"That's right," Dave replied. "Millie, by sorting and distributing the mail each morning, produces logical 'modules' of mail. It just makes the whole process much easier."

"That's a great analogy Dave, thanks" I said, "In terms of modular programming, that means that when we write code, we should place code that performs a single task or action into a function of its own. For instance, if we write a program to calculate payroll, all of the code to calculate the Federal Withholding Tax should be placed in a function of its own. Similarly, the code to calculate the State Withholding Tax should be placed in a function of its own. This process has traditionally been described as Modular programming, although the concepts and techniques have been enhanced quite a bit by modern Object-oriented programming languages such as JavaScript."

What is a function?

"So in theory," Bob said, "a function is code that performs a single task or action?"

"That's right Bob," I said. "Last week, all of the code that we wrote for the Grades Calculation project went into the same, general area of the Grades JavaScript file. By the end of today's class, we'll have taken that code, and re-distributed much of it into separate functions. For instance, all of the code that performs the calculation for the final grade of an English student will be placed in a function of its own called calculateEnglishStudent(). In a similar way, the code to perform the calculation for the final grade of a Math student will be placed in a function of its own called calculateMathStudent(), and the code to perform the calculation for the final grade of a Science student will be placed in a function of its own called calculateScienceStudent()."

"I see what you're getting at now," Ward said, "If the code to calculate the final grade for a math student is in a function of its own, I would think finding it, and making changes to it, would be much easier."

"Right on the mark Ward," I said. "Not only is code that is broken down and placed in functions like this easier to find and modify, when it's also bundled in the form of an object---something we'll do in coming weeks---it can be easily re-used in other applications."

"What's that?" Peter asked.

"The write() function of the Document object is a perfect example of that," I said. "It's probably no exaggeration to say that millions of JavaScript programs use the code in the write() function of the Document object--yet the code in the write() method was written just once."

I gave everyone a chance to take in what I was saying.

"Are there any rules or guidelines for writing functions?" Steve asked. "Do you write them from scratch right away--or do you place all of your code in the main area of your JavaScript file, and then at some point, move the code out of there into separate functions?"

"With a little experience Steve," I said, "you'll find yourself writing functions of your own right from the very start of your program. It seems strange to you now, because for the last five weeks, we've dealt with just the single area of our JavaScript file--but the more programs you write, the more natural placing code in your own functions will become. Just remember---place code that performs a single task into a function of its own. Needless to say, we haven't done that yet with the Grades Calculation project---but that's because we first needed to concentrate on learning the fundamentals of the JavaScript language and how to create a working program before we could worry about making our program more readable, efficient and easy to modify. For the remainder of today's class we'll worry about all of that, and in next week's class, we'll learn how the functions we create today can be placed in files of their own that can then be incorporated into programs written by other programmers."

"Just like the write() function of the Document object?" Kate asked.

"You hit the nail on the head Kate," I said, "Programmers who write good code, and are insightful enough to place that code in separate JavaScript files are rewarded by having their code used by hundreds of other programmers--not only by programmers in their own companies but by programmers all over the world. We'll learn more on how to create code and place it in those type of files in the coming weeks."

"I can imagine that's quite an ego trip," Ward said, "having your code used like that---but it's also quite an incentive for me to learn this language."

"I have just one question," Mary said, "if we take all of the code out of the main area of our program and place it in those other functions you mentioned, what will be left in the main area of our program?"

"We won't take all of the code out of the main area of our JavaScript program," I answered. "The main area of the program is required, and it will contain the code that 'calls' or requests the execution of the code contained in those functions we write. The code in the main area of our JavaScript program frequently resembles the outline of a book---with each call to a function appearing as a chapter heading."

Creating your own Functions…

"This all sounds very exciting," Rhonda said. "So how do we create functions of our own, and what do we name them?"

"You can name your functions virtually anything you want Rhonda," I said, "but be sure to pick a meaningful name. As far as how to create them, for this week anyway, functions of our own must be defined within the same JavaScript file as the code that calls them. They can either be 'on top of' or 'on the bottom of' the main area of our program---my personal preference. In coming weeks, we'll see that functions can also be defined in the <head> section of our HTML document, and for that matter, in separate files."

"The <head> section?", Kate asked.

"We haven't looked at the <head> section yet," I said, "but we will in a few weeks, I promise. And that's when I'll show you how to write, and call, JavaScript code in separate files."

I waited for signs of confusion before continuing.

"…if you have more than one custom function, it's a good idea to separate them with a blank line. Let's examine a now familiar JavaScript program containing just a single line of code, and then we'll modify it to include a custom function of our own."

I then displayed this code on the classroom projector.

```
<! Example6-1 -->
<html>
<body>
<script type="text/javascript">

document.write("I love JavaScript!")

</script>
</body>
</html>
```

"Look familiar?" I asked, "This is the first JavaScript program we wrote in the course. As you know, it displays the message 'I love JavaScript' in the Browser Window. Let's see how we can take the code to display that message out of the main area of our JavaScript program--and place it in a function of its own which we'll call displayMessage. .."

I then modified the code to look like this…

```
<! Example6-2 -->
<html>
```

```
<body>
<script type="text/javascript">

displayMessage()                        //Call to Custom Function

function displayMessage() {             //Function begins here
    document.write("I love JavaScript!")
}                                       //Function ends here

</script>
</body>
</html>
```

I then saved the program as '**Example6-2.htm**" and opened it up within Internet Explorer. The following screenshot was displayed on the classroom projector.

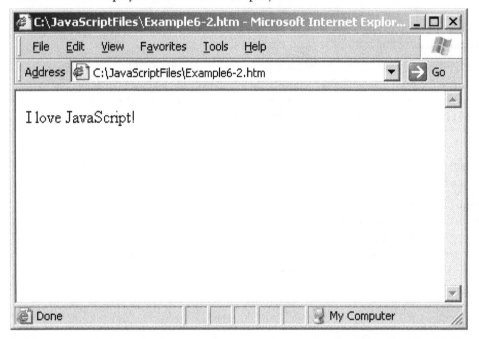

"This program behaves in the same manner as the previous version did," I said, "but in this version of the program, the JavaScript instruction to display the message 'I love JavaScript' is no longer being executed directly from the main area of our program--instead, the instruction is executed from a function called displayMessage(), and this is the code that tells JavaScript to execute the code in the displayMessage() function..."

```
displayMessage()                        //Call to Custom Function
```

"Notice," I continued, "that the code to 'call' or execute the displayMessage() function references the name of the function precisely--function names are case sensitive. Notice also that the displayMessage() function follows the main area of our program---although it could just as easily be located 'above' it, like this..."

```
<! Example6-3 -->
<html>
<body>
<script type="text/javascript">

function displayMessage() {             //Function begins here
    document.write("I love JavaScript!")
}                                       //Function ends here

displayMessage()                        //Call to Custom Function

</script>
</body>
</html>
```

"As I mentioned," I said, "I prefer to place my function definitions after the code that 'calls' or executes them."

"Can you explain what's going on with that first line of code in the function?" Kathy said. "It's like nothing we've ever seen before."

"You're right Kathy," I said. "it will take some explaining. The first line of a function, which is sometimes called the function header, sometimes called the function definition, sometimes called the function signature, is different from anything we've seen so far. Let's take a look..."

```
function displayMessage() {
```

"...From left to right, we have the name of the function, followed by a pair of parentheses within which any Parameters to the function are specified with a name."

Function Parameters and Arguments

"What's a parameter," Bob asked.

"Remember the prompt function?" I said. "The prompt function is defined with a parameter for the prompt that is to appear in the Prompt Popup Box, and also a parameter for the default value that is to appear in its Text Box."

'I remember," Bob said.

"A parameter," I said, "is just a qualifier to a function, something which in some way provides additional information to the function as to how it should behave. A function that is defined with one or more parameters is seeking qualifying information from the code that calls it, and any code that executes that function is required to supply that qualifying information. Parameters are specified in the function header within parentheses. If the parentheses are empty, as is the case with our displayMessage() function, that means the function is defined without parameters--so the code 'calling' the function need not worry about supplying it with qualifying information. "

> **Note: You will also hear the term arguments used interchangeably with parameters. Technically, functions are defined with parameters, and the qualifying information itself is 'passed' to the function as an argument. There's a subtle difference.**

"Are parameters the same as arguments, such as the ones we've been passing to some of the functions we've executed---like write() for instance?" Linda asked.

"You're right Linda," I said, "arguments are the actual values that we pass to a function. Many programmers use the terms arguments and parameters interchangeably, and really, only a computer scientist would argue with you. In theory, parameters are the names that appear in a Function header, and arguments are the actual values that are passed to the function by the code that calls it. For each parameter in the function's header, there must be an argument passed to it."

"So parameters appear in the function header, and arguments are the actual values passed to the function when it is called?" Dave said. "

"Perfect Dave," I said, "I..."

"I know," Rhonda said laughing, "you couldn't have said it any better yourself!"

"Can we modify the displayMessage() function to include a parameter?" Linda asked.

"I don't see why not," I answered. "Let's do this--let's modify the displayMessage() function to allow the programmer to pass an argument specifying his or her favorite programming language. I thought for a moment, and then displayed this code on the classroom projector.

I thought for a moment: "Let's modify the displayMessage() function so that it accepts a single argument..."

```
<! Example6-4 -->
<html>
<body>
<script type="text/javascript">

displayMessage("JavaScript")
displayMessage("Visual Basic")
displayMessage("C#")

function displayMessage(language) {
  document.write(language + "<br>")
}
```

```
</script>
</body>
</html>
```

I then saved the program as "Example6-4.htm", and opened it up within Internet Explorer. The following screenshot was displayed on the classroom projector.

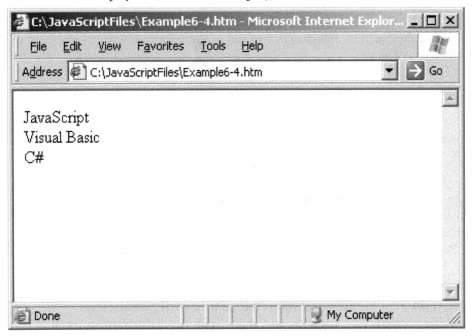

"As you can see," I said, "the previous version of this program featured a displayMessage() function that was 'hard coded' to display the message 'I love JavaScript'. In this version of the program, the displayMessage() function is much more dynamic, defined with a single parameter, which is then used by the function to display the user's favorite (or multiple favorite) programming languages."

I waited a moment before continuing.

"Let's take a look at the new header for the displayMessage() function," I said. "Here's the original function header..."

```
function displayMessage() {
```

"and here's the new function header declared with a parameter..."

```
function displayMessage(language) {
```

"Within the parentheses," I continued, "we are telling JavaScript that the displayMessage() function will accept a single parameter called language."

"Let's examine the code to call the displayMessage() function." I said. "Calling a function that requires a parameter is easy, provided you know the function's signature."

"Signature?" Joe asked.

"The function's signature is the number of arguments required," I said. "Here we know that we need to pass displayMessage() just a single argument, and we do that---actually executing it three times with different values for the argument---with this code..."

```
displayMessage("JavaScript")
displayMessage("Visual Basic")
displayMessage("C#")
```

"I'm a little confused as to what the displayMessage() function does with the argument once it receives it from the calling code," Barbara said. "Can you clear that up?"

"I'll try Barbara," I answered, "Let's look at the code from the body of the **Example6-3** program, in which the program was 'hard coded' to display JavaScript as its favorite language..."

```
document.write("I love JavaScript!")
```

"...and here's the modified code, which uses the parameter 'language' as an argument to the write() function of the document object..."

```
document.write(language + "<br>")
```

"The value for the argument 'language' is used as an argument for the write() function of the document object," I said. "Notice also how we append the '<br>' tag to the end of the language parameter so that we generate a new line in the event the function is executed multiple time."

"Is 'language' a variable?" Lou asked. "And if so, why isn't it declared within the body of the function?"

"Parameters are a lot like variables," I said, "but they don't need to be declared within the body of the function since they are really declared within the function header."

"That makes sense," Barbara said, "I have another question. Is it possible to create a function that accepts more than one argument, and if so, how does JavaScript know which parameter is which when the code that calls the function passes the arguments.."

"Another good question," I said. "Yes, it is possible to design a function that accepts more than one argument. In JavaScript, arguments are passed positionally. That means that if the function's header specifies two parameters, JavaScript assumes that the first argument passed to the function is the first parameter, the second argument passed to the function is the second parameter, and so on. Let me show you exactly what I mean by modifying the code we just wrote to accept two parameters..."

I then modified the code from **Example6-4** to look like this, and displayed it on the classroom projector.

```
<! Example6-5 -->
<html>
<body>
<script type="text/javascript">

displayMessage("JavaScript","a bunch")
displayMessage("Visual Basic","lots")
displayMessage("C#","a little bit")

function displayMessage(language, howMuch) {
document.write("I love " + language + " " + howMuch + "<br>")
}

</script>
</body>
</html>
```

"Notice the difference in the function header for displayMessage," I said. "It's now defined with two parameters---language and howMuch. Both of these parameters are used, in the body of the function, as arguments to the write() function of the Document object..."

```
function displayMessage(language, howMuch) {
document.write("I love " + language + " " + howMuch + "<br>")
}
```

"...also, as you would expect, if the function header now specifies two parameters, the call to the function must specify two arguments, which appear after the function name within parentheses, separated by a comma. Notice that because the parameters in the displayMessage() function are used as arguments to the write() function of the Document object, these arguments are really String arguments, and so they must be enclosed within quotation marks..."

```
displayMessage("JavaScript","a bunch")
displayMessage("Visual Basic","lots")
displayMessage("C#","a little bit")
```

I then saved the program as "**Example6-5.htm**", and opened it up within Internet Explorer. The following screenshot was displayed on the classroom projector.

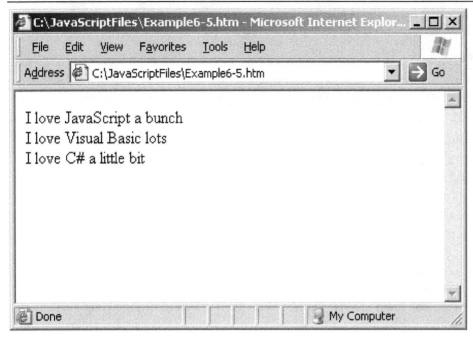

"Now the calling program can not only designate a favorite language, but also an assessment as to how much the user likes it," I said.

"I can see," Ward said, "that two parameters make this function even more flexible. This program is pretty neat."

"You're right Ward," I said, "the more parameters a function accepts, the more flexible it can be. Of course, the more parameters a function accepts the more complex the code in the function needs to be to handle the multiple arguments that it will receive. Later on today, we'll create functions for the Grades Calculation project that will accept several parameters---and you'll see what I mean."

"I have a problem," Peter said, "I've been coding this with you, and I'm not seeing anything when I open my source file within Internet Explorer."

A quick trip to Peter's workstation---and a look at his source file---revealed the problem. The capitalization of the name of his parameters in the function header didn't exactly match their usage in the body of the function.

"You spelled 'howMuch' using mixed case in your function header," I said, "but you spelled it entirely in lower case within the body of the function. Remember, JavaScript is case sensitive---you must match the spelling of variables, object name, parameters right down to upper and lower case---and if you don't, the program won't do anything. Also, unfortunately, you won't receive an error message to give you a clue to the problem."

"Suppose we had forgotten to supply the function call with two arguments?" Lou said, "What would have happened? Would the program not give us any results?"

"Let's see," I said, as I displayed this modified code on the classroom projector...

```
<! Example6-6 -->
<html>
<body>
<script type="text/javascript">

displayMessage("JavaScript","a bunch")
displayMessage("Visual Basic","lots")
displayMessage("C#")

function displayMessage(language, howMuch) {
  document.write("I love " + language + " " + howMuch + "<br>")
}

</script>
</body>
</html>
```

"Notice," I said, "that my 3rd invocation of the displayMessage() function is missing the second argument--the howMuch argument. Let's see what happens when Internet Explorer executes the JavaScript code."

I then saved the program as "**Example6-6.htm**", and opened it up within Internet Explorer. The following screenshot was displayed on the classroom projector.

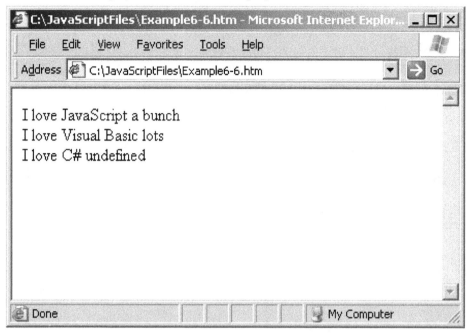

"*undefined*?", Rhonda said.

"That's right Rhonda," I said, "the displayMessage() function is expecting two arguments. When it didn't get the second argument, it used the default value of the parameter---undefined---in the write() method of the Document object."

"I know other programming languages support something called overloaded functions," Dave said, "does Javascript?"

"Wonderful question Dave," I said, "unfortunately not."

"What's an overloaded function?" Valerie asked.

"Overloaded functions," I said, "are functions having the same name---but different signatures, that is the number of arguments. Overloaded functions typically perform the same general work--but due to the varying arguments, do it a little differently. As I said, JavaScript doesn't support overloaded functions."

I waited a moment before continuing.

"Right now," I said, "I'd like to discuss an alternative way of passing arguments to a function."

"What do you mean?" Rhonda asked.

"So far," I replied, "we've passed String literals to the displayMessage() function we've designed."

"What else can we pass?" Chuck asked.

"We can pass the value of a variable," I said. "let me show you."

I then displayed this code on the classroom projector.

```
<! Example6-7 -->
<html>
<body>
<script type="text/javascript">

favorite = "JavaScript"
intensity = "enormously"

displayMessage(favorite, intensity)
```

```
function displayMessage(language, howMuch) {
    document.write("I love " + language + " " + howMuch + "<br>")
}

</script>
</body>
</html>
```

I then saved the program as "**Example6-7.htm**", and opened it up within Internet Explorer. The following screenshot was displayed on the classroom projector.

Don't Forget: If typing these examples and exercises isn't something you want to do, feel free to follow this link to find and download the completed solutions for all of the examples and exercises in the book. Just click on the JavaScript book, then follow the link entitled exercises ☺

http://www.johnsmiley.com/main/books.htm

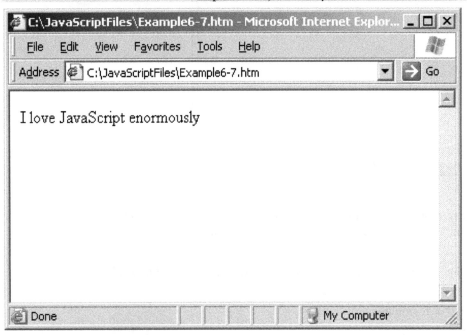

"This version of the program," I said, "displays just a single message in the Browser Window, but aside from that, behaves in the same manner as the other version did. However, we've changed the code by first declaring two variables called *favorite* and *intensity*, assigning them values ..."

```
favorite = "JavaScript"
intensity = "enormously"
```

"and then passing them as arguments to the displayMessage() function..."

```
displayMessage(favorite, intensity)
```

"...doing so has no impact on the execution of the function---the function doesn't really care if a String literal is passed to it as an argument or a variable is passed."

In JavaScript, Arguments are passed by Value

"Suppose," Linda said, "that for some reason, within the body of the function, we change the value of the passed argument---does that have any effect on the value of the variable in the code that called it?"

"I'm not sure I know what Linda is asking," Rhonda said.

"Let me try to explain, Rhonda" I said. "In some programming languages, when a change is made to the value of a parameter that is passed to it via a variable, the value of the variable itself back in the code that called it is also changed."

"Do you mean," Valerie asked. "that changing the value of the parameter language within the displayMessage function would change the value of the variable favorite?"

"Exactly right Valerie," I answered.

I gave everyone a moment to think about that.

"Is that a good thing?" Joe asked.

"Some programmers find this a convenient way of arriving at a programming solution," I said. "In those other languages, variables passed as arguments can either be passed by value or by reference. By value simply means that the actual value of the variable is passed to the function as an argument, and in that case, changing the parameter within the body of the function has *no* impact on the variable in the calling code. When those other languages pass a variable as an argument to a function by reference, it isn't the actual value of the variable that is passed to the function, but the memory address of the variable. That means that when the function changes the value of the parameter, it directly updates the value of the variable back in the calling code."

"What about JavaScript?" Mary asked. "Does it pass arguments by Value or by Reference."

"JavaScript variables are passed by value---that means that if a variable is passed as an argument to a function, changing the value of the parameter within the body of the function has no impact on the value of the variable in the code that calls the function."

"Can we see an example of this?"

I then displayed this code on the classroom projector...

```
<! Example6-8 -->
<html>
<body>
<script type="text/javascript">

favorite = "JavaScript"
intensity = "enormously"

displayMessage(favorite, intensity)
document.write("The value of favorite is now " + favorite)

function displayMessage(favorite, intensity) {
   document.write("I love " + favorite + " " + intensity + "<br>")
   favorite = "VB.Net"
   document.write("The value of favorite in displayMessage is " + favorite + "<br>")
}

</script>
</body>
</html>
```

I then saved the program as "**Example6-8.htm**", and opened it up within Internet Explorer. The following screenshot was displayed on the classroom projector.

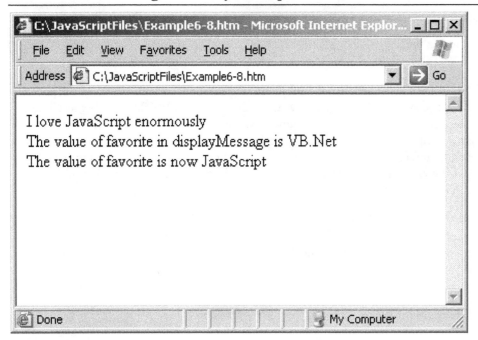

"Let me explain what's going on here," I said. "As we did in Example6-7, we declared two variables called favorite and intensity, and initialized both of them with values…"

favorite = "JavaScript"
intensity = "enormously"

"---we then passed the variables as arguments to the displayMessage() function…"

displayMessage(favorite, intensity)

"We didn't need to do this to prove that JavaScript passes variables by value" I said, "but notice that we've changed the names of the parameters within the function's header. We're still accepting two String parameters, but in this version of the program we've named them with the same names as the variables in the main() function…"

function displayMessage(favorite, intensity) {

"I just noticed that," Peter said.

"Can we do that?" Ward asked. "Shouldn't the names of the *parameters* be different from the *variables* in the calling code?"

"They don't have to be," I said, "I know that in Example6-7, the parameter names were different from the names of the variables in the main part of our program, but there's no rule that they have to be. JavaScript considers the variables declared in the main part of our code and the parameters in the displayMessage() function to be different animals---they're actually stored in different memory locations. Whenever variables or parameters are declared with identical names, in different 'parts' of the program as they are here, they are said to be 'shadowed'. You need to understand which one you are working with. In the displayMessage function, any reference to the favorite or intensity parameters is a reference to the parameters declared within the function. In the main portion of the program, any reference to the favorite or intensity variables is a reference to the variables declared there. We prove that by executing this line of code within the displayMessage() function which causes the value of the passed argument--JavaScript---to be displayed in our Internet Browser…"

document.write("I love " + favorite + " " + intensity + "<br>")

"With this line of code, we then change the value of the favorite *parameter* to 'VB.Net'…"

favorite = "VB.Net"

"…You might be inclined to believe that we have also changed the value of the favorite *variable* in the main part of our program, but you'll see in a moment we haven't. First, we prove that the value of the favorite *parameter* has indeed been changed by executing this line of code…"

document.write("The value of favorite in displayMessage is " + favorite + "<br>")

"... which displays, in the Internet Browser window, the altered value of the favorite *parameter*, which is now 'VB.Net'. The displayMessage() function ends, and this line of code is then executed from the body of the main part of our code, proving that the value of the favorite variable in the main() function has *not* changed."

document.write("The value of favorite is now " + favorite)

'We've proven," I concluded, "that changing the value of the favorite parameter within the displayMessage() function has had no impact on the value of the favorite variable in the main part of our program."

"I think I understand what's going on here," Rhonda said. "even though the variables in the main part of our program and the parameters in the displayMessage() function have the same names, they're really separate entities, aren't they?"

"That's right Rhonda," I said. "Both the variables and the parameters are declared 'local' to each function in which they appear."

Variable Scope

"You've used the term local several times this morning," Blaine said. "Can you tell us exactly what it means?"

"Local is a term that refers to the scope of a variable," I said. "A variable's scope describes what other parts of your program can 'see' the variable. A local variable is simply one declared within a function---or, as we'll see next week, one declared in something called a class function. A variable declared within a function can be seen or accessed only by code within that same function."

"So a local variable is one declared within a function?" Kate asked.

"That's basically correct Kate," I said. "Although technically, a local variable is one declared within a block--that is, within a pair of braces. That means that if you declare a variable within the braces of an If statement, the variable can only be seen by the code within the If statement."

"What about the variables declared in the main part of our program?" Linda asked. "They don't appear to belong to any function."

"You're right Linda," I answered, "those variables can be seen and accessed by code anywhere within our program---and that includes any function. Those variables are Global variables."

"Are you saying that code in a function *can* change the value of a Global variable declared in the main portion of the program?" Kate asked.

"Absolutely Kate," I said, "but not vice versa---code in the main portion of the program can't 'see' variables declared within a function. Furthermore, code in one function cannot see or access variables declared in another function."

"Didn't you say that arguments are passed by value?" Rhonda asked.

"This notion of the scope of Local and Global variables is different from that of passed arguments," I said. "Values of variables passed as arguments to a function can't be changed by the called function---but what we're talking about here is a different concept. Here, we're talking about code that has access to variables that have been declared elsewhere in a program."

"While we're on this topic," Dave said, "you should caution the class about declaring a variable in a function that has the same name as a Global variable. That can really cause some problems."

"Absolutely Dave correct Dave," I agreed. "JavaScript does permit you to declare a variable in a function having the same name as an already declared Global variable. If you do so, JavaScript will presume that you are working with the variable declared in the function. If that's your intent, wonderful--but if you think you are actually working with the Global variable, then you may be in for some frustrating work as you try to figure out why your program isn't working as you think it should. The bottom line---don't name your Local variables with the same name as a Global Variable. In fact, some programmers I know 'prefix' the name of their Global variables with the 'g_' characters to prevent accidentally using a Global variable when they really meant to use a Local variable."

Variable Lifetime

"I've heard some programmers at work refer to the lifetime of a variable," Valerie said. "Is lifetime the same as scope?"

"Not exactly," I replied, "but the two terms are related. Scope affects what parts of our program can see the variable. Lifetime, on the other hand, affects how 'long' your variable lives. A variable or parameter declared as a local within a function has local scope, and can only be seen by other code within that function. It is also 'born' when its declaration statement within the function is executed and dies after the last line of code in the function is executed. A variable declared in the main part of the program dies when the program itself ends---in other words, when the Internet Browser window is closed."

The Return Type

"When I write functions in Java," Dave said, "I'm required to specify a return type---even if the function doesn't return a value. We didn't do that here."

"Good point Dave," I said, "In programming languages, many times, functions perform some sort of processing, and then return a value of some kind to the code that calls them. The return value can be used to provide an answer of some kind to he calling program. Sometimes it is also used to inform the calling program as to the success or failure of the operation performed in the function. The return type will ordinarily be either a number or a String---although it can also be a JavaScript object or a Boolean Data Type."

"So the displayMessage() function performs some kind of processing, but doesn't return a value to the code that calls it, is that right?" Steve asked.

"That's exactly right Steve," I said.

"I'm a bit confused," Rhonda said.

"Sometimes," I said, "I compare functions to favors that you might ask a friend to do for you. Perhaps you ask your friend to feed your fish while you're away on vacation, and because you tend to be a worrier, you request a 'return value' in the form of a phone call or an email from your friend to confirm that he or she actually fed the fish. On the other hand, your friend may be the type of person who never forgets to do anything---in which case, your mind is at ease, and no 'return value' is necessary."

"So sometimes," Kate said, "functions return a value, and sometimes they do not?"

"Exactly Kate," I said, "and it's entirely up to the designer of the function to decide if the function will return a value or not. In the case of the displayMessage() function we just wrote, did we return a value?"

Kate emphatically said 'no'.

"That's right, we didn't return a value from the displayMessage() function," I said, "but we could have. In the case of displayMessage(), I didn't think it was really necessary."

"I'm trying to recall if we've executed any functions which return a value?" Lou asked.

"I think we have Lou," Linda said. "When we executed the parseInt() function last week, it returned a numeric value which we then assigned to a variable."

"That's right, I forgot about that," Lou said.

"Can we see how to write a function of our own that returns a value?" Barbara asked.

"Sure thing Barbara," I said. "We can modify the displayMessage() function we wrote in Example6_2 to return a value---in this case, a Boolean Data Type..."

I then displayed this code on the classroom projector.

```
<! Example6-9 -->
<html>
<body>
<script type="text/javascript">

var retval

retval = displayMessage()
document.write("The value of retval is " + retval)

function displayMessage() {
  document.write("I love JavaScript!" + "<br>")
  return true
}
```

```
</script>
</body>
</html>
```

I then saved the program as "**Example6-9.htm**", and opened it up within Internet Explorer. The following screenshot was displayed on the classroom projector.

Don't Forget: If typing these examples and exercises isn't something you want to do, feel free to follow this link to find and download the completed solutions for all of the examples and exercises in the book. Just click on the JavaScript book, then follow the link entitled exercises ☺

http://www.johnsmiley.com/main/books.htm

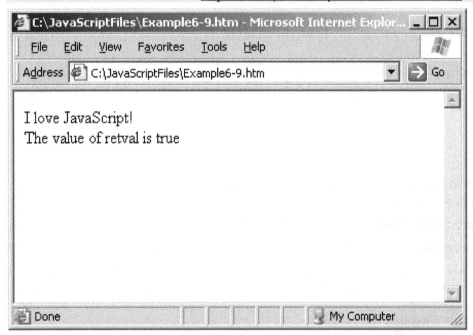

"Returning a value from a function in JavaScript," I said, "is a bit simpler than in other languages where we would have to change the function header to reflect the returned value. In JavaScript, all we need to do is return the value, and we do that somewhere within the body of the function--usually the last statement---by executing a return statement. Here's the statement that returns a Boolean return value, in this case, True..."

return true

"...As you can see, all we need to do is execute the return statement, followed by the value you wish to return to the calling code."

> **Caution: The Boolean value 'true' is spelled in all lower case letters. Spelling it in any other way will not work.**

"What does the code that calls the function do with the return value?" Kate asked.

"it can do one of three things with it," I answered. "It can store the return value in a variable; it can use the return value in an expression, for instance, as an argument to the write() function of the Document object; or interestingly enough, it can choose to ignore the return value simply by executing the function and not doing anything at all with the return value."

I waited a moment before continuing.

"...In this example code, we declared a variable called *retval* into which we stored the return value from the function call."

var retval

"...having declared the retval variable, we now execute the displayMessage() function--but notice how we place the 'call' of the function to the right of the assignment operator (=)---in this way, after the displayMessage() function executes, its return value is immediately stored in the variable *retval*..."

retval = displayMessage()

"…finally, we display the return value stored in the retval variable in our Browser window by using the write() function of the Document object..."

```
document.write("The value of retval is " + retval)
```

"I should mention here," I said, "that instead of storing the return value of displayMessage() in a variable the way we just did here, we could have used the return value directly as an argument to the write() function of the System object, like this…"

```
<! Example6-10 -->
<html>
<body>
<script type="text/javascript">
document.write("The value of the return value is " + displayMessage())

function displayMessage() {
  document.write("I love JavaScript!" + "<br>")
  return true
}
</script>
</body>
</html>
```

"…this version of the code is a bit trickier to follow, but many JavaScript programmers love the compact nature of this style of code--just something to watch out for."

"I'm surprised," Rhonda said, "I actually understand what's going on here."

"Can a function return more than one value?" Chuck asked.

"Excellent question Chuck," I replied, "The answer is 'no'. A function is limited to returning just a single return value--however, it is possible to return something called an Array. An Array is a data structure which is a collection of variables. So, you see, there is a way 'around' the limitation of returning just a single return value. Time permitting, we'll learn more about Arrays towards the end of this course."

We had been working for quite some time, and so I suggested we all take a break before completing our first 'hands on' exercises of the day.

Using functions to fine tune your code

Fifteen minutes later, after returning from break, I resumed class by reminding my students that the main benefit in creating functions of our own---custom functions as I call them---is that doing so promotes program modularity

"Remember," I said, "modularity means that, as much as possible, we create functions in our programs that perform one task and one task only. In the long run, this makes our programs easier to read, understand, and to modify in the future. Creating custom functions allows our code to be more easily understood and used by other programmers-- and that's a big benefit in commercial programming shops. In today's first exercise, I have a pretty extensive exercise for you to complete---this exercise isn't at all modular. There's a lot of code to it, and as you write it, you'll find that all of it is being placed within the main portion of our program. As you complete the exercise, try to think of ways that you could use custom functions to make the program modular--that's exactly what we'll be doing in the next exercise."

I then distributed the exercise for the class to complete.

Exercise 6-1---The Smiley National Bank program with all of the code in the main part of the program

In this exercise, you'll write a program for a mythical Bank that allows the user of the program to display his/her bank balance, or to make deposits and withdrawals from their account.

1. Use Notepad (if you are using Windows) and enter the following code.

```
<! Practice6-1 -- >
<html>
<body>
<script type="text/javascript">
```

```
var balance = 0
var newBalance = 0
var adjustment = 0
var response = ""
var moreBankingBusiness = ""

moreBankingBusiness = prompt("Do you want to do some banking?","Yes")
moreBankingBusiness = moreBankingBusiness.toUpperCase()

while (moreBankingBusiness == "YES") {

  response = prompt("What would you like to do? (1=Deposit, 2=Withdraw, 3=Get Balance)","")

  if (response == null) {
    alert("You clicked on the Cancel button")
    exit
  }

  if (response == "") {
    alert("You must make an entry in the Text Box")
    exit
  }

  if (parseInt(response) < 1 || parseInt( response) > 3) {
    alert(response + " - is not a valid answer")
    exit
  }

  //1 is a Deposit
  if (parseInt(response) == 1) {
    adjustment = parseFloat(prompt("Enter the Deposit Amount",""))
    newBalance = balance + adjustment
    alert("*** SMILEY NATIONAL BANK ***\n\n" +
      "Old Balance is: " + balance + "\n" +
      "Adjustment is: +" + adjustment + "\n" +
      "New Balance is: " + newBalance + "\n")
  }


  //2 is a Withdrawal
  if (parseInt(response) == 2) {
    adjustment = parseFloat(prompt("Enter the Withdrawal Amount",""))
    newBalance = balance - adjustment
    alert("*** SMILEY NATIONAL BANK ***\n\n" +
      "Old Balance is: " + balance + "\n" +
      "Adjustment is: -" + adjustment + "\n" +
      "New Balance is: " + newBalance + "\n")
  }
  // 3 is a Balance Inquiry
  if (parseInt(response) == 3) {
    alert("*** SMILEY NATIONAL BANK ***\n\n" +
    "Your Current Balance is: " + balance )
  }

  balance = newBalance

  moreBankingBusiness = prompt("Do you have more banking business?","Yes")
  moreBankingBusiness = moreBankingBusiness.toUpperCase()

}

alert("Thanks for banking with us!")
```

```
</script>
</body>
</html>
```

2. Save your source file as **'Practice6-1.htm'** in the \JavaScriptFiles\Practice folder (select File-Save As from Notepad's Menu Bar). Be sure to save your source file with the file name extension 'htm'.

3. Use Internet Explorer to Open your Source File.

4. The program will ask you if you wish to do some banking. Because we specified 'Yes' as the default for the Prompt Popup Box, 'Yes' is already in the Text Box.

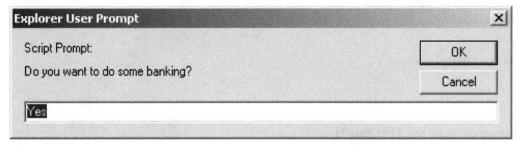

5. Now click on the OK button. The program will then ask you what you wish to do--Make a Deposit, Make a Withdrawal, or Get a Balance. Type '1' into the TextBox to indicate you wish to Make a Deposit.

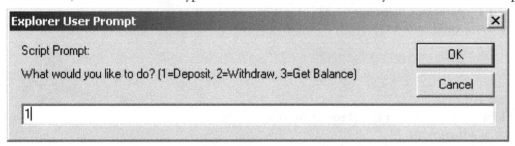

6. Now click on the OK button. The program will then ask you how much you wish to deposit into your account. Enter '50' into the TextBox to indicate your deposit amount.

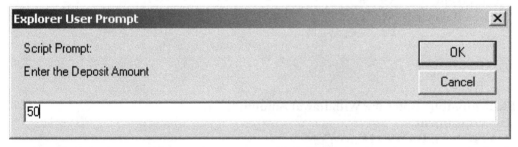

7. Now click on the OK button. The program will display a confirmation message, indicating your deposit amount and your old and new balance.

8. After clicking on the OK button, the program will then ask if you have more banking business. Because we specified 'Yes' as the default for the Prompt Popup Box, 'Yes' is already in the Text Box.

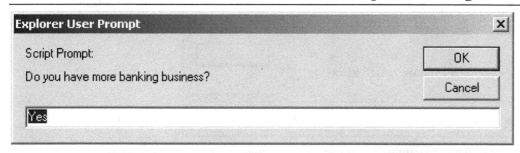

9. Answer 'Yes' by clicking on the on the OK button. The program will then ask you what you wish to do--Make a Deposit, Make a Withdrawal, or Get a Balance. Type '2' into the TextBox to indicate you wish to Make a Withdrawal.

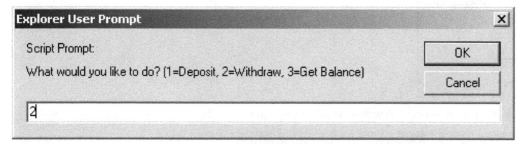

10. Now click on the OK button. The program will then ask you how much you wish to withdraw. Enter '20' into the TextBox to indicate your withdrawal amount.

11. Now click on the OK button. The program will display a confirmation message, indicating your transaction (withdrawals are designated with a negative transaction amount) and your old and new balances.

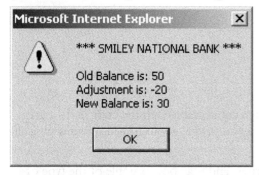

12. After clicking on the OK button, the program will then ask if you have more banking business. Answer 'Yes'.

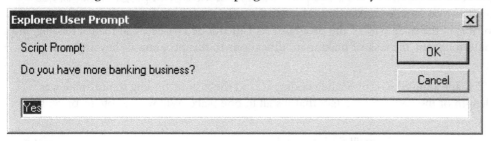

13. Now click on the OK button. The program will then ask you what you wish to do-- Make a Deposit, Make a Withdrawal, or Get a Balance. Type '3' into the TextBox to indicate you wish to display the current balance.

14. Now click on the OK button. The program will then display the current balance of your account.

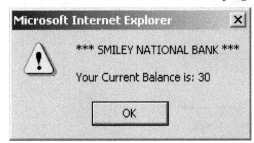

15. After clicking on the OK button, the program will then ask if you have more banking business. Answer 'No'.

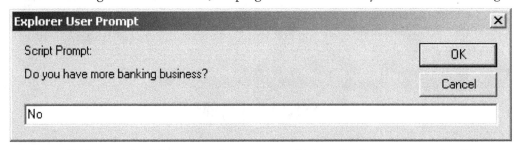

16. After clicking on the OK button, the program will then display a message thanking you for using it. After clicking on the OK button, the program will end.

Discussion

Although this program was very tedious to type, everyone was pretty much comfortable with the code in it---except for a reference to parseFloat(), there really wasn't anything new in the program, and in about fifteen minutes time all of my students had successfully coded the exercise.

"This program," I said, "is one we'll be working with in quite a few exercises, and is a good example of the type of program you may be asked to develop in the future. It's also a good example of the type of program that can be enhanced significantly by writing custom functions. As you undoubtedly noticed while you wrote the program, there's a lot of code---and all of it is in the main part of the program. As I mentioned earlier, that makes reading and understand the code difficult, and toughens the task of making modifications to this program if they are ever required."

"I agree with that," Kate said, "I made a mistake or two while coding it, and the task of finding the mistake was certainly compounded by the length of the code and the fact that it's all in one place. Will we be able to break this code up modules?"

"I think so Kate," I said. "If we examine the code, we'll find that we're performing three distinct functions---making a deposit, making a withdrawal, and displaying a balance. Those three functions, according to what we've learned today about modularity, should be in three separate custom functions---that's what we'll be doing in the next exercise. Before we start with that, do you have any questions about anything in this code? I suspect you may have done a double take when you saw the reference to the parseFloat() function."

```
adjustment = parseFloat(prompt("Enter the Deposit Amount",""))
```

"I was wondering about that," Valerie said.

"I presume that the parseFloat() is similar to the parseInt() function," Dave said, "except that it converts a String into a number that can store a decimal part. An Integer is a whole number----parseFloat() enables us to handle a Deposit or Withdrawal that isn't a whole number, such as 12 dollars and 34 cents."

"Excellent Dave," I said, "that's exactly right. If we used parseInt() to convert the String value in the Prompt Box that the user provides us, JavaScript would truncate or ignore whatever is to the right of the decimal point--we would lose part of the number."

There was a momentary period of silence.

"Except for parseFloat()," Steve said, "I think just about everything in this program is something we've done before, but I was a little confused about the two variables--- *oldBalance* and *balance*. Are these two variables required because we chose to display both the old balance and the new balance whenever the user made a transaction?"

"That's exactly the reason Steve," I answered. "It isn't until after we display a confirmation of the user's transaction that we actually calculate a new balance for them---for that reason, we need to keep in our program's memory both the old balance and the new balance in order to display both of these values in the alert box. The old balance is no problem--it's stored in the balance variable. To calculate the new balance, we perform one of two lines of code, depending upon the transaction type. If a deposit was made we perform this calculation..."

```
newBalance = balance + adjustment
```

"...and if the user makes a withdrawal we perform this calculation..."

```
newBalance = balance - adjustment
```

"...regardless of the type of transaction, though, just before asking the user if he or she has more banking business, we must set the value of the balance variable equal to the value of the newBalance variable..."

```
balance = newBalance
moreBankingBusiness = prompt("Do you have more banking business?","Yes")
moreBankingBusiness = moreBankingBusiness.toUpperCase()
```

"Makes sense to me," Steve answered. "Thanks for the explanation."

I waited to see if there were more questions before continuing.

"Ok," I said, "let's take a shot at modifying this program to use three custom functions--one for a Deposit, one for a Withdrawal, and one to display a balance. There will still be some code in the main part of our program--we're not moving it all into custom functions--but the main part of our program will appear more condensed this time around, with calls to the three functions. When all is said and done, the new version of the program should behave identically to the one we just wrote--but you should find the program easier to read and much easier to modify."

No one had any questions about what we were about to do, and so I handed out this exercise for my class to complete.

Exercise 6-2--The Smiley National Bank program with three custom functions

In this exercise, you'll modify the program you wrote in Exercise 6-1, taking much of the code in the main() function and placing it in one of three custom functions you'll create.

1. Use Notepad (if you are using Windows) and enter the following code.

```
<! Practice6-2 -- >
<html>
<body>
<script type="text/javascript">

var balance = 0
var newBalance = 0
var adjustment = 0
```

```javascript
var response = ""
var moreBankingBusiness = ""

moreBankingBusiness = prompt("Do you want to do some banking?","Yes")
moreBankingBusiness = moreBankingBusiness.toUpperCase()

while (moreBankingBusiness == "YES") {

response = prompt("What would you like to do? (1=Deposit, 2=Withdraw, 3=Get Balance)","")

if (response == null) {
alert("You clicked on the Cancel button")
exit
}

if (response == "") {
alert("You must make an entry in the Text Box")
exit
}

if (parseInt(response) < 1 || parseInt( response) > 3) {
alert(response + " - is not a valid answer")
exit
}

if (parseInt(response) == 1) {
makeDeposit()
}

if (parseInt(response) == 2) {
makeWithdrawal()
}

if (parseInt(response) == 3) {
getBalance()
}

balance = newBalance

moreBankingBusiness = prompt("Do you have more banking business?","Yes")
moreBankingBusiness = moreBankingBusiness.toUpperCase()

}

alert("Thanks for banking with us!")
function makeDeposit() {

  adjustment = parseFloat(prompt("Enter the Deposit Amount",""))
  newBalance = balance + adjustment;
  alert("*** SMILEY NATIONAL BANK ***\n\n" +
  "Old Balance is: " + balance + "\n" +
  "Adjustment is: +" + adjustment + "\n" +
  "New Balance is: " + newBalance + "\n")
}

function makeWithdrawal() {
  adjustment = parseFloat(prompt("Enter the Withdrawal Amount",""))
  newBalance = balance - adjustment
  alert("*** SMILEY NATIONAL BANK ***\n\n" +
  "Old Balance is: " + balance + "\n" +
  "Adjustment is: -" + adjustment + "\n" +
  "New Balance is: " + newBalance + "\n")
}

function getBalance() {
  alert("*** SMILEY NATIONAL BANK ***\n\n" +
```

```
   "Your Current Balance is: " + balance )
}
</script>
</body>
</html>
```

2. Save your source file as '**Practice6-2.htm**' in the \JavaScriptFiles\Practice folder (select File-Save As from Notepad's Menu Bar). Be sure to save your source file with the file name extension 'htm'.

3. Use Internet Explorer to Open your Source File.

4. The program will ask you if you wish to do some banking. Because we specified 'Yes' as the default for the Prompt Popup Box, 'Yes' is already in the Text Box.

5. Now click on the OK button. The program will then ask you what you wish to do-- Make a Deposit, Make a Withdrawal, or Get a Balance. Type '1' into the TextBox to indicate you wish to Make a Deposit.

6. Now click on the OK button. The program will then ask you how much you wish to deposit into your account. Enter '50' into the TextBox to indicate your deposit amount.

7. Now click on the OK button. The program will display a confirmation message, indicating your deposit amount and your old and new balance.

8. After clicking on the OK button, the program will then ask if you have more banking business. Because we specified 'Yes' as the default for the Prompt Popup Box, 'Yes' is already in the Text Box.

9. Now click on the OK button. The program will then ask you what you wish to do-- Make a Deposit, Make a Withdrawal, or Get a Balance. Type '2' into the TextBox to indicate you wish to Make a Withdrawal.

10. Now click on the OK button. The program will then ask you how much you wish to withdraw. Enter '20' into the TextBox to indicate your withdrawal amount.

11. Now click on the OK button. The program will display a confirmation message, indicating your transaction (withdrawals are designated with a negative transaction amount) and your old and new balance.

12. After clicking on the OK button, the program will then ask if you have more banking business. Answer 'Yes'.

13. Now click on the OK button. The program will then ask you what you wish to do-- Make a Deposit, Make a Withdrawal, or Get a Balance. Type '3' into the TextBox to indicate you wish to display the current balance.

14. Now click on the OK button. The program will then display the current balance of your account.

15. After clicking on the OK button, the program will then ask if you have more banking business. Answer 'No'.

16. After clicking on the OK button, the program will then display a message thanking you for using it. After clicking on the OK button, the program will end.

Discussion

During the completion of this exercise, the question as to the most efficient way to modify the code from the previous exercise came up. Many of my students created a new JavaScript source file, and then 'copied and pasted' the old code into the new file. Then they modified the old code for the new exercise. Copying and pasting is not without its perils, however, and this method of creating the Practice6-2 source file was probably no quicker than just creating the code from scratch.

"This program should behave the same as the previous version, is that correct?" Rhonda asked.

"That's right Rhonda," I said. I could tell from her face that something wasn't right. I paid a quick visit to her PC, and discovered that even though she had properly created the three custom functions, she had failed to 'call' them from the main part of her program. Therefore, the program wasn't permitting her to do any banking business.

After getting Rhonda back on track I said: "The behavior of the program hasn't changed. What we've done is take the code to make a deposit, a withdrawal, and display a balance out of the main part of the program and move it into three custom functions called makeDeposit(), makeWithdrawal() and displayBalance()."

I waited for more questions, but everyone seemed satisfied with what they had done so far.

"With the remaining time we have left today," I said, as I glanced at the classroom clock, "I'd like to make changes to the Grades Calculation program we wrote last week by adding several custom functions to the program."

I then distributed the final exercise of the day for the class to complete.

Exercise 6-3---The Grades Calculation Project with Custom Functions

In this exercise, you'll modify the Grades Calculation program by taking some of the code currently residing in the main part of the program and creating several custom functions: whatKindOfStudent(), calculateEnglishGrade(), calculateMathGrade(), calculateScienceGrade(), and three functions to display the grades of the three student types.

1. Using Notepad (if you are using Windows) locate and open the Grades.htm source file you worked on last week. (It should be in the \JavaScriptFiles\Grades folder)

2. Modify your code so that it looks like this.

```
<! Grades -- >
<html>
<body>
<script type="text/javascript">

var ENGLISH_MIDTERM_PERCENTAGE = .25
var ENGLISH_FINALEXAM_PERCENTAGE = .25
var ENGLISH_RESEARCH_PERCENTAGE = .30
var ENGLISH_PRESENTATION_PERCENTAGE = .20
var MATH_MIDTERM_PERCENTAGE = .50
var MATH_FINALEXAM_PERCENTAGE = .50
var SCIENCE_MIDTERM_PERCENTAGE = .40
var SCIENCE_FINALEXAM_PERCENTAGE = .40
var SCIENCE_RESEARCH_PERCENTAGE = .20
var midterm = 0
var finalExamGrade = 0
var research = 0
var presentation = 0
var finalNumericGrade = 0
var finalLetterGrade = ""
var response = ""
var moreGradesToCalculate = ""

moreGradesToCalculate = prompt("Do you want to calculate a grade?","Yes")
moreGradesToCalculate = moreGradesToCalculate.toUpperCase()

while (moreGradesToCalculate == "YES") {

  response=whatKindOfStudent()

  // Student type is valid, now let's calculate the grade

  switch(parseInt(response)) {

    // Case 1 is an English Student
    case 1:
      calculateEnglishGrade()
      displayEnglishGrade()
      break

    // Case 2 is a Math Student
    case 2:
      calculateMathGrade()
      displayMathGrade()
      break

    // Case 3 is a Science Student
    case 3:
      calculateScienceGrade()
      displayScienceGrade()
      break

    default:
      alert(response + " - is not a valid student type")
  }

  moreGradesToCalculate = prompt("Do you have another grade to calculate?","Yes")
  moreGradesToCalculate = moreGradesToCalculate.toUpperCase()
}

alert("Thanks for using the Grades Calculation program!")
```

```
function whatKindOfStudent() {
  // What type of student are we calculating?
  response = prompt("Enter student type (1=English, 2=Math, 3=Science)","")
  if (response == null) {
    alert("You clicked on the Cancel button")
    exit
  }

  if (response == "") {
    alert("You must make an entry in the Text Box")
    exit
  }

  if (parseInt(response) < 1 || parseInt( response) > 3) {
    alert(response + " - is not a valid student type")
    exit
  }

  return response
} //End of whatKindOfStudent

function calculateEnglishGrade() {
  midterm = parseInt(prompt("Enter the Midterm Grade",""))
  finalExamGrade = parseInt(prompt("Enter the Final Examination Grade","" ))
  research = parseInt(prompt("Enter the Research Grade",""))
  presentation = parseInt(prompt("Enter the Presentation Grade",""))
  finalNumericGrade =
    (midterm * ENGLISH_MIDTERM_PERCENTAGE) +
    (finalExamGrade * ENGLISH_FINALEXAM_PERCENTAGE) +
    (research * ENGLISH_RESEARCH_PERCENTAGE) +
    (presentation * ENGLISH_PRESENTATION_PERCENTAGE)
  if (finalNumericGrade >= 93)
    finalLetterGrade = "A"
  else
  if ((finalNumericGrade >= 85) & (finalNumericGrade < 93))
    finalLetterGrade = "B"
  else
  if ((finalNumericGrade >= 78) & (finalNumericGrade < 85))
    finalLetterGrade = "C"
  else
  if ((finalNumericGrade >= 70) & (finalNumericGrade < 78))
    finalLetterGrade = "D"
  else
  if (finalNumericGrade < 70)
    finalLetterGrade = "F"
  }

function calculateMathGrade() {
  midterm = parseInt(prompt("Enter the Midterm Grade","" ))
  finalExamGrade = parseInt(prompt("Enter the Final Examination Grade",""))
  finalNumericGrade =
    (midterm * MATH_MIDTERM_PERCENTAGE) +
    (finalExamGrade * MATH_FINALEXAM_PERCENTAGE)
  if (finalNumericGrade >= 90)
    finalLetterGrade = "A"
  else
  if ((finalNumericGrade >= 83) & (finalNumericGrade < 90))
    finalLetterGrade = "B"
  else
```

```javascript
    if ((finalNumericGrade >= 76) & (finalNumericGrade < 83))
      finalLetterGrade = "C"
    else
    if ((finalNumericGrade >= 65) & (finalNumericGrade < 76))
      finalLetterGrade = "D"
    else
    if (finalNumericGrade < 65)
      finalLetterGrade = "F"
    }
function calculateScienceGrade() {
  midterm = parseInt(prompt("Enter the Midterm Grade",""))
  finalExamGrade = parseInt(prompt("Enter the Final Examination Grade",""))
  research = parseInt(prompt("Enter the Research Grade",""))
  finalNumericGrade =
    (midterm * SCIENCE_MIDTERM_PERCENTAGE) +
    (finalExamGrade * SCIENCE_FINALEXAM_PERCENTAGE) +
    (research * SCIENCE_RESEARCH_PERCENTAGE)
  if (finalNumericGrade >= 90)
      finalLetterGrade = "A"
  else
  if ((finalNumericGrade >= 80) & (finalNumericGrade < 90))
    finalLetterGrade = "B"
  else
  if ((finalNumericGrade >= 70) & (finalNumericGrade < 80))
    finalLetterGrade = "C"
  else
  if ((finalNumericGrade >= 60) & (finalNumericGrade < 70))
    finalLetterGrade = "D"
  else
  if (finalNumericGrade < 60)
    finalLetterGrade = "F"
  }
function displayEnglishGrade() {
  alert("*** ENGLISH STUDENT ***\n\n" +
    "Midterm grade is: " + midterm + "\n" +
    "Final Exam is: " + finalExamGrade + "\n" +
    "Research grade is: " + research + "\n" +
    "Presentation grade is: " + presentation + "\n\n" +
    "Final Numeric Grade is: " + finalNumericGrade + "\n" +
    "Final Letter Grade is: " + finalLetterGrade)
}
function displayMathGrade() {
  alert("*** MATH STUDENT ***\n\n" +
    "Midterm grade is: " + midterm + "\n" +
    "Final Exam is: " + finalExamGrade + "\n\n" +
    "Final Numeric Grade is: " + finalNumericGrade + "\n" +
    "Final Letter Grade is: " + finalLetterGrade)
}
function displayScienceGrade() {
  alert("*** SCIENCE STUDENT ***\n\n" +
    "Midterm grade is: " + midterm + "\n" +
    "Final Exam is: " + finalExamGrade + "\n" +
    "Research grade is: " + research + "\n\n" +
    "Final Numeric Grade is: " + finalNumericGrade + "\n" +
```

```
        "Final Letter Grade is: " + finalLetterGrade)
}
</script>
</body>
</html>
```

3. Save your source file as '**Grades.htm**' in the \JavaScriptFiles\Grades folder (select File-Save As from Notepad's Menu Bar). Be sure to save your source file with the file name extension 'htm'.

4. Use Internet Explorer to Open your Source File.

5. The program should ask you if you have a grade to calculate.

6. Answer 'Yes', and then calculate the grade for an English student. Enter 70 for the midterm, 80 for the final examination, 90 for the research grade and 100 for the presentation. A final numeric grade of 84.5 should be displayed--with a letter grade of 'C'.

7. After the message box is displayed with the calculated grade, the program should ask you if you have more grades to calculate.

8. Answer yes, and then calculate the grade for a Math student. Enter 70 for the midterm and 80 for the final examination. A final numeric grade of 75 should be displayed--with a letter grade of 'D'.

9. After the message box is displayed with the calculated grade, the program should ask you if you have more grades to calculate.

10. Answer yes, and then calculate the grade for a Science student. Enter 70 for the midterm, 80 for the final examination. and 90 for the research grade. A final numeric grade of 78 should be displayed--with a letter grade of 'C'. After the message box is displayed with the calculate grade, the program should ask you if you have more grades to calculate.

11. Answer no--you should be thanked for using the program, and then the program should end.

Discussion

"Wow, that was intense," Rhonda said, "my program works, and amazingly, I think I actually understand what we did here--essentially, we've taken a bunch of code out of the main part of our program, and put it into one of several custom functions."

"Exactly right Rhonda," I said. "We created several custom functions:

- whatKindOfStudent()
- calculateEnglishStudent()
- calculateMathStudent()
- calculateScienceStudent()
- displayEnglishGrade()
- displayMathGrade()
- displayScienceGrade()

"As much as possible, I think the program is now pretty modular, although I'm sure one of you might be able to suggest the creation of some additional functions."

"I think the program is very modular," Kate said. "We have a function to determine the type of student for whom the user wishes to calculate a final grade, three functions for the calculation for each one of the three different student types, plus three functions for the display of the various Grade."

"The number of lines of code in the main part of the program has really been reduced," I said. "Possibly the most important code remaining there is a loop that asks the user if he or she wants to calculate a grade, and based on their response that they do, we execute the whatKindOfStudent() function and assign its return value to a response variable…"

```
while (moreGradesToCalculate == "YES") {
  response=whatKindOfStudent()
```

"What does the return value of the whatKindOfStudent() function indicate?" Chuck asked.

"The whatKindOfStudent() function prompts the user for a number from 1 to 3 indicating the type of student for which they wish to calculate a grade," I said. "That number is then returned to the calling code, which assigns it to the response variable. Based on the value of the response variable, we then call one of the three custom functions we wrote to calculate the student's grade, and execute the appropriate display function...."

```
switch(parseInt(response)) {

  // Case 1 is an English Student
  case 1:
    calculateEnglishGrade()
    displayEnglishGrade()
    break
```

"Each one of the three calculate functions is fairly well encapsulated," I said.

"Encapsulated?" Kathy asked.

"Encapsulated," I said, "means that everything that is needed to perform the calculations, including prompting the user for the component pieces of the grade, is included in the function. Not all programmers would write these functions like this--they might very well include a separate function to prompt the user for the grade components, then execute one of the calculate functions, followed by the display functions.."

"Why is that?" Ward asked. "Is there something wrong with the way we've done it."

"There's a science and art to designing functions," I said. "No two people are likely to write their program in the same way, which is one of the things I love about teaching programming. The reason that some programmers would choose to write a separate function to prompt the user for input is that eventually we will no longer use the prompt() function to prompt the user for the grade components. Instead, we'll build a User Interface consisting of an HTML Form---complete with Textboxes, Radio Buttons and Buttons, and that's how the user will let us know what kind of student they wish to calculate, and provide us with the component grade pieces. Some programmers would argue that we've built too much dependence upon a particular input function into the Calculate functions, and that eventually we'll have to change it. That may be correct---we will have to change it, but in this classroom environment, that will be great experience."

"Something I found pretty interesting," Joe said, "is how you chose to create functions to display the grades. Why didn't you just display the grades from within the various calculate functions?"

"Calculating a grade and displaying a grade are different tasks," I said. "Separating the code for each makes sense-- especially if you consider the fact that the manner in which we are displaying the information for Frank Olley is completely arbitrary---he didn't really care how the display of the information looked."

"In other words," Dave said smiling, "he may want it changed as soon as he sees it. Placing the code to display the grades in functions separate from the calculation functions will make modifying the code easier."

"Excellently stated Dave," I said.

It had been an extremely long, and interesting, class. No one had any further questions, and so I dismissed class for the day.

Summary

In this chapter, we learned about the concept of program modularity, and the benefits of creating custom functions in our JavaScript programs. We discussed details of creating our own functions, Return types of functions, and how to define functions to accept one or more parameters. We finished the chapter by modifying the Grades Calculation project to include several custom functions.

Chapter 7---Creating Your Own Objects In JavaScript

In Chapter 6, we began the process of learning how to introduce modularity into the programs we write by creating custom functions in our programs. Once defined, these functions were then 'called' from the main part of our JavaScript program file. In this chapter, we take modularity several steps further by first learning how to call these functions from another JavaScript file---then learn how to create what is known as a JavaScript class. A class is a template from an 'object' can be created. Creating objects from classes is the name of the game in Object-oriented programming languages such as JavaScript, and by the end of today's class you'll see why. Techniques you learn today will make your programs easier to work with, the number of lines of code in your main JavaScript program shrinks, and overall, your programs become easier to follow, maintain and modify. Plus, the code you place in your JavaScript Classes is available to be used by hundreds, even thousands, of other programmers in the company or even throughout the world. This is truly object oriented programming.

Calling Functions from External Files

"Early on in our course," I said, as I began our seventh class, "I mentioned to you that JavaScript is an Object-Oriented programming language, in which in we work with standard classes and objects that make the job of writing a program much easier. I also told you that at some point, you would be able to design classes of your own from which objects could be created. However, I warned you that it would be some time before you could do this. Well, today's the day. Up until now, we've used functions of standard JavaScript objects, such as the write() function of the document object. In today's class, you'll learn how to design and create classes of your own from which programs will be able to 'instantiate' objects. Before we do that, however, I want to show you how to separate the functions you write from your main JavaScript file and place them in a file of their own."

"What does that accomplish," Rhonda asked.

"It makes our programs even more modular," I said, "and makes the functions that we write more reusable. Functions that are contained in a file of their own can be accessed by many other programs---not just the program that contains the function code. An additional benefit is that if we place the function code in an external file, if the code within the function needs to be modified, only one file needs to be modified--the file containing the function code. If we embed the function code in the same file as the code that 'calls' it, the function code may be found in many--hundreds, even thousands--of JavaScript program files."

I could see some confusion in the faces of my students.

"Let's take a look at the code we wrote last week in which we created a function that displays a message and also returns a value...

```
<! Example6-10 -->
<html>
<body>
<script type="text/javascript">

document.write("The value of the return value is " + displayMessage())

function displayMessage() {
  document.write("I love JavaScript!" + "<br>")
return true
}

</script>
</body>
</html>
```

I then opened the program within Internet Explorer. The following screenshot was displayed on the classroom projector.

"Nothing special here," I said, "we've seen this before. But now what I want to do is take the function out of this program and put it in a file of its own."

"A separate file?" Kate asked.

"That's right Kate," I said. "We can take the function and place it in a separate file. It cuts down on the size of the main program, and makes it less cluttered."

"Does the file require a special name?" Blaine asked.

"We can name it anything we like," I said, "although it's my habit to place functions that will run from an external file like this in a file named functions.js."

Using Notepad, I then copied and pasted the code for the function displayMessage() into a file, and saved it as functions.js...

"As you can see," I said, "all I've done is take the code for the function displayMessage() and place it in an external JavaScript file. An external JavaScript file can contain more than one function--although this one contains just one. Later on today, we'll place several *JavaScript classes* into an external JavaScript file, just like this one."

"I notice," Dave said, "that there's no HTML code present in the external file."

"Great observation Dave," I said, "external JavaScript files may contain only JavaScript code. The JavaScript comment that you see is perfectly legal here---but if we included an HTML tag of any kind, we would generate an error when our Internet Browser tried to deal with it."

"So the file name extension .js stands for JavaScript?" Valerie asked.

"That's right Valerie," I said, "The .js file name extension is not required, but it is a convention."

> **NOTE: The .js file name extension for an External JavaScript file is not required---but it is a convention.**

"I suppose our next step will be to remove the function from our main program?" Mary asked.

"You read my mind Mary," I said. "We need to remove the function code from our .html program file--and when we do that, we also need to include a reference to our external JavaScript file in our HTML program so that our Internet Browser can find the function when we call it. Here's our modified HTML program..."

I then modified **Example6-10** to look like this...

```
<! Example7-1 -->
<html>
<head>
<script src='functions.js'></script>
</head>
<body>
<script type="text/javascript">
document.write("The value of the return value is " + displayMessage())

</script>
</body>
</html>
```

and saved it as "**Example7-1.htm**". When I opened it within Internet Explorer, the following screenshot was displayed on the classroom projector.

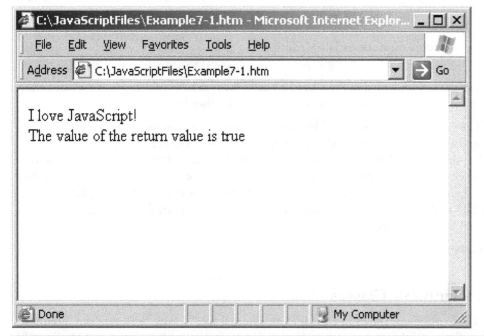

Don't Forget: If typing these examples and exercises isn't something you want to do, feel free to follow this link to find and download the completed solutions for all of the examples and exercises in the book. Just click on the JavaScript book, then follow the link entitled exercises ☺

http://www.johnsmiley.com/main/books.htm

"As you can see," I said, "this version of the program produces the same results as Example6-10. The difference is that the code for the function displayMessage() is contained not in the HTML source file but in an external JavaScript file. Let's take a look at the code that tells our Internet Browser where to 'find' the displayMessage() function. It's really just a single line of code which I've placed in a section of our html program we haven't seen before, the <head> section..."

```
<head>
<script src='functions.js'></script>
</head>
```

"We've seen the script tag before," I said, "but the src attribute is new to us. It tells our Internet Browser the location of any external JavaScript files."

"Could we have more than one?" Chuck asked.

"Yes we could," I said, "if we have more than one external JavaScript file that we wish to reference in our program, then we would have multiple script tags, like this..."

```
<head>
<script src='functions.js'></script>
<script src='functions2.js'></script>
<script src='functions3.js'></script>
</head>
```

"How does our Internet Browser know where to find our external JavaScript file?", Linda asked. "We haven't specified a location---only the file name."

"Good question Linda," I said. "By default, our Internet Browser looks for any externally referenced files in the same folder as the .html code it is running. Since we saved the file functions.js in the same folder as Example7-1.html, our Internet Browser looked for it there. If we wanted to, we could fully qualify the file name with a path and folder, like this..."

```
<head>
<script src='c:\JavaScriptFiles\functions.js'></script>
</head>
```

"...also, if the external JavaScript file is located on a Web Server, you can use the URL---Uniform Address Locator--otherwise known as a Web Address like this..."

```
<head>
<script src='http://www.johnsmiley.com/functions.js'></script>
</head>
```

"I still don't understand why the script tag is included in the <head> tag," Dave said. "Could we have included the reference to the external JavaScript file in the <body> tag like we did with our other JavaScript code?"

"Good question Dave," I said. "The answer is yes---we could include the reference within the body tag, as long as the reference to the file comes *before* any code that may call the function. On the other hand, by placing the reference to the external file in the <head> tag, I am certain that the code in the external JavaScript is loaded into my computer's memory before the code in the <body> tag is executed---in other words, I'm taking no chances that I can accidentally call my function before I've told my Internet Browser where it's located. Besides, by placing all references to external JavaScript files in the <head> tag, I've made my main program even tidier---I just need to look in one place to find all external JavaScript references."

I paused a moment before continuing.

Creating Objects from Instantiable Classes

"Now that we've seen how easy it is to place our function code into an external file," I said, "let's turn our attention to creating something called a class from which we can instantiate objects which possess Properties and Methods.."

"Classes? Objects? Properties? Methods? Instantiate?" Rhonda asked.

"Let's start with the last term first," I said. "Instantiate is a word that means to create an object from a class. Objects we've seen a little bit of already---for instance, the document object, whose write() method we use to write text to our Internet Browser window. Methods we've also seen before---this is behavior that is programmed into an Object, such as the write() method of the document object. Finally, characteristics of an object are given the technical term 'Property'."

"So what's a Class?" Blaine asked.

"A class is just a model for an object," I answered, "much like an architectural blue print is a model for a house or a building. And just as is the case with a blue print, where many 'instances' of a house can be built from a single blue print, from one JavaScript class, many instances of an object can be created."

"So we're talking about creating classes---blue prints or models of objects---of our own?" Linda asked.

"That's right Linda," I answered. "Today we'll learn how to create JavaScript classes of our own, and by the end of today's class, we'll have designed and coded several which will model real-world objects."

"This sounds exciting?" Ward said, "what kind of real-world objects can be modeled using JavaScript Classes?"

"In the real world of programming," I said, "classes are used to model employees, students, inventory, database records, to name a few. In today's class, we'll create a class to model a bank transaction, and of course, we'll also be creating a class to model the English, Math and Science students here at the university."

"This process sounds to me like it may not be all that easy." Rhonda said.

Creating Classes is an extension of Modular Programming

"I don't want to make creating classes sound too easy," I said, "but I think you'll find that it's just an extension of the modular programming process we learned about and practiced last week when we broke our code up into modules by creating custom functions. Creating classes is a matter of determining what real-world objects need to be represented in your program, and in apportioning variables and methods to each one. In many ways, this is nearly complete with the Grades Calculation project. I think we all realize by now that the project is modeling a real-world student. The bottom line is that if you are comfortable with what we did last week concerning function creation, you'll have no trouble going through the mechanics of creating classes. Experience will help you identify the objects you need to model in your program--along with the characteristics and behavior of that object that you need to simulate as well."

> **Note: A method is nothing more than a function that is defined within a JavaScript class. A property is just a variable defined within a JavaScript class.**

Objects possess data (Properties) that simulate object characteristics

"What do you mean by characteristics of an object?" Blaine asked. "Can you give us an example of an object's characteristics"

"Yes I can Blaine," I said, "For instance, if we design a class to represent a real world employee in a corporation, we would want to design a class capable of representing the employee's name, address, social security number, and salary, to name a few characteristics. The characteristics of the employee object are represented and stored 'inside' the object by the implementation of variables."

"And those characteristics are called Properties of an object?" Valerie asked.

"Perfect Valerie," I answered.

Objects have behavior

"That makes sense to me," Linda said, "but what about an object's behavior that you mentioned? What kind of behavior can an object possess?"

"Well," I said, thinking for a moment, "an employee has certain kinds of behaviors---such as working on a particular task, attending meetings, traveling to a customer site, taking a vacation day--these kinds of behavior---the proper term is methods---can be simulated in an object by the implementation of a class function, the kind that we wrote last week."

"I see," Kate said, "but wouldn't the code for that be pretty complex. I'd hate to have to write it."

"You're right Kate," I said, "that code can be pretty complex to write, but the beauty of objects is that if you are a newly hired junior programmer in your company, you're most likely not the person who has to design the Employee class and those hard to write methods. It's the designer of the Employee class that needs to worry about the details of the code to model that behavior. The beauty of a class is that once it's written, it can be used over and over again by hundreds, even thousands of other programmers--both junior and experienced programmers. You see, all of the really difficult code necessary to implement the behavior of the object resides within the class itself. A programmer who wants to use the Employee object—just like we've been using the document object to execute its write() method---only needs to execute the object's method in order to implement the behavior."

"So the programmer who designs the class from which an object is created isn't necessarily the programmer who will later use the object in a program?" Ward asked.

"That's right Ward," I said. "It's usually senior level programmers who design the classes from which objects in a corporate environment are created. I know programmers who spend all of their time designing Classes just like that---and never write any code that actually creates any of those objects."

"So what happens after the class is designed," Steve asked.

"Usually," I answered, "the class is saved in an external JavaScript file, placed in a folder, advertised and made available to other programmers in the company or corporation. And if the JavaScript class you design is really good, it may be used by programmers all over the world."

"I think you mentioned this a minute ago, but I may have missed it," Mary said, If characteristics of an object are implemented via variables, how is the behavior of an object implemented?"

"Behavior in an object is implemented via methods," I said, "just like the functions we wrote last week. A function that appears within a class is given a special name called a method."

"I'm anxious to see one of these classes," Linda said, "Can you show us one?"

"Sure thing Linda," I said, "Let's create a class called Banner designed to display the user's favorite programming language in the Internet Browser window. The class will contain just a single attribute called favoriteProgram, implemented via a variable, and it will possess just one kind of behavior, display, designed to display that single attribute."

I then displayed this code on the classroom projector---and saved it as **'Banner.js'**.

```
//Banner class
function Banner() {

  this.favoriteProgram=""
  this.display=display

  function display() {
    document.write("I love " + this.favoriteProgram + "!<br>")
  }

}
```

"Wow, am I confused." Mary said.

"I expected to see the word class somewhere," Dave added, "that's what Java uses to designate a class."

"Always remember," I said smiling, "JavaScript is not Java. JavaScript doesn't use the keyword 'class' in its class definition. Classes are actually implemented using the keyword function."

"How can you tell it's a class then?" Rhonda asked.

"By the word 'this'," I said, "notice that there are three of them in the definition of the Banner class."

I looked around the classroom for signs of confusion--and saw plenty of it.

"Let's take a closer look at the code in the Banner class," I said. "The first line of code looks to be an ordinary function definition--but as I mentioned a moment ago, JavaScript implements classes using the keyword function. This function is actually the definition of something JavaScript, and other Object Oriented languages, call a Constructor...."

```
function Banner() {
```

Constructors

"A Constructor," I continued, " is the code that gives 'birth' to the object. Everything that we see here is actually coded inside of the Banner class's Constructor..."

"Constructor method?" Linda asked. "I'm afraid I'm confused."

"A Constructor method," I said, "contains code that is automatically executed each time an instance of our object is created."

"Kind of like a start-up Macro in Microsoft Word," Valerie added.

"Constructor methods are very similar," I said. "Code that you want to be executed when an instance of an object is created from a class you place inside a special method called a Constructor Method. Constructor methods are named with the same name as the Class."

"What kind of code goes into a Constructor method?" Joe asked.

"Any kind of code that in some way initializes our object," I said.

"Initializes?" Rhonda asked.

"That's right Rhonda," I said, "For instance, if the class is used to gain access to records in a database, the Constructor method is an ideal location to place code that finds and opens the database. Other types of initialization code is to set attributes of the object--Instance Variables---to default values, if that's appropriate. For instance, if your class has a currentDate Instance Variable, you could place code in its Constructor method to interrogate the System date on the user's PC, and set the value of the currentDate Instance Variable accordingly."

"I see," Kate said. "that makes sense."

"That next line of code," Valerie said, "looks like a variable declaration—is it?"

this.favoriteProgram=""

"You can think of it that way Valerie," I said. "although to be specific, it's really the declaration for the one and only property in our Banner class---favoriteProgram. Notice several things. First, we don't use the keyword 'var' to designate the Property. Secondly, we initialize the favoriteProgram Property to an empty string. Finally, the declaration for the property begins with the word 'this', followed by a period."

"What does 'this' mean?" Mary asked.

"That's really the million dollar question," I answered, "and the answer may be a bit confusing, so hold on. In a moment, we'll see how to create an 'instance' of an object from the Banner class---a Banner object. In fact, we'll see that it's possible to create many Banner objects within the same program. That's where the word 'this' in our class definition comes in. It tells JavaScript that each instance of the class---each Banner object---needs its own 'copy' of the favoriteProgram Property."

"In other words," Dave said, "'this' refers to a particular Banner object."

"Exactly Dave," I said. "Each Banner object has its own 'copy' of the favoriteProgram Property---and its the keyword 'this' that tells JavaScript that this property is what is known as an instance Property."

"What about that next line?" Mary asked. "Is that also a Property declaration?"

this.display

"No Mary," I answered, "This is our way of letting JavaScript know that we are defining a method called display, which we then define as a function like this..."

```
function display() {
  document.write("I love " + this.favoriteProgram + "!<br>")
}
```

"That first line of code," Dave said, "in C++ would be the equivalent of a function prototype."

"Good point Dave," I said. "It is similar. For those of you not familiar with C++, a function prototype is more or less a 'preannouncement' that a function with that name will be defined later on in the program."

"That makes sense," I heard Kate say.

"As I think you can see," I said, "the implementation of this method is very much like the functions we learned to code last week. The display() method merely displays the value of the Instance Variable favoriteProgram in our Internet Browser using the write() method of the document object."

"I notice that we need to preface the Instance Variable name favoriteProgram with the word 'this', Rhonda said.

"That's right Rhonda," I said.

I paused a moment before continuing.

"Of course, what makes this code special," I said, "is that it isn't code from the Banner class itself that will execute the display() method but code from our JavaScript program which will first create an instance of the Banner object which will then execute this method."

"When you say an object is created from the Banner class," Dave said, "does that mean that each object gets its own copy of each of the Instance Variables and methods to work with?"

"That's right Dave," I said. "Later on in today's class, we'll see that it's possible to create, in a program, more than one object from the same class. When that happens, each object has separate 'copies' of each of the Instance Variables and methods defined in the class. In this way, there's no danger of one object 'stepping on the foot' of the other."

"Are we going to execute this class?" Rhonda asked. "I can't wait to see how this works."

"We can't directly execute the Banner class from within our Internet Browser," I said, "Remember, Instantiable Classes are intended to have objects built from their 'blueprint' created in other JavaScript programs that call them. Let me show you."

Creating objects from your classes

"In order to create an instance of a Banner object from our Banner class," I said, "we must first create a JavaScript program. This program will look like the others that we've coded in the course so far. What you'll find strange, I'm sure, is the code necessary to create or instantiate the Banner object. Take a look…"

I then displayed this code on the classroom projector.

```
<! Example7-2 -->
<html>
<head>
<script src='Banner.js'></script>
</head>
<body>
<script type="text/javascript">

var x = new Banner()
x.favoriteProgram = "JavaScript"
x.display()

</script>
</body>
</html>
```

I then saved the program as "**Example7-2.htm**".

I could see much confusion on the faces of many of my students---Mary was hardly alone.

"Let's take a look at this code line by line," I said. "As you can see, this JavaScript program begins almost identically to Example7-1…"

```
<! Example7-2 -->
<html>
<head>
<script src='Banner.js'></script>
</head>
<body>
<script type="text/javascript">
```

"As was the case with Example7-1," I said, "where we included a reference to the JavaScript external file containing the function we would be executing, here we include a reference to the external JavaScript file containing the definition of our Banner class."

"What's going on with that next line of code?" Kathy asked. "It looks like a variable declaration."

"This line of code looks just like a variable declaration, doesn't it," I said…

```
var x = new Banner()
```

"…in fact, it is. However, instead of declaring a numeric or string Data Type for our variable, what we are doing instead is declaring a variable that will be a Banner type."

"Can you do that?" Ward asked.

"Yes we can," I said. "When you declare an ordinary numeric JavaScript variable, JavaScript allocates space in the computer's memory for a numeric Data Type--the same applies for a String variable. When you declare a variable of type Banner, JavaScript allocates space in the computer's memory for the Banner object's Instance Variables and for its method definitions. "

"That's right," Dave said excitedly, "you did say that each object gets a 'copy' of the class's Instance Variables and methods. So that's how it's done."

"That's right Dave," I said. "This syntax looks very confusing at first, but that's what's going on--we're telling JavaScript to allocate enough 'room' in the PC's memory for a Banner object. By the way, notice the use of the word 'new'--it alerts JavaScript that we want to create an 'instance' of a Banner object."

"What's x?" Lou asked.

"x is just the name of the variable," I said. "Hereafter, the instance of the Banner object we're about to create will be referred to by this name. But let's not forget the rest of the line--we also need to follow the variable name x with an equal sign, followed by the keyword 'new' followed by the name of the Banner class, followed by an empty pair of parentheses."

"What's the significance of the empty set of parentheses?" Linda asked.

"Do you remember Linda," I said, "that our definition of the Banner class was implemented using a function named Banner? It just so happens that the Banner function header was defined with no arguments..."

function Banner() {

"...in other words, an empty set of parentheses. So, in order to create our Banner object, we must execute the function contained within the Banner class that creates the object--and we must be sure to execute it using the proper signature. Technically, we're executing the Constructor method of the Banner class."

I gave everyone a further chance to study the line of code that declares, and then creates an instance of a Banner object. It had been my experience that this single line of code may be the most confusing single concept for beginner JavaScript programmers.

"You're right, this syntax is pretty confusing," Kate said. "Seeing a Class name that we've defined ourselves specified as the type declaration is strange."

"I agree Kate," I said, "it is strange at first, but believe me, once you get used to it, declaring variables to refer to instances of your own classes will become second nature to you. As I think I've mentioned before, that's the name of the game in JavaScript, and JavaScript programmers are forever defining classes with attributes and behavior, and then instantiating objects from these classes in their programs. In class 'lingo', attributes are called properties and behavior is implemented by class methods."

Changing an Object's Attributes

"Can you go over how to change an object's attribute," Mary asked. "It seemed like you used an assignment statement, but I was a little confused by the syntax."

"Good question Mary," I said. "Once you've declared an instance of your class's object, you can easily set--by that I mean change---one of its attributes just by changing the value of the Instance Variable that implements that attribute. Remember, behind the scenes, the attributes or characteristics of an object are really just Instance Variables defined in the object's class. Changing the attributes of an object is easy, but we can't just assign a value to the Instance Variable, we need to assign a value to the Instance Variable associated with this particular object. Because of that, we need to use a special notation called Object Dot Notation."

"Object Dot Notation?" Rhonda asked. "This is getting more complicated."

"It's not bad at all, Rhonda," I replied. "Object Dot Notation is just a way of telling JavaScript the name of the object whose Instance Variable we wish to update. With Object Dot Notation, we first specify the name of the variable that we used to declare an instance of our object, followed by a 'dot' or a period, followed by the name of the Instance Variable that implements the attribute. After that, we're basically working with a ordinary JavaScript assignment statement, in that we use the equal sign assignment operator, followed by the value we wish to assign to the Instance Variable...."

x.favoriteProgram = "JavaScript"

"So what we've done here is change the value of the Instance Variable 'favoriteProgram' inside the Banner class?" Steve asked.

"That's close Steve," I said, "but more specifically, we've changed the value of the Instance Variable 'favoriteProgram' within a particular instance of the Banner object referenced by the variable 'x'. Remember, each object has its own 'copy' of every Instance Variable and method in the memory. It's a subtle distinction, I know, but the distinction will become important later on today when we learn that we can create another type of variable within a class called a Class Variable. A Class Variable is a variable that is shared by every instance of an object instantiated from that class."

"I assume we can retrieve the value of an object's attribute using the same Object Dot Notation?" Ward asked.

"That's right Ward," I said. "we could display the value of the favoriteProgram attribute using this syntax…"

`document.write(x.favoriteProgram)`

"I see," Linda said, "really, except for the name of the object variable and the 'dot', this syntax is just like working with a variable."

"That's a good way of thinking about it," I said.

Everyone seemed to understand how to change, and view, the value of an Object's attribute.

Calling an Object's Methods

"Calling the method for an Object that we've declared," I said, "should be familiar to you--it's the same way that we execute methods of the standard JavaScript objects, such as the document object. Once again, we use Object Dot Notation, specifying the name of our object variable, followed by a 'dot', followed by the name of the method we wish to execute…"

`x.display()`

"What's the purpose of the empty set of parentheses following the method name?" Mary asked.

"Any arguments required by the method appear within the parentheses," I said. "We defined the display() method of the Banner class to require no parameters---the empty set of parentheses are required when no arguments are required."

"I'm anxious to see Banner class in action," Rhonda said. "What do we need to do."

"All we need to do," I said, "is open up **Example7-2.htm** in our Internet Explorer." I did exactly that, and the following screenshot was displayed on the classroom projector.

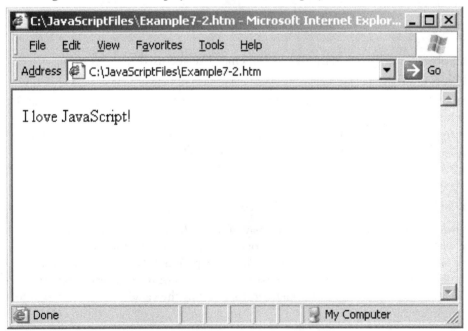

"Does everyone realize what's happened here?" I asked. "The code in Example7_1 created an instance of a Banner object from the Banner class, set the value of its favoriteProgram attribute, and then executed its display() method."

"Pretty cool," Kate said.

"I don't want to be a 'downer' about all of this," Rhonda said, "but couldn't we have just executed all of this code from a single JavaScript program. What has this really bought us? Quite honestly, I think it's complicated things."

"That's usually the first reaction that beginners have," I said. "You're right in that we could have placed all of the code we executed in a single JavaScript program. But many years of experience has shown that modular programming---and in JavaScript that means creating objects---leads to better programs. I think as the day progresses you'll begin to understand that placing code in classes whose objects are then instantiated actually 'uncomplicates' programs."

Creating multiple objects from your classes

"Is it possible to create more than one instance of the same object in the startup class?" Bob asked. "For instance, suppose I was creating an instance of that Employee object you were describing earlier, and I wanted to 'instantiate' an object for every employee in a particular department."

"Yes it is possible," I said. "You just need to declare more than one object variable, like this…"

I then displayed the following code on the classroom projector….

```
<! Example7-3 -->
<html>
<head>
<script src='Banner.js'></script>
</head>
<body>
<script type="text/javascript">

var x = new Banner()
var y = new Banner()

x.favoriteProgram = "JavaScript"
x.display()

y.favoriteProgram = "C#"
y.display()

</script>
</body>
</html>
```

…saved it as '**Example7-3.htm**' and opened it up within Internet Explorer. The following screenshot was displayed on the classroom projector.

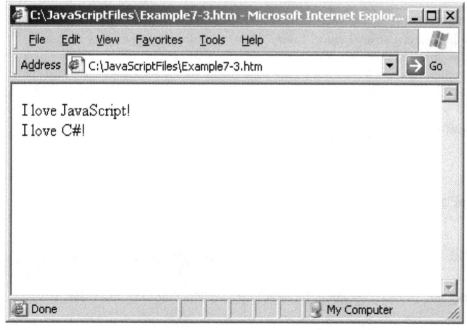

"What we've done here," I said, "is to declare two instances of the Banner object…"

```
var x = new Banner()
var y = new Banner()
```

"I wouldn't have thought that was possible to have two object instances of the same class in a program," Blaine said.

"It's no problem," I said. "because we're using distinct variable names, and as I mentioned earlier, each instance of an object is maintained separately in the computer's memory. Keeping the object and its attributes in separate locations of memory keeps one object from being confused with another. When we modify the attribute value of an object, JavaScript knows exactly which object to act upon by the object variable name we use..."

```
x.favoriteProgram = "JavaScript"
x.display()
```

```
y.favoriteProgram = "C#"
y.display()
```

"That's pretty amazing," Rhonda said. "Is there a limit to the number of objects you can instantiate?"

"The number of objects you can instantiate," I said, "is limited only by the available memory in your computer---since that's where the objects are maintained. In some large commercial applications, it's not unusual to have thousands of objects in memory at one time."

Constructors with Arguments

"Is it possible to create a Constructor method that has one or more arguments?" Peter asked.

"Yes it is Peter," I said, "you frequently see examples like that on the Internet. All you need to do is give some thought as to the number and type of arguments that your Constructor will accept---and be sure that when you create the object from the class using the new keyword, that you supply the proper number and type of arguments. I should mention that creating a Constructor with Arguments allows you to supply the initial value of your object's Properties when the object is created. Let me show you by creating a Class called Banner2." I then displayed the following code on the classroom projector....

```
//Banner2 Class

function Banner2(x) {

  this.favoriteProgram=x
  this.display=display

  function display() {
    document.write("I love " + this.favoriteProgram + "!<br>")
  }

}
```

"Because the Banner2 Constructor is expecting an argument," I said, "when we create the object using the 'new' keyword, we need to supply the value for that argument..."

```
<! Example7-4 -->
<html>
<head>
<script src='Banner2.js'></script>
</head>
<body>
<script type="text/javascript">

var x = new Banner2("JavaScript")
x.display()

</script>
</body>
</html>
```

I then saved it as '**Example7-4.htm**' and opened it up within Internet Explorer. The following screenshot was displayed on the classroom projector.

"As you can see," I said, "the bottom line hasn't changed---our program still displays 'I love JavaScript! in our Internet Browser. The difference with this version of the program is that we're setting values for the Class properties via the Constructor---not by setting the Property values directly the way we did in Examples 7-2 and 7-3."

"I see that," Dave said. "For my money, coding a Constructor to accept arguments has no obvious benefits."

"I agree Dave," I said.

Dave had a question: "I know that other languages such as Java, C++ and C# provide for something called overloaded functions and overloaded Constructors. Does JavaScript?"

"No Dave," I said, "JavaScript doesn't currently *support* overloaded functions or Constructors."

"What's an overloaded function or Constructor?" Rhonda asked.

"Overloaded functions are functions having the same name--but with different 'signatures', that is the number of arguments expected. In some programming languages, you can define functions with the same name--and the program knows which one to execute by matching the call statement to the function using the number of arguments supplied. JavaScript doesn't do that. In JavaScript, a program can't have functions--or Constructor methods--with the same name."

Class Variables

"I mentioned earlier," I said, "that each object and its attributes or Instance Variables, are maintained in separate locations in the computer's memory. This protects the data in one object from being confused with the data of another object. There's another type of variable you can declare in a class called a Class Variable which allows you to share its value with every instance of an object created from that class."

"I was just about to ask if such a thing was possible," Dave said. "I've worked with other languages where that was possible, and it can be a pretty beneficial feature."

"When you say share," Kate asked, "you mean that each object can see the value of the variable, and update it as well?"

> **NOTE: Class Variables 'share' their data with every instance of the object created from the class**

"That's right Kate," I said, "as Dave said, this can be a very beneficial feature. Class Variables are a great way for objects of the same class to share data."

"Is that important?" Mary asked. "Is that something that's commonly required?"

"It can be," I said. "For instance, have you ever worked with an accounting program? One part of an accounting program typically is used to generate invoices to your customers, and it's customary to assign a unique invoice number to each invoice. If you write the accounting program using JavaScript, each invoice can be an object, and you could create a Class Variable called nextInvoiceNumber which would enable each object to access the next available invoice number when the invoice object is created."

"I see what you mean," Valerie said, "that makes sense. By storing the value of the next invoice number in a Class Variable, each instance of the object can 'get at' the value, plus increment the value by one after they use it."

"Excellent Valerie," I said.

"Can we add a Class Variable to the Banner class to see how it works?" Steve asked.

"Sure Steve," I said. "Do you remember that in Example7-3, we created two Banner objects, both of which were 'alive' at the same time. Suppose we want each object to be able to know how many Banner objects are currently 'alive'? A Class Variable is an ideal way to do that."

"How exactly would we do that?" Peter asked.

"We can declare a Class Variable in the Banner class," I said, "and then, within the Constructor Method of the Banner class, increment the value of that Class Variable by 1. Since the Constructor method is automatically executed each time an object of the class is created, the value of the Class Variable should always reflect the number of Banner objects that are currently in existence."

I then modified the Banner class to look like this, and displayed it on the classroom projector.

```
//Banner3 class
function Banner3() {

  Banner3.numberOfBannerObjects

  this.favoriteProgram=""
  this.display=display
  this.howMany=howMany

  if (isNaN(Banner3.numberOfBannerObjects)) {
    Banner3.numberOfBannerObjects = 0
  }

  Banner3.numberOfBannerObjects++

  function display() {
    document.write("I love " + this.favoriteProgram + "!<br>")
  }

  function howMany() {
    document.write("The number of Banner objects is " +
    Banner3.numberOfBannerObjects + "<hr>")
  }

}
```

"Let's take a look at the new code in the Banner class," I said. "We've added a Class Variable called numberOfBannerObjects, added some lines of code in the Constructor methods, and created a new method called howMany(). Let's take a look at the declaration of the Class Variable first. A Class Variable is very much like an Instance Variable--- what differentiates a Class Variable from an Instance Variable is that its declaration is preceded by the name of the class, followed by a period..."

```
Banner3.numberOfBannerObjects
```

"So that's how we know we are dealing with a Class Variable and not an Instance Variable?" Blaine asked.

"That's right Blaine," I said.

"That makes sense," Dave said, "since a Class variable really belongs to the Class---not to a particular object instantiated from the class."

"Absolutely," I said. "Notice one thing--we didn't initialize the value of our Class variable to zero. We don't want to initialize the value of our Class variable because if we do, then whenever an object is created from this class, it will presume the 'starting' value of the variable is zero, not the actual value that is being updated by the various objects using it. For that reason, Class variables are not initialized with values." I waited a moment before continuing.

"We also needed to write code to increment the value of the numberOfBannerObjects Class Variable by using the Increment (++) operator. But first, we have to execute this code..."

```
if (isNaN(Banner3.numberOfBannerObjects)) {
Banner3.numberOfBannerObjects = 0
}
```

"What's going on with that isNaN function?" Dave asked.

"Good question Dave," I said. "Because we didn't initialize the value of the numberOfBannerObjects class variable, it's value isn't anything---in computer jargon, it's called NaN, which stands for Not-A-Number. If we try to add 1 to a variable whose value is Not-A-Number, we get Not-A-Number again. Fortunately, JavaScript allows us to determine if a variable's value is Not-A-Number using the isNaN function. If the return value of the isNaN function is true, then we know we are dealing with an uninitialized Class Variable, and we then set its value to 0. In actuality, this condition will only exist if no Banner3 objects have been created from the Banner3 class. After that, the value of the Class Variable will be equal to the number of Banner3 objects that currently exist. Regardless, the next line of code takes the value of the numberOfBannerObjects Class variable and increments it by one..."

```
Banner3.numberOfBannerObjects++
```

"...Finally, here's the code for the new method called howMany(). This method will be used by client programs to display the number of Banner objects that are currently 'alive'..."

```
function howMany() {
   document.write("The number of Banner objects is " +
   Banner3.numberOfBannerObjects + "<hr>")
}
```

"Notice in the howMany() method," I said, "that we precede the Class Variable name with the name of our class---Banner3---not the keyword 'this', as we do with Instance Variables."

"What's that <hr> tag I see with the write() method of the document object?" Linda asked.

"I was about to ask about that," Rhonda said.

"Those of you who took my HTML class will recognize that as the Horizontal Rule tag," I said. "It 'draws' a horizontal line in our Browser window. You'll see it visually in just a second."

I waited a moment before continuing.

"Now let's write the code to see the effect of the Class Variable in action." I said. "What we'll do is create two Banner objects, and then execute the howMany() method of each one. If the code is working properly, it should report to us the number of Banner objects in existence at the time the code runs..."

I then displayed this code on the classroom projector.

```
<! Example7-5 -->
<html>
<head>
<script src='Banner3.js'></script>
</head>
<body>
<script type="text/javascript">

var x = new Banner3()
x.favoriteProgram = "JavaScript"
x.display()
x.howMany()

var y = new Banner3()
y.favoriteProgram = "C#"
y.display()
y.howMany()

</script>
</body>
</html>
```

I then saved it as '**Example7-5.htm**' and opened it up within Internet Explorer. The following screenshot was displayed on the classroom projector.

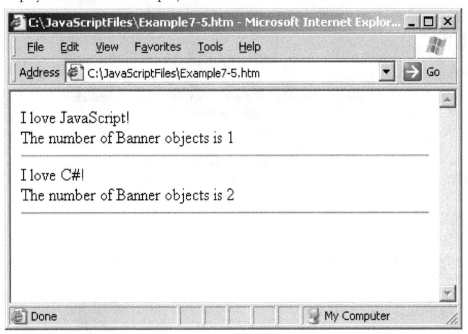

"Do you see what's happened here?" I asked. "After we create the first instance of the Banner3 object using this syntax..."

```
var x = new Banner3()
x.favoriteProgram = "JavaScript"
```

"...the value of the Class Variable numberOfBannerObjects is incremented by 1 (giving us 1) when the Banner3's Constructor Method is executed. Executing the howMany() method displays the value of that Class Variable (1) in our Internet Browser..."

```
x.howMany()
```

"...this syntax is then used to create a second instance of the Banner object..."

```
var y = new Banner3()
y.favoriteProgram = "C#"
```

"...this results in the value of the Class Variable numberOfBannerObjects being incremented by 1 (giving us 2) when the single argument version of the Constructor method is executed. Executing the howMany() method displays the value of the Class Variable (2) in our Browser's Window."

```
y.howMany()
```

"From this example, " Dave said, "I can see that both of our Banner objects can 'see' the value of the Class Variable numberOfBannerObjects, but can either of the objects modify its value?"

"Good question Dave," I said, "The objects themselves cannot modify the value of the Class Variable--except through methods that are defined in the class itself. In this case, the only method defined to update the value of the Class Variable is the Constructor method. However, take a look at this code..."

I then modified the code from **Example7_5** to look like this...

```
<! Example7-6 -->
<html>
<head>
<script src='Banner3.js'></script>
</head>
<body>
<script type="text/javascript">

var x = new Banner3()
x.howMany()
```

var y = new Banner3()
y.howMany()

Banner3.numberOfBannerObjects = 0

x.howMany()
y.howMany()

</script>
</body>
</html>

"Although we can't directly update the value of the Class Variable using this syntax..."

x.numberOfBannerObjects = 0

"...we can update it using this syntax..."

Banner3.numberOfBannerObjects = 0

I then saved the program as '**Example7-6.htm**' and opened it up within Internet Explorer. The following screenshot was displayed on the classroom projector.

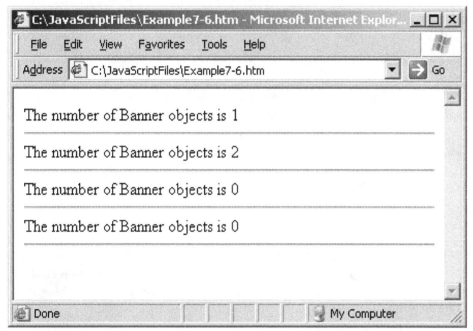

"I know this code is a bit confusing," I said, "but it does illustrate the ability of our program to directly modify the value of a Class Variable. As we did in Example7-5, here we've also created two Banner3 objects. The first Banner3 object is created using this syntax..."

var x = new Banner3()

"...and as a result, the Constructor method of the Banner3 object is executed, incrementing the value of the Class Variable numberOfBannerObjects from 0 to 1. Executing the howMany() method of the first Banner3 Object results in the message 'The number of Banner objects is 1' being displayed in our Internet Browser window..."

x.howMany()

"...the second Banner object is then created using this syntax..."

var y = new Banner3()

"...and once again, the Constructor method is executed, incrementing the value of the Class Variable numberOfBannerObjects from 1 to 2. Executing the howMany() method of the second Object results in the message 'The number of Banner objects is 2' being displayed in our Internet Browser window..."

y.howMany()

"...with this line of code, we gain direct access to the Class Variable numberOfBannerObjects, and update it to 0 using an assignment statement..."

Banner3.numberOfBannerObjects = 0

"...Has the value of the Class Variable really been updated? It has, and we can prove that by executing the howMany() method of the second Banner object, resulting in the message 'The number of Banner objects is 0' being displayed in our Internet Browser window..."

x.howMany()

"...By the way, notice how if we use the second object to display the value of the Class Variable, the result is still the same, we get the same results in the Browser Window when we execute the howMany() method of the second Banner object..."

y.howMany()

"I'm convinced, there really is just the single Class Variable called numberOfBannerObjects shared among all the objects created from the class," Rhonda said. "I think I'm really beginning to understand this. But isn't there a potential problem here?"

"How so Rhonda?," I asked.

"Well," she continued, "the Class Variable numberOfBannerObjects was intended to keep track of the number of Banner objects in existence, and our code was able to subvert that by directly updating the value of the Class Variable. If other objects are dependent upon the value of numberOfBannerObjects, being able to change the value the we did here seems more than a little dangerous to me."

"You raise some good points Rhonda," I said. " Unfortunately, this 'end around' that you saw here can't be stopped. The current version of JavaScript has no way to stop it."

"This is all great stuff," Rhonda said, "but I'd be lying if I didn't say that I would feel a lot more confident about creating my own classes and objects if I had a chance to work with them a little bit. Will we have time to do that today?"

"Absolutely," I said. "I have a series of exercises for you to complete that will give you plenty of practice in creating classes and objects. We'll start by taking the Smiley National Bank program we created last week, and modifying it to use objects. Then, towards the end of today's class, you'll modify the Grades Calculation project to use objects also."

We had been working a long time without a break, and so I asked everyone to take a fifteen minute break. When my students returned, I distributed this exercise for them to complete.

Exercise 7-1 Create the BankTransaction Instantiable Class for the Smiley National Bank

In this exercise, you'll take the code you wrote last week in Practice6_2, and include it in a BankTransaction class. This class will then be used by a client program you'll write in Exercise 7-2 to instantiate BankTransaction objects which will handle the details of making Deposits, Withdrawals, and displaying Bank Balances.

1. Use Notepad (if you are using Windows) and enter the following code.

```
//BankTransaction Class
function BankTransaction() {

    this.newBalance = 0
    this.adjustment = 0
    BankTransaction.Balance

    this.makeDeposit=makeDeposit
    this.makeWithdrawal=makeWithdrawal
    this.getBalance = getBalance

    function makeDeposit() {
      if (isNaN(BankTransaction.Balance)) {
        BankTransaction.Balance = 0
      }
      this.adjustment = parseFloat(prompt("Enter the Deposit Amount",""))
      this.newBalance = BankTransaction.Balance + this.adjustment
      alert("*** SMILEY NATIONAL BANK ***\n\n" +
        "Old Balance is: " + BankTransaction.Balance + "\n" +
        "Adjustment is: +" + this.adjustment + "\n" +
```

```
        "New Balance is: " + this.newBalance + "\n")
     BankTransaction.Balance = this.newBalance
  }
  function makeWithdrawal() {
     this.adjustment = parseFloat(prompt("Enter the Withdrawal Amount",""))
     this.newBalance = BankTransaction.Balance - this.adjustment
     alert("*** SMILEY NATIONAL BANK ***\n\n" +
     "Old Balance is: " + BankTransaction.Balance + "\n" +
     "Adjustment is: -" + this.adjustment + "\n" +
     "New Balance is: " + this.newBalance + "\n")
     BankTransaction.Balance = this.newBalance
  }
  function getBalance() {
     alert("*** SMILEY NATIONAL BANK ***\n\n" +
     "Your Current Balance is: " + BankTransaction.Balance )
  }
}
```

2. Save your source file as **'BankTransaction.js'** in the \JavaScriptFiles\Practice folder (select File-Save As from Notepad's Menu Bar). Be sure to save your source file with the file name extension 'js'.

3. Since this class is not directly executable, in order to test it, we'll need to write code to create instances of its Objects. We'll do that in Exercise 7-2.

Discussion

Creating the BankTransaction Instantiable class took us about fifteen minutes to complete. Much to my surprise, most of the students seemed comfortable completing the exercise---I think they were beginning to enjoy working with objects..

"Somehow I thought this would be more confusing," Rhonda said, "but I think I've surprised myself by more or less understanding what's going on here. Not only that, but I'm beginning to get the sense that the changes we've made to the Smiley National Bank application are doing exactly what you said they would do--make the program easier to read, follow, and modify in the future. If I'm correct, what we've done in this Exercise is take a bunch of code out of Practice6_2, and include it in an Instantiable object called BankTransaction. Is that right?"

"That's right Rhonda," I said. "We've taken some—but not all---of the code we had in written in Practice6_2---and included it in a BankTransaction class, from which we will create objects within a 'client' program. BankTransaction contains three variables. Two of the variables, *adjustment* and *newBalance*, are Instance Variables, which means that each object created from the class has a separate copy of them. One variable however, *Balance*, is a Class Variable."

"A Class Variable can be seen by every objects of that class," Ward said, "plus, it exists for as long as any object of that class is alive."

"That's excellent Ward," I said.

"Why is Balance declared as a Class Variable?" Peter asked.

"Designating Balance as a Class Variable," I said, "will enable our client program to keep a 'running total' of the bank account balance as it is updated by various objects."

"How many methods are there in the BankTransaction class," Chuck asked.

"The BankTransaction class has three methods," I said, "makeDeposit(), makeWithdrawal() and getBalance()). The code in each of these methods hasn't changed *much* from that found in the methods in Practice6_2---basically, all we've done is move the code into methods in an Instantiable class. We did, however, have to deal with the issue of our Class Variable Balance not being initialized---which we handled by checking for a Not-A-Number condition..."

```
if (isNaN(BankTransaction.Balance)) {
   BankTransaction.Balance = 0
}
```

"...and since Balance is a Class Variable, any references to the Balance variable needs to be prefaced with the Class Name, as is illustrated here in the getBalance() method..."

```
function getBalance() {
  alert("*** SMILEY NATIONAL BANK ***\n\n" +
  "Your Current Balance is: " + BankTransaction.Balance )
}
```

"Aside from these," I said, "I think the code is little changed from the way it appeared in Exercise 6-2."

"You're right," Valerie said, "I was a little amazed at that myself---it seems that the work we did last week in creating custom methods for this application enabled us to create the BankTransaction Class pretty easily."

I waited a moment to see if there were any questions. No one had any, and so I distributed this exercise to create the client program in which we would instantiate objects from the BankTransaction class we just created.

Exercise 7-2---The Smiley National Bank client programming using BankTransaction objects

In this exercise, you'll create a client program to instantiate objects from the BankTransaction class you created in Exercise 7-1.

1. Use Notepad (if you are using Windows) and enter the following code.

```
<! Practice7-1 -- >
<html>
<head>
<script src='BankTransaction.js'></script>
</head>
<body>
<script type="text/javascript">

var response = ""
var moreBankingBusiness = ""

moreBankingBusiness = prompt("Do you want to do some banking?","Yes")
moreBankingBusiness = moreBankingBusiness.toUpperCase()

while (moreBankingBusiness == "YES") {

  response = prompt("What would you like to do? (1=Deposit, 2=Withdraw, 3=Get Balance)","")

  if (response == null) {
    alert("You clicked on the Cancel button")
    exit
  }

  if (response == "") {
    alert("You must make an entry in the Text Box")
    exit
  }

  if (parseInt(response) < 1 || parseInt( response) > 3) {
    alert(response + " - is not a valid answer")
    exit
  }

  if (parseInt(response) == 1) {
    var transaction = new BankTransaction()
    transaction.makeDeposit()
  }

  if (parseInt(response) == 2) {
    var transaction = new BankTransaction()
    transaction.makeWithdrawal()
  }
```

```
  if (parseInt(response) == 3) {
    var transaction = new BankTransaction()
    transaction.getBalance()
  }

  moreBankingBusiness = prompt("Do you have more banking business?","Yes")
  moreBankingBusiness = moreBankingBusiness.toUpperCase()

}

alert("Thanks for banking with us!")

</script>
</body>
</html>
```

2. The program will ask you if you wish to do some banking. Because we specified 'Yes' as the default for the Prompt Popup Box, 'Yes' is already in the Text Box.

3. Now click on the OK button. The program will then ask you what you wish to do-- Make a Deposit, Make a Withdrawal, or Get a Balance. Type '1' into the TextBox to indicate you wish to Make a Deposit.

4. Now click on the OK button. The program will then ask you how much you wish to deposit into your account. Enter '50' into the TextBox to indicate your deposit amount.

5. Now click on the OK button. The program will display a confirmation message, indicating your deposit amount and your old and new balance.

6. After clicking on the OK button, the program will then ask if you have more banking business. Because we specified 'Yes' as the default for the Prompt Popup Box, 'Yes' is already in the Text Box.

7. Now click on the OK button. The program will then ask you what you wish to do-- Make a Deposit, Make a Withdrawal, or Get a Balance. Type '2' into the TextBox to indicate you wish to Make a Withdrawal.

8. Now click on the OK button. The program will then ask you how much you wish to withdraw. Enter '20' into the TextBox to indicate your withdrawal amount.

9. Now click on the OK button. The program will display a confirmation message, indicating your transaction (withdrawals are designated with a negative transaction amount) and your old and new balance.

10. After clicking on the OK button, the program will then ask if you have more banking business. Answer 'Yes'.

11. Now click on the OK button. The program will then ask you what you wish to do-- Make a Deposit, Make a Withdrawal, or Get a Balance. Type '3' into the TextBox to indicate you wish to display the current balance.

12. Now click on the OK button. The program will then display the current balance of your account.

13. After clicking on the OK button, the program will then ask if you have more banking business. Answer 'No'.

14. After clicking on the OK button, the program will then display a message thanking you for using it. After clicking on the OK button, the program will end.

Discussion

"This program behaves in an identical manner to the code in Practice6-1," I said. "the difference is in the way the code is implemented, with this version using a client program to create instances of the BankTransaction Class we created in Exercise 7-1. Crucial to that working properly, we must include a reference to the BankTransaction class in our code. We do that here...."

```
<head>
<script src='BankTransaction.js'></script>
</head>
```

"...In this version of the program, it's the BankTransaction object that does the majority of the work. This client program creates objects, and based on the type of banking business the user wishes to do, executes one of the three methods of the BankTransaction class..."

```
if (parseInt(response) == 1) {
  var transaction = new BankTransaction()
  transaction.makeDeposit()
}

if (parseInt(response) == 2) {
  var transaction = new BankTransaction()
```

```
  transaction.makeWithdrawal()
}
if (parseInt(response) == 3) {
  var transaction = new BankTransaction()
  transaction.getBalance()
}
```

"We've really taken the notion of modular programming to its extreme, by creating classes and objects, haven't we?" Dave commented.

"That's right, Dave" I said. "By 'encapsulating' the code for making deposits, withdrawals and displaying balances in the BankTransaction object, all any client program using our object needs to know is how to instantiate the object, and what methods to execute. It's pretty easy, isn't it?"

I waited to see if there were any questions---but it seemed like everyone was OK.

"Will we be modifying the Grades Calculation Project to use objects today?" Joe asked.

"That's our next step Joe," I said. "Any suggestions as to how we can 'turn' the code in the existing Grades.htm file into an Instantiable class?"

"I guess we could create a single class called Student," Mary said, "having the same methods that we created last week in the form of functions. That's essentially what we just did with the Banking program."

"That's a possibility," I agreed.

"From what I've been reading about Object oriented programming," Dave said, "I think we need at least three classes---one for each of the three different types of students."

"Is that right?" Rhonda said, turning to Dave, but addressing her question to me.

"Dave's on the right track," I said. "It makes the most sense to create a separate class for each type of student. Mary, I'd have no objection if you created a single class called Student---I mean you wouldn't really be wrong, but you'll see that creating three student classes is the way to go."

"Sounds great," Rhonda said, "I'm ready to start!"

"Is there more than one way to design the classes in this project?" Blaine asked. "I hadn't thought of using three classes at all---I was thinking of just a single Student class."

"That's a good question Blaine," I said, "I want to emphasize that while there are some agreed upon 'rules' for the construction of objects, believe me, if we asked five programmers to review the requirements for this project, and asked them to design classes based on them, I bet we would come up with five different object models. As I frequently say, in the world of programming, there are many ways to paint a picture, and there's rarely a single, correct solution to a problem."

"Can we get going on this," Rhonda repeated impatiently. "This sounds like great fun to me, and I'm anxious to get started."

I then distributed this exercise for the class to complete.

Exercise 7-3---Create the EnglishStudent Instantiable Class

In this exercise, you'll create the EnglishStudent class for the Grades Calculation project. This class will allow a client program to create an object which will prompt the user for information necessary to calculate the final grade for an English student.

1. Use Notepad (if you are using Windows) and enter the following code.

```
//EnglishStudent Class
function EnglishStudent() {

  this.ENGLISH_MIDTERM_PERCENTAGE = .25
  this.ENGLISH_FINALEXAM_PERCENTAGE = .25
  this.ENGLISH_RESEARCH_PERCENTAGE = .30
  this.ENGLISH_PRESENTATION_PERCENTAGE = .20
  this.midterm = 0
  this.finalExamGrade = 0
```

```
    this.research = 0
    this.presentation = 0
    this.finalNumericGrade = 0
    this.finalLetterGrade = ""

    this.calculate=calculate
    this.displayGrade=displayGrade

    document.write("EnglishStudent's Constructor")

    function calculate() {
      this.midterm = parseInt(prompt("Enter the Midterm Grade",""))
      this.finalExamGrade = parseInt(prompt("Enter the Final Examination Grade","" ))
      this.research = parseInt(prompt("Enter the Research Grade",""))
      this.presentation = parseInt(prompt("Enter the Presentation Grade",""))
      this.finalNumericGrade =
        (this.midterm * this.ENGLISH_MIDTERM_PERCENTAGE) +
        (this.finalExamGrade * this.ENGLISH_FINALEXAM_PERCENTAGE) +
        (this.research * this.ENGLISH_RESEARCH_PERCENTAGE) +
        (this.presentation * this.ENGLISH_PRESENTATION_PERCENTAGE)
      if (this.finalNumericGrade >= 93)
        this.finalLetterGrade = "A"
      else
      if ((this.finalNumericGrade >= 85) & (this.finalNumericGrade < 93))
        this.finalLetterGrade = "B"
      else
      if ((this.finalNumericGrade >= 78) & (this.finalNumericGrade < 85))
        this.finalLetterGrade = "C"
      else
      if ((this.finalNumericGrade >= 70) & (this.finalNumericGrade < 78))
        this.finalLetterGrade = "D"
      else
      if (this.finalNumericGrade < 70)
        this.finalLetterGrade = "F"
    }
    function displayGrade() {
      alert("*** ENGLISH STUDENT ***\n\n" +
        "Midterm grade is: " + this.midterm + "\n" +
        "Final Exam is: " + this.finalExamGrade + "\n" +
        "Research grade is: " + this.research + "\n" +
        "Presentation grade is: " + this.presentation + "\n\n" +
        "Final Numeric Grade is: " + this.finalNumericGrade + "\n" +
        "Final Letter Grade is: " + this.finalLetterGrade)
    }
}
```

2. Save your source file as **'EnglishStudent.js'** in the \JavaScriptFiles\Grades folder (select File-Save As from Notepad's Menu Bar). Be sure to save your source file with the file name extension 'js'.

3. You won't be able to test your EnglishStudent class for a while---remember, an Instantiable class cannot be run directly from within your Internet Browser. You'll be creating an EnglishStudent object from this class via the startup Grades.htm program, which you'll modify in Exercise 7-7.

Discussion

No one had any trouble creating the EnglishStudent class, although I did notice a student or two try to open it up directly from within their Internet Browser---something you can't do since the EnglishStudent class is an Instantiable class.

"I noticed that you changed the name of the method calculateEnglishGrade() to calculate()," Dave said, "Is there a reason for that?"

"There's an object oriented programming term called 'polymorphism'," I said, "which means it's OK---even preferable---to have identically named methods in different classes, provided the methods perform the same function. Since each one of our student classes has a method to perform a grade calculation, I thought it made sense to give each one of the methods the same name. Therefore, we'll have a calculate() method in each one of the three student classes."

"Why are we executing the write() method of the document object in the Constructor method," Linda said. "Why is that? Is that really necessary."

"Whenever I'm developing a new application," I said, "I like to place code in the Constructor methods of my classes to display a message to my Internet Browser window. That way, when I run the program, I can see if, and when, my objects are being created. This can sometimes help you understand how your programming is behaving. At any rate, it can't hurt---provided we remember to remove the code from the Constructor methods prior to delivering the final version of the program to Frank Olley."

There were no other questions, and so we moved onto creating the MathStudent class.

Exercise 7-4 Create the MathStudent Instantiable Class

In this exercise, you'll create the MathStudent class for the Grades Calculation project. This class will allow a client program to create an object which will prompt the user for information necessary to calculate the final grade for a Math student.

1. Use Notepad (if you are using Windows) and enter the following code.

```
//MathStudent Class
function MathStudent() {

  this.MATH_MIDTERM_PERCENTAGE = .50
  this.MATH_FINALEXAM_PERCENTAGE = .50
  this.midterm = 0
  this.finalExamGrade = 0
  this.finalNumericGrade = 0
  this.finalLetterGrade = ""

  this.calculate=calculate
  this.displayGrade=displayGrade

  document.write("MathStudent's Constructor")

  function calculate() {
    this.midterm = parseInt(prompt("Enter the Midterm Grade",""))
    this.finalExamGrade = parseInt(prompt("Enter the Final Examination Grade","" ))
    this.finalNumericGrade =
      (this.midterm * this.MATH_MIDTERM_PERCENTAGE) +
      (this.finalExamGrade * this.MATH_FINALEXAM_PERCENTAGE)
    if (this.finalNumericGrade >= 90)
      this.finalLetterGrade = "A"
    else
    if ((this.finalNumericGrade >= 83) & (this.finalNumericGrade < 90))
      this.finalLetterGrade = "B"
    else
    if ((this.finalNumericGrade >= 76) & (this.finalNumericGrade < 83))
      this.finalLetterGrade = "C"
    else
    if ((this.finalNumericGrade >= 65) & (this.finalNumericGrade < 76))
      this.finalLetterGrade = "D"
    else
    if (this.finalNumericGrade < 65)
      this.finalLetterGrade = "F"
  }

  function displayGrade() {
    alert("*** MATH STUDENT ***\n\n" +
```

```
        "Midterm grade is: " + this.midterm + "\n" +
        "Final Exam is: " + this.finalExamGrade + "\n\n" +
        "Final Numeric Grade is: " + this.finalNumericGrade + "\n" +
        "Final Letter Grade is: " + this.finalLetterGrade)
   }
}
```

2. Save your source file as '**MathStudent.js**' in the \JavaScriptFiles\Grades folder (select File-Save As from Notepad's Menu Bar). Be sure to save your source file with the file name extension 'js'.

3. You won't be able to test your MathStudent class for a while---remember, an Instantiable class cannot be run directly from within your Internet Browser. You'll be creating an MathStudent object from this class via the startup Grades.htm program, which you'll modify in Exercise 7-7.

Discussion

Again, there were no major problems in completing the exercise, and to my surprise, absolutely no questions. We then moved onto the next exercise—the creation of the ScienceStudent class.

Exercise 7-5 Create the ScienceStudent Instantiable Class

In this exercise, you'll create the ScienceStudent class for the Grades Calculation project. This class will allow a client program to create an object which will prompt the user for information necessary to calculate the final grade for a Science student.

1. Use Notepad (if you are using Windows) and enter the following code.

```
//ScienceStudent Class

function ScienceStudent() {

  this.SCIENCE_MIDTERM_PERCENTAGE = .40
  this.SCIENCE_FINALEXAM_PERCENTAGE = .40
  this.SCIENCE_RESEARCH_PERCENTAGE = .20
  this.midterm = 0
  this.finalExamGrade = 0
  this.research = 0
  this.finalNumericGrade = 0
  this.finalLetterGrade = ""

  this.calculate=calculate
  this.displayGrade=displayGrade

  document.write("ScienceStudent's Constructor")

  function calculate() {
    this.midterm = parseInt(prompt("Enter the Midterm Grade",""))
    this.finalExamGrade = parseInt(prompt("Enter the Final Examination Grade",""))
    this.research = parseInt(prompt("Enter the Research Grade",""))
    this.finalNumericGrade =
      (this.midterm * this.SCIENCE_MIDTERM_PERCENTAGE) +
      (this.finalExamGrade * this.SCIENCE_FINALEXAM_PERCENTAGE) +
      (this.research * this.SCIENCE_RESEARCH_PERCENTAGE)
    if (this.finalNumericGrade >= 90)
      this.finalLetterGrade = "A"
    else
    if ((this.finalNumericGrade >= 80) & (this.finalNumericGrade < 90))
      this.finalLetterGrade = "B"
    else
    if ((this.finalNumericGrade >= 70) & (this.finalNumericGrade < 80))
      this.finalLetterGrade = "C"
    else
    if ((this.finalNumericGrade >= 60) & (this.finalNumericGrade < 70))
      this.finalLetterGrade = "D"
```

```
    else
    if (this.finalNumericGrade < 60)
      this.finalLetterGrade = "F"
  }
  function displayGrade() {
    alert("*** SCIENCE STUDENT ***\n\n" +
      "Midterm grade is: " + this.midterm + "\n" +
      "Final Exam is: " + this.finalExamGrade + "\n" +
      "Research grade is: " + this.research + "\n\n" +
      "Final Numeric Grade is: " + this.finalNumericGrade + "\n" +
      "Final Letter Grade is: " + this.finalLetterGrade)
  }
}
```

2. Save your source file as **'ScienceStudent.js'** in the \JavaScriptFiles\Grades folder (select File-Save As from Notepad's Menu Bar). Be sure to save your source file with the file name extension 'js'.

3. You won't be able to test your ScienceStudent class for a while---remember, an Instantiable class cannot be run directly from within your Internet Browser. You'll be creating an ScienceStudent object from this class via the startup Grades.htm program, which you'll modify in Exercise 7-7.

Discussion

"These three classes have been very similar," I said. "with just minor differences in the way the final grade is calculated."

"Is it time to modify Grades.htm?" Steve asked?

"Not quite yet Steve," I said. "Remember our first topic in today's class---calling functions from external files?"

"So we're going to take one of the functions out of Grades.htm and place it in a file of its own?" Dave asked.

"That's right Dave," I said.

"I thought we were converting all of the functions in Grades.htm to classes," Mary said.

"All but one of them Mary," I said. "There's one function---the WhatKindOfStudent() function---that doesn't obviously lend itself to the creation of a class. Typically. classes represent 'things', such as an EnglishStudent, an Employee, a Department. WhatKindOfStudent sounds like...well, like a function. For that reason, in the next exercise, you'll create a file called functions.js, and place the WhatKindOfStudent function from Grades.htm in it."

There were no questions, and so I distributed this exercise for the class to complete.

Exercise 7-6 Create the WhatKindOfStudent function

In this exercise, you'll create the functions.js external file---and place the WhatKindOfStudent function in it.

1. Use Notepad (if you are using Windows) and enter the following code.

```
//functions.js
function whatKindOfStudent() {
// What type of student are we calculating?
response = prompt("Enter student type (1=English, 2=Math, 3=Science)","")
if (response == null) {
  alert("You clicked on the Cancel button")
  exit
}

if (response == "") {
  alert("You must make an entry in the Text Box")
  exit
}

if (parseInt(response) < 1 || parseInt( response) > 3) {
  alert(response + " - is not a valid student type")
```

```
    exit
}
return response
} //End of whatKindOfStudent function
```

2. Save your source file as '**functions.js**' in the \JavaScriptFiles\Grades folder (select File-Save As from Notepad's Menu Bar). Be sure to save your source file with the file name extension 'js'.

3. As was the case with the coding of the three Student classes, you won't be able to test your whatKindOfStudent function until we open the modified Grades.htm within Internet Explorer in Exercise 7-7.

Discussion

No one had any problem completing this exercise---at least not to this point. Once again, the results of this exercise wouldn't be obvious until we complete the next exercise.

"As you can see," I said, "all we've done is place the whatKindOfStudent() function in a file called functions.js. If in the future we need to create additional functions for us in our programs, we'll place them here."

Exercise 7-7 Modify the Grades Calculation program to use Instantiable objects

In this exercise, you'll modify the Grades.htm file from last week to create objects from the Instantiable Classes you just created. In addition. Grades.htm will also execute the externally located whatKindOfStudent() function.

1. Using Notepad (if you are using Windows) locate and open the **Grades.htm** source file you worked on last week. (It should be in the \JavaScriptFiles\Grades folder)

2. Modify your code so that it looks like this.

```
<! Grades-- >
<html>
<head>
<script src='EnglishStudent.js'></script>
<script src='MathStudent.js'></script>
<script src='ScienceStudent.js'></script>
<script src='functions.js'></script>
</head>
<body>
<script type="text/javascript">

var response = ""
var moreGradesToCalculate = ""

moreGradesToCalculate = prompt("Do you want to calculate a grade?","Yes")
moreGradesToCalculate = moreGradesToCalculate.toUpperCase()

while (moreGradesToCalculate == "YES") {

  response=whatKindOfStudent()

  // Student type is valid, now let's calculate the grade

  switch(parseInt(response)) {

    // Case 1 is an English Student
    case 1:
      var x = new EnglishStudent()
      x.calculate()
      x.displayGrade()
      break

    // Case 2 is a Math Student
    case 2:
      var y = new MathStudent()
      y.calculate()
      y.displayGrade()
      break
```

```
    // Case 3 is a Science Student
    case 3:
      var z = new ScienceStudent()
      z.calculate()
      z.displayGrade()
      break

    default:
      alert(response + " - is not a valid student type")
  }

  moreGradesToCalculate = prompt("Do you have another grade to calculate?","Yes")
  moreGradesToCalculate = moreGradesToCalculate.toUpperCase()
}

alert("Thanks for using the Grades Calculation program!")

</script>
</body>
</html>
```

3. Use Internet Explorer to Open your Source File.

4. The program should ask you if you have a grade to calculate.

5. Answer 'Yes', and then calculate the grade for an English student. Enter 70 for the midterm, 80 for the final examination, 90 for the research grade and 100 for the presentation. A final numeric grade of 84.5 should be displayed--with a letter grade of 'C'.

6. After the message box is displayed with the calculated grade, the program should ask you if you have more grades to calculate.

7. Answer yes, and then calculate the grade for a Math student. Enter 70 for the midterm and 80 for the final examination. A final numeric grade of 75 should be displayed--with a letter grade of 'D'.

8. After the message box is displayed with the calculated grade, the program should ask you if you have more grades to calculate.

9. Answer yes, and then calculate the grade for a Science student. Enter 70 for the midterm, 80 for the final examination. and 90 for the research grade. A final numeric grade of 78 should be displayed--with a letter grade of 'C'. After the message box is displayed with the calculate grade, the program should ask you if you have more grades to calculate.

10. Answer no--you should be thanked for using the program, and then the program should end.

Discussion

Changing the Grades Class to use Instantiable objects was pretty tedious---it took most of my students about 15 minutes to complete the exercise. Despite that, there were no major problems, and I think most everyone understood what was going on.

"In the final analysis," Ward said, "we took a bunch of the code from the Grades.htm file, and placed it in the EnglishStudent, MathStudent, ScienceStudent classes, and the whatKindOfStudent functions. Is that right? Grades.htm really has very little code in it now."

"That's right Ward," I said, "The number of lines of code in the Grades.htm file itself has been drastically reduced--moved into one of three classes or the external function file. What that means is that the code is easier to read, understand and maintain."

"How so?" Rhonda asked.

"Let me ask you this question," I said. "If Frank Olley walked into our classroom right now, and told you that the calculation of the final grade for an English Student needs to be changed, can you tell where we would need to change?"

"That's easy," Dave said. "That code is in the EnglishStudent class--in fact, it's in the calculate() method of the EnglishStudent class."

"I couldn't have said it better myself Dave," I said. "Anything related to the English Student now resides in a single file---the EnglishStudent class."

I waited a moment before beginning the discussion of the code.

"Crucial to Grades.htm being able to find our function and classes," I said, "is to include a reference to them in the <head> section of our program..."

```
<head>
<script src='EnglishStudent.js'></script>
<script src='MathStudent.js'></script>
<script src='ScienceStudent.js'></script>
<script src='functions.js'></script>
</head>
```

"If we had wanted to," I said, "we could have included all of our classes in the same file---actually, we could have included all of our classes and function in the same file--but I prefer to keep them separate. Notice how we still execute the whatKindOfStudent() function, but the code for the function is no longer in Grades.htm..."

```
response=whatKindOfStudent()
```

Can you review the code that instantiates the various student objects?" Barbara said.

"Sure thing Barbara," I said, "here it is…"

```
switch(parseInt(response)) {
    // Case 1 is an English Student
    case 1:
      var x = new EnglishStudent()
      x.calculate()
      x.displayGrade()
      break

    // Case 2 is a Math Student
    case 2:
      var y = new MathStudent()
      y.calculate()
      y.displayGrade()
      break

    // Case 3 is a Science Student
    case 3:
      var z = new ScienceStudent()
      z.calculate()
      z.displayGrade()
      break
```

"All of the code necessary to instantiate the EnglishStudent, MathStudent, or ScienceStudent objects is contained within this Switch structure. The test condition for the Switch structure is the user's response of 1, 2 or 3 in an InputBox. If the user's response is 1, we declare an instance of the EnglishStudent object, using the object variable x. We could probably have chosen a more descriptive variable name, but x is fine for now.."

```
var x = new EnglishStudent()
```

"…we then execute the calculate() method of the EnglishStudent object using this code…"

```
x.calculate()
```

"…followed by the execution of the DisplayGrade() method...."

```
x.displayGrade()
```

"In the same way, if the user's response is 2, we execute the code necessary to create an instance of the MathStudent object, execute its calculate() method, followed by its displayGrade() method..."

```
    // Case 2 is a Math Student
    case 2:
      var y = new MathStudent()
      y.calculate()
      y.displayGrade()
      break
```

"Lastly," I said, "the code for the Science Student..."

```
// Case 3 is a Science Student
case 3:
  var z = new ScienceStudent()
  z.calculate()
  z.displayGrade()
  break
```

I waited to see if anyone had any questions, but there were none.

"This class has been a very productive one," I said, "in that we learned how to code classes, and create objects from them which gives us access to the object's data and behavior. Next week we'll learn that sometimes in our haste to give a client program access to an object's data, we permit too much access--which can have some pretty nasty effects on the data integrity of our objects. We'll learn how to correct that problem next week."

With that, I dismissed the class for the day.

Summary

In this chapter, we learned how we can create Classes—that is, classes from which objects can be created. These objects can have attributes, which are implemented via instance and Class Variables within the class, and behavior, which is implemented via class methods or functions. Classes cannot be executed directly like a JavaScript program---their objects must be created from within another JavaScript program. Objects are created using the New keyword.

Classes have a special type of methods. The Constructor method is a method with the same name as the class, and its code is guaranteed to execute when an object of the class is first created.

Chapter 8---Controlling Access To The Data In Your Object

In Chapter 7, we learned how to create Instantiable classes, which are classes from which other objects can be created. These objects are just like the standard JavaScript objects, such as the document object, that we've been working with all along. Instantiable objects possess characteristics or attributes, which are created via Instance and Class variables. An Instantiable object's attributes can be read or updated by the JavaScript client program that creates the object. Instantiable objects also possess certain types of behavior, which are created via methods. An Instantiable object's methods can be executed by the JavaScript class (program) that creates it.

In this Chapter, we'll learn that while it's great that the JavaScript program that creates an Instantiable object can access and update the object's Instance and Class variables, it's not always desirable for these variables to be directly updateable by the client program. The same can be said of client programs that execute the object's methods. There may be cases where some methods of the Instantiable class need to be 'hidden' from the client program. We'll learn that there are ways to deal with these potential problems.

Controlling Access to your Object's data

"Last week," I said, as I began our eighth class, "we learned how to create Instantiable classes, which are classes from which objects can be created. We learned how we can design an Instantiable class to model a real-world object, complete with characteristics or attributes, and behaviors. When an object is created from an Instantiable class, the JavaScript class creating the object can read and update the object's attributes, and trigger its behavior by executing its methods. In today's class, we'll continue studying Instantiable Class creation which we began last week."

"I wouldn't have thought there was a lot more to cover with Instantiable Classes," Mary said, "I thought we were pretty much done with this topic last week."

"In terms of Instantiable classes," I said, "what we've done so far has been fine--but in today's class, we'll learn that the Instantiable Classes we created last week, while fully functional, may have some potential data problems."

"Data problems?" Rhonda asked. "That sounds serious. Do you mean that there are problems with the classes we created last week?"

"There's no need to be alarmed Rhonda," I said. "In terms of the mechanics of creating Instantiable Classes, everything we did last week was just fine. But in our excitement with learning how to use a JavaScript class to model an object, its attributes and its behavior, we didn't consider, in the least, whether the data in the object needs to be protected, and if so, how to protect it?"

"Protecting the data?" Peter asked. "I'm afraid I don't understand. From whom do we need to protect data?"

"That's a great question Peter," I said. "It may be difficult for you to fathom right now, but the JavaScript programs you will later write, particularly if you are writing programs to run in a commercial environment, have potential for 'exposing' data that is sensitive."

"Such as?" Ward asked.

"In a *Customer* object, sensitive data would be customer account numbers and social security numbers," I said. "In an *Employee* object, sensitive data would be employee salary information or employee performance appraisals. These are all examples of data that, if the designer of the Instantiable class is not careful, can wind up in the hands of the wrong person. It seems that nearly every week there's a story in the newspaper about sensitive data finding its way into the wrong hands. This is something we need to consider when we design our Instantiable classes."

"How do we do that?" Blaine asked. "Can you give us an example?"

"Sure thing Blaine," I said. "Every class we've created so far in the course has had all of its variables be accessible by client programs---as well as all of its methods. To illustrate, let's take a look at the code that we wrote last week to implement the attributes of the EnglishStudent Class..."

```
this.ENGLISH_MIDTERM_PERCENTAGE = .25
this.ENGLISH_FINALEXAM_PERCENTAGE = .25
this.ENGLISH_RESEARCH_PERCENTAGE = .30
this.ENGLISH_PRESENTATION_PERCENTAGE = .20
this.midterm = 0
this.finalExamGrade = 0
```

```
this.research = 0
this.presentation = 0
this.finalNumericGrade = 0
this.finalLetterGrade = ""
```

"Because of the word 'this'," Rhonda said, "all of these variables are Instance Variables. Is that right?"

"That's my point exactly Rhonda," I said, "When we created the EnglishStudent class last week, each one of the variables within the class was declared in such a way that any client program can read and update them. In JavaScript, Instance Variables declared with the keyword 'this' are called Public Instance Variables."

> **Note: In JavaScript, Instance Variables declared with the keyword 'this' are called Public Instance Variables.**

"Is that a problem?" Steve asked. "Don't we want the program that creates our object to be able to work directly with the object's attributes and methods?"

"Certainly the methods Steve," I said, "but perhaps not all of the attributes. For instance, is it 'OK' if our client program directly updates the *midterm* attribute of the EnglishStudent class, like this?"

```
<! Example8-1 -->
<html>
<head>
<script src='EnglishStudent.js'></script>
</head>
<body>
<script type="text/javascript">

var x = new EnglishStudent()
x.midterm = 99

</script>
</body>
</html>
```

I could see Steve (and the other students) pondering this.

"Now we're starting to get into dangerous territory," I said. "Allowing a program to create an object, and then update the component pieces of the English student's final grade is fine, but by design, only the calculate() method of the EnglishStudent object should determine the final numeric grade. To allow a programmer to directly update the finalNumericGrade or finalLetterGrade of the EnglishStudent object is to invite problems."

"Like what?" Rhonda asked.

"The only way that a final grade should be calculated," I said, "is via the code that the designer of the object wrote. Do you see that by permitting the user of the object to directly update the *finalNumericGrade* or *finalLetterGrade* attributes, we've allowed him or her to 'bypass' the correct calculation. This can lead to results that are incorrect at best, and fraudulent at worst."

"In other words," Dave said, "a programmer could update the final grade for a student by bypassing the code in the calculate() method of the EnglishStudent object."

"That's right Dave," I said. "and it's something that has happened. For instance, suppose an unscrupulous programmer decides to alter the formula for the calculation of the English Student grade, by changing the value of the ENGLISH_MIDTERM_PERCENTAGE from 25% to 90% for a friend who stopped attending class halfway through the course?"

```
<! Example8-2 -->
<html>
<head>
<script src='EnglishStudent.js'></script>
</head>
<body>
<script type="text/javascript">
```

```
var x = new EnglishStudent()
x.ENGLISH_MIDTERM_PERCENTAGE = .90
x.calculate()
x.displayGrade()

</script>
</body>
</html>
```

"Watch what happens now," I said, as I saved the program as '**Example8-2.htm**' opened it within Internet Explorer, entered 100 for the Midterm grade, 0 for the Final Exam, 0 for Research and 0 for Presentation.

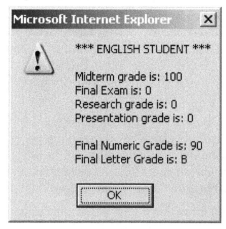

"As you can see," I said, "despite these lackluster grade components, the unscrupulous programmer's friend still achieved a final numeric grade of 90, and a letter grade of 'B'."

"That's amazing," I heard Rhonda say, "he was really able to subvert the correct calculation."

"I see your point," Dave said, "the *ENGLISH_MIDTERM_PERCENTAGE* Instance Variable is really not intended to be updated in this manner---the results can be catastrophic."

"That's right Dave," I said, "in fact, if JavaScript supported it, we would have defined *ENGLISH_MIDTERM_PERCENTAGE* as a Constant, a memory placeholder like a variable, but one that can't be changed from its initial value. As it is, we've made a design mistake in permitting the client program to update this variable. As I said before, fraudulent activity like this is the worst case scenario. But even if the programmer doesn't intend to do something dishonest like this, allowing the programmer to directly work with an attribute that can only be updated properly by complex code is a big mistake. Remember, one of the great things about objects, is that they allow the developer of the object to shield the complexities of a task from the programmer who needs to use the object. In the real-world of programming, programmers work with objects like this all the time--and the objects are many times more complex than that of an English Student calculation at a university. Programmers are developing object oriented programs today to monitor switches in a nuclear power plant or values on the Space Shuttle just before launch. Can you imagine what the dire affects might be if the designer of one of those objects accidentally permitted the programmer using the object to directly update one of the object's attributes?"

"I think I get the point," Valerie said, "certain attributes of an object should NOT be updateable by the programmer using the object."

"That's right Valerie," I said, "and some attributes are best not seen as well. My point is that access to an object's attributes and methods is something the designer of the class needs to give careful thought before distributing the class for use by other programmers."

I waited a moment before continuing.

"I'm not sure that there is a consensus among class designers," I said, "but I think it's safe to say that some attributes, but not all, can be directly accessible by the program creating the object, and therefore should be designated with the keyword 'this' prefix. Other attributes can be visible to the program creating the object, but should not be directly updateable by it. Other attributes should be invisible to certain users of the program creating the object, and still others should be totally invisible to the program creating the object--accessible only by code within methods of the object itself. These attributes should be declared as variables without the keyword 'this.'"

"Can you give us an example of each one of these categories?" Kate asked. "I'm afraid I'm still not getting it?"

"Let's imagine," I said, "that a programmer at XYZ University designs a Student class to model the university's real-world Student, and that the Student Class has this list of attributes…"

```
function Student() {

this.studentID = ""
this.name = ""
this.address = ""
this.age = 0
this.SSN = ""
this.GPA = 0
```

"…SSN is the student's Social Security Number and GPA is the student's Grade Point Average. Let's further suppose that the designer of the Student class coded the Constructor method so that when a Student Object is created, the value of the studentID attribute is used to locate student information in a database record, and to assign values to the rest of the Student Class attributes. Finally, let's suppose that another programmer at the University finds the Student Class, and decides to use it in a program she is writing which is designed to permit a work-study student to update student address and age information."

"I see some potential problems with this Student Class right away?" Dave said. "Because we used the keyword 'this' in the declaration statement for the Instance attributes, each one of them is a Public Instance Variable and can be accessed and updated by the client program using them. That means there's nothing stopping that program from creating a Student object whose Constructor method then retrieves the student information from a database record and exposes private information about the student--such as Social Security Number and Grade Point Average."

"I see what Dave is saying," Steve added. "From the scenario you've described, I think that the client program using the Student object should have full access--by that I mean read and update--to just two attributes, the *address* and *age* attributes. Furthermore, I would suggest read-only access to the studentID and name attributes--we don't want either of those attributes being changed by accident. Finally, I would suggest that both SSN and GPA should be totally invisible to the user of the Student object--at least in this particular case."

"I agree with both Dave and Steve," Rhonda said. "But how can we do all of that in JavaScript--hide some attributes and make others 'invisible'?"

"We can do that Rhonda," I said. "By declaring an Instance attribute *without* the keyword 'this' we create a Private Instance Variable. By doing so, we can prevent the client program from being able to access the attribute at all, and in a moment, you'll see that we can also use special methods to selectively restrict what the client program using our object can do with the data inside of it. Before we do that, let's create a Student class with the attributes I just listed, and create a method called display() to display its data."

"Will we be accessing data in a database today?" Rhonda asked excitedly.

"No Rhonda," I said, "working with data from a database within JavaScript is beyond the scope of this introductory course. Instead of 'looking' up the student's information in a database record, we'll simulate its lookup by assigning a set of default values to the object's attributes via its Constructor method."

I then displayed the code for the Student class on the classroom projector…

```
//Student Class
function Student() {

this.studentID = ""
this.name = ""
this.address = ""
this.age = 0
this.SSN = ""
this.GPA = 0

this.display=display

this.studentID = "123"
this.name = "Mary Smith"
this.address = "22 Twain Drive"
this.age = 22
```

```
this.SSN = "111-22-3333"
this.GPA = 2.01

function display() {
  alert("*** STUDENT RECORD ***\n\n" +
    "StudentID: " + this.studentID + "\n" +
    "Name: " + this.name + "\n" +
    "Address: " + this.address + "\n" +
    "Age: " + this.age + "\n\n" +
    "SSN: " + this.SSN + "\n" +
    "GPA: " + this.GPA)
}

}
```

"Here's the Student Class," I said, "As you can see, the Student Class contains the six attributes we discussed. Notice that all six Instance Variables are Public Instance Variables---declared using the 'this' prefix. This means that a client program has access to these Instance Variables. Notice also that the Student class has two methods--the Constructor Method, in which we placed code to assign a set of default values to each one of the six attributes of the class so that we can experiment a bit with Student Objects created from the class. As I mentioned earlier, ordinarily we would obtain this information from a data source such as a database, but that's beyond the scope of this introductory course, so we'll just 'pretend' to do so via the Constructor method. The second method is the display() method which displays the values of the attributes in a JavaScript message box. Now let's create a client program, and write the code necessary to instantiate a Student object from this class…"

```
<! Example8-3 -->
<html>
<head>
<script src='Student.js'></script>
</head>
<body>
<script type="text/javascript">

var x = new Student()
x.display()

</script>
</body>
</html>
```

I then saved the program as '**Example8-3.htm**'and opened it within Internet Explorer. The following screenshot was displayed on the classroom projector.

"Can anyone tell me what this code did?" I asked.

"What we've done here," Chuck said, "is to create a Student object, initialize the values of all six attributes via its Constructor method, and then display those values in a message box via the Object's display() method."

"That's excellent Chuck," I said. "Any other comments about the program?

"Right now," Dave said, "the data in this class is very much 'unprotected'. The user of the Student object is able to access every Instance attribute of the Student class."

"Absolutely right Dave," I said, "We had previously agreed that we didn't want a client program to have access to the student's Social Security Number or Grade Point Average--and both of these values are now prominently displayed in the message box. Worse yet, the user of this Student object can directly update both of those attributes--- something we also said we didn't want to happen. Let's see how easy it is to change that Grade Point Average for Mary Smith…"

I then displayed this modified code on the classroom projector…

```
<! Example8-4 -->
<html>
<head>
<script src='Student.js'></script>
</head>
<body>
<script type="text/javascript">

var x = new Student()
x.GPA = 4.0
x.display()

</script>
</body>
</html>
```

I then saved the program as '**Example8-4.htm**' and opened it within Internet Explorer. The following screenshot was displayed on the classroom projector.

"Wow," Kate said, "we've really done that Mary Smith a favor---her Grade Point Average went from 2.01 to 4.0. I see what you mean by allowing the client program full access to the *gpa* attribute of the Student Class."

"I had totally forgotten we could update these attributes directly using Object Dot Notation," Ward said, "but as you indicated, by declaring the Instance Variables as Public, we've enabled full access to the Instance Variables in the Student Class."

"So what's our alternative again?, Mary asked.

"The alternative Mary," I answered, "is to declare our Instance Variables as Private---without the keyword 'this'."

"What will we use instead?" Kate asked.

"We'll declare them like we would an ordinary variable," I said, "by using the keyword 'var'."

I waited for a moment before continuing.

"Again," I said, "that will make the Instance Variables Private to the class. Private access means that the Instance Variable can be used only by code located within the same class as the Instance Variable."

I gave everyone a chance to ponder that statement for a moment.

"That seems pretty worthless, doesn't it?" Mary said. "What's the use of having an attribute if it can't be seen or updated from outside the Instantiable class."

"We'll see in a moment," I said, "how this technique is the perfect way to 'protect' data within our object. What we do is to declare the Instance Variables Private--but provide Public methods to access and modify them. Right now, I'd like to show you what happens if we define our Instance Variables as Private by using the keyword 'var'..."

I then modified the code in the Student Class to look like this...

```
//Student Class

function Student() {

var studentID = ""
var name = ""
var address = ""
var age = 0
var SSN = ""
var GPA = 0

this.display=display

studentID = "123"
name = "Mary Smith"
address = "22 Twain Drive"
age = 22
SSN = "111-22-3333"
GPA = 2.01

function display() {
  alert("*** STUDENT RECORD ***\n\n" +
    "StudentID: " + studentID + "\n" +
    "Name: " + name + "\n" +
    "Address: " + address + "\n" +
    "Age: " + age + "\n\n" +
    "SSN: " + SSN + "\n" +
    "GPA: " + GPA)
}

}
```

"By declaring our Instance Variables as Private," I said, "we're now preventing the code from the Example8-4 program from being able to access these Instance Variables. Look at what happens when we re-run program Example8-4..."

I then opened **Example8-4.htm** within Internet Explorer. The following screenshot was displayed on the classroom projector.

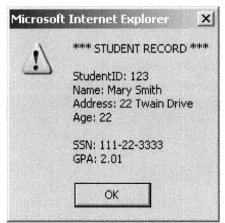

"What happened?" I heard Rhonda say. "Mary Smith's GPA hasn't changed. It's still 2.01."

"Exactly Rhonda," I answered. "Although our code told JavaScript to update the *gpa* Instance Variable to 4.0, since that Instance Variable was declared as Private in the Student class, JavaScript couldn't perform the update--as a result, the display() method of the Student class displayed the initial value of the gpa Instance Variable as set by the Constructor method."

"Interesting," Dave said. "No error message? I think in Java, an attempt to work with a Private Instance Variable would generate a compiler error."

"You're right about the compiler error in Java Dave," I said, "but as you've probably noted with our experience in JavaScript so far, it's not a language that produces a lot of error messages. Here, in essence, JavaScript basically ignored our request to update a Private Instance Variable."

"I see that Private Access means we can't update the value of an Instance Variable," Rhonda said, "but does it also mean we can't 'see' their values as well?"

"That's right Rhonda," I said, "we can neither directly see nor update Private Instance Variables. However, and this is where the 'trick' comes in, we can *indirectly* see and update them, provided that a Public method of the Student Class is written to enable us to do that. For instance, the display() method of the Student class is a Public method that permits us to 'see' the Private Instance Variables."

"I see what you mean," Mary said. "Even though the Instance Variables of the Student Class are now declared as Private, the Public display() method allows us to 'see' the values of the Student Class's Instance Variables."

"That's right Mary," I said.

"But suppose," Mary continued "we want to be able to update the Instance Variables as well as see them?"

"Then we need to write a Public method to permit that as well," I said. "The point is that instead of allowing a client program to directly view or update an Instance Variable, we write a Public method that permits viewing or updating. You'll see the benefits of doing so in just a few minutes."

Instance Variables--Public or Private?

"Should all of our Instance Variables be declared as Private" Linda asked.

"That's a good question Linda," I said. "In the JavaScript world, it's considered best to create Private Instance Variables, and many programmers follow this guideline, declaring all of their Instance Variables as Private, and writing Public methods to provide access to the Private Instance Variables and their values. On the other hand, you will find programmers who declare all of their Instance Variables as Public. You'll also find programmers who pick and choose--declaring some Instance Variables as Public and some as Private, depending upon the particular attribute of an object the Instance Variable represents."

"What's your recommendation?" Steve asked.

"My recommendation," I said, "is to declare your Instance Variables as Private, and write Public methods to access them. You'll find the same recommendation from most experienced JavaScript programmers, although certainly you will find experienced programmers declaring Public Instance Variables at times. The bottom line is that the JavaScript language allows you to create Public Instance Variables--if you choose to do so, that's up to you. However, it may be something that a prospective employer frowns upon, since Public Instance Variables can cause data integrity problems, the type we just saw with the Student Class example."

"I'm still having problems with this concept of Private Instance Variables and Public methods," Chuck said. "In the Student Class we just wrote, is the display() method the type of Public method you are talking about?"

"Good question Chuck," I said. "Any function declared using the 'this' keyword is a Public method. However, typically, the Public methods I'm referring to are specially named methods called get() and set() methods. Get() methods are Public methods that permit a client program to 'get' or retrieve the value of a Private Instance Variable. Set() methods are Public methods that permit a client program to 'set' or update the value of a Private Instance Variable."

"So we should code a pair of Get() and Set() Public methods for each Instance Variable?" Linda asked.

"If you declare your Instance Variables as Private," I said, "in order to provide both read and update ability to your client program, you will need a Get() and Set() Public method for each one. Without them, there's no way that the client program can access the Object's attribute represented by that Instance Variable. As you'll see in a minute, you can place code in the Get() method to determine if the client program requesting the value of the Private Instance

Variable really should have it, and code in the Set() method to determine if the client program attempting to update the value of the Private Instance Variable should be able to do so."

"That would come in very handy with the *SSN* and *GPA* attributes of the Student Class," Mary said.

"Absolutely," I said. "The Set() method is a great place to place code to verify if the client program has the authority to update the Private Instance Variable. Code in the Set() method can also be used to perform validation on the proposed update before the Instance Variable is actually changed, and the Object set to an Invalid state."

"Validation code?" Rhonda asked. "Invalid state? What do you mean?"

"The 'State' of an object are the values of the data that represent the object," I said. "An object must always maintain its data in a valid state. In Example8_4, although we saw how a client program can inappropriately change the value of the GPA Instance Variable, still, the value of GPA was set to a value that is consistent with a Grade Point Average. With a Public Instance Variable, it's easy for a client program to make a mistake and cause the object's state to become invalid like this…"

```
<! Example8-5 -->
<html>
<head>
<script src='Student.js'></script>
</head>
<body>
<script type="text/javascript">

var x = new Student()
x.age = -6 // OOPS! Negative Age?

</script>
</body>
</html>
```

Using Set and Get Statements

"Does anyone see a problem here?" I asked.

"I do," Rhonda called out. "You've assigned a negative number to the Student Object's age attribute. I'm sure you didn't mean to do that. Is that what you mean by Invalid State."

"You're absolutely right Rhonda," I said, "I didn't intend to do that, but if the age Instance Variable is declared with Public Access, there's absolutely no way to prevent this. And now the Student Object does have an Invalid state---one of its attributes makes no sense. The Student's age cannot be negative."

"A Set method could prevent this from happening?" Lou asked.

"That's right Lou," I said. "Using a Set Method---also called a Mutator method, we can alert the user if the update they've attempted to make to a Private Instance Variable is invalid. By the way, Get Methods, which permit the retrieval of the value of a Private Instance Variable, are also called Accessor methods. Take a look at this code…"

I then modified the code in the Student class to look like this…

```
//Student Class
function Student() {

var studentID = ""
var name = ""
var address = ""
var age = 0
var SSN = ""
var GPA = 0

this.display=display
this.setAddress=setAddress
this.getAddress=getAddress
this.setAge=setAge
this.getAge=getAge
```

```
studentID = "123"
name = "Mary Smith"
address = "22 Twain Drive"
age = 22
SSN = "111-22-3333"
GPA = 2.01
function setAddress(temp) {
  address = temp
}
function getAddress() {
  return address
}
function setAge(temp) {
  if (parseInt(temp) < 1) {
    alert("Invalid Age: " + temp + " Program Terminating")
    exit
  }
else
  age = temp
}
function getAge() {
  return age
}


function display() {
  alert("*** STUDENT RECORD ***\n\n" +
    "StudentID: " + studentID + "\n" +
    "Name: " + name + "\n" +
    "Address: " + address + "\n" +
    "Age: " + age)
}
}
```

"What we've done here," I said, "is to declare a Get() and Set() method for two of our Instance Variables---*address* and *age.*"

"Are those the Accessor and Mutator methods you mentioned?" Valerie asked.

"That's right Valerie," I answered. "Get() methods are also called Accessor methods, and permit the client program to retrieve the value of a Private Instance Variable. Set() methods are also called Mutator methods, and permit the client program to update the value of a Private Instance Variable."

"Is there anything magical about the name of the Get and Set methods?" Ward asked. "Could we name them anything we want."

"Great question Ward," I said, "Yes--you can name them anything you want--although by convention, methods designed to return the value of a Private Instance Variable begin with the word 'get', followed by the name of the Instance Variable. Methods desired to update a Private Instance Variable begin with the word 'set', followed by the name of the Instance Variable."

"Why didn't we create Accessor and Mutator methods for all of the Private Instance Variables?" Kate asked.

"Didn't you say that was your recommendation."

"Not quite Kate," I replied. "My recommendation is to create Private Instance Variables for every attribute of the object, but to create Accessor and Mutator methods only where necessary. Since we are not interested in providing our client program with direct access to the Student Object's other four attributes, it makes no sense to write Accessor or Mutator methods for those Instance Variables---this way, there's no way the our client program can view them or update them."

"Except through the Public display() method," Dave said, "and I notice that you've modified that method--it no longer displays the SSN or GPA Instance Variables."

"That's right Dave," I said. "Does everyone see the benefits of declaring our Instance Variables as Private?"

"I think I do," Linda said, "but isn't providing Accessor and Mutator methods the same as making the Instance Variable Public in the first place?"

"That's the argument that some programmers make," I said, "but that's only true if no validation is being performed in the Accessor or Mutator methods. You have to remember that when a direct retrieval or update is made to a Public Instance Variable by a client program, there's nothing that the Object can do to stop it. Accessor and Mutator methods, on the other hand, are much 'smarter'. For instance, code in an Accessor method can determine the identity of the user of the client program, and make a decision as to whether he or she can see the data. Code in a Mutator method can be written to validate the proposed update BEFORE it occurs."

"I'm convinced," Linda said. "Can we take a closer look at the Accessor and Mutator methods before we test this code."

"Sure thing Linda," I said, "Let's take a look at the Mutator methods first. Remember, we created Mutator methods only for the age and address Private Instance Variables."

"That means that the other four Private Instance Variables can't be updated?" Linda asked.

"That's right," I said, "if we declare an Instance Variable as Private, without a Mutator method or some other Public method that updates it, the Instance Variable is 'shut off' from the client program."

"So it's up to the designer of the object to decide if an Accessor or Mutator method will be written for each Private Instance Variable?" Joe asked.

"Exactly," I answered. "If no access to the Private Instance Variable is required, then neither an Accessor or Mutator method will be written. If the Private Instance Variable's value can be seen but not updated, then only an Accessor method will be written."

Mutator Methods

"Where's the Mutator method for the address attribute?" Blaine asked. "Is that the setAddress() method?"

"That's right Blaine," I said, as I displayed it on the classroom projector. "Mutator methods by convention begin with the prefix 'set'."

```
function setAddress(temp) {
  address = temp
}
```

"Is there anything 'special about a Mutator method?" Barbara asked. "*setAddress* looks like an ordinary method to me."

"Barbara's right," I said, "Mutator methods are just ordinary methods, with code that permits the user of the object to update the value of a Private Instance Variable. This is accomplish by the client program passing the proposed updated value of the Private Instance Variable as an argument to the Mutator method. Notice that setAddress() is declared to accept a single argument called 'temp'---this argument, when passed to the method, is then assigned to the Private Instance Variable called address."

"So that's how it works," Rhonda said. "The address Instance Variable is declared Private, but even so, code within the class itself has full access to it."

"You have the idea now Rhonda," I said. "Notice that there was no validation code in the setAddress() method--- however, the Mutator method for the age attribute is a bit more complicated..."

```
function setAge(temp) {
  if (parseInt(temp) < 1) {
    alert("Invalid Age: " + temp + " Program Terminating")
    exit
  }
else
  age = temp
}
```

"….as was the case with the *setAddress()* Mutator method, *setAge()* also accepts a single argument, although this one will be an Integer, using an If statement, to handle the negative number that we 'accidentally' assigned to the age attribute in Example 8-5. We've seen how the parseInt() method works---it will take the value of the passed argument, and 'convert' it to an Integer which then can be compared to the number one. If the value of the passed argument is less than one, we display a message to the user, and execute the exit statement, otherwise we assign the value of the passed argument to the Private Instance Variable called *age.*"

"What's the impact of executing the exit statement within the Mutator method?" Dave asked.

"Will it end the program--or just destroy the Student object?"

"Executing the exit method of the System object ends the entire program," I said.

"Is there a more elegant way of handling the error than that?" Linda asked.

"Yes there is," I said, "we could have defined the Mutator method to return a value to the client program."

"So Mutator methods cam return a value?" Bob asked.

"Mutator methods can return a value just like any other method," I said. "In the case of setAge(), we could have chosen to return a value to the client program indicating the success or failure of the update. Traditionally, a return value of 0 indicates success, and some other value, such as -1, indicates failure."

Everyone seemed anxious to see the Mutator method of the Student class in action--but first, we needed to examine the Accessor methods of the Student Class.

Accessor Methods

"Let's take a look at the two Accessor methods we created, getAddress() and getAge(). As you can see, by convention, Accessor methods are named beginning with the prefix 'get'. Accessor methods return the value of the Private Instance Variable as a return value to the client program that calls them. Here's the getAddress() Accessor method…"

```
function getAddress() {
    return address
}
```

"…and here's the getAge() Accessor method…"

```
function getAge() {
    return age
}
```

"We had no reason to do so," I continued, "but it's within the Accessor method that we can write code to determine if the client program should have access to the value of the Private Instance Variable. One way to do so would be to require the client program to supply, as an argument, a password."
I waited to see if there were any questions, but there were none.

"I'm anxious to see how the Mutator and Accessor methods work," Rhonda said.

"Rhonda's right," I said, "it's time to test the Accessor and Mutator methods of the Student Class. Let's see if we can assign a negative value to the age attribute of the Student object…"

Don't Forget: If typing these examples and exercises isn't something you want to do, feel free to follow this link to find and download the completed solutions for all of the examples and exercises in the book. Just click on the JavaScript book, then follow the link entitled exercises ☺

http://www.johnsmiley.com/main/books.htm

I then displayed this code on the classroom projector…

```
<! Example8-6 -->
<html>
<head>
<script src='Student.js'></script>
</head>
<body>
<script type="text/javascript">
```

```
var x = new Student()
x.setAddress("222 Elm Street")
x.setAge(-6)
x.display()

</script>
</body>
</html>
```

"Here's code that creates an instance of a Student object," I said, "and then uses the Mutator methods setAddress() and setAge() to update the Private Instance Variables of address and age. Notice how we're passing values for both via arguments to the respective Mutators."

"I was about to say," Kate said, "that there is no assignment statement in the code---I forgot that we no longer assign a value directly to an Instance Variable--instead we pass a value as an argument to the Mutator method."

"Does everyone notice that I've made the mistake that I made earlier," I continued, "by 'accidentally' passing a negative number as an argument to the setAge() Mutator method. Let's see if the Mutator catches it..."

I then saved the program as '**Example8-6.htm**' and opened it within Internet Explorer. The following screenshot was displayed on the classroom projector.

"Impressive," I heard Steve say. "Looks like the Mutator method really worked."

I then clicked on the OK button, and the program ended.

"The *setAge()* Mutator detected a value less than 1," I said, "and displayed the message box. When I clicked on the OK button, the program then ended. Now let's see how the program behaves if we pass it a good value for the age attribute..."

I then displayed this code on the classroom projector...

```
<! Example8-7 -->
<html>
<head>
<script src='Student.js'></script>
</head>
<body>
<script type="text/javascript">

var x = new Student()
x.setAddress("222 Elm Street")
x.setAge(46)
x.display()

</script>
</body>
</html>
```

I then saved the program as '**Example8-7.htm**' and opened it within Internet Explorer. The following screenshot was displayed on the classroom projector.

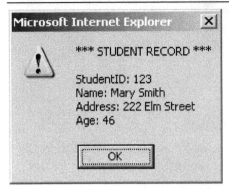

"Does everyone see how the two Mutator methods have allowed us to update the Private Instance Variables address and age?" I asked.

"I'm fine with that," Linda said, "but we haven't used the Accessor methods, have we? We used the Public display() method of the Student object to display the values for the address and age Instance Variables. Can we see how the Accessor methods in action?"

"That's a good point Linda," I said. "Let's do that."

I then displayed this code on the classroom projector.

```
<! Example8-8 -->
<html>
<head>
<script src='Student.js'></script>
</head>
<body>
<script type="text/javascript">

var x = new Student()
x.setAddress("222 Elm Street")
x.setAge(46)

document.write("The value of age is: " + x.getAge() + <br>")
document.write("The value of address is: " + x.getAddress() + <br>")

</script>
</body>
</html>
```

"Where are the Accessor methods for age?" Rhonda asked. "I'm not seeing them."

"They're in these two lines of code," I said. "You may have missed them because their return values are being used as an argument to the write() method of the Document object..."

```
document.write("The value of age is: " + x.getAge() + <br>")
document.write("The value of address is: " + x.getAddress() + <br>")
```

I then saved the program as '**Example8-8.htm**' and opened it within Internet Explorer. The following screenshot was displayed on the classroom projector.

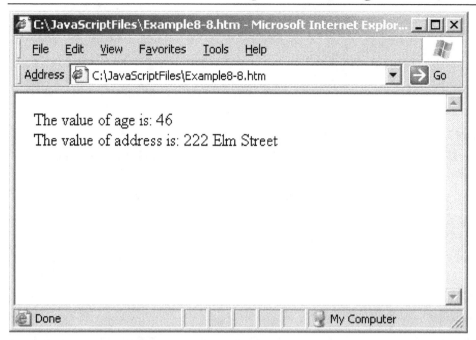

"I see," Rhonda said. "The Accessor methods worked great!"

We had been working for some time, and so I suggested we take a break prior to examining the Grades Calculation project for data integrity issues. While my class was out of the room, I placed a quick phone call to coordinate a visit with a special guest.

Let's analyze the Grades Calculation project for Data Integrity

Fifteen minutes later I resumed class by explaining that it was now time to examine the Grades Calculation project for data integrity concerns, the type that we had been studying all morning.

"Does anyone see any Data Integrity problems with the Grades Calculation project?" I asked. "Don't forget, you'll need to examine all of the classes in the project."

I gave everyone a few minutes to find and load up their own versions of the Grades Calculation project on their PC's.

"The first thing that strikes me as being suspect, at least based on what we learned this morning," Dave said, "is that the Instance Variables in the EnglishStudent, MathStudent and ScienceStudent classes are defined as Public. That means that a client program can, in theory, directly access those Instance Variables."

"Absolutely correct," I replied. "That's definitely something that we'll need to correct."

"Does that mean that we'll need to write Accessor and Mutator methods for each of the Instance Variables?" Joe asked.

"Not necessarily," I replied. "Right now, the display() method is used to display the values of the Instance Variables for the Student Object. For that reason, we could choose *NOT* to create an Accessor method for each one. It all depends upon whether we believe there will *ever* be a need for a client program to directly read the value of any of the various student object Instance Variables."

"What about Mutator methods?" Dave asked. "Do we need to code one of those for each Instance Variable in each of the various Student classes? If I remember correctly, the values for these Instance Variables are assigned when each class's calculate() method is executed. Does the fact that no client program needs to directly update the Instance Variables eliminate the need to code a Mutator method."

"Ultimately," I said, "the values for these Instance Variables are coming from the user of the program. In cases like that, I like to code a Mutator method."

"That's right," Linda said, "the Mutator method will be a great place to put the validation code we'll need for the *midterm*, *finalExamGrade*, *research* and *presentation* Instance Variables. Just like the negative number that we assigned to the age attribute a few minutes ago, each one of the Instance Variables of the various Student classes in the Grades calculation project can have invalid grades assigned to them by the user. Isn't the Mutator method the place for that code."

"Absolutely Linda," I said, "that's another reason to code a Mutator method for these Instance Variables. You're right---at this point, the user can specify a negative number for a student's midterm, and our program will calculate a final grade anyway. We'll definitely need to correct that as well. One more thing--I'd suggest coding the Mutator methods as Private---this will ensure that only code within the class can update the Instance Variables."

"Can we do that?" Ward asked, "I mean code a method as Private, just like our Instance Variables."

"Yes we can," I said, "it works the same way. Without the keyword 'this', a method in a class is Private to the class, and can only be accessed by code within the class."

"Will anything we do in the next few minutes require a change to the Grades.htm file itself?" Kate asked.

"No it won't," I said, "we're making changes to the internals of the EnglishStudent, MathStudent and ScienceStudent classes---that's the beauty of Object-Oriented programming."

We then spent the next few minutes agreeing on what everyone believed would be the final versions of the various Student Classes (they didn't realize they would change after we learned about Inheritance the following week). We agreed that for every Student Class we would ..."

1. Modify all of the Instance Variables to have Private Access

2. Create a Mutator method for the *midterm, finalExamGrade, research* and *presentation* Instance Variables. We agreed to incorporate validation code in the Mutator methods, with valid grades ranging from 0 to 100. Since these Mutator methods would be executed only by code within the Student classes themselves, we agreed to create them as Private methods.

3. There was no need to code a Mutator for either the *finalNumericGrade* or the *finalLetterGrade* Instance Variables.

4. Modify the code in the calculate() method to accept input values from the user, and assign them to the Private Instance Variables of the class via the newly written Mutator methods, instead of directly updating the Private Instance Variables. The finalNumericGrade and finalLetterGrade Instance Variables would continue to be updated directly via the calculate() method.

5. Finally, I suggested that I thought it would be a good idea to code an Accessor method for the *finalNumericGrade* and *finalLetterGrade* Instance Variables. I envisioned that we would need both of these when we developed our Graphical User Interface a few weeks from now.

Exercise 8-1 Modify the EnglishStudent Class

In this exercise, you'll modify the EnglishStudent class you created last week.

1. Using Notepad (if you are using Windows) locate and open the EnglishStudent.js source file you worked on last week. (It should be in the \JavaScriptFiles\Grades folder)

2. Modify your code so that it looks like this.

```
//EnglishStudent Class

function EnglishStudent() {

var ENGLISH_MIDTERM_PERCENTAGE = .25
var ENGLISH_FINALEXAM_PERCENTAGE = .25
var ENGLISH_RESEARCH_PERCENTAGE = .30
var ENGLISH_PRESENTATION_PERCENTAGE = .20
var midterm = 0
var finalExamGrade = 0
var research = 0
var presentation = 0
var finalNumericGrade = 0
var finalLetterGrade = ""

this.calculate=calculate
this.displayGrade=displayGrade
this.getFinalNumericGrade=getFinalNumericGrade
this.getFinalLetterGrade=getFinalLetterGrade
```

```
this.setMidterm=setMidterm
this.setFinalExamGrade=setFinalExamGrade
this.setResearch=setResearch
this.setPresentation=setPresentation

function setMidterm(temp) {
  if (parseInt(temp) < 0 | parseInt(temp) > 100) {
    alert("Invalid Midterm Grade (" + temp + ") Program Terminating")
    exit
  }
  else
    midterm = temp
}

function setFinalExamGrade(temp) {
  if (parseInt(temp) < 0 | parseInt(temp) > 100) {
    alert("Invalid Final Exam Grade (" + temp + ") Program Terminating")
    exit
  }
  else
    finalExamGrade= temp
}

function setResearch(temp) {
  if (temp < 0 | temp > 100) {
    alert("Invalid Research Grade (" + temp + ") Program Terminating")
    exit
  }
  else
    research = temp
}

function setPresentation(temp) {
  if (temp < 0 | temp > 100) {
    alert("Invalid Presentation Grade (" + temp + ") Program Terminating")
    exit
  }
  else
    presentation = temp
}

function getFinalNumericGrade() {
return finalNumericGrade
}

function getFinalLetterGrade() {
return finalLetterGrade
}

function calculate() {
  setMidterm(parseInt(prompt("Enter the Midterm Grade","")))
  setFinalExamGrade(parseInt(prompt("Enter the Final Examination Grade","" )))
  setResearch(parseInt(prompt("Enter the Research Grade","")))
  setPresentation(parseInt(prompt("Enter the Presentation Grade","")))
  finalNumericGrade =
    (midterm * ENGLISH_MIDTERM_PERCENTAGE) +
    (finalExamGrade * ENGLISH_FINALEXAM_PERCENTAGE) +
    (research * ENGLISH_RESEARCH_PERCENTAGE) +
    (presentation * ENGLISH_PRESENTATION_PERCENTAGE)
  if (finalNumericGrade >= 93)
    finalLetterGrade = "A"
```

```
    else
    if ((finalNumericGrade >= 85) & (finalNumericGrade < 93))
        finalLetterGrade = "B"
    else
    if ((finalNumericGrade >= 78) & (finalNumericGrade < 85))
        finalLetterGrade = "C"
    else
    if ((finalNumericGrade >= 70) & (finalNumericGrade < 78))
        finalLetterGrade = "D"
    else
    if (finalNumericGrade < 70)
        finalLetterGrade = "F"
}
function displayGrade() {
    alert("*** ENGLISH STUDENT ***\n\n" +
        "Midterm grade is: " + midterm + "\n" +
        "Final Exam is: " + finalExamGrade + "\n" +
        "Research grade is: " + research + "\n" +
        "Presentation grade is: " + presentation + "\n\n" +
        "Final Numeric Grade is: " + finalNumericGrade + "\n" +
        "Final Letter Grade is: " + finalLetterGrade)
}
}
```

2. Save your source file as **'EnglishStudent.js'** in the \JavaScriptFiles\Grades folder (select File-Save As from Notepad's Menu Bar). Be sure to save your source file with the file name extension 'js'.
3. You won't be testing your modified EnglishStudent class until we have completed the work on the other classes in the project.

Discussion

No one had any problems completing their work on the EnglishStudent class, and so we moved onto the next exercise.

Exercise 8-2 Modify the MathStudent Class

In this exercise, you'll modify the MathStudent class you created last week.
1. Using Notepad (if you are using Windows) locate and open the MathStudent.js source file you worked on last week. (It should be in the \JavaScriptFiles\Grades folder)
2. Modify your code so that it looks like this.

```
//MathStudent Class

function MathStudent() {

var MATH_MIDTERM_PERCENTAGE = .50
var MATH_FINALEXAM_PERCENTAGE = .50
var midterm = 0
var finalExamGrade = 0
var finalNumericGrade = 0
var finalLetterGrade = ""

this.calculate=calculate
this.displayGrade=displayGrade
this.getFinalNumericGrade=getFinalNumericGrade
this.getFinalLetterGrade=getFinalLetterGrade
this.setMidterm=setMidterm
this.setFinalExamGrade=setFinalExamGrade

function setMidterm(temp) {
    if (parseInt(temp) < 0 | parseInt(temp) > 100) {
        alert("Invalid Midterm Grade (" + temp + ") Program Terminating")
```

```
      exit
    }
    else
      midterm = temp
}
function setFinalExamGrade(temp) {
  if (parseInt(temp) < 0 | parseInt(temp) > 100) {
    alert("Invalid Final Exam Grade (" + temp + ") Program Terminating")
    exit
  }
  else
    finalExamGrade= temp
}
function getFinalNumericGrade() {
  return finalNumericGrade
}
function getFinalLetterGrade() {
  return finalLetterGrade
}
function calculate() {
  setMidterm(parseInt(prompt("Enter the Midterm Grade","")))
  setFinalExamGrade(parseInt(prompt("Enter the Final Examination Grade","" )))
  finalNumericGrade =
    (midterm * MATH_MIDTERM_PERCENTAGE) +
    (finalExamGrade * MATH_FINALEXAM_PERCENTAGE)
  if (finalNumericGrade >= 90)
    finalLetterGrade = "A"
  else
  if ((finalNumericGrade >= 83) & (finalNumericGrade < 90))
    finalLetterGrade = "B"
  else
  if ((finalNumericGrade >= 76) & (finalNumericGrade < 83))
    finalLetterGrade = "C"
  else
  if ((finalNumericGrade >= 65) & (finalNumericGrade < 76))
    finalLetterGrade = "D"
  else
  if (finalNumericGrade < 65)
    finalLetterGrade = "F"
  }
function displayGrade() {
  alert("*** MATH STUDENT ***\n\n" +
    "Midterm grade is: " + midterm + "\n" +
    "Final Exam is: " + finalExamGrade + "\n\n" +
    "Final Numeric Grade is: " + finalNumericGrade + "\n" +
    "Final Letter Grade is: " + finalLetterGrade)
}
}
```

3. Save your source file as '**MathStudent.js**' in the \JavaScriptFiles\Grades folder (select File-Save As from Notepad's Menu Bar). Be sure to save your source file with the file name extension 'js'.

4. You won't be testing your modified MathStudent class until we have completed the work on the other classes in the project.

Discussion

Again, there were no problems completing the exercise, and so we moved onto updating the ScienceStudent class.

Exercise 8-3 Modify the ScienceStudent Class

In this exercise, you'll modify the ScienceStudent class you created last week.

1. Using Notepad (if you are using Windows) locate and open the ScienceStudent.js source file you worked on last week. (It should be in the \JavarScriptfiles\Grades folder)
2. Modify your code so that it looks like this.

```
//ScienceStudent Class
function ScienceStudent() {

var SCIENCE_MIDTERM_PERCENTAGE = .40
var SCIENCE_FINALEXAM_PERCENTAGE = .40
var SCIENCE_RESEARCH_PERCENTAGE = .20

var midterm = 0
var finalExamGrade = 0
var research = 0
var finalNumericGrade = 0
var finalLetterGrade = ""

this.calculate=calculate
this.displayGrade=displayGrade
this.getFinalNumericGrade=getFinalNumericGrade
this.getFinalLetterGrade=getFinalLetterGrade
this.setMidterm=setMidterm
this.setFinalExamGrade=setFinalExamGrade
this.setResearch=setResearch

function setMidterm(temp) {
  if (parseInt(temp) < 0 | parseInt(temp) > 100) {
    alert("Invalid Midterm Grade (" + temp + ") Program Terminating")
    exit
  }
  else
    midterm = temp
}

function setFinalExamGrade(temp) {
  if (parseInt(temp) < 0 | parseInt(temp) > 100) {
    alert("Invalid Final Exam Grade (" + temp + ") Program Terminating")
    exit
  }
  else
    finalExamGrade= temp
}

function setResearch(temp) {
  if (temp < 0 | temp > 100) {
    alert("Invalid Research Grade (" + temp + ") Program Terminaing")
    exit
  }
  else
    research = temp
}

function getFinalNumericGrade() {
  return finalNumericGrade
}
```

```
function getFinalLetterGrade() {
  return finalLetterGrade
}

function calculate() {
  setMidterm(parseInt(prompt("Enter the Midterm Grade","")))
  setFinalExamGrade(parseInt(prompt("Enter the Final Examination Grade","" )))
  setResearch(parseInt(prompt("Enter the Research Grade","")))
  finalNumericGrade =
    (midterm * SCIENCE_MIDTERM_PERCENTAGE) +
    (finalExamGrade * SCIENCE_FINALEXAM_PERCENTAGE) +
    (research * SCIENCE_RESEARCH_PERCENTAGE)
  if (finalNumericGrade >= 90)
    finalLetterGrade = "A"
  else
  if ((finalNumericGrade >= 80) & (finalNumericGrade < 90))
    finalLetterGrade = "B"
  else
  if ((finalNumericGrade >= 70) & (finalNumericGrade < 80))
    finalLetterGrade = "C"
  else
  if ((finalNumericGrade >= 60) & (finalNumericGrade < 70))
    finalLetterGrade = "D"
  else
  if (finalNumericGrade < 60)
    finalLetterGrade = "F"
}

function displayGrade() {
  alert("*** SCIENCE STUDENT ***\n\n" +
    "Midterm grade is: " + midterm + "\n" +
    "Final Exam is: " + finalExamGrade + "\n" +
    "Research grade is: " + research + "\n\n" +
    "Final Numeric Grade is: " + finalNumericGrade + "\n" +
    "Final Letter Grade is: " + finalLetterGrade)
}

}
}
```

3. Save your source file as '**ScienceStudent.js**' in the \JavaScriptFiles\Grades folder (select File-Save As from Notepad's Menu Bar). Be sure to save your source file with the file name extension 'js'.

4. Use Internet Explorer to Open your Grades.htm Source File.

5. The program should ask you if you have a grade to calculate.

6. Answer 'Yes', and then calculate the grade for an English student. Enter 70 for the midterm, 80 for the final examination, 90 for the research grade and 100 for the presentation. A final numeric grade of 84.5 should be displayed--with a letter grade of 'C'.

7. After the message box is displayed with the calculated grade, the program should ask you if you have more grades to calculate.

8. Answer yes, and then calculate the grade for a Math student. Enter 70 for the midterm and 80 for the final examination. A final numeric grade of 75 should be displayed--with a letter grade of 'D'.

9. After the message box is displayed with the calculated grade, the program should ask you if you have more grades to calculate.

10. Answer yes, and then calculate the grade for a Science student. Enter 70 for the midterm, 80 for the final examination. and 90 for the research grade. A final numeric grade of 78 should be displayed--with a letter grade of 'C'. After the message box is displayed with the calculate grade, the program should ask you if you have more grades to calculate.

11. Answer no--you should be thanked for using the program, and then the program should end.

Discussion

I think most everyone in the class was surprised that we could change the EnglishStudent, MathStudent and ScienceStudent classes, without the need to change the Grades.htm program. or DisplayGrade classes.

"This is the beauty of Object Oriented programming," I said, "provided you do it right. We encapsulated the main features of the program into our objects---there's very little left in the Grades.htm program, so little in fact that when the internal workings of our objects change, there's no need to change the main program."

"That is pretty amazing," Ward said, "I'm beginning to really like the Object oriented features of JavaScript."

A surprise visit from Frank Olley

"So am I," came a voice from outside my classroom door. Unknown to the students in the class, Frank Olley had been outside, and had just witnessed the execution of the Grades Calculation project from the hallway. I had phoned Frank during the break, to confirm some aspects of the validation of the component grades (I wanted to be sure that valid grades ranged from 0 to 100) and when I found out he was on campus, I invited him down for a demo.

"I've got to tell you," Frank said, "I'm most impressed with the progress you've made with the program in such a short time. In fact, I love it so much, I'd like you to install it on my PC today--but John tells me you still have some work to do on it."

I could see that the students in the class were just about to burst with pride.

Frank then spent some time admiring the work of the individual students. About ten minutes later, I dismissed class for the day.

Summary

The entirety of this Chapter was spent dealing with a topic that is extremely important in the world of Java-- protecting the data in your objects from accidental or willful manipulation that can cause the state of your objects to become invalid.

We learned that the primary means of protecting your data is to declare your Instance Variables as Private, which allows only code within the class itself to view or update the variable. Having done that, if you wish client programs (those creating instances of your object) to be able to see or update these Instance Variables, you need to write Accessor and Mutator methods.

Accessor methods enable a client program to 'see' the values of your Instance Variables. Mutator methods enable a client program to 'update' the values of your Instance Variables.

Chapter 9---Arrays

In this chapter, we'll learn about one of the most fundamental data structures in the world of programming--Arrays. Arrays are collections of variables, each having the same name, but a unique Index. Arrays permit a programmer to easily solve certain types of problems that would otherwise be extremely tedious to code.

Why Arrays

I began our ninth class by telling my students that the entirety of today's class would be devoted to the topic of Arrays.

"Is an Array similar to a regular variable?" Dave asked.

"Yes they are Dave," I said. "We've learned that a variable is a single piece of data stored in the computer's memory and given a name. In JavaScript, an Array is an object containing a collection of variables. I sometimes call Arrays a family of variables, stored in the computer's memory, with each 'member' of the Array having the same name, but possessing a unique number called a Subscript which is used to identify it. Individual members of an Array are called elements of the Array."

> **NOTE: You sometimes see the terms Subscript and Index used interchangeably.**

"In the world of programming," I continued, "certain kinds of programming problems can more easily be solved using Arrays--in fact, it's probably safe to say that there are certain types of programming problems that could not be solved without the use of Arrays."

"What kinds of problems?" Chuck asked, his curiosity obviously aroused..

"In general Chuck," I said, "problems where there is a requirement to manipulate large amounts of data, and where the data isn't really unique so much as there are just huge volumes of it."

"Could you give us an example of something like that?" Kate asked.

I thought for a moment, and then said. "Let's suppose Kate that you are a weather meteorologist, and armed with the knowledge of JavaScript that you have picked up in this class, you decide to write a JavaScript program to keep track of 365 days' worth of daily high temperature readings."

"That sounds interesting," Ward said, "that's an awful lot of data---at least more than we're used to."

"Furthermore," I continued, "let's presume that Kate would also like to calculate the yearly average for her temperature readings. From what we've learned so far in the class we know that we could declare and store these temperature readings in 365 separate variables called highTemperature1 through highTemperature365."

"I agree, that would do the trick," Dave said, "but who really wants to code 365 variable declaration statements, plus the 365 assignment statements to store the value of the variable. Plus, the calculation for the yearly average would require that we sum each and every one of those variables---what a tedious exercise that would be. Is this where an Array can help us?"

"That's exactly the case Dave," I answered. "Let's think about this for a moment. Each one of the 365 recorded high temperature readings really represent the same thing---a temperature reading. What's different about each one? Only the day that the temperature is recorded. You'll see in a few minutes that an Array is a much better choice than an ordinary variable in which to store those 365 temperature readings---in fact, you'll be surprised to learn that an Array declaration to store 365 high temperature readings is just a single line of code."

"Amazing," I heard Valerie say.

"Not only does an Array eliminate the need to declare 365 separate variables," I continued, "but once the values for the year's temperature readings are stored in the Array, it's a simple process to use a For Loop to access each individual element of the Array, retrieving the value, adding it to an accumulator variable, and then calculating an average temperature. Believe it or not, we can do that in about five lines of code."

"I can't wait to see this in action," Steve said.

"Let me give you another example," I said. "On Wednesday evenings, I teach a Database Administration class here at the university. Last Wednesday, I gave a quiz to each one of the six students in the class. What would you say if I asked you to write a JavaScript program to calculate the overall class average for that quiz. Based on what you've learned in the first nine weeks of the course, and excluding what we've discussed so far about Arrays, do you have any idea as to how we could calculate the class average?"

"I guess," Rhonda suggested, "that one way would be to borrow the functionality that we are currently using with the Grades Calculation program."

"How's that Rhonda?" I asked.

"Well, we could prompt the user of the program to enter quiz grades for each one of the six students," she replied.

"Since you told us to discount today's discussion of Arrays, the best I can suggest is to declare six variables---one to represent the quiz grades for each one of the students---and to assign the user's input to one of those variables. Once the user has entered all six student grades, we can then sum the values of the variables and divide by six to calculate an overall class average."

"Based on what we've learned in the first nine weeks of class Rhonda, that's an excellent approach," I said.

"However, once you learn more about Arrays, I bet you'll come to the conclusion that this method, as effective as it is, is what I term the "brute force method."

I gave everyone a chance to ponder that statement. "Now suppose I told you that my Database Management class doesn't have just six students---it really has 150 students. Would that change your approach to solving the problem?"

"I would think we need to find a better approach to solving the problem than this," Rhonda replied. "I really don't want to have to declare 150 variables! There must be a better way."

"Absolutely Rhonda," I said, "and we'll see shortly that the 'better approach' you sense must exist is to use an Array instead of individual variables. But before we start to discuss Arrays in detail, I think it's a good idea if we first code up the solution to the problem using the 'brute force' method. That will allow us to see how tedious programming would be without Arrays."

I then distributed this exercise for the class to complete.

Don't Forget: If typing these examples and exercises isn't something you want to do, feel free to follow this link to find and download the completed solutions for all of the examples and exercises in the book. Just click on the JavaScript book, then follow the link entitled exercises ☺

http://www.johnsmiley.com/main/books.htm

Exercise 9-1 Brute Force---Life without Arrays

In this exercise, you'll write a program that prompts the user for six quiz grades, then calculates and displays the grades plus the overall class average in the Internet Browser.

1. Use Notepad (if you are using Windows) and enter the following code.

```
<! Practice9-1 -->
<html>
<body>
<script type="text/javascript">

var grade1 = 0
var grade2 = 0
var grade3 = 0
var grade4 = 0
var grade5 = 0
var grade6 = 0
var accumulator = 0
var counter = 6
var average = 0.0

grade1 = prompt("What is the first grade?","")
grade2 = prompt("What is the second grade?","")
grade3 = prompt("What is the third grade?","")
grade4 = prompt("What is the fourth grade?","")
grade5 = prompt("What is the fifth grade?","")
grade6 = prompt("What is the sixth grade?","")
```

```
accumulator = parseInt(grade1) + parseInt(grade2) + parseInt(grade3) +
              parseInt(grade4) + parseInt(grade5) + parseInt(grade6)
average = accumulator / counter

document.write(grade1 + "<br>")
document.write(grade2 + "<br>")
document.write(grade3 + "<br>")
document.write(grade4 + "<br>")
document.write(grade5 + "<br>")
document.write(grade6 + "<p>")

document.write("The class average is " + average)

</script>
</body>
</html>
```

2. Save your source file as '**Practice9-1.htm**' in the \JavaScriptFiles\Practice folder (select File-Save As from Notepad's Menu Bar). Be sure to save your source file with the file name extension 'htm'.

3. Use Internet Explorer to Open your Source File.

4. The program will prompt you for six grades. Enter 82 for the first grade, 90 for the second, 64 for the third, 80 for the fourth, 95 for the fifth and 75 for the sixth.

5. The program will then display the grades, plus the calculated overall class average, which is 81.

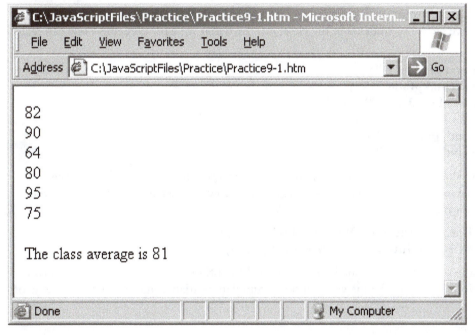

Discussion

Everyone agreed that the code in this exercise did what every good program must do---it worked. Beyond that, it had been an extremely tedious exercise to code.

"Brute force is right," Peter said. "What a boring program to write! I can't wait to see how an Array can improve upon this."

"We'll see that in a minute Peter," I said. "but first, let's take a look at the code first---much of which will be pretty familiar to you, as we're using the same technique we use in the Grades Calculation Project. As usual, the first thing we do is to declare the variables that we will need to use in our program. We have six local variables in the main() method..."

```
var grade1 = 0
var grade2 = 0
var grade3 = 0
var grade4 = 0
```

```
var grade5 = 0
var grade6 = 0
```

"Notice that we've declared a variable for each one of the six quiz grades," I continued, "and we've initialized each one of them to 0. In addition, I've introduced two special types of variables in this code. The first variable, appropriately named accumulator, is called an accumulator. It's really just an ordinary variable that is used to sum values---in this case, we'll use the accumulator to sum the values of the six grade variables…"

```
var accumulator = 0
```

"…the second special type of variable is called a counter, which we've named counter, and like the accumulator variable, a counter variable is just an ordinary variable that is used to count something--in this case, we're using it to count the number of students in the class. We could get fancier than this, but for now, since we will eventually divide the value of counter into accumulator to arrive at a class average, we immediately assign the number 6 to the counter variable…"

```
var counter = 6
```

"…we also declare a variable called average, into which we will store the class average. Since this variable can conceivably contain a fraction, we assign it a fractional value, but that's not really necessary…"

```
var average = 0.0
```

I went on to explain that in the next section of code, we used the prompt() method to prompt the user for each of the six quiz grades for the class.

"Notice that the return value of the user's response is assigned to a unique variable," I said. "This is where the problem arises---if all of a sudden we have 150 students in the class, not the 6 that we have here, this code can really balloon in size…"

```
grade1 = prompt("What is the first grade?","")
grade2 = prompt("What is the second grade?","")
grade3 = prompt("What is the third grade?","")
grade4 = prompt("What is the fourth grade?","")
grade5 = prompt("What is the fifth grade?","")
grade6 = prompt("What is the sixth grade?","")
```

"…Here's the code that assigns a value to the accumulator variable. As we progress through today's class, the code to work with the accumulator variable will become a little more elegant. For now, we just assign it the sum of the values of each one of the six grade variables…"

```
accumulator = parseInt(grade1) + parseInt(grade2) + parseInt(grade3) +
              parseInt(grade4) + parseInt(grade5) + parseInt(grade6)
```

"…This line of code is probably the most important one in the program," I continued, "in that it assigns the class average to the average variable. Notice that we take the value of the accumulator variable, and divide by the value of the counter variable…"

```
average = accumulator / counter
```

"Is there anything magical about the names of those two variables, the accumulator and counter variables?" Joe asked.

"Not at all Joe," I answered, "we can name them anything we want."

I paused before continuing.

"This next section of code displays the values of the individual grades," I said, "This is another problematic section of code if the number of students in the class should increase as we would need to add additional lines of code"

```
document.write(grade1 + "<br>")
document.write(grade2 + "<br>")
document.write(grade3 + "<br>")
document.write(grade4 + "<br>")
document.write(grade5 + "<br>")
document.write(grade6 + "<p>")
```

"Finally," I said, "this line of code displays the class average..."

document.write("The class average is " + average)

I checked the room for signs of confusion, but no one seemed to be having any trouble understanding what we had just done.

"I think you're all pretty comfortable with this code," I said. "There's really nothing in this code that we haven't seen before."

I then made this suggestion.

"Now I'd like each one of you to modify this code to calculate the class average for a course with 500 students," I said.

"I hope you're kidding," Joe said smiling.

"Well, I am...but suppose we really needed to calculate the average for a class with 500 students. Could we do it?" I asked.

Everyone agreed that modifying the code to calculate the average for a course of 500 students would be a real nightmare.

"We would need 500 prompts to the user and 500 variables in which to store their responses," Kate said. "Plus, we would need multiple lines of code to sum the values of the 500 variables and assign them to the accumulator variable."

What's an Array?

"All of your points are excellent ones, Kate" I said. "Examining the 'brute force' method gives us a chance to see the types of problems that can be more easily solved using Array processing."

"Is an Array a separate Data Type, like an Integer or a String?" Peter asked.

"In JavaScript," I said, "an Array is actually a collection of variables containing values. In JavaScript, you can have Integer and String Arrays and as we'll see later, even Object Arrays."

"I'm still a little confused as to exactly what an Array is," Rhonda said. "Do you have any analogies up your sleeve that might make this a little clearer."

"In the past when I've taught Arrays," I said, "many of my students have found my analogy of an Array to a hotel to be pretty useful."

"A hotel?" Rhonda asked.

"That's right, Rhonda" I said. "Just about everyone at one time or other has stayed in a hotel or motel. As you know, a variable is just a storage location in your computer's memory. Getting back to the hotel analogy, think of an ordinary variable as a storage location consisting of just a single floor. An Array, on the other hand, is a storage location having more than just one floor--with each floor having its own unique floor number."

"Just like a hotel," Joe said. "I see what you mean."

"I'm not much of an artist," I said, "but here's a graphic depiction of what I mean."

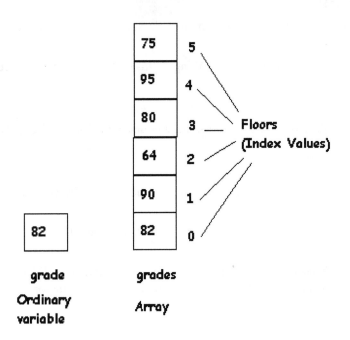

"This drawing is an attempt to illustrate the difference between an ordinary variable and an Array," I said. "On the left side of the drawing, we have an ordinary Integer variable called grades, with an assigned value of 82. On the right side of the drawing, we have an Array of Integer variables called grades, the Array containing 6 elements, each element having its own value. As you can see, the ordinary variable grade can hold only one value at a time. The Integer Array, on the other hand, can hold all 6 quiz grades at one time."

"What are those numbers to the right of the grades in the Array?" Barbara asked.

"In keeping with our hotel analogy," I said. "those are the floor numbers of the 'hotel', or in computer terms, the Array Subscript or Index values. A Subscript uniquely identifies the element within the Array---each element has a subscript, and subscripts cannot be duplicated. This ensures that once a value is entered into an element of the Array, you'll later be able to retrieve that value by using its subscript."

"Why does the first element of the Array begin with zero?" Ward asked. "Why doesn't it begin with one?"

"Let me guess, that's the basement!" Rhonda said, obviously joking.

"In a way Rhonda, you're right," I replied. "In the computer world, many things begin with the number zero instead of one, and Array element numbers are one of them. In JavaScript, the first element of an Array begins with the number zero--it's just something that you'll need to get used to."

Declaring and Initializing an Array

"How do you declare an Array?" Steve asked.

"Like this," I said.

```
var grades = new Array(6)
```

or

```
var grades = new Array()
```

"Why are there two forms of the declaration?" Ward asked. "Is there a preferred method to declaring the Array."

"When we declare our Array," I said, "we may or may not know how many elements the Array will eventually hold. If we do, it's a good idea to tell JavaScript right up front. If we don't--and you'll see later on why that may be the case---an empty set of parentheses tells JavaScript that we don't know how many elements the Array will hold. Either way is acceptable."

"I'm a bit confused," Lou said. "The new keyword---is that the same keyword we use when we create instances of objects?"

"That's right Lou," I said. "In JavaScript, behind the scenes, Arrays are really objects. Here we are telling JavaScript, with a single statement, that we are declaring an Integer Array called grades, and that it will have a total of six elements or 'floors'..."

"I want to be certain I'm clear about this," Kate said. "Is the number six the number of elements in the Array, or the 'top' floor of the hotel?"

"That's is a key distinction Kate" I said, "In JavaScript, the number within parentheses---it represents the total number of elements in the Array, which is not the same as the 'top floor'. This Array has six elements, with its subscripts numbered from 0 through 5."

Adding data to the Elements of an Array

"So how do we get values into the Array," Rhonda asked. "How do we initialize an Array? Like we do a variable?"

"In JavaScript," I said, "there are actually several ways to initialize an Array. One way is to include the data values for the Array as part of its declaration, in which case JavaScript infers the size of the Array from the data values in the declaration. We'll take a look at that method in a few minutes. The other way is to assign the values of array elements one by one."

"How do we assign a value to an individual element of an Array?" Steve asked. "And once we have values in the Array elements, how can we retrieve the value from one of those elements?"

"Working with Array elements isn't much different than working with an ordinary variable," I said. "The difference is that we need to reference the element number within the Array by using its Subscript within brackets. For example, if we had an Array called grades, this code would be used to assign the value of 64 to element number 2..."

grades[2] = 82

"By the way," I cautioned, "the Array element with a Subscript equal to 2 is actually the third element in the Array. Remember, element numbers start with zero, not one. Therefore, the first element in the Array has a Subscript of 0, the second element has a Subscript of 1, and so forth."

"Are Array values referred to in the same way?" Steve asked. "using the Subscript number within brackets?"

"That's right Steve," I replied. "Again, as was the case with the assignment statement, just reference the Subscript of the Array element within brackets. For instance, you can use this syntax to display the value of element number 0 of the grades Array in the Internet Browser..."

document.write(grade[0])

"This isn't too bad at all," Kathy said, "I must confess, when I first heard the term 'Array' I thought it would be a lot more complicated than this."

"I've been experimenting with an Array of my own," Rhonda said, "but nothing seems to be working."

I took a walk to Rhonda's PC, and quickly saw the problem.

"I see what the problem is Rhonda," I said, "Your Array declaration is fine, but JavaScript is very sensitive as to the spelling of the word Array---you spelled 'array' without a capital A..."

int rhonda[] = new array(10)

"...it should read..."

int rhonda[] = new Array(10)

"That did the trick," she said, obviously happy at the result."

"I've been experimenting a little bit also," Dave said, "and I discovered that even when I declare an Array to contain 6 elements, if I add a seventh--or more---JavaScript permits it. I would think that it would generate an error---or just not run the program."

"Good point Dave," I said, "As I mentioned earlier, it's optional to include the number of elements in the Array as part of its declaration. So optional, in fact, that JavaScript doesn't really use the number you specify to later validate the data you place in the Array. As you discovered, JavaScript doesn't hold you to that initial declaration."

"Can we use other than a numeric literal to refer to the Array's subscript?" Dave asked.

"You can use any expression within the brackets, as long as the expression evaluates to a valid Subscript." I explained.

"I'm not sure I'm following this," Chuck said.

"For instance," I explained, "if you have a variable called counter containing an Integer value, and that value represents a valid Subscript in the grades Array, this is a valid assignment statement that uses the value of the variable---not an actual number to represent the subscript..."

grades(counter) = 80

"The ability to do this," I said, "will come in very handy in the exercise we're about to complete, as it will enable us to use loop processing to quickly access all of the elements of an Array."

I waited for questions, but there were none. I think everyone, for the moment anyway, felt pretty comfortable declaring and working with Arrays.

"I have an exercise for you to complete which will give you a chance to use an Array to perform the same average calculation we did in the last exercise using the 'brute force' method--but I think you'll enjoy it a whole lot more."

I then distributed this exercise for the class to complete.

Exercise 9-2 Our First Look at Arrays

In this exercise, you'll create your first Array.

1. Use Notepad (if you are using Windows) and enter the following code.

```
<! Practice9-2 -->
<html>
<body>
<script type="text/javascript">

var grades = new Array(6)
var accumulator = 0
var counter = 6
var average = 0.0

grades[0] = 82
grades[1] = 90
grades[2] = 64
grades[3] = 80
grades[4] = 95
grades[5] = 75

accumulator = grades[0] + grades[1] + grades[2] +
              grades[3] + grades[4] + grades[5]
average = accumulator / counter

document.write(grades[0] + "<br>")
document.write(grades[1] + "<br>")
document.write(grades[2] + "<br>")
document.write(grades[3] + "<br>")
document.write(grades[4] + "<br>")
document.write(grades[5] + "<p>")

document.write("The class average is " + average)

</script>
</body>
</html>
```

2. Save your source file as **'Practice9-2.htm'** in the \JavaScriptFiles\Practice folder (select File-Save As from Notepad's Menu Bar). Be sure to save your source file with the file name extension 'htm'.
3. Use Internet Explorer to Open your Source File.
4. The program will then display each of the six grades, plus the calculated overall class average, which is 81.

Discussion

Except for a student or two who confused the parentheses with square brackets, no one had any trouble completing this exercise.

"As you can see," I said, "the results of this program are identical to that in Exercise 9-1---the display of 6 grades, plus the calculated overall class average. Of course, this version uses an Array, so let's take a closer look at that code now. It's this line of code that declares a six element Array called grades. And as you know by now, that means the first element in the Array has a subscript of 0 and the last element has a subscript of 5. By the way, I didn't mention this before, but it's a good idea to name Arrays using the plural form of a noun--that enables programmers reading your code to recognize immediately that the variable is actually an Array..."

```
var grades = new Array(6)
```

"...Using an Array here, we've reduced the number of lines of code necessary to declare the variables to store our six grades from six to one. As was the case with Exercise 9-1, these next three lines of code declare our accumulator variable, our counter variable and our average variable. Once again, we initialize the value of our counter variable to 6, although shortly you'll see there's a more elegant way to keep track of the number of grades to use in our average calculation. For now, we initialize it to 6..."

```
var accumulator = 0
var counter = 6
var average = 0.0
```

"...You probably remember that the previous version of this program assigned values to variables named grade1 through grade6---this version also assigns values to 6 memory locations, but this time we assign values to individual elements of the grades Array. In the next exercise, we'll learn that there's a more compact method for assigning values to Array elements..."

```
grades[0] = 82
grades[1] = 90
grades[2] = 64
grades[3] = 80
grades[4] = 95
grades[5] = 75
```

"...as we did in Exercise 9-1, we then sum the values of all six grades and assign the result to the accumulator variable. This time we refer to the individual elements of the grades Array..."

```
accumulator = grades[0] + grades[1] + grades[2] +
              grades[3] + grades[4] + grades[5]
```

"...and with this line of code calculate the overall class average..."

```
average = accumulator / counter
```

"This next section of code is similar to that in Exercise 9-1---it displays the values of the individual grades using the write() method of the document object to do so..."

```
document.write(grades[0] + "<br>")
document.write(grades[1] + "<br>")
document.write(grades[2] + "<br>")
document.write(grades[3] + "<br>")
document.write(grades[4] + "<br>")
document.write(grades[5] + "<p>")
```

"...finally, this line of code displays the calculated class average..."

```
document.write("The class average is " + average)
```

The wonders of Array processing

"So far," Ward said, "from what I've seen of Array processing, I can see that it reduces the number of variables we need to declare in our program, but quite honestly, I don't see what the big deal is all about. Everything we did in this exercise was very similar to what we did in Exercise 9-1--however, instead of referencing individual variable names we referenced element of an Array. There was still quite a bit of tedious typing referring to individual elements of the Array."

"I agree with Ward," Lou said. "Surely there's got to be an easier way to assign values to an Array? And once we have the values in the Array, what then? Suppose we have an Array with 365 elements---like the daily high temperature readings you mentioned earlier. Would we need to code 365 separate assignment statements?"

"Glad you asked that Lou," I said. "There is a shorter form of assigning values to an Array, and its one to which I alluded earlier when I said there's a method to declare and initialize an Array just by assigning values to it. Check out this code…"

```
var grades = new Array(82,90,64,80,95,75)
```

"Notice that the values for the Array elements are contained within the parentheses," I said. "Now, with a single line of code, we have both declared an Array called grades, and initialized it with values. How does JavaScript know how 'large' to size the Array? The six values within the parentheses tell JavaScript that the grades Array should have six elements."

"This is an improvement," Ward persisted. "but I still say 'big deal'. I see that this method will reduce the number of lines of code required to assign values to the elements of an Array. But what else can Arrays do for me? Why is it that the programmers at work always tell me they couldn't live without them? If I still need to refer to each and every element within the Array individually, I still have quite a bit of work ahead of me."

"Arrays allow you to use Loop processing to quickly refer to each element in the Array," I said. "and that can be a big time saver. This exercise, I believe, will illustrate why the programmers at your workplace love Arrays so much."

I then distributed this exercise for the class to complete.

Exercise 9-3 The wonders of Array processing

In this exercise, you'll modify the code from exercise 9-3, using a JavaScript For Loop to quickly and easily access the elements of an Array.

1. Use Notepad (if you are using Windows) and enter the following code.

```
<! Practice9-3 -->
<html>
<body>
<script type="text/javascript">

var grades = new Array(82,90,64,80,95,75)
var accumulator = 0
var counter = 0
var average = 0.0

for (row = 0; row < grades.length; row++) {
  document.write (grades[row] + "<br>")
  accumulator = accumulator + grades[row]
  counter++
}

average = accumulator / counter
document.write("<br>The class average is " + average)

</script>
</body>
</html>
```

2. Save your source file as '**Practice9-3.htm**' in the \JavaScriptFiles\Practice folder (select File-Save As from Notepad's Menu Bar). Be sure to save your source file with the file name extension 'htm'.
3. Use Internet Explorer to Open your Source File.
4. Execute the program. The program will then display each of the six grades, plus the calculated overall class average, which is 81.

Discussion

"OK, I'm beginning to see the light," Ward said. "This version of the program is certainly a lot more streamlined than the other code, and I'm happy to see we never directly referred to an individual element of the Array."

"I'm not quite sure I understand what's happening," Rhonda said, "Can you explain the code to us?."

"Sure thing Rhonda," I said. "This time, instead of declaring and initializing the grades Array using the new statement, we declare and initialize the Array in a single statement by assigning values to each one of the six elements of the grades Array..."

```
var grades = new Array(82,90,64,80,95,75)
```

"...as before, we declare variables for the accumulator, counter and average. But notice that this time, the counter variable is assigned a value of 0, not 6. We'll be arriving at a value for the counter variable a little later on in the code., and it will make our program much more flexible in being able to deal with different numbers of quiz grades to calculate..."

```
var accumulator = 0
var counter = 0
var average = 0.0
```

"At this point in our program," I continued, "the grades Array now has six elements, with values assigned to each. In the previous version of this program, we then used the write() method of the document object to display the values for each element of the Array, using six separate executions of the write() method. The problem with that version-and it's one that bothered the heck out of Ward---is that if the number of students in the class increases, we're going to have to increase the number of elements in the Array, and write another line of code to display that student's grade. That's why this next section of code is so powerful--it uses a JavaScript For loop to access every element in the grades Array, displaying its value in our Internet Browser window, then adds its value to the accumulator variable and increments the value of the counter variable by one..."

```
for (row = 0; row < grades.length; row++) {
  document.write (grades[row] + "<br>")
  accumulator = accumulator + grades[row]
  counter++
}
```

"...the wonderful thing about this code is that it works, without modification, regardless of the number of elements in the Array."

"Are you saying," Linda said, "that if we changes the declaration of the grades Array to have 250 student grades, this code wouldn't need to be changed?"

"That's exactly right Linda," I said.

"I'm a little confused," Rhonda said, "how are we specifying the subscript for the Array element in the write() method of the document object?"

"Do you remember a little earlier I said that we could refer to an Array's subscript using a variable?" I said. "That's what we're doing here, by using the *row* variable, which is the Loop Control variable for the For Loop. As you can see, *row* is initialized to zero, which is the value for the first element of the Array, and we then increment row by one each time the For loop executes. The For loop continues to execute while the value of the row variable is less than the length attribute of the grades Array..."

```
for (row = 0; row < grades.length; row++) {
```

"Length attribute?" Linda asked. "What's that?"

"Do you remember a few minutes ago I mentioned that in JavaScript, Arrays are actually objects?" I said. "As a byproduct of that, each Array that we declare has a *length* attribute, which tells us exactly how many elements are in the Array. By specifying that the For loop should continue to execute while the value of the *row* Loop Control variable is less than the *length* attribute of the Array, we ensure that we access each and every element of the Array."

"Powerful," Ward said.

"I'm afraid I still don't see how the subscript for the individual Array elements is being specified," Rhonda said. "Is it because we are using the loop control variable row within the brackets?"

"That's exactly right Rhonda," I said. "The Loop control variable is used, within brackets, to specify the Subscript of the Array element we wish to display in our Internet Browser. Each time the body of the For Loop is executed, an incrementing value of 'row' is used as the subscript for the Array element..."

```
document.write (grades[row] + "<br>")
```

"After we have displayed the value of the Array element in our Internet Browser, we then add it to the current value of the variable *accumulator,*" I continued. "In this way, the *accumulator* variable maintains a 'running total' of the value of the Array elements we have displayed in the Internet Browser."

```
accumulator = accumulator + grades[row]
```

"To make things easier to understand," I said, "visualize that the first time the body of the For Loop is executed, the value of the row variable is zero. That means that this statement is interpreted by JavaScript like this…"

```
accumulator = accumulator + grades[0]
```

"…This statement in turn is then interpreted by JavaScript like this…"

```
accumulator = 0 + 90
```

"The second time through the loop," I continued, "the value of row in incremented, making it 1, and the statement is then interpreted by JavaScript like this…"
accumulator = accumulator + grades[1]

"or.."

```
accumulator = 90 + 91
```

I then explained that this process is repeated until all the For Loop terminates, and all the elements of the Array had been processed.

"We can't forget the role of the counter variable in the process," I said. "It's this line of code that increments the value of the counter variable, each time the For Loop is executed. When the For Loop terminates, the value of the counter variable is equal to the number of elements in the Array…"

```
counter++
```

"Finally, this section of code is virtually identical to the previous versions, displaying a blank line in our Internet Browser, calculating the average, and displaying it in the Internet Browser as well. The big difference here is that the value of the counter variable is assigned within the For Loop, not at the time the counter variable is declared …"

```
average = accumulator / counter
document.write("<br>The class average is " + average)
```

Using an Array for Averaging

"I would really love to see Arrays used with the code we wrote in Exercise 9-1," Mary said. "Is it possible to use Arrays there, even when the user is being prompted for grades to calculate?"

"Yes it is possible," I said. I hadn't really considered having the class do this, but it sounded like a great idea, and so, after a few minutes of thought, I distributed this exercise for the class to complete.

Exercise 9-4 Using Arrays with Interactive Processing

In this exercise, you'll modify the program you wrote in Exercise 9-1, using Arrays to make the process of calculating the average of six grades much easier.

1. Use Notepad (if you are using Windows) and enter the following code.

```
<! Practice9-4 -->
<html>
<body>
<script type="text/javascript">

var grades = new Array(6)
var accumulator = 0
var counter = 0
var average = 0.0
var moreGradesToCalculate = ""

moreGradesToCalculate = prompt("Do you want to calculate a grade?","Yes")
moreGradesToCalculate = moreGradesToCalculate.toUpperCase()

while (moreGradesToCalculate == "YES") {
  grades[counter] = parseInt(prompt("What is the grade?",""))
```

```
      moreGradesToCalculate = prompt("Do you have more grades to calculate?","Yes")
      moreGradesToCalculate = moreGradesToCalculate.toUpperCase()
      counter++
}

for (row = 0; row < grades.length; row++) {
   document.write (grades[row] + "<br>")
   accumulator = accumulator + grades[row]
}

average = accumulator / grades.length
document.write("<br>The class average is " + average)

</script>
</body>
</html>
```

2. Save your source file as '**Practice9-4.htm**' in the \JavaScriptFiles\Practice folder (select File-Save As from Notepad's Menu Bar). Be sure to save your source file with the file name extension 'htm'.
3. Use Internet Explorer to Open your Source File.
4. The program will ask if you if you have grades to enter. Answer yes.
5. The program will then prompt you for a grade. Enter 82.
6. The program will then ask if you have more grades to enter. Answer yes.
7. The program will then prompt you for a grade. Enter 90, and continue entering grades in this manner (64 for the third grade, 80 for the fourth, 95 for the fifth, and 75 for the sixth).
8. After entering the sixth grade, the program will ask if you have more grades to enter. Answer no. The program will then display the calculated average, which is 81.

Discussion

"As you can see," I said, "the changes between this version of the program and the one from Exercise 9-1 are pretty dramatic---using Arrays to process a series of grades like this is a great deal easier than using six variables."

"I see that," Steve said, "and I can also see that we 'married' the methodologies from Exercise 9-1 and Exercise 9-3 to write a program that allows the user to load values into the elements of the Array themselves, instead of the program doing so within code."

"That's right Steve," I said. "Much of the code in this program is found in Exercise 9-1--- the main difference is that the user's input of a quiz grade is assigned to an element of an Array instead of to a dedicated variable. Let's take a look at the code now. As we did in Exercise 9-3, the first thing we did was declare an Array called *grades* containing six elements, plus variables for the accumulator, counter and average..."

```
var grades = new Array(6)
var accumulator = 0
var counter = 0
var average = 0.0
```

"This String variable," I said, "moreGradesToCalculate, you should recognize from the Grades Calculation project as a variable we use in a While Loop test expression to determine if we should continue processing the loop to prompt the user for more grades.."

```
var moreGradesToCalculate = ""
```

"This section of code asks the user if he or she has a grade to enter, takes their response and using the toUpperCase() method, 'converts' it to upper case..."

```
moreGradesToCalculate = prompt("Do you want to calculate a grade?","Yes")
moreGradesToCalculate = moreGradesToCalculate.toUpperCase()
```

"This section of code establishes a While loop, in which the user is prompted for a grade, then asked if they have any others to input...."

```
while (moreGradesToCalculate == "YES") {
```

"...This line of code is crucial, in that it uses the value of the counter variable to establish the Subscript number as the user's value for a grade is then added as an element to the Array..."

```
grades[counter] = parseInt(prompt("What is the grade?",""))
```

"...Now it's time to ask the user if they have more grades to enter--once again, their response is 'converted' to upper case, then stored in the moreGradesToCalculate variable..."

```
moreGradesToCalculate = prompt("Do you have more grades to calculate?","Yes")
moreGradesToCalculate = moreGradesToCalculate.toUpperCase()
```

"...This line of code is also crucial---it's here that we increment the value of the counter variable so that if the user does have another grade to input, we load that value into the next element in the grades Array. We'll also use the value of the counter variable later to calculate the class average..."

```
counter++
```

"...The While loop continues to execute until the user indicates they have no more grades to input. At that point, we have an Array loaded with grade values, and it's time to read the values in the grades Array, and calculate an average, just as we did in Exercise 9-3. In fact, this code is nearly identical to that in Exercise 9-3, in which we use a For loop to move through the elements of the grades Array, and to calculate an average.."

```
for (row = 0; row < grades.length; row++) {
  document.write (grades[row] + "<br>")
  accumulator = accumulator + grades[row]
}
average = accumulator / grades.length
alert("The class average is " + average)
```

"Does anyone see where the code varies from Exercise 9-3?" I asked.

"I do," Linda said, "your calculation of the average variable is slightly different. In this exercise, you are dividing the accumulator variable by the length attribute of the grades Array---not the counter variable."

"Excellent observation Linda," I said, "you're absolutely correct. I wanted to show you that the value of the counter variable and the length attribute of our Array are identical. You can use either one to calculate the average variable."

A Problem with our Array

I waited to see if there were any questions--but no one seemed to have any problems understanding what was going on, and so I continued.

"I just noticed a slight problem," Rhonda said. "When I ran the program and entered only one quiz grade, the program displayed one grade followed by five lines reading 'undefined', and displayed an average reading 'NaN'. I think it was expecting me to enter 6 grades."

"That's right Rhonda," I said, "this version of the program 'works' only if the user enters six or more grades. I'm afraid specifying an array size of 6 has hurt us here."

I then ran the program myself, and instead of entering six grades, I entered the first grade--82--then told the program that I had no more grades to enter. The following screenshot was displayed on the classroom projector.

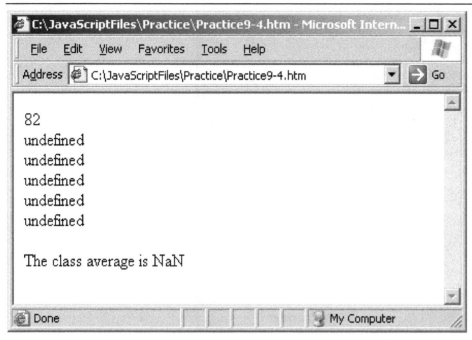

"That's exactly what happened to me," Rhonda said. "What happened? What are all of those 'undefined' lines?"

"I'm afraid the problem is that we declared our Array to contain 6 elements," I said, "that was my mistake. We should only specify a size for an Array when we are absolutely sure of the number of elements that it will contain. Although we only entered one value into the array, the length attribute was still set at 6---based on our declaration. As a result, the code that loops through each element of the array to calculate the accumulator is erroneous. Remember, we initialized the grades Array to 6 elements---and since we only loaded one element to the grades Array, it's this code, using the length attribute of the Array, that poses the problem…"

```
for (row = 0; row < grades.length; row++) {
  document.write (grades[row] + "<br>")
  accumulator = accumulator + grades[row]
}
```

"What's wrong with the code?" Blaine asked.

"The code presumes that the Array has been fully loaded," I said, "because it uses the length attribute of the grades Array to determine the end point of the For Loop."

"And the length attribute returns a value equal to the number of elements in the Array--not the number of elements that have had values loaded to them," Dave said.

"Dave's right," Linda said, "What can we do to fix this problem?"

"The fix is very easy Linda," I said, "all we need to do is change our Array declaration. If we're unsure of the number of elements our Array will hold, we should declare it with an empty set of parentheses, like this…"

```
var grades = new Array()
```

"Now let's run the program again," I said, "I think our results will be much better." I did exactly that, entered a single grade, and the following screen shot was displayed on the classroom projector…

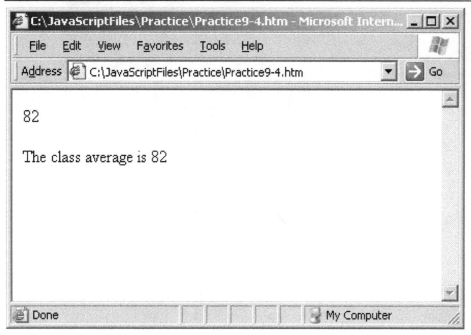

"That's better," Ward said.

Multiple dimensioned Arrays

We were making great progress on what can be a difficult topic, when I began my discussion of multidimensional Arrays.

"All of the Arrays that we've seen so far, have been one-dimensional Arrays," I explained. "now it's time to discuss multidimensional Arrays."

"Dare I ask the difference?" said Kathy tentatively.

"They say a picture is worth a thousand words," I said. "Let's use Notepad to see the difference. In Notepad, one-dimensional Arrays appear as a single column of data. Two-dimensional Arrays appear as rows and columns of data, much like a Worksheet. For instance..." I said, as I displayed this file on the classroom projector:

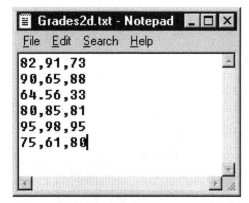

"This is a two-dimensional text file," I explained. "This file contains not only the original quiz grades we worked with in our exercises so far today, but two other quiz grades as well."

"So the first column of numbers are scores from the first quiz, the second column scores from the second quiz, and the third column scores from the third quiz" Ward asked.

"That's right," I replied. "Each row represents a 'record' of three quiz scores for one student---and each column represents a different quiz."

"You mentioned the word multidimensional a minute ago," Joe said. "and you just said this is the depiction for a two-dimensional Array. Does that mean you can have an Array with more than two dimensions."

"Yes you can Joe," I answered. "Creating an Array with more than two dimensions is easy in JavaScript--visualizing one is something else, and requires a little imagination---but JavaScript doesn't limit you to a two-dimensional Array. JavaScript, in fact, allows you to declare an Array with up to 255 dimensions."

"So far," Kathy said, "both types of Arrays you've shown us, the one-dimensional and two-dimensional varieties, have represented some real world object. What kind of real-world object would you represent with a three-dimensional Array?"

"One classic example," I said, "is a farm. We can use a three-dimensional Array to represent a farmer's crops. A farmer plants crops in fields (the first dimension), and within a field, he or she plants crops in rows (the second dimension) and columns (the third dimension). Try to imagine a farm that has ten fields, each field made up of one hundred rows and columns,. A three-dimensional Array is a perfect way to represent the crop plants in a particular row and column of a field on the farm."

I gave everyone a chance to visualize this.

"Is there any limitation as to how large an Array can be?" Steve asked.

"In theory no," I said, "but as we saw just a few minutes ago when we ran out of memory by declaring a huge one-dimensional Array, there is a practical limitation in terms of your PC's memory. Multi-dimensional Arrays, in particular, can use up the available memory in your computer very quickly. Each dimension that you add to an Array geometrically increases the storage requirements for the Array."

I sensed that my students were becoming tense with this discussion of multi-dimensional Arrays and so I sought to comfort them a bit.

"Don't worry," I told everyone, "in the real-world of programming, most of your work will be with one and two dimensional Arrays---just remember that everything you learn today about two-dimensional Arrays can be applied to an Array with three or more dimensions."

"How are two dimensional Arrays declared?" Joe asked.

"It's a two step process," I said, "Think of it this way. First, we declare the 'row' part of the two-dimensional array. Then, for each row element, we assign it the declaration of a 'column' part of the two-dimensional array, which is itself another Array."

I gave everyone a chance to let this sink in.

"In other words," Dave said, "a two-dimensional Array is really an Array whose elements are themselves defined as an Array."

"That's excellent Dave," I said, "I couldn't have said it better myself. Let's take a look at the declaration of a two-dimensional Array called grades for the file we just viewed in Notepad that contains scores for three quizzes for six different students..."

```
var grades = new Array(6)
grades[0] = new Array(3)
grades[1] = new Array(3)
grades[2] = new Array(3)
grades[3] = new Array(3)
grades[4] = new Array(3)
grades[5] = new Array(3)
```

I gave everyone a moment to let this settle in.

"By convention," I said, "for a two-dimensional Array, the declaration for the 'rows' appears first, followed by the declaration for the 'column' for each one of the 'rows', although there's no requirement to do it that way."

"So the number 6 in the first Array declaration refers to the number of rows in the Array, and the number 3 thereafter refers to the number of columns?" Barbara asked.

"That's right," I said. "With this declaration, JavaScript initializes a two-dimensional Array, the first dimension having six elements---with the lowest Subscript being 0, and the highest subscript being 5. The second dimension has three elements--with the lowest Subscript being 0, and the highest being 2. Let me ask you a question: If this Array were actually a worksheet, how many 'cells' would it contain?"

"Eighteen," Dave said. "Just multiply the two size figures--six by three is eighteen."

"That's right Dave," I said. "A two dimensional Array containing six rows and three columns contains a total of eighteen elements--each element holding a quiz score. You can see why I said earlier that each dimension you add to an Array increases its storage requirements geometrically."

"Am I correct in assuming that we could also declare this two dimensional array with no numbers in the parentheses?" Kate asked.

"That's right Kate," I said, "as is the case with a one-dimensional array, the size of the Array is optional. We could just as easily declare this array like this..."

```
var grades = new Array()
grades[0] = new Array()
grades[1] = new Array()
grades[2] = new Array()
grades[3] = new Array()
grades[4] = new Array()
grades[5] = new Array()
```

"...in which case the number of elements in the Array is really unknown---and unlimited."

"How do we refer to individual elements within a multi-dimensional Array?" Peter asked. "Is it similar to referring to the elements of a one-dimensional Array?"

"It is similar," I answered. "As we've seen, one-dimensional Arrays are referenced by using a single Subscript within brackets. Two-dimensional Array elements are referenced by using two Subscripts--one for each dimension. For example, to refer to the third quiz grade for the second student, we would use this notation…"

```
grades[1] [2] = 88
```

"The number within the first pair of brackets," I said, "refers to the first dimension--or row---of the Array, and that's the dimension that represents students. Don't forget, subscript 1 is actually the second row, or student, in the Array. The number within the second set of brackets refers to the second dimension---or column--of the Array, and that's the dimension that represents quizzes. Subscript 2 is the third quiz score."

I looked for signs of confusion in the faces of my students, but happily, I didn't see any. I suggested that now would be a great time for them to complete an exercise to get their feet wet by working with a two-dimensional Array.

Exercise 9-5 A Two-Dimensional Array

In this exercise, you'll create your first two-dimensional Array.

1. Use Notepad (if you are using Windows) and enter the following code.

```
<! Practice9-5 -->
<html>
<body>
<script type="text/javascript">

var grades = new Array(6)
grades[0] = new Array(3)
grades[1] = new Array(3)
grades[2] = new Array(3)
grades[3] = new Array(3)
grades[4] = new Array(3)
grades[5] = new Array(3)

grades[0] [0] = 82
grades[0] [1] = 91
grades[0] [2] = 73

grades[1] [0] = 90
grades[1] [1] = 65
grades[1] [2] = 88

grades[2] [0] = 64
grades[2] [1] = 56
grades[2] [2] = 33

grades[3] [0] = 80
grades[3] [1] = 85
grades[3] [2] = 81
```

```
grades[4] [0] = 95
grades[4] [1] = 98
grades[4] [2] = 95

grades[5] [0] = 75
grades[5] [1] = 61
grades[5] [2] = 80

for (row = 0; row < grades.length; row++) {
  for (col = 0; col < grades[row].length; col++) {
    document.write (grades[row][col] + " ")
  }
document.write ("<br>")
}

</script>
</body>
</html>
```

2. Save your source file as **'Practice9-5.htm'** in the \JavaScriptFiles\Practice folder (select File-Save As from Notepad's Menu Bar). Be sure to save your source file with the file name extension 'htm'.

3. Use Internet Explorer to Open your Source File.

4. The program will display the three quiz grades for the six students in row and column format.

Discussion

I immediately ran the program myself and the following screen was displayed on the classroom projector:

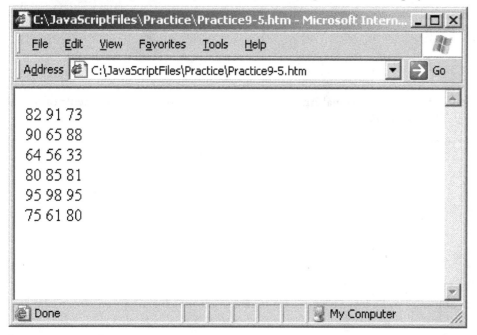

"As you can see," I said, "what we've done is write code to load the three quiz grades for six students into a two-dimensional Array, and then display them in the Internet Browser."

"This is pretty impressive," Rhonda said. "although I must confess, I'm not real clear with how you did this."

"Don't worry Rhonda," I said, "I'll be glad to explain it."

"Those first seven lines of code, are those the declaration for the two-dimensional Array?" Peter asked.

"Yes they are Peter," I replied. "First we declare the 'row' portion of the Array..."

var grades = new Array(6)

"...then for each row in the Array, we then declare the 'column' portion of the Array as a 3 element Array of its own..."

```
grades[0] = new Array(3)
grades[1] = new Array(3)
grades[2] = new Array(3)
grades[3] = new Array(3)
grades[4] = new Array(3)
grades[5] = new Array(3)
```

"Once we've declared the Array," I said, "this next section of code initializes each element of the Array----here, one line of code at a time..."

```
grades[0] [0] = 82
grades[0] [1] = 91
grades[0] [2] = 73

grades[1] [0] = 90
grades[1] [1] = 65
grades[1] [2] = 88

grades[2] [0] = 64
grades[2] [1] = 56
grades[2] [2] = 33

grades[3] [0] = 80
grades[3] [1] = 85
grades[3] [2] = 81

grades[4] [0] = 95
grades[4] [1] = 98
grades[4] [2] = 95

grades[5] [0] = 75
grades[5] [1] = 61
grades[5] [2] = 80
```

"Is it possible to initialize the elements of a two dimensional Array the same way we initialized the elements of the one-dimensional Array in Exercise 9-3?" Dave asked.

"Yes it is Dave," I said, "here's the syntax..."

```
int grades[] [] = {
{ 82, 91, 73},
{ 90, 65, 88},
{ 64, 56, 33},
{ 80, 85, 81},
{ 95, 98, 95},
{ 75, 61, 80}
}
```

"...Some students find this syntax confusing, so I'll leave it up to you to determine which syntax you wish to use."

I paused before continuing.

"...Now, with our two-dimensional Array loaded with values, all that remains is to navigate through the eighteen elements of the Array and display them in our Internet Browser. This next section of code is similar to the code we saw in Exercise 9-4, but because we are dealing with an Array that has not just one dimension but two, the technique is more complex, requiring us to use something called nested For loops..."

```
for (row = 0; row < grades.length; row++) {
  for (col = 0; col < grades[row].length; col++) {
    document.write (grades[row][col] + " ")
  }
document.write ("<br>")
}
```

"This is where I became totally lost when I did the exercise," Kate said. "You say this is a Nested For Loop? I think I've heard some programmers at work use that term. It sounds very complicated."

"Nested For Loops can be intimidating Kate," I said. "but if you just remember that a nested For Loop is nothing more than a loop whose body itself contains a For Loop I think you'll be OK."

I paused a moment to give everyone in the class to realize what I had just said.

"A nested For Loop is a For Loop that contains another For Loop in its body," I repeated. "The first For Loop structure is called the 'Outer Loop', and the For Loop that appears in its body is called the 'Inner Loop'. If you check the code, you'll see that each For loop has its own unique Loop control variable. I've named the Loop control variable of the outer loop 'row', and the Loop control variable of the inner loop 'column'. This is because the Outer loop is intended to process the columns in the two-dimensional Array, and the Inner Loop is intended to process the rows. Think of these For Loops almost like a mouse pointer which is directing a screen cursor to various positions within the Array."

"This is confusing," Rhonda chimed in. "I keep trying to visualize what's going on with the code but..."

"I think if you take it a step at a time, you'll be fine," I said. "and that's exactly what we're going to be doing in a minute. Notice that the outer loop has a body consisting of three lines of code---another For Loop, a write() method and another write() method. The Inner loop has a body consisting of just one line of code--the write() method."

"Isn't the write() method *part* of the body of the inner loop?" Barbara asked.

"No it's not," I said. "The Inner loop--the one that uses col as the Loop control variable---has just one line of code in it, the write() method."

I paused for a moment before continuing.

"You'll see in a minute," I said, "as we step through this code that the body of the inner loop will be executed a total of eighteen times, while the body of the outer loop will be executed just six times."

"Is that because there are 6 rows of data in the Array?" Dave asked.

"Exactly Dave," I said.

"But there are only three columns in the Array," Blaine said, "Why would the inner loop be executed 18 times. Shouldn't it be executed just three times?"

"That's a good question Blaine," I responded. "The Inner Loop is executed three times---but each time the outer loop is executed, which is six times, the Inner Loop is once again executed three times. Six multiplied by three is 18--that's the total number of times the inner loop is executed."

"It also happens to be the number of elements in the Array," Dave said proudly..

I saw a great deal of confusion on the faces of my students.

"Don't worry if you feel a little overwhelmed by this right now," I said. "I think this will all make a lot more sense to you in a few moments. Let's get back to the body of the inner loop now---amazingly, it consists of just this single line of code..."

```
document.write (grades[row][col] + " ")
```

"All in all, this line of code will be executed a total 18 times," I explained, "which as Dave pointed out is the total number of elements, or quiz grades, in our two dimensional Array. Using nested For loops, the values of the two Loop control variables, row and col, are varied to point to each element in the Array, and displayed in the Internet Browser window..."

```
for (row = 0; row < grades.length; row++) {
  for (col = 0; col < grades[row].length; col++) {
```

"Again, the first loop is known as the Outer loop," I continued, "and we use it to 'move' through the rows in the Array. We initialize its Loop Control variable--row---to 0, and for its termination point, we use the length attribute of the grades Array, which is six. Ultimately, JavaScript interprets this line of code to look like this..."

```
for (row = 0; row < 6; row++) {
```

"That means that the outer loop is executed six times, is that right?" Chuck asked.

"Exactly right Chuck," I said. "Now let's take a look at the Inner loop which is used to process the columns in the Array..."

```
for (col = 0; col < grades[row].length; col++) {
```

"...I want you to notice the length attribute as we use it here. We used the length attribute in the outer loop also, and in that case, it returned a value equal to the number of rows in the Array. In this case, we're asking JavaScript to return the length attribute for a particular row of the Array, and that's why we used the qualifier 'row' here. Ultimately, JavaScript interprets this code to look like this..."

```
for (col = 0; col < 3; col++)
```

"And that's why the inner loop is executed three times?" Chuck asked.

"That's right Chuck," I said.

I then displayed this table on the classroom projector.

"Maybe this will help," I said. "to give you an appreciation for the sequence of code execution. This table shows the statements that are being executed, the values of the *row* and *col* Loop Control variables, the Array element that is being pointed to by the value of *row* and *col*, the value of that Array element, and the result of the execution of the statement..."

Statement	row	col	grades	Value of grades	Comment
For (int row...)	0				1st execution of outer loop
For (int col...)	0	0	0,0	82	1st execution of inner loop
write(grades[row] [col]	0	0	0,0	82	Displays 82 in Internet Browser
For (int col...) by 1.	0	1	0,1	91	2nd execution of inner loop. Value of col is incremented by 1.
write(grades[row] [col]	0	1	0,1	91	Displays 91 in Internet Browser
For (int col...) by 1.	0	2	0,2	73	3rd execution of inner loop. Value of col is incremented by 1.
write(grades[row] [col]	0	2	0,2	73	Displays 73 in the Internet Browser
write(" ")	0	2	0,2	73	New line is generated in the Internet Browser
For (int row...) incremented by 1.	1				2nd execution of outer loop. Value of row is
For (int col...)	1	0	1,0	90	1st execution of inner loop
write(grades[row] [col]	1	0	1,0	90	Displays 90 in Internet Browser
For (int col...) by 1.	1	1	1,1	65	2nd execution of inner loop. Value of col is incremented by 1.
write(grades[row] [col]	1	1	1,1	65	Displays 65 in Internet Browser
For (int col...) by 1.	1	2	1,2	88	3rd execution of inner loop. Value of col is incremented by 1.
write(grades[row] [col]	1	2	1,2	88	Displays 88 in the Internet Browser
write(" ")	1	2	1,2	88	New line is generated in the Internet Browser
For (int row...) incremented by 1.	2				3rd execution of outer loop. Value of row is
For (int col...)	2	0	2,0	64	1st execution of inner loop
write(grades[row] [col]	2	0	2,0	64	Displays 64 in Internet Browser
For (int col...) by 1.	2	1	2,1	56	2nd execution of inner loop. Value of col is incremented by 1.
write(grades[row] [col]	2	1	2,1	56	Displays 56 in Internet Browser
For (int col...) by 1.	2	2	2,2	33	3rd execution of inner loop. Value of col is incremented by 1.
write(grades[row] [col]	2	2	2,2	33	Displays 33 in the Internet Browser

write(" ")	2	2	2,2	33	New line is generated in the Internet Browser
For (int row...) incremented by 1.	3				4th execution of outer loop. Value of row is
For (int col...)	3	0	3,0	80	1st execution of inner loop
write(grades[row] [col]	3	0	3,0	80	Displays 80 in Internet Browser
For (int col...) by 1.	3	1	3,1	85	2nd execution of inner loop. Value of col is incremented
write(grades[row] [col]	3	1	3,1	85	Displays 85 in Internet Browser
For (int col...) by 1.	3	2	3,2	81	3rd execution of inner loop. Value of col is incremented
write(grades[row] [col]	3	2	3,2	81	Displays 81 in the Internet Browser
write(" ")	3	2	3,2	81	New line is generated in the Internet Browser
For (int row...) incremented by 1.	4				5th execution of outer loop. Value of row is
For (int col...)	4	0	4,0	95	1st execution of inner loop
write(grades[row] [col]	4	0	4,0	95	Displays 95 in Internet Browser
For (int col...) by 1.	4	1	4,1	98	2nd execution of inner loop. Value of col is incremented
write(grades[row] [col]	4	1	4,1	98	Displays 98 in Internet Browser
For (int col...) by 1.	4	2	4,2	95	3rd execution of inner loop. Value of col is incremented
write(grades[row] [col]	4	2	4,2	95	Displays 95 in the Internet Browser
write(" ")	4	2	4,2	95	New line is generated in the Internet Browser
For (int row...) incremented by 1.	5				6th execution of outer loop. Value of row is
For (int col...)	5	0	5,0	75	1st execution of inner loop
write(grades[row] [col]	5	0	5,0	75	Displays 55 in Internet Browser
For (int col...) by 1.	5	1	5,1	61	2nd execution of inner loop. Value of col is incremented
write(grades[row] [col]	5	1	5,1	61	Displays 61 in Internet Browser
For (int col...) by 1.	5	2	5,2	80	3rd execution of inner loop. Value of col is incremented
write(grades[row] [col]	5	2	5,2	80	Displays 80 in the Internet Browser
write(" ")	5	2	5,2	80	New line is generated in the Internet Browser

We then spent the next few minutes going over the table.

"I hope that helped," I said, as I scanned the faces of my students for signs of confusion.

"Yes it did," Ward said, "I have just one question. Why did we use the write() method in the body of the inner loop to print the values of the individual elements of the Array---and then the write() method again in the outer loop?"

"That was for formatting purposes," I said. "The write() method within the inner loop doesn't generate a new line character---if we had included the <br> tag within the inner loop as we did within the outer loop, we would have had a single column of values displayed in the Internet Browser, with each value appearing on a line by itself. As a result, the 'cursor' in the Internet Browser remains on the same line. We did execute the write() method with the <br> tag in the outer loop --but only at the 'end' of each row--as the last statement in the body of the inner loop."

Creating Arrays of Objects

That explanation satisfied Ward and the other students, and so before continuing onto the next topic of creating Arrays of objects, I asked everyone to take a fifteen minute break.

"Something that's asked of me all the time," I said, after resuming from break, "is whether it's possible to create an Array of objects in JavaScript."

"You mean like the Student objects we've been working with throughout the class?" Mary asked.

"That's right Mary," I said, "that kind of object. The answer is yes---in fact, creating an Array of objects is easy to do. Do you remember the Banner object we worked with several weeks ago? Let's create an Array of Banner objects."

I then displayed this code on the classroom projector.

```
<! Example9-1 -->
<html>
<head>
<script src='Banner.js'></script>
</head>
<body>
<script type="text/javascript">

var x = new Array()

x[0] = new Banner()
x[0].favoriteProgram = "JavaScript"
x[0].display()

x[1] = new Banner()
x[1].favoriteProgram = "Visual Basic"
x[1].display()

for (row = 0; row < x.length; row++) {
   document.write(x[row].favoriteProgram + "<br>")
}

</script>
</body>
</html>
```

I then saved it as '**Example9-1.htm**' and opened it up within Internet Explorer. The following screenshot was displayed on the classroom projector.

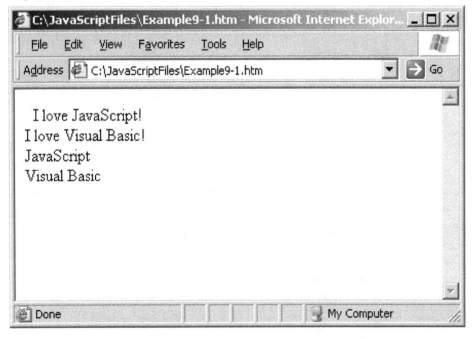

"Working with an Array of objects is a little different than working with an Array of JavaScript Data Types, such as Integer or String" I said. "It's really a two step process. First, we need to declare the Array, and then we need to go about the business of actually creating the objects, just as we would normally--but because we're dealing with an Array of objects, we need to use subscript values when we refer to the object. Let's start with the Array declaration. This line of code declares our Array--notice how we've not defined a size for the Array--from what we've seen this morning, it's safer not to do so..."

```
var x = new Array()
```

"…with the Array declared, we can then go about creating the Banner objects themselves--but we need to tell JavaScript where in the Array this object, once created, will be referenced. In this case, it's element number 0…"

```
x[0] = new Banner()
```

"With the Banner object now created, and referenced as element 0 of the x Array, we can now work with the object just like we normally would--we just need to remember to reference the element number any time we refer to the object. With this line of code we set the favoriteProgram attribute of the Banner object to 'Java'…"

```
x[0].favoriteProgram = "JavaScript"
```

"…and then execute its display() method…:"

```
x[0].display()
```

"Just to prove that we can have multiple Banner objects 'alive' at the same time, this code creates a second Banner object, establishes it as element 1 of the x Array, sets its favoriteProgram attribute to 'Visual Basic' and then executes its display() method…"

```
x[1] = new Banner()
x[1].favoriteProgram = "Visual Basic"
x[1].display()
```

"So we have two Banner objects loaded in our Array?" Mary asked.

"You can think of it that way Mary," I said. "In reality, the Array contains a reference---a memory address really--- pointing to both objects. The important thing is that when we refer to an element in the Array, JavaScript can find the Banner object we intend to work with in the computer's memory--along with any attributes that belong to that particular object. That's why we can use the For…Loop logic we've been employing in today's class to display the *favoriteProgram* attribute of every Banner object referenced by our Array…"

```
for (row = 0; row < x.length; row++) {
  document.write(x[row].favoriteProgram + "<br>")
}
```

"That is really neat," Blaine said. "I'm beginning to like Arrays more and more--too bad we can't include one in the Grades Calculate project."

"I don't see why we can't," I said. "Frank Olley never requested it, but I don't think he would mind if we calculated an overall average for every student's grade entered into the program, just like in the practice exercises we've been doing today.. I think an Array would be a perfect way to do that."

I then distributed this exercise for the class to complete.

Exercise 9-6 Modify the Grades Calculation Project to use an Array

In this exercise, you'll modify the Grades class to include Array processing to calculate an overall class average.

1. Using Notepad (if you are using Windows) locate and open the Grades.htm source file. (It should be in the \JavaScriptFiles\Grades folder)
2. Modify your code so that it looks like this.

```
<! Grades-- >
<html>
<head>
<script src='EnglishStudent.js'></script>
<script src='MathStudent.js'></script>
<script src='ScienceStudent.js'></script>
<script src='functions.js'></script>
```

```
</head>
<body>
<script type="text/javascript">

var response = ""
var moreGradesToCalculate = ""
var grades = new Array()
var accumulator = 0
var counter = 0
var average = 0

moreGradesToCalculate = prompt("Do you want to calculate a grade?","Yes")
moreGradesToCalculate = moreGradesToCalculate.toUpperCase()

while (moreGradesToCalculate == "YES") {

 response=whatKindOfStudent()

 // Student type is valid, now let's calculate the grade

 switch(parseInt(response)) {

  // Case 1 is an English Student
  case 1:
   var x = new EnglishStudent()
   x.calculate()
   x.displayGrade()
   grades[counter] = x.getFinalNumericGrade()
   counter++
   break

  // Case 2 is a Math Student
  case 2:
   var y = new MathStudent()
   y.calculate()
   y.displayGrade()
   grades[counter] = y.getFinalNumericGrade()
   counter++
   break

  // Case 3 is a Science Student
  case 3:
   var z = new ScienceStudent()
   z.calculate()
   z.displayGrade()
   grades[counter] = z.getFinalNumericGrade()
   counter++
   break

  default:
   alert(response + " - is not a valid student type")
 }
moreGradesToCalculate = prompt("Do you have another grade to calculate?","Yes")
moreGradesToCalculate = moreGradesToCalculate.toUpperCase()
}

for (row = 0; row < grades.length; row++) {
 accumulator = accumulator + grades[row]
}

average = accumulator / grades.length
alert("The class average is " + average)
alert("Thanks for using the Grades Calculation program!")
```

```
</script>
</body>
</html>
```

3. Save your source file as '**Grades.htm**' in the \JavaScriptFiles\Grades folder (select File-Save As from Notepad's Menu Bar). Be sure to save your source file with the file name extension 'htm'.

4. Use Internet Explorer to Open your Source File.

5. Test your program thoroughly. After you start your program, it should ask you if you have a grade to calculate.

6. Answer 'Yes', and then calculate the grade for an English student. Enter 70 for the midterm, 80 for the final examination, 90 for the research grade and 100 for the presentation. A final numeric grade of 84.5 should be displayed--with a letter grade of 'C'.

7. After the message box is displayed with the calculated grade, the program should ask you if you have more grades to calculate.

8. Answer yes, and then calculate the grade for a Math student. Enter 70 for the midterm and 80 for the final examination. A final numeric grade of 75 should be displayed--with a letter grade of 'D'.

9. After the message box is displayed with the calculated grade, the program should ask you if you have more grades to calculate.

10. Answer yes, and then calculate the grade for a Science student. Enter 70 for the midterm, 80 for the final examination. and 90 for the research grade. A final numeric grade of 78 should be displayed--with a letter grade of 'C'. After the message box is displayed with the calculate grade, the program should ask you if you have more grades to calculate.

11. Answer no--an overall average of 79.16 will be displayed in a message box.

Discussion

Making the modifications to the code in the Grades class required careful attention to detail---but in the end, everyone was able to complete the exercise without a great deal of trouble. Rhonda did have one problem though.

"What's wrong Rhonda?" I asked, as I made my way to her workstation.

"My program's not doing anything," she answered.

True enough---as soon as we tried to bring up her version of Grades.htm in her Internet Browser, 'nothing' seemed to happen.

"JavaScript is very poor with error messages," I said, "a change that you've made to your project is causing a problem somewhere."

I displayed her code on the classroom projector, starting with the Student classes, which had no obvious problems. I then brought up the Grades.htm file---and Dave saw it almost immediately.

"I did the same thing last week," he said.

"What's that Dave?" Rhonda said anxiously.

"Your call to the getFinalNumbericGrade," he said, "you forgot the pair of parentheses at the end."

Sure enough, Rhonda had done exactly that. Her code looked like this...

```
grades[counter] = x.getFinalNumericGrade
```

when it should have looked like this

```
grades[counter] = x.getFinalNumericGrade()
```

"I discovered last week," Dave said, "that when you fail to include the closing parenthesis, you assign the actual text of the method to the variable, in this case to an Array element of grades---pretty strange, I must say."

"Great job picking that up Dave," I said, as Rhonda fixed her program and ran it successfully.

I waited a moment before continuing.

"I'm not sure that the changes we've just made to the Grades Calculation project are something Frank Olley requires," I said, "but I think they will add greatly to your learning experience---and it didn't require all that much additional code. Our first step was to declare a grades Array to store the values of the individual calculated final grades. We declared grades as an Array with no size specified in order to accommodate any number of grades that a user will calculate in this program…"

```
var grades = new Array()
var accumulator = 0
var counter = 0
var average = 0.0
```

"…We needed to modify our existing code to add the student's calculated grade as an element of the grades Array. To do that, all we needed to do was to add a line of code to each of the individual Case statements to add the *finalNumericGrade* attribute of the various student objects to the Array, using the current value of the counter variable to specify the subscript. Here's the code to do that for the EnglishStudent object…"

```
case 1:
 var x = new EnglishStudent()
 x.calculate()
 x.displayGrade()
 grades[counter] = x.getFinalNumericGrade()
```

"…once we have the student's grade in the grades Array, we need to increment the value of the counter variable so that the next student's grade is assigned to the next available location in the Array…"

```
counter++
```

"…This process of adding an element to the grades Array continues for each student calculated. Finally, when the user indicates there are no more grades to calculate, now it's time to move through the elements of the Array, calculate the average, and display it…"

```
for (row = 0; row < grades.length; row++) {
 accumulator = accumulator + grades[row]
}
average = accumulator / grades.length
alert("The class average is " + average)
```

"Seeing the Array used in the Grades Calculation program really helped me," Rhonda said.

I waited to see if there were any questions, but there were none. I then dismissed class for the day.

Summary

In this chapter, you learned just about everything you could want to know about Array processing, and more. In particular, we learned about the various types of Arrays and also about Array dimensions. Arrays are a frequent source of confusion for new programmers and I hope our coverage of them will make your future work with them easier.

Specifically, we saw:
· Why Arrays are useful in making our code easier to write and use
· Different types of Arrays: one dimensional and multi-dimensional Array
· How Arrays can reduce the amount of hard-coding we write in our projects.

In the next chapter, we'll explore some of the common errors that can occur in JavaScript programming, and examine ways to make allowances for problems that might occur when our programs run.

Chapter 10---Exception Handling

In this chapter, you'll follow my university class as we learn how to avoid some of the common mistakes that beginner JavaScript programmers make. Plus, you'll also learn how to detect and handle the errors that slip through your fingers.

Common Beginner Errors

I began our tenth class by explaining that as a teacher of computer programming, it's frequently tempting to show my students examples of bad code early on in a class in an effort to show them what 'not' to do. However, after many years of teaching, I have learned that there's a huge danger in illustrating bad code or code that contains errors too early in the class.

"For that reason," I said, "I try to wait until we've established a strong foundation in good coding techniques before discussing the types of errors you can make which can quickly ruin your programming reputation. In today's class, we'll examine the types of common errors that beginners make and then learn how to implement Error Handling techniques in our JavaScript programs to detect handle the errors that can occur anyway even in the best of programs."

"What kinds of errors are you talking about detecting?" Dave asked. "I assume you mean runtime errors---you're not talking about compiler errors."

"That's a good point Dave," I said. "There are actually three kinds of errors that we'll be discussing today. The first kind are Load-time errors, and those are the errors which are detected by the JavaScript Interpreter as it attempts to execute our program. Load-time errors prevent us from ever getting to the point where we can run our program. The second kind are run-time errors. These are the kinds of error that the JavaScript compiler can't detect, and which unfortunately occur when we run our program. Runtime errors display nasty error messages to the user of our program. The third kind of errors are the most dangerous. These are logic errors, and they are not detected by the compiler, nor, for the most part, do they cause your program to 'bomb' or abnormally terminate at run time. Logic errors are programming mistakes that can cause horrific results--such as generating a paycheck for an employee for one million dollars instead of one thousand dollars, or ordering a dosage of medicine for a patient that is incorrect, or opening a valve or an engine of the space shuttle prematurely. Logic errors can be very difficult to track down--in fact, there are programs that have run for years with subtle logic errors that went unnoticed."

> **Note: To turn 'on' the JavaScript Error dialog box in the Internet Explorer, first click on the Tools tab of the menu and select Internet Options. This will open the Internet Options window. Click on the Advanced tab. Locate the check box for "Display a notification about every script error" and make sure it is checked. Then click OK.**

Load-Time Errors--When NOTHING seems to happen

"Let's start by examining the common types of JavaScript Load-time errors that you are likely to make," I said.

"What are Load-time errors?" Rhonda asked. "Is that when 'nothing' seems to happen?"

"Right you are Rhonda," I said, "that's exactly what they are. When you open your JavaScript html page in your Internet Browser, JavaScript takes a quick look at the code and if it sees anything obviously wrong, it simply won't 'load' the page into your Internet Browser. For the most part, Load-time errors are simply typos in our code."

"We've all made those during the class," Dave said.

Misspelling Object Names

"Yes we have," I agreed. "If nothing seems to happen with your JavaScript program, take a look at the lower left hand corner of your Browser Window---you should see a yellow exclamation point..."

> **Note: Depending upon the Internet Browser you are using, you may receive an immediate message box indicating the error.**

"...in the lower left hand portion of our Browser window telling us that something is wrong. Let me code a simple JavaScript program that has an *intentional typo*, just to verify that everyone knows what I mean."

Don't Forget: If typing these examples and exercises isn't something you want to do, feel free to follow this link to find and download the completed solutions for all of the examples and exercises in the book. Just click on the JavaScript book, then follow the link entitled exercises ☺

http://www.johnsmiley.com/main/books.htm

```
<! Example10-1 -->
<html>
<body>
<script type="text/javascript">

var x = 22

docment.write("The value of x is " + x)

</script>
</body>
</html>
```

"Does everyone see the typo," I asked. "I've spelled the name of the 'document' object as 'docment' instead--as a result, nothing seems to happen when I load up this program in my Internet Browser, however, note the yellow exclamation point in the lower left hand portion of the Browser window..."

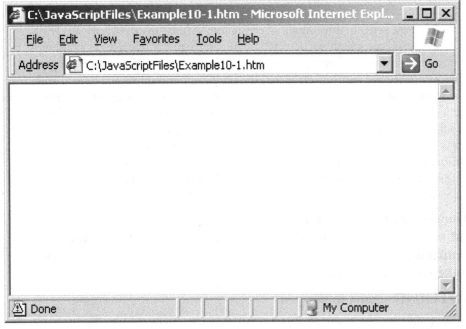

"If we click on that exclamation point," I said, "we should see a clue as to the error..."

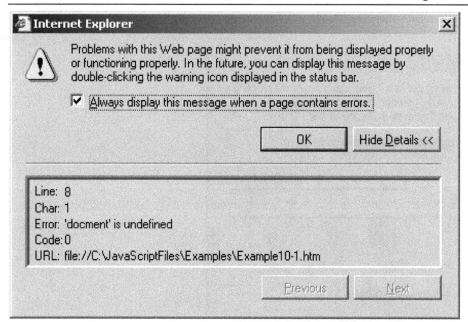

"There's our clue," I said, "docmnt is undefined, and Javascript also gives us the line in our source file where it encountered the problem. Of course, if it's the middle of the night, you could stare at docmnt for a long time and not realize what the problem is--that's why it's always good to have someone else take a look at your code if you can't resolve the issue. By the way, if you want to be certain you are seeing all of your error messages, be sure to check 'on' the box that says 'Always display this message when a page contains errors'---otherwise, your Internet Browser may suppress error messages that occur."

> **Note: To be certain you are seeing all of your error messages, be sure to check 'on' the box that says 'Always display this message when a page contains errors'---otherwise, your Internet Browser may suppress error messages that occur, and you will have to close and then re-open your Browser window to see them.**

"So will all Load-time errors be typos like this?" Ward asked.

"You could also get a Load-time error if you reference an external file, such as a class or a function file, that can't be found," I said. "Here's some code that references the Banner object we worked with last week---notice that I've misspelled the name of 'Banner.js' in the <head> section..."

```
<! Example10-2 -->
<html>
<head>
<script src='Bnner.js'></script>
</head>
<body>
<script type="text/javascript">

var x = new Array()

x[0] = new Banner()
x[0].favoriteProgram = "JavaScript"
x[0].display()

x[1] = new Banner()
x[1].favoriteProgram = "Visual Basic"
x[1].display()

for (row = 0; row < x.length; row++) {
document.write(x[row].favoriteProgram + "<br>")
}

</script>
</body>
</html>
```

"...If I try to open this program in my Internet Browser, I'll see this Load-time error displayed in the Error window..."

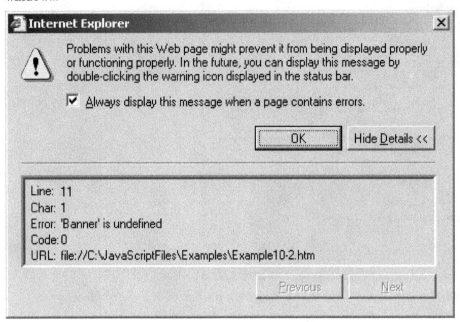

"...Notice that the error message doesn't tell us that it can't find the file 'Bnner.js'---it tells us that the Banner class referenced in Line 11 is undefined. It's up to us to figure out that the file name referenced is wrong. By the way, we would get this same error message if we spelled the name of 'Banner.js' correctly--but it didn't appear in the same folder location as our program."

Braces (and parentheses) must occur in matching pairs

"Another common error that beginner programmers make," I said, "which can generate a Load-time error deals with braces, brackets, and parentheses."

I noticed a lot of affirmative nodding of heads in the class.

"I have to admit," Linda said, "I did find the whole issue of braces and parentheses confusing at first--all of those curly braces can really be confusing."

"I don't blame you," I said. "by the way, that's a good reason to indent your code. Another way to eliminate this error altogether is to double check your code to ensure that you have the same number of right and left curly braces and parentheses."

"In a JavaScript program," I continued, "there are numerous instances where you need to include braces, parentheses and brackets. If you use braces in your code, be sure you have the *same* number of right and left braces. If you use parentheses in your code, be sure you have the same number of right and left parentheses. If you use brackets in your code, be sure to have the same number of right and left brackets. Take a look at this code..."

```
<! Example10-3 -->
<html>
<body>
<script type="text/javascript">

var counter = 0

if (counter == 0) {
   document.write("The value of counter is equal to 0")
}
}

</script>
</body>
</html>
```

"I don't whether you notice or not," I said, "but there's an 'extra' right brace in the code---notice that we have only one left brace, but two right braces--that's a problem."

"What kind of error message will you get if you make this kind of mistake?" Rhonda asked. "Is it as 'user friendly' as some of the others we've seen this morning?"

"Let's see Rhonda," I said. I opened the program in Internet Explorer. 'Nothing' appeared to happen--but we did see the yellow exclamation point in the lower left hand corner of my Internet Browser Window indicating there was an error on the Page.. When I double clicked on it, this error message was displayed.

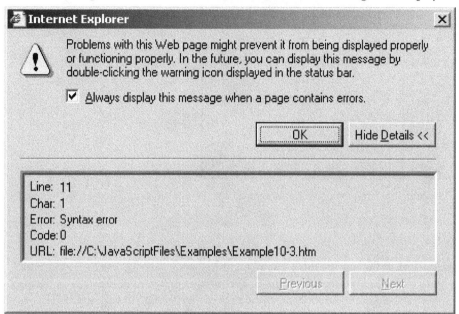

"Syntax error?" I heard Steve say.

"Although it's not a very user friendly message," I said, "Syntax error does alert us to the fact that we have broken some rule of coding---and Line 11, Character 1 is exactly where the 'extra' brace is located."

"If we forget to correctly code a closing brace," Linda asked, "what will happen?"

"Good question Linda," I answered, "let's see." I then modified Example10-3 to look like this...

```
<! Example10-4 -->
<html>
<body>
<script type="text/javascript">

var counter = 0

if (counter == 0) {
   document.write("The value of counter is equal to 0")

</script>
</body>
</html>
```

saved it as '**Example10-4.htm**' and opened it up within Internet Explorer. Here was the error message that was displayed.

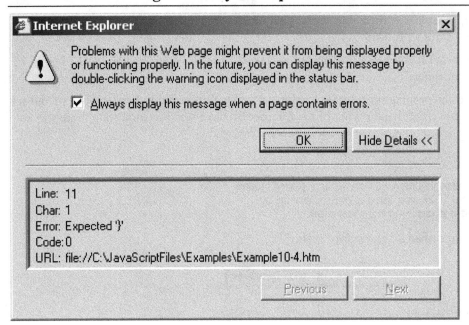

"The error message is telling us that JavaScript is expecting a right brace at Line 11," Kate said, "that makes sense."

"As far as error messages go," I said, "this one isn't bad."

Runtime Errors

"The two types of errors that we've examined so far this morning have been Load-time errors," I said. "Load-time errors, though sometimes a nuisance to correct, do little to tarnish the image of your program in the eyes of the user since the user should never see them--they should all be uncovered in the process of testing your program. There's really no excuse to permit a program with a Load-time error to make its way into your user's hands, since all the programmer really needs to do is to load the program in their Internet Browser to verify that it runs. Unfortunately, there are some types of errors that escape the watchful eye of the JavaScript Interpreter and don't show up until run time when an unsuspecting user is interacting with your program. These types of errors are called run-time errors, and usually result in your program displaying an error message, with a cryptic message to the user asking them if they would like to Debug the program. Regardless of whether he or she chooses that option (and if they do, they will be very confused), the program will abnormally terminate or 'bomb' as we sometimes call it. Runtime errors are serious, and can sometimes result in the user of your program losing hours of work.

JavaScript is Case sensitive

"Probably the most common types of Interpreter errors," I said, "are caused by the case sensitivity of JavaScript. In JavaScript, just about everything is case sensitive. The names of classes, such as document and Array,, the names of methods, and the names of variables are all case sensitive. This can give programmers, especially those who have experience in other languages that are not case sensitive, a lot of trouble. Improperly referencing the name of a class, a method or a variable in your program will generate a 'cannot resolve symbol' Interpreter error. Remember, any reference to a class name, the method of a class, or to a variable that you declare in your program must match case exactly. For instance, if we declare a variable called *counter* (in lower case) and then attempt to increment its value like this...

```
<! Example10-5 -->
<html>
<body>
<script type="text/javascript">

var counter = 0
Counter++

</script>
</body>
</html>
```

"...we'll generate a Runtime error indicating that an Object is expected' at Line 6."

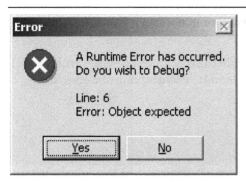

"What does that mean?" Rhonda asked. "What object?"

"We declared counter in lower case letters," I said, "but then we tried to refer to the variable with an initial Capital letter. Because JavaScript is case sensitive, it considers these to be two separate entities. The bit about the object is JavaScript's way of saying it doesn't know what we're talking about. Are we referring to a variable? A class? An object derived from a class?"

"In other words," Dave said, "JavaScript is very confused."

"Exactly Dave," I said, grateful for the bailout. "In a similar manner, if we declare a variable called 'x' in lower case letters, but then later refer to it as 'X' in upper case letters..."

```
<! Example10-6 -->
<html>
<body>
<script type="text/javascript">

var x = 22
document.write("The value of x is " + X)

</script>
</body>
</html>
```

"...you may see this runtime error."

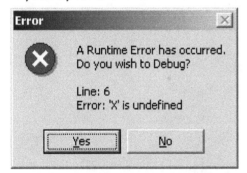

"Notice how the message box indicates a Runtime error has occurred," I said. "The last thing we want to have happen--and I can't emphasize this strong enough, is for the user to see this message. It's confusing, and worse yet, if the user clicks on the 'Yes' button saying they wish to Debug the program, depending upon what software is installed on their PC, there can be even more confusion."

"What do you mean?" Mary asked.

"For instance Mary," I said, "if a version of Microsoft's Visual Studio is installed on the user's PC when he or she clicks on the 'Yes' button, the Visual Studio programming environment will open with our JavaScript source code in it. Most users won't be able to make any sense out of this---and as a result, your program will forever be known as the program which bombed or in some way 'hurt' their PC."

"Aside from ensuring that our code is foolproof," Peter said, "is there any way to stop the Runtime Error message box from displaying?"

"Good question Peter," I said, "we'll see later on this morning that there is a way to 'intercept' runtime errors, and to display a more user friendly message to our user---one that doesn't have the choice of 'Debug'. Before we see how to do that, though, let's continue examining some of the errors that beginners commonly make."

Forgetting the left and right parentheses for the condition in an If structure generates a Runtime error. Parentheses are required.

"An error that is closely related to the one we just examined," I said, "is one that I see a lot of beginners make, and it concerns the If statement. Beginners tend to forget that the test condition for an If statement must be enclosed within parentheses."

"Ah yes," I heard Joe say.

"What's that?" Rhonda asked. "Test expression?"

"That's right Rhonda," I said. "Let me show you an example."

I then displayed this code on the classroom projector.

"This code," I said, "uses an If statement to determine if the value of the counter variable is 0."

```
<! Example10-7 -->
<html>
<body>
<script type="text/javascript">

var counter = 0

if (counter == 0) {
  document.write("The value of counter is equal to 0")
}

</script>
</body>
</html>
```

"Notice," I said, "how the test condition 'counter == 0' is *properly* enclosed within parentheses…"

```
if (counter == 0)
```

"Oh my gosh," Rhonda said, "you're right, I totally forgot about having to do that--what kind of error message will forgetting to do so generate?"

"Let me show you," I said, as I changed the code in **Example10-7** to look like this…

```
<! Example10-8 -->
<html>
<body>
<script type="text/javascript">

var counter = 0

if counter == 0 {
  document.write("The value of counter is equal to 0")
}

</script>
</body>
</html>
```

"Notice how the test expression is no longer enclosed within parentheses," I said. "Now let's open this program within Internet Explorer and see what error message it generates."

I did so, and the following error message was displayed on the classroom projector.

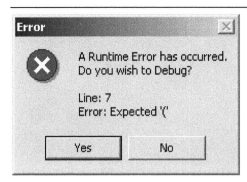

"This error message is not quite as clear as some of the other error messages we've seen," I said, "but it does point us in the right direction by listing the line of code in error, and by telling us that JavaScript is expecting a right parentheses."

I waited to see if there were any questions.

"Are there any other runtime errors that you'll be discussing today?" Steve asked.

"The two that we've covered this morning," I answered, "are probably the two most common, but I need to emphasize that there are literally dozens of different kinds of runtime errors that can occur in our programs. That's why it's so important to implement some form of Exception handling that we'll discuss in a few minutes."

Logic Errors

"You've talked about Load-time errors and Runtime errors," Barbara said, "Are those the two types of Errors we may encounter in our JavaScript programs?"

"Like it or not," I said, "there are times when we make a mistake in our program when no Error message is generated. Obviously, when a message box pops up indicating there is a problem with our program, we (or the user) will notice it. Unfortunately, there's another type of error, called logic errors, which are much more serious. Logic errors do not result in your program abnormally terminating. In fact, the program seems to be working just fine. Logic errors produce incorrect results, which if they are lucky enough to be detected by the user, minimize their damage. However, many logic errors are not discovered by the user for a long period of time, in which case the damage done by them is multiplied. As you can imagine, logic errors can drastically impact your programming career and reputation."

"What can we do about Logic Errors?" Rhonda said. "These sound really dangerous."

"They are dangerous Rhonda," I said, "about all you can do is pay careful attention to the Logic errors I demonstrate in the next half hour, make a mental note, and do your best to avoid them."

Referring to an Array element that doesn't exist

"As we learned last week," I said, "JavaScript doesn't enforce a lot of rules when it comes to Arrays. For instance, in some programming languages, defining an Array with a size of 6 elements and trying to add a seventh like this would generate a runtime error..."

```
<! Example10-9 -->
<html>
<body>
<script type="text/javascript">

var grades = new Array(6)
var accumulator = 0
var counter = 6
var average = 0.0

grades[0] = 82
grades[1] = 90
grades[2] = 64
grades[3] = 80
grades[4] = 95
grades[5] = 75
grades[6] = 44
```

```
accumulator = grades[0] + grades[1] + grades[2] +
              grades[3] + grades[4] + grades[5]
average = accumulator / counter

document.write(grades[0] + "<br>")
document.write(grades[1] + "<br>")
document.write(grades[2] + "<br>")
document.write(grades[3] + "<br>")
document.write(grades[4] + "<br>")
document.write(grades[5] + "<p>")

document.write("The class average is " + average)

</script>
</body>
</html>
```

"What I've *accidentally* done is to declare an Array with a size of 6 elements, and then assign a value to grades[6], which is really the 7th element in the Array. In some programming languages, this would produce a runtime error---JavaScript ignores it, runs the program and displays a perfect answer..."

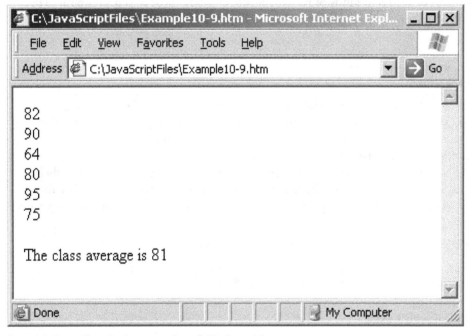

"So this is really a logic error then," Kathy said.

"That's right Kathy," I said, "if a programmer reviewed this code, and looked at it thoroughly, they'd have to wonder why they are assigning a value to element 6, but not using it elsewhere in the code. In fact, some programming languages produces messages to the effect that a variable has been assigned a value but thereafter has never been used."

"But JavaScript doesn't do that?" Rhonda said.

"Exactly Rhonda," I said, "you can therefore get yourself in a bit more trouble using JavaScript than some other languages. About the only time you'll produce a discernible error in JavaScript using Arrays is if you refer to an element of an Array that hasn't been assigned a value, like this..."

```
<! Example10-10 -->
<html>
<body>
<script type="text/javascript">

var grades = new Array(6)
var accumulator = 0
var counter = 6
var average = 0.0
```

```
grades[0] = 82
grades[1] = 90
grades[2] = 64
grades[3] = 80
grades[4] = 95
grades[5] = 75
document.write(grades[0] + "<br>")
document.write(grades[1] + "<br>")
document.write(grades[2] + "<br>")
document.write(grades[3] + "<br>")
document.write(grades[4] + "<br>")
document.write(grades[5] + "<br>")
document.write(grades[6] + "<p>")

accumulator = grades[0] + grades[1] + grades[2] +
              grades[3] + grades[4] + grades[5] + grades[6]

average = accumulator / counter

document.write("The class average is " + average)

</script>
</body>
</html>
```

"Notice how I've referred to Array element 6 when I've never assigned anything to it," I said. "Watch what happens when I load this program into my Internet Browser..."

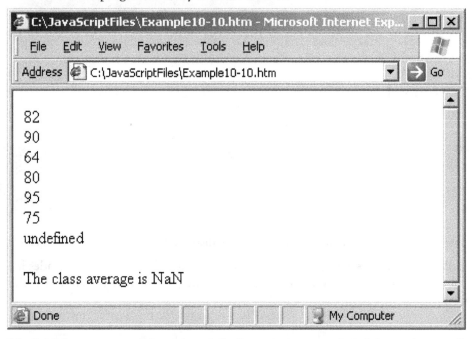

"As I think you can see," I continued, "referencing an unassigned Array element displayed 'undefined' in our Browser's window..."

```
document.write(grades[6] + "<p>")
```

"and using that undefined value in this calculation resulted in our accumulator value being assigned a value of NaN--or not a number...."

```
accumulator = grades[0] + grades[1] + grades[2] +
grades[3] + grades[4] + grades[5] + grades[6]
```

"...which also led to NaN being assigned as the class average..."

```
average = accumulator / counter
```

"I see," Rhonda said, "wow, is that dangerous. I almost wish JavaScript would produce an error message, rather than let something subtle like this slip through."

"Many programmers feel that way," I said. "You sometimes hear that JavaScript is not 'strongly typed'---what that means is that it doesn't force programmers to follow conventions that other programming languages do. This can sometimes be a detriment, particularly in terms of detecting errors."

Forgetting to Increment a Counter Variable

"Forgetting to increment a counter variable," I said, "is one of the most common Logic errors I see."

"Counter variable?" Steve asked.

I continued by explaining that many of the programs we had written during the course, particularly those we wrote last week when dealing with arrays, depended heavily upon declaring, incrementing and examining a counter variable somewhere within a program.

"Counter variables," I explained, "are variables that you declare to do exactly that: count something. For example, last week in Exercise 9-3, we wrote code that loaded the values of six quiz grades to an array. We then used a For Loop to access each element of the array, add its value to an accumulator variable, increment a counter, and finally calculate an average. Here's the code from Exercise 9-3..."

```
<! Practice9-3 -->
<html>
<body>
<script type="text/javascript">

var grades = new Array(82,90,64,80,95,75)
var accumulator = 0
var counter = 0
var average = 0.0

for (row = 0; row < grades.length; row++) {
  document.write (grades[row] + "<br>")
  accumulator = accumulator + grades[row]
  counter++
}

average = accumulator / counter
document.write("<br>The class average is " + average)

</script>
</body>
</html>
```

I then opened the program in my Internet Browser---and an average of 81 was displayed on the classroom projector.

"Crucial to this program correctly calculating the class average," I said, "is knowing the number of student grades in the array. In order to keep track of that number, we declared a variable called counter, and incremented it by 1 each time we added an element to the array..".

```
counter++
```

"...Had we forgotten to increment this counter variable, a number of problems could have resulted. Most often, we get a result of NaN. Let me show you..."

I then deleted the line of code that increments the counter so that the program looked like this...

```
<! Example10-11 -->
<html>
<body>
<script type="text/javascript">

var grades = new Array(82,90,64,80,95,75)
var accumulator = 0
var counter = 0
var average = 0.0
```

```
for (row = 0; row < grades.length; row++) {
  document.write (grades[row] + "<br>")
  accumulator = accumulator + grades[row]
}

average = accumulator / counter
document.write("<br>The class average is " + average)

</script>
</body>
</html>
```

I then saved the program as '**Example10-11.htm**' and loaded it within my Internet Browser. The following screen shot was displayed on the classroom projector.

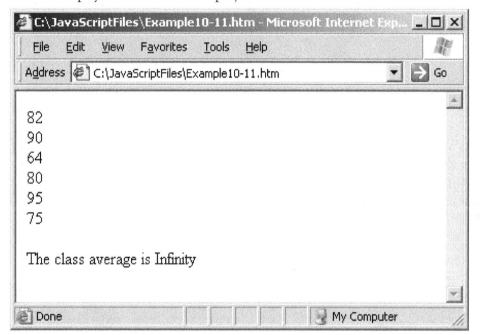

"There's the NaN result I said might occur," I continued. "In some programming languages, this would generate a runtime Division By Zero errors---however, in JavaScript, we get a result of NaN, or sometimes a result of Infinity. Either way, you don't want the user of your program calling you complaining about a result of NaN, so remember that it's vitally important to increment the value of any counter variables you declare."

Forgetting to Add to an Accumulator

"Forgetting to add values to an accumulator," I said, "is similar to forgetting to increment a counter variable. A counter variable is used to count the instances of something---like the number of quizzes taken or the number of employees in a company. An accumulator variable is a little different in that it is used to hold the running total of something---such as the total scores of all of the quiz grades taken or the total value of all employee salaries in a company. In the same example we used to illustrate the problem with a counter variable," I said, "we also added the value of the quiz grade to an accumulator variable. If we had forgotten to add the grade to the accumulator variable, we would have displayed an incorrect average in our Internet Browser window---most likely zero."

"And there goes our reputation!" Rhonda said.

"That's right, Rhonda" I agreed. "It only takes a few mistakes to tarnish it."

I displayed the code from Example10-11 on the classroom projector and highlighted the line of code where we added the grade to the accumulator variable.

```
accumulator = accumulator + grades[row]
```

"Forgetting to add a value to the accumulator variable is a very common type of JavaScript error," I explained.

"What kind of error would this generate again?" Ward asked.

"The program would run," I said, "but most likely the program would display an average of zero."

I then *deleted* the line of code where we add the value of the quiz grade to the accumulator variable, *added back* the line of code to correctly increment the counter variable so that it looked like this...

```
<! Practice10-12 -->
<html>
<body>
<script type="text/javascript">

var grades = new Array(82,90,64,80,95,75)
var accumulator = 0
var counter = 0
var average = 0.0

for (row = 0; row < grades.length; row++) {
  document.write (grades[row] + "<br>")
  counter++
}

average = accumulator / counter
document.write("<br>The class average is " + average)

</script>
</body>
</html>
```

I then saved the program as '**Example10-12.htm**' and opened it within my Internet Browser. The following screen shot was displayed on the classroom projector.

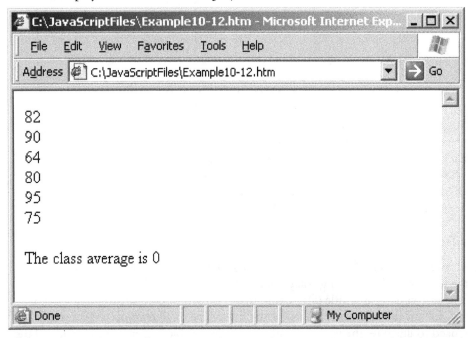

"As you can see," I said, "because we forgot to increment the value of the accumulator variable, its value was equal to its initial value of zero. Therefore, when we divided it by the value of the counter variable--which in this case was 6---our result was zero. The program didn't bomb--but it did result in an incorrect answer."

"So this is a logic error," Valerie said, "since the program didn't bomb?"

'That's right Valerie," I said. "and as you can all see, an error like this can be far worse than a run-time error, particularly if an unsuspecting user takes the result at face value."

Not providing a way for a while structure to end

"Another type of run-time error that is common for beginners," I said, "is to code a While Loop, and forget to provide a way for it to ultimately end. A few weeks ago, we wrote this code, in Exercise 5-7, to display the floor numbers of a hotel..."

```
<! Practice5-7 -->
<html>
<body>
<script type="text/javascript">

var counter = 2

document.write("The floors in the hotel are...<br>")

while (counter < 21) {
document.write (counter + "<br>")
counter++
}

</script>
</body>
</html>
```

"Beginners," I continued, "frequently forget that in a While Loop, it's important to include, somewhere within the body of the loop, code which enables the loop to eventually end--otherwise we have what is known as an endless loop. In this case of this code, we told JavaScript to continue executing the loop while the value of the counter variable is less than 21. Since we initialized the counter variable to 2, this means if we didn't place some code in the body of the loop to do 'something' to cause the value of the counter variable to become 21 or greater, the loop would never end. What we did, of course, was write this line of code which increments the value of the counter variable every time the body of the loop is executed..."

```
counter++
```

"And what happens if we forget to increment the counter variable?" Joe asked.

"We'll create a program that will display the number 2 indefinitely---in other words, an infinite loop," I said, as I did exactly that---forget to increment the counter variable.

```
<! Example10-13 -->
<html>
<body>
<script type="text/javascript">

var counter = 2

document.write("The floors in the hotel are...<br>")

while (counter < 21) {
  document.write (counter + "<br>")
}

</script>
</body>
</html>
```

I then saved the program as '**Example10-13.htm**' and opened it within Internet Explorer. Immediately, a warning message was displayed.

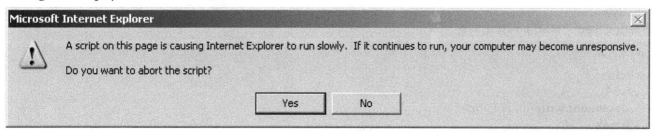

"What's going on?" Rhonda asked.

"Whenever a program is executing an infinite loop," I answered, "it tends to consume a lot of your computer's CPU cycles--that's this warning message is telling us. The infinite loop may cause our computer to run slowly. Whenever you see this warning message from a JavaScript program that you've written, it should be an alert to you that your code has a problem."

"Should we click on the 'No' button?" Peter asked.

"If we don't," I said, "we'll have a problem, and we'll need to use the Windows Task Manager to 'kill' our script. If we click on the 'Yes' button, our program will stop running, although we'll still be able to see the display of our hotel 'floors' in the Internet Browser."

I then clicked on the 'No' button, and true to my prediction, the number 2 was being 'infinitely' displayed in my Internet Browser.

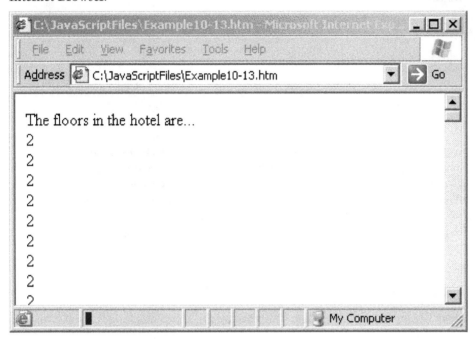

"So that's an infinite loop," Rhonda said, "and all because we forgot one little line of code."

Forgetting to code a break statement when one is needed in a switch structure can cause unpredictable results

"This next 'error' isn't so much an error as it is a JavaScript feature," I said. "but it's a feature that can trip many beginners up--that is, when coding a Switch structure, once a Case statement evaluates to True, the code in every succeeding Case statement is also executed."

"That's why we use the Break statement, isn't it?" Dave asked.

"That's right Dave," I said. "The break statement is normally included as the last statement of a Case statement to tell JavaScript to 'skip' the remainder of the Case statements if the Case statement is found to be true. Here's a program that uses a Switch statement to evaluate the value of the variable 'x'. Depending upon the value of the variable, the program displays one of several alternative messages to the JavaScript Console. Notice the break statement in each of the Case statements."

```
<! Example10-14 -->
<html>
<body>
<script type="text/javascript">

var x = 2

switch(x) {
  case 1:
    document.write("x is 1<br>")
    break
  case 2:
    document.write("x is 2<br>")
    break
  case 3:
    document.write("x is 3<br>")
```

```
    break
  default:
    document.write("x is not 1, 2 or 3<br>")
    break
}

</script>
</body>
</html>
```

"...This program, when run, will display the message 'x is 2' in our Internet Browser window. .."

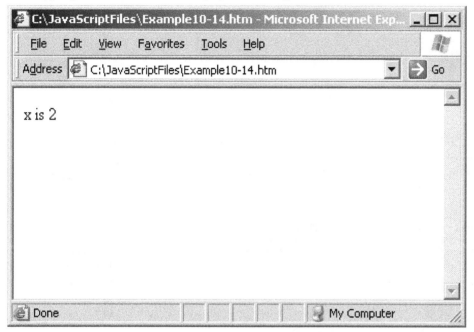

"...If however, we remove the break statements from the program, so that it looks like this..."

```
<! Example10-15 -->
<html>
<body>
<script type="text/javascript">

var x = 2

switch(x) {
  case 1:
    document.write("x is 1<br>")
  case 2:
    document.write("x is 2<br>")
  case 3:
    document.write("x is 3<br>")
  default:
    document.write("x is not 1, 2 or 3<br>")
}

</script>
</body>
</html>
```

"...we get a different result. When we save and execute this version of the program, because of our failure to include a break statement, we get multiple messages displayed in our Internet Browser window."

I then saved the program as '**Example10-15.htm**' and opened it within Internet Explorer, and the following screen shot was displayed on the classroom projector.

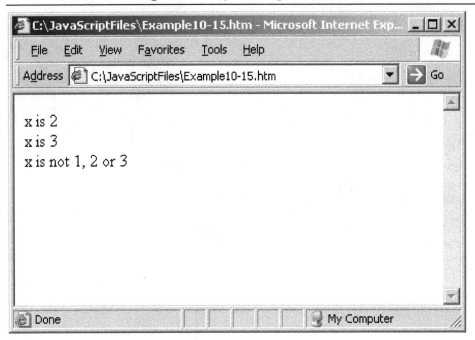

"As you can see, forgetting to code the break statements led to the execution of each one of the Case statements following the first Case statement that evaluated to True."

Confusing the equality operator (==) with the assignment operator (=) generates Nothing

"This is an error I see all the time from beginners," I said, "and occurs when beginners confuse the equality operator(==) with the assignment operator (=), usually in the test expression of an If statements. Here's the code we just examined with a properly formatted test expression checking to see if the value of the counter variable is 0 …"

```
<! Example10-16 -->
<html>
<body>
<script type="text/javascript">

var counter = 0

if (counter == 0) {
  document.write("The value of counter is equal to 0")
}

</script>
</body>
</html>
```

"…Notice how we check the value of counter against the numeric literal 0 by using the equality operator(==)…"

```
if (counter == 0)
```

"It's relatively easy," I said, "especially for those you have programmed in other languages to confuse the equality operator(==) with the assignment operator(=) and code the test expression like this instead…"

```
if (counter = 0)
```

"If we code a program that includes a test expression formatted like this…"

```
<! Example10-17 -->
<html>
<body>
<script type="text/javascript">

var counter = 0

if (counter = 0) {
  document.write("The value of counter is equal to 0")
}
```

```
</script>
</body>
</html>
```

"…we will get this…"

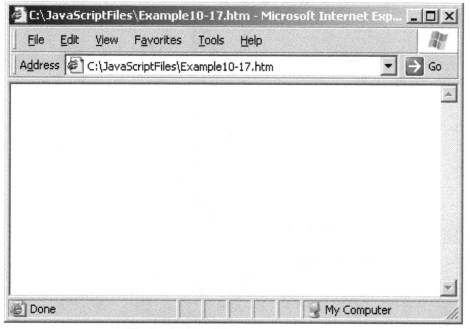

"Nothing did happen?" Rhonda said.

"That's right Rhonda," I said, "what we did was execute an assignment statement within an If statement. Unlike some other programming languages, JavaScript permitted it, and the program ended."

"Wow, I've got to be careful with that one," Blaine said. "That's something that I've been guilty of on more than one occasion."

Forgetting to specify the return value for a function you write doesn't produce an error but...

"An error related to a function," I continued, "occurs when we write a function that will return value, but forget to return a value within the function. Take a look at this code. Here, we've created a function called 'test', which accepts two numeric arguments, sums them, then returns the sum as a return value. Notice that the last line of the function properly uses the return statement to return a numeric value to the code that calls it..."

```
<! Example10-18 -->
<html>
<body>
<script type="text/javascript">
document.write("The sum of 13 and 22 is " + test(13,22))

function test(x,y) {
  z = x + y
  return z
}
</script>
</body>
</html>
```

"..and this is result when we open our program within our Internet Browser..."

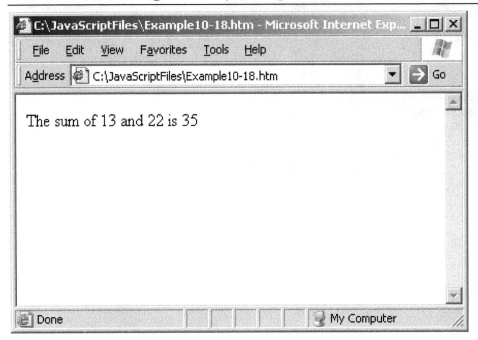

"…however, if we forget to code the return statement, like this…"

```
<! Example10-19 -->
<html>
<body>
<script type="text/javascript">

document.write("The sum of 13 and 22 is " + test(13,22))

function test(x,y) {
z = x + y
}

</script>
</body>
</html>
```

"…when we load the program within Internet Explorer, we'll see this…"

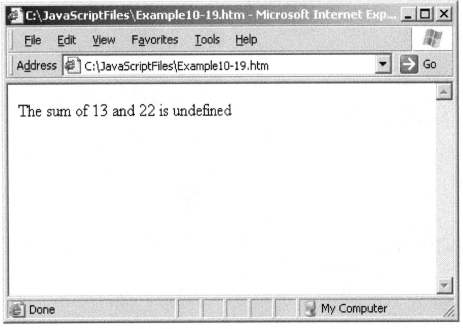

"As you can see," I said, "the program runs, no error is generated, but instead of displaying the sum of the numbers 13 and 22, we display the word 'undefined' instead. This can be pretty embarrassing if someone has paid you to write this code. The bottom line, is whenever you write a function that you intend to return a value, be sure to include the return statement."

I waited for questions but there were none.

"When we return from break," I said, "we'll be examining ways that we can use JavaScript Error Handling routines to detect run-time errors."

JavaScript Error Handling

After break, I told my students that during the first part of our class, we had intentionally created errors to cause our programs to bomb. During the last half of our class, we would be examining ways of gracefully handling those errors in such a way that our programs just don't stop in mid-stream.

"As we discussed," I said, "nothing can ruin your reputation faster than having one of your customers tell a prospective client that he or she loves your programs---but it's too bad they 'bomb' once in a while. As you can imagine, this can be very bad for business!"

I explained that it isn't always possible to write a program that will never produce a run-time error. It's possible for the user to introduce data, via a Prompt Box, which causes a run-time error. You might also write a program that reads data from a disk file, the name and location of which is specified by the user at run time.

"Suppose," I said, "the user of your program indicates that the file is located on a diskette, but then forgets to insert the disk into the diskette drive?"

"I do that all the time," Rhonda said. "Will that cause our program to bomb?"

"It can," I said, "since our program is attempting to open a file that doesn't exist."

"That generates an error?" Ward asked. "I'm surprised---when I do that while using Microsoft Word, a warning message is displayed."

"That's exactly the point, Ward" I replied. "The programmers who wrote Microsoft Word implemented Error Handling in their program, intercepting the run-time error that is triggered, and substituting in its place a more user-friendly message. That's the warning message you see in Word. Most importantly, though, Microsoft Word continues running instead of coming to a grinding halt--which is what we want our JavaScript program to do. Remember, when a JavaScript program comes to a jarring stop, it can result in the loss of hours of work on the part of the user."

"So we can do something like that in our JavaScript program?" Barbara asked. "I mean, intercept those error messages we saw earlier and replace them with user-friendly messages of our own."

"Yes we can," I said. "As you'll see, it's actually pretty easy to 'intercept' both those nasty JavaScript runtime and Load-time error messages and replace them with more soothing, user-friendly messages that appear as warning messages. Let's begin our look at JavaScript Error Handling by completing an exercise in which we intentionally cause a Runtime error."

I then distributed this exercise to the class.

Exercise 10-1 Intentionally Generate an Error

In this exercise, you'll write a program that intentionally generates an Error by calling a function that doesn't exist. But don't worry--in the next exercise, you'll implement Error Handling to gracefully handle it.
1. Use Notepad (if you are using Windows) and enter the following code.

```
<! Practice10-1 -->
<html>
<body>
<script type="text/javascript">

var response

response = prompt("What is the flavor of your favorite ice cream?", "")

displayflavor(response)
```

```
function displayFlavor(favorite) {
    document.write("I agree--I love " + favorite + " also!" + "<br>")
}

</script>
</body>
</html>
```

2. Save your source file as **'Practice10-1.htm'** in the \JavaScriptfiles\Practice folder (select File-Save As from Notepad's Menu Bar). Be sure to save your source file with the file name extension 'htm'.

3. Open up your source file within Internet Explorer.

4. Execute your program. Enter the flavor of your favorite ice cream, then click on the OK button. You should see this error message.

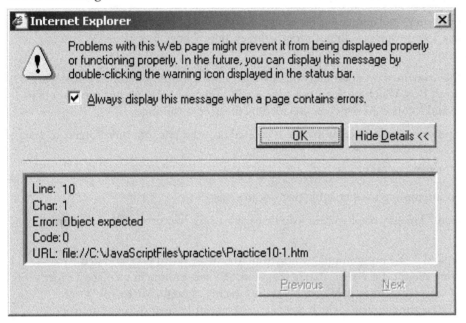

Discussion

"What we've done here," I said, "is to write some innocent looking code that prompts the user for their favorite ice cream, then passes their response as an argument to a function which should then display a message congratulating them on their good taste! Certainly, there's nothing obvious in the code that would suggest the program would have a problem---again, Case Sensitivity in JavaScript is very subtle. It isn't until the program is run that we generate this error. Once the error is displayed, there's really nothing the user can do but to click on the OK button---at which time our program simply stops running. As you can see, a program that terminates abnormally can be pretty nasty."

"So will we be able to prevent this type of problem?" Kate asked.

"Yes Kate," I answered, "there is a way to 'intercept' JavaScript Exceptions so that when they do occur, the program doesn't come to a grinding halt."

JavaScript Exceptions

"Is a JavaScript exception the same as a JavaScript error?" Steve asked. "I think you've used both terms in the last few minutes."

"The JavaScript language," I said, "prefers to call its errors Exceptions. In fact, when a JavaScript error occurs, an Exception Object is created. Once the Exception Object is created, we then have access to its attributes, which can provide information to us about the Exception."

"The Exception Object is an object that we don't have to create ourselves?" Kate asked.

"That's right Kate," I said, "when the error is generated, JavaScript automatically creates the Exception Object for us."

"What can we do when a JavaScript error occurs?" Ward asked.

Ignore the Exception

"One thing we can do is to ignore the error," I said.

"What's that?" Ward asked, not sure that he had heard be correctly.

"We can ignore the error," I said, "and just let the program bomb. This is an alternative that many JavaScript programmers choose.

"Is it OK to ignore exceptions?" Mary asked.

"As you gain experience in JavaScript," I said, "you'll see that most of the code you write won't trigger exceptions. You'll also learn the kind of code that is likely to trigger an exception, such as code that opens external files or databases---this is the kind of code that can trigger run-time exceptions. The point is, not every piece of code you write needs to be written to handle exceptions--but for that code which your experience (and testing) has revealed capable of triggering an exception, that's the code that needs to include error handling code---and that means coding a Try-Catch-Finally block."

Handle the Exception with Try-Catch-Finally blocks

"Try-Catch-Finally Block?" Kate said. "Is that what you just said."

"That's right Kate," I replied. "A Try-Catch-Finally Block. The idea is to 'try' the code in the 'Try' block that may cause an exception and then use the 'Catch' block to specify the code to execute if an exception should occur."

"So that's the reason it's called a Try block?" Mary asked.

"That's the reason Mary," I said.

"What about the Finally block?" Steve asked.

"The Finally block specifies code that is to be executed whether an exception occurs or not," I said. "Usually, this is code that performs some kind of housekeeping function such as closing files, or thanking the user for using our program."

"Are you going to show us an example of the Try-Catch-Finally block?" Rhonda asked.

"Even better," I said, "I'm going to give you a chance to work with them on your own by modifying the code from Exercise 10-1 to include Exception Handling."

I then distributed this exercise for the class to complete.

Exercise 10-2 Try-Catch-Finally Block

In this exercise, you'll modify the program from Exercise 10-1 to use a Try-Catch-Finally block to deal with the error that resulted in Exercise 10-1.

1. Use Notepad (if you are using Windows) and enter the following code.

```
<! Practice10-2 -->
<html>
<body>
<script type="text/javascript">

var response

response = prompt("What is the flavor of your favorite ice cream?", "")

try {
  displayflavor(response)
}

catch(exception) {
  alert("An Unexpected error has occurred.\n\n" +
      "Error Description: " + exception.description + "\n\n" +
      "Please contact John Smiley at johnsmiley@johnsmiley.com.\n\n" +
      "Click OK to continue.")
}
```

```
finally {
  alert("Thank you for using my program!")
}
function displayFlavor(favorite) {
  document.write("I agree--I love " + favorite + " also!" + "<br>")
}

</script>
</body>
</html>
```

2. Save your source file as '**Practice10-2.htm**' in the \JavaScriptFiles\Practice folder (select File-Save As from Notepad's Menu Bar). Be sure to save your source file with the file name extension 'htm'.

3. Open up your source file within your Internet Browser.

4. Execute your program. Enter the flavor of your favorite ice cream, then click on the OK button. This time, instead of that nasty JavaScript error message, the program will display a more user friendly warning message, asking the user to contact John Smiley, and to click the OK button.

5. Click on the OK button, and you should see a message box thanking you for using the program.

Discussion

I immediately ran the program and the following screen shot was displayed on the classroom projector…

I then clicked on the OK button, and this screen shot was displayed on the classroom projector.

"That's the Finally block kicking in," Dave said.

"Absolutely right Dave," I said. "But before I discuss the Finally block, let me explain what we've done here. We've used a Try block to 'intercept' the exception before it displayed that generic JavaScript error message. The code in the Try-block is the code we tell JavaScript may cause an exception…"

```
try {
  displayflavor(response)
}
```

"… If an exception occurs, then execution of the program will jump to the Catch block. In our case, we have coded the Catch block tell JavaScript to display a much more user-friendly error message..."

```
catch(exception) {
  alert("An Unexpected error has occurred.\n\n" +
      "Error Description: " + exception.description + "\n\n" +
      "Please contact John Smiley at johnsmiley@johnsmiley.com.\n\n" +
```

```
      "Click OK to continue.")
}
```

"Understandably," I said, "this syntax is confusing. What we're doing is telling the Catch block that we are expecting an Exception object to be created--that's what this line of code does…"

```
catch(exception)
```

"By the way, there's nothing magical about the word 'exception' in the argument list. You may also see this used…"

```
catch(e)
```

"…and this will also work…"

```
catch(Rhonda)
```

That seemed to amuse Rhonda---I think she enjoyed being called exceptional :)

"If you use something other than exception with the catch Block," I said, "be sure to change the object name within the catch block. For instance, if we use 'rhonda' as our exception object name, we need to change it in our alert function, like this…"

```
"Error Description: " + rhonda.description + "\n\n" +
```

"Can you explain the 'Finally' block?" Mary asked. "When does it get executed?"

"The Finally block is executed regardless of whether an exception is generated or not," I answered. "In other words, the code in the Finally block is executed both when an exception occurs and also when no exception occurs. In this case, we included a message thanking the user for working with our program…"

```
finally {
   alert("Thank you for using my program!")
}
```

"…if we were to go back into our program, and call the *displayFlavor* function with the correct name, you would see the message congratulating us on our good taste in ice cream, and also the alert message thanking us for using the program."

I did exactly that, changing this line of code

```
displayflavor(response)
```

to this

```
displayFlavor(response)
```

As predicted, the program asked me for my favorite ice cream. I answered 'Vanilla', clicked on the OK button, saw a congratulator message, and an alert message thanking me for using the program.

"I see how it works now," Mary asked. "Thanks!"

I scanned the room for signs of confusion--but didn't see any.

> **Note: There is an older style of Exception Handling called 'On Error', which I will not be covering here. Try-Catch-Finally is newer and the preferred method**

Can we modify the Grades Calculation Project?

"Can we modify the Grades Calculation Project?" Kate asked, "to provide for Exception Handling?"

"Yes we can." I said, "However, at this point, I'm a little reluctant to expend much energy in doing so. The Grades Calculation project is going to undergo some overhauling as we add a Graphical User Interface in the next few weeks---placing Exception Handling code in the classes that make up the project at this point may be premature."

I then dismissed class for the day. I told my students that during the evening hours I would be placing a shore-to-ship call to Rose and Jack to see how they were coming along with the ocean tests on their company's new ocean liner.

Summary

This chapter was designed to show you the various types of errors that all programmers---especially beginners---can make in their programs. We've actually covered two different types of errors here: mistakes made by programmers, such as forgetting to open or close a file, and errors that are not the result of a programming mistake—such as a missing, renamed, or moved file.

We learned that you can't always code for every eventuality. You could put Exception handlers in every part of your program, trying to 'intercept' every error that you think of. That's one extreme. We learned that you should definitely code a Try-Catch-Finally block in any part of your program that has proven troublesome during your testing phase.

And now a word or two of advice. Everyone makes mistakes when they start programming. Never let this discourage you. When you first learn something new, it's a strange and awkward experience, as you become familiar with it.

But in the same way it's a new and exciting time. Never let the frustrations of learning something new thwart that excitement. As time goes by, experience will help you make less mistakes.

Chapter 11---Developing A Graphical User Interface

At this point in our JavaScript journey, we've learned how to develop a working JavaScript program that solves the problem of calculating grades for Frank Olley, Robin Aronstrom and David Burton. The program, while fully functional, lacks a Graphical User Interface, also known as a GUI. In this chapter, you'll follow my university class as we create a Graphical User Interface for the Grades Calculation project.

Building a Graphical User Interface

I began our next to last class by telling my students that my shore-to-ship call to Jack and Rose had gone well and that they had assured me they would be returning in time for next Saturday's final class. Both would be returning to the United States on the maiden voyage of the ocean liner that they had helped engineer.

"Talk about following through with the SDLC," Dave said. "They helped design the ship, now they're participating in the implementation, and feedback and maintenance phases also!"

"That's a good point, Dave" I said. "We'll be doing the same thing next week when we deliver the Grades Calculation project to Frank Olley of the English Department."

I continued by explaining that although, in fact, we had already completed the Grades Calculation project, and I'm sure Frank Olley would be pleased with what we had done so far, starting in today's class, and wrapping up next week with our final class, we would be developing a Graphical User Interface.

"Graphical User Interface?" Rhonda asked. "Haven't we already done that already? Our program runs within an Internet Browser---it looks pretty graphical to me."

"Rhonda," I answered, "you're correct when you say our program runs within an Internet Browser, but it lacks the polish and style that using some of the HTML GUI elements can give it. For instance, it doesn't have any buttons."

"Buttons?" Kate asked. "You mean the types of buttons that appear in a Microsoft Windows program? Are you talking about writing a Windows program?"

"Not a Microsoft Windows program," I said, "but a program that has windows elements---which will contain Buttons, Checkboxes, Radio Buttons, and Text Fields, to name a few. These GUI features can all be implemented using HTML GUI elements."

"Why HTML?" Ward asked. "This is a JavaScript class."

"Don't forget Ward," I replied, "JavaScript is a language that is run within an HTML page. Our GUI will be created using HTML code, with JavaScript blended within it."

Designing our GUI

"I understand now," Blaine said. "Do we have any idea what our GUI will look like."

> **Note: A shortcut term for a Graphical User Interface is a GUI (pronounced Goo-Ey)**

"We developed a sketch of the interface for the Grades Calculation project way back in Week 1," I said. "I polished it up a bit prior to today's class. Let's take a look at it, and see if it meets with your approval."

I then displayed this sketch of our GUI on the classroom projector.

Don't Forget: If typing these examples and exercises isn't something you want to do, feel free to follow this link to find and download the completed solutions for all of the examples and exercises in the book. Just click on the JavaScript book, then follow the link entitled exercises ☺

http://www.johnsmiley.com/main/books.htm

○ **English Student**   **Midterm**   ▢

○ **Math Student**   **Final Exam**   ▢

○ **Science Student**   **Research Paper** ▢

                            Presentation   ▢

▢ **Calculate Grade**

▢ **Reset**

"This is an illustration of our proposed GUI," I said. "The surrounding rectangle represents what HTML calls a Form, and the Labels, circles and rectangles that you see within the Form represent other HTML GUI elements, which we'll be discussing today. Interestingly, each one of those elements is actually an HTML object that we will create or instantiate. Collectively, these GUI elements are part of something called the Document Object Model, or DOM for short."

"Is that Document the same as the document object we've been working with using the write method?" Kate asked.

"That's excellent Kate," I said, "it is the same document object. Up to now, all we've really done with the Document Object Model is to use the document object's write method--but there's a whole lot more to it, as you'll see in today's class, and even more so, in next week's class when we start to work with events and methods of our GUI elements."

"When you say create an object," Bob asked "do you mean to create objects from the classes we've created ourselves, such as EnglishStudent by using the *new* keyword?"

"We don't need to do that Bob," I said. "HTML GUI elements can be referenced in the same way that the document object can be---we don't need to create instances of them, we just use them."

I paused a moment before continuing.

"...the border that you see around my drawing is called an HTML Form. In HTML, the Form acts as a 'container' for other GUI elements, and for the Grades Calculation Project, we'll be placing four HTML elements 'upon' it--- Labels, Radio Buttons, Buttons and Text Fields."

Note: A Form acts as a container for other GUI elements

"What are those three round circles?" Rhonda asked.

"The three 'round circles'," I said, "represent HTML Radio Buttons. Radio Buttons are a GUI element that permit the user of our program to specify, via a mouse click, a True/False or a Yes/No answer."

"Why are they called Radio Buttons?" Joe asked.

"They're called Radio Buttons," I said. "because they mimic the behavior of old-time radios, where you pushed a button to select a radio channel. On a radio with five buttons, one button was always depressed or selected, but only one button---never more than one. The Radio Button HTML GUI element is displayed on a HTML Form with a circle and a caption or descriptive Label next to it. Radio Buttons can be 'selected' when the user clicks their mouse on it. Once the Radio Button is selected, a small black dot is displayed within it."

Note: Only one Radio Button in a Radio Button Group can be selected at one time

"So you're saying that of the three Radio Buttons that we see here on the Form, only one can be selected at one time?" Chuck asked.

"That's right Chuck," I agreed. "When the user selects a Radio Button, that Radio Button will become 'selected' and the Radio Button previously selected will become 'unselected'. The idea here, with the Grades Calculation project, is that the user will select one of the three Radio buttons to select the type of student for which they wish to calculate a grade."

"What about those empty rectangles on the Form?" Mary asked. "What do they represent?"

"The empty rectangles," I said, "represent HTML Text Fields. Text Fields---also called Text Boxes---are much like the text boxes we displayed during the course when we executed the prompt method."

"What will we be using Text Fields for?" Rhonda asked.

"They'll be used by the user of our program to enter values for the Midterm, Final Exam, Research Paper and Presentation grades." I said. "Once these values are entered into a text box, the idea is that the user will then click on the Calculate button to trigger the calculation of the student's final grade."

"But not all student types require all four component grades," Dave said. "Will that be a problem?"

"No," I answered, "next week, when we build some 'intelligence' into our GUI, you'll see that, based upon the Radio Button that the user selects, we'll display only those Text Fields that are required to calculate that particular type of grade."

"So if the user selects a Math Student," Linda said, "only the Text Fields for Midterm and Final Exam will be displayed?"

"That's right Linda," I said. "That will be something we program into our GUI next week when we learn about GUI event procedures."

"It appears that we have two buttons, one called Calculate and one called Reset," Rhonda said. "Are both of those Form elements?"

"Yes they are," I said. "Both buttons are HTML Form elements."

"What about those identifying captions?" Steve asked. "Are they HTML elements?"

"That's a good observation Steve," I said. "however, HTML does not have a distinct Label element. Four of the identifying captions that appear on the Form--Midterm, Final Exam, Research Paper and Presentation---are ordinary HTML text---something that we learned how to do in our Introductory HTML class. The other captions that you see--Calculate, Reset, and the captions appearing to the right of the three Radio Buttons are actually attributes of the Button and Radio Button objects."

"What are identifying captions used for?" Peter asked.

"Captions are used to provide instructions to the user," I said, "or to identify other objects, such as our Text Fields. For instance, the Midterm caption identifies the Text Field to be used for the input of the Midterm grade."
I waited a moment to see if there were any other questions--we had discussed, more or less, all of the features of the Form.

"How and where will we be displaying the student's calculated grade?" Barbara asked. "In the current version of the Grades Calculation program, we're displaying it in an Alert Box. Should we display the grade somewhere on the Form?"

"That's a great question Barbara," I said, "I would like to display the student's grade on the Form itself. Let's update the sketch to include that."

I then updated my sketch, and displayed it on the classroom projector.

"Now," I said, "the user will select a type of student, enter component grades into the appropriate Text Field, click on the Calculate Grade button, and the student's numeric and letter grade will appear as text on the Form."

"Since we're on the subject of identifying captions," Ward said, "I would suggest providing some captions to categorize what the Radio Buttons and TextFields represent."

I wasn't quite sure what Ward meant--so I asked him update my sketch. After he was done, he displayed it on the classroom projector.

Student Type   **Grades**   **ENGLISH STUDENT**

● English Student   Midterm | 70 |

○ Math Student   Final Exam | 80 |

○ Science Student   Research Paper | 90 |

                        Presentation | 100 |

| Calculate Grade | Numeric Grade: 84.5

| Reset | Letter Grade: C

"Ah yes, I see what you mean Ward," I said. "You're right---that is a better design."

Creating our GUI

"These objects that we'll be creating to form our GUI?" Lou asked. "Will we be creating these within the Grades.htm file? Or will this code go into a class file?"

"That's a good question Lou," I said, "Typically, the code for the creation of a GUI is placed in the startup .htm file. However, I'd like to suggest that we create a new startup .htm file, and call it GradesGUI.htm."

"I don't mind saying that the prospect of creating a GUI seems a bit overwhelming to me," he said.

"Like everything else we've done in the class Lou," I said, "I think you'll see that if we take this a step at a time, we'll be just fine. Let's start by examining the sketch for our GUI, identifying the HTML GUI elements, and listing the objects that will be used to create them, along with the ."

I then displayed this list on the classroom projector.

HTML Object	GUI Element	Object Name
Button	Calculate Button	btnCalculate
	Reset Button	btnRest
Radio	English Radio Button	radEnglish
	Math Radio Button	radMath
	Science Radio Button	radScience
Text Field	Student Type	txtStudentType
	Midterm text box	txtMidterm
	Final Exam text box	txtFinal
	Research Paper text box	txtResearch
	Presentation text box	txtPresentation
	Numeric Grade	txtNumericGrade
	Letter Grade	txtLetterGrade

Ordinary Text	STUDENT TYPE:
	GRADES:
	Midterm
	Final Exam
	Research Paper
	Presentation
Form	The entire window

"Can you go over the process of creating the GUI again?" Linda asked.

"Sure thing Linda," I said. "Within GradesGUI.htm, we'll create an HTML form, use HTML Table Rows to place HTML objects within it, and then give our objects names. When we load GradesGUI.htm from within our Internet Browser, our GUI will be displayed---and hopefully, it will look just like the GUI we've sketched. Once the GUI is displayed, it's there for the user to interact with it--and next week we'll learn how to make the GUI communicate with our program by writing code in event handlers.."

"Why is that necessary?" Mary asked.

"Event handlers," I said, "enable our program to know which objects on the Form the user has interacted with. That's how we'll know if the user clicks on the Math Student Radio Button, what value he or she enters as the Midterm grade, and when they click on the Calculate button. Without event handlers, we have a displayed GUI, but nothing else. But we'll learn more about that next week when we learn how to create our event handlers, and place code within them."

Setting Up the Top-Level Component--the Form

"So where do we start?" Linda asked. "What's our first step?"

"We start by creating an HTML Form," I said. "Creating a Form is necessary in order for the event procedures we code next week to work properly. Once we've created the Form, we'll then place other HTML GUI objects 'upon' it."

I paused for a moment before continuing.

"I'd like to demonstrate this process," I continued, "by creating an example program called GUIV1.htm. V1 stands for version 1, as we will be creating multiple versions of this GUI program over the course of the next few minutes."

I then displayed this code on the classroom projector.

```
<! GUIV1 -- >
<html>
<head>
  <title>GUIV1</title>
</head>
<body>
  <form name="myForm">
  </form>
</body>
</html>
```

"Nothing terrifically fancy here," I said, as I saved the program as **'GUIV1.htm'** and opened it up within my Internet Browser.

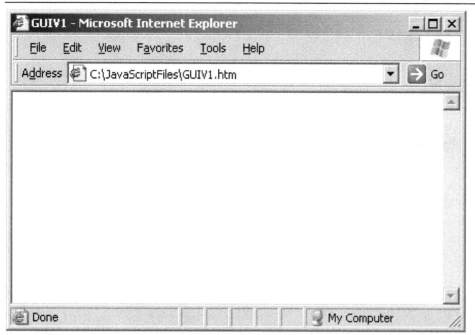

"There's *nothing* there," Rhonda exclaimed.

"Well, you're right," I said hesitantly. "We really haven't specified much to happen here---although note that the title bar in our Internet Browser Window does read 'GUIV1 Let's examine the few lines of code we have written here. As we've done throughout the class, our first line of code is a comment line..."

<! GUIV1 -- >

"...this is followed by the <html> tag, and the <head> tag, something you've seen before. The next line of code, however, is new to you--it's the <title> tag, and it's used to give a title to our Internet Browser's window..."

```
<html>
<head>
  <title>GUIV1</title>
</head>
```

"That is a nice feature," Rhonda said, "I was wondering how to do that--and now I know."

"We follow up the <title> tag with the now familiar <body> tag. In HTML, the <body> tag is used to designate what we want displayed in our Browser window. This window won't be displaying anything yet--but we are specifying that a Form, with the name 'myForm' be created."

```
<body>
  <form name="myForm">
  </form>
</body>
```

"...finally, here's the ending <html> tag..."

```
</html>
```

"Why don't we 'see' the form in our Browser window," Dave asked. "The display appears to be just an empty Internet Browser Window."

"HTML Forms are invisible Dave," I said, "In HTML, Forms are used to allow a user to interact with a program using GUI elements, and to report those elements to a program running on a Web Server. Although we won't learn how to interact with such a program in this class, it's a good idea to get used to working with our GUI elements using HTML Forms. However, as you point out, there's no visible evidence that we have coded a form here."

"I have a question that I've been meaning to ask for a couple of weeks now," Kate said. "Is there any way to specify the 'size' of our Browser Window when it opens?"

"Yes there is Kate," I said, "we can execute the resizeTo() method of our Browser's Window object, specifying the height and width of the window, by placing this code within the <body> tag of our program."

```
<script type="text/javascript">
  window.resizeTo(500,450)
</script>
```

"I should caution you though," I continued, "I find pre-defined windows like this to be a bit on the clumsy side. My preference is to present the user with a full window, and let them decide if it needs to be resized. I design my programs--and GUI Forms--accordingly."

Adding HTML Components to the Form

"I don't know about anyone else," Rhonda said, "but I can't wait to create one of those GUI Objects you were talking about earlier. What's next? How do we place Buttons, Radio Buttons, Text Fields and captions on our Form? Will we be adding those GUI elements soon?"

Buttons

"Yes we will," I said. "Right now in fact. Let's modify the code we just wrote in GUIV1 to include three Buttons."

I then displayed this code on the classroom projector.

```
<! GUIV2 -- >
<html>
<head>
  <title>GUIV2</title>
</head>
<body>
  <form name="myForm">
    <input type="button" name="btn1" value="Button1">
    <input type="button" name="btn2" value="Button2">
    <input type="button" name="btn3" value="Button3">
    <input type="button" name="btn4" value="Button4">
    <input type="button" name="btn5" value="Button5">
    <input type="button" name="btn6" value="Button6">
  </form>
</body>
</html>
```

"Before I explain the code we just wrote," I said, "I'd like to show you what it does. As they say, a picture is worth a thousand words!"

I then saved the program as '**GUIV2.htm**' and opened it up within my Internet Browser. The following screenshot was displayed on the classroom project.

Don't Forget: If typing these examples and exercises isn't something you want to do, feel free to follow this link to find and download the completed solutions for all of the examples and exercises in the book. Just click on the JavaScript book, then follow the link entitled exercises ☺

http://www.johnsmiley.com/main/books.htm

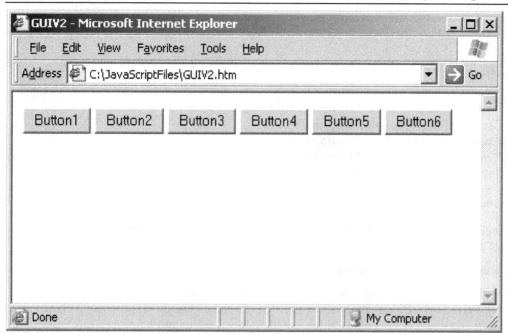

"As you can see," I said, "we now have the same window--and invisible Form---that we had before, but this time we have six buttons placed on it."

I then used my mouse pointer to resize the window.

"See how the buttons have been rearranged?" I asked.

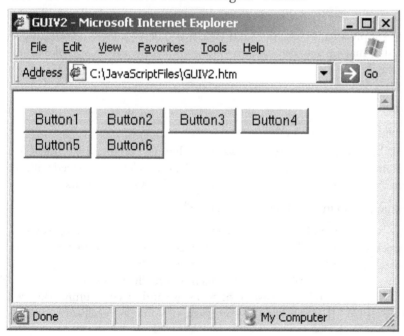

"Wow, how did that happen?" Linda asked. "The buttons rearranged themselves. And we didn't have to write any code to do that?"

"I'm not sure if that's a good feature or a bad one," Ward said. "If we spend a lot of time designing our GUI--do we really want our GUI Elements moving all over the place?"

"The rearrangement of the buttons was done for us automatically," I said, "and is a function of our Internet Browser."

"Is there anything we can do to prevent this?" Ward asked.

"Yes there is Ward," I said, "We can create an HTML table which will enable us to more permanently locate---or anchor---our GUI elements within our Form. I'll be showing you how to do that shortly. However, before I do, let's take a close look at the code in GUIV2 now---particular that within the <body> tags. Unlike our previous example, which had no code whatsoever between the <form> tags, this code specifies the code to create six HTML buttons..."

```
<body>
 <form name="myForm">
  <input type="button" name="btn1" value="Button1">
  <input type="button" name="btn2" value="Button2">
  <input type="button" name="btn3" value="Button3">
  <input type="button" name="btn4" value="Button4">
  <input type="button" name="btn5" value="Button5">
  <input type="button" name="btn6" value="Button6">
 </form>
</body>
```

"This syntax may be a bit confusing for you," I said, "so let's isolate our attention to the code that we executed to create the first button in our Form that is captioned 'Button1'. Here's the code..."

```
<input type="button" name="btn1" value="Button1">
```

"...In keeping with the theme that our GUI elements are part of a Form which is intended to be used for input, it makes some sense that the GUI elements we learn about today will be included within an <input> tag. HTML Buttons are designated by specifying a type parameter of 'button. Although it's not required to name our button, we then supplied a unique name for the button by providing a value for the name parameter. Finally, to designate a caption for the button, we supplied it via the value parameter."

I gave everyone a chance to soak this in.

"...Notice that we have named our button with the prefix 'btn'--this makes our code a lot more readable."

"You said the name parameter is not required?" Chuck asked.

"That's right Chuck," I said. "You don't need to supply a name for your GUI elements unless you will be referring to them within your program code. With buttons, that may or may not happen---but to be on the safe side, I like to specify a name for all of my GUI elements anyway."

Using Tables to 'anchor' our GUI Elements

"You mentioned that there's a way to anchor our GUI elements?" Ward asked

"That's right Ward," I said. "We can build an HTML Table consisting of rows and columns, and then place our GUI elements within cells of the Table. Unlike the buttons we saw in the previous example, GUI elements placed within the Cells of an HTML Table tend to stay where we place them--at least relative to the other GUI elements."

"A Table?" Rhonda asked. "Is that what we learned to do in our Basic HTML class?"

"That's right Rhonda," I said. "An HTML Table is very much like a Spreadsheet. It consists of one or more Rows, and within each Row, there are cells. We can arrange our GUI elements within the Cells of an HTML in such a way that even though our Internet Browser may resize our display window, the arrangement of the cells doesn't get altered. I'd like to modify the code we just wrote---in which we placed six buttons horizontally in our Internet Browser Window to instead display 6 buttons arranged in a table consisting of two rows and three columns. Before I do that, however, let's see how easy it is to create an HTML Table--by the way, some of you may recall seeing this in our Basic HTML class..."

I then displayed this code on the classroom projector.

```
<! GUIV3 -- >
<html>
<head>
<title>GUIV3</title>
</head>

<body>
 <form name="myForm">
  <table border="1">
   <tr>
    <td>Row 1, Column 1</td>
```

```
        <td>Row 1, Column 2</td>
        <td>Row 1, Column 3</td>
      </tr>
      <tr>
        <td>Row 2, Column 1</td>
        <td>Row 2, Column 2</td>
        <td>Row 2, Column 3</td>
      </tr>
    </table>
  </form>
</body>
</html>
```

saved it as **'GUIV3.htm"** and opened up the program in my Internet Browser. The following screenshot was displayed on the classroom projector.

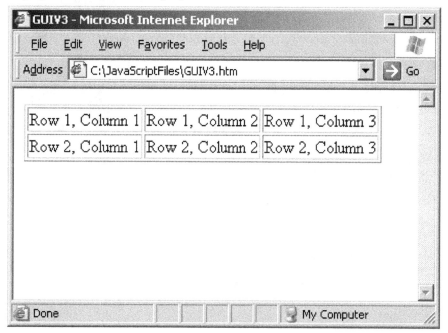

"As you can see," I said, "we now have a table consisting of two rows with three cells in each row. You can also think of this as a table consisting of two rows and three columns, although there really is no such thing as an HTML Table column."

"I'm a little confused as to the code that produced this," Rhonda said, "can you go over it?"

"Sure thing Rhonda," I said, "I'll be glad to. First off, notice that we created our Table within a Form, using a <table> tag..."

```
<form name="myForm">
  <table border="1">
```

"I've included a value for the border attribute of 1," I said, "which tells HTML that I want a border of 1 pixel around the borders of my table and cells. For those of you unfamiliar with the term, a pixel is just a dot on the display monitor. 1 pixel as thin a border as we can get. Shortly, we'll see that we can specify the width of our Table using either a fixed number of pixels, or a percentage of the display screen. For now, we'll just accept the default."

> **Note: If the user adjusts their window size, the fixed width table remains at 200 pixels wide and the percentage table adjusts itself to the window area. Some people prefer to use the percentage value so the table will adjust itself to the screen size of any resolution.**

I looked for signs of confusion before continuing.

"Our next step," I said, "is to define an HTML Table Row using the <tr> tag. As is the case with the <table> tag, the Table Row tag also supports a width attribute, which allows us to specify the width of our Table Row, again in either pixels or a percentage of the screen. For now, we'll just accept the default--the same way we did for the <table> tag..."

<tr>

"...Now this is where things can get confusing. Within the <tr> tag, we need to specify the 3 cells that will be contained in this row. We do that by using the <td> tag, which stands for Table Cell. As you can see, we have three sets of <td> and </td> tags to designate the cells, followed by a close Table Row </tr> tag..."

```
<td>Row 1, Column 1</td>
<td>Row 1, Column 2</td>
<td>Row 1, Column 3</td>
</tr>
```

Note: You may be wondering why the tag for a Table Cell isn't <tc>. So am I :)

"Notice," I continued, "that between the opening Table Cell tag <td> and the closing Table Cell tag </td> appears the text that we want to appear in the cell. All we need to do is enclose it within the pair of tags. In a minute, we'll take this code and add HTML buttons to the cells instead."

"Is that the technique we'll use to create the identifying captions you spoke of earlier?" Linda asked.

"Very good Linda," I said, "that's exactly what we'll do."

"Does the Table Cell tag also have a width attribute?" Dave asked.

"Yes it does Dave," I said, "we can experiment with that in our next example."

"Is the remainder of the code devoted to creating the second row and its cells?" Peter asked.

"Excellent Peter," I said, "that's exactly what we're doing. Let's take a look..."

```
<tr>
    <td>Row 2, Column 1</td>
    <td>Row 2, Column 2</td>
    <td>Row 2, Column 3</td>
  </tr>
</table>
```

"Notice," I said, "that our three cells are enclosed within a pair of Table Row <tr> tags. Notice also the closing Table </table> tag."

"This doesn't look as difficult as I thought it would," Rhonda said. "And you say that adding buttons to the cells is relatively easy."

"Yes it is Rhonda," I said. "Let add buttons to the table we just created."

I then displayed this modified code on the classroom projector.

```
<! GUIV4 -- >
<html>
<head>
<title>GUIV4</title>
</head>
<body>
  <form name="myForm">
    <table border="1">
      <tr>
        <td><input type="button" name="btn1" value="Button1"></td>
        <td><input type="button" name="btn2" value="Button2"></td>
        <td><input type="button" name="btn3" value="Button3"></td>
      </tr>
      <tr>
        <td><input type="button" name="btn4" value="Button4"></td>
        <td><input type="button" name="btn5" value="Button5"></td>
        <td><input type="button" name="btn6" value="Button6"></td>
```

```
      </tr>
   </table>
   </form>
</body>
</html>
```

saved it as **'GUIV4.htm"** and opened up the program in my Internet Browser. The following screenshot was displayed on the classroom projector.

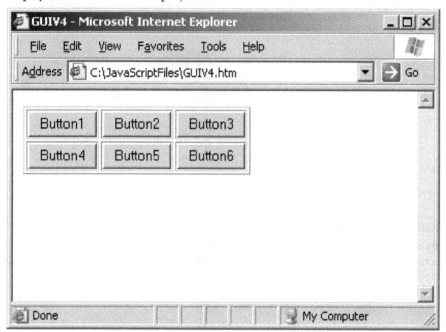

"As you can see," I said, "we now have two rows of buttons, consisting of three cells each. All we needed to do was to place the <input> tag for the buttons between the two Table Data <td> tags..."

<td><input type="button" name="btn1" value="Button1"></td>

"Notice," I said, "that we don't have a lot of control over the placement of the buttons within the Table Row since we didn't specify a width parameter for either the rows or cells--we'll do that in our next example."

"What happens if we resize our Browser window?" Mary asked

"Good question Mary," I said, "let's see."

I then resized my Browser Window---try as I might, I could not get the button arrangement of two rows and three columns to change.

"Notice what happened," I pointed out. "When I resized the Browser window, scroll bars appeared. Our second row of buttons is still in place---right under the first row. Does everyone see the difference when we used a Table to 'anchor' our buttons?"

"I do," Ward volunteered, "when we initially placed buttons on the Form without the benefit of rows and cells, the buttons moved from the second row to the first row. I can see that if you want the relative positions of your GUI elements to stay the same, a Table is the way to do."

"Are you going to show us how to work with the width parameter of the table and the table rows?" Mary asked.

"I'll be glad to Mary," I said, "But before I do, let me point out how well our little program behaved with no width specified for either the Table or for the Table rows. Browsers generally do a good job of displaying the table and its cells by examining the data in the cells, and adjusting the width of the columns and cells accordingly. However, if you want to, you can adjust the width of the Table, its rows, and its cells. I must warn you, I've had a lot more success setting the width of the Table and the width of its cells, but not the Table rows. For now, let me show you how easy it is to adjust the width of a Table by modifying the example we just coded so that the Table fills 70% of the screen."

I then modified the code from the **GUIV4** example to look like this...

```
<! GUIV5 -- >
<html>
<head>
<title>GUIV5</title>
</head>

</head>

<body>
  <form name="myForm">
    <table border="1" width="70%">
      <tr>
        <td><input type="button" name="btn1" value="Button1"></td>
        <td><input type="button" name="btn2" value="Button2"></td>
        <td><input type="button" name="btn3" value="Button3"></td>
      </tr>
      <tr>
        <td><input type="button" name="btn4" value="Button4"></td>
        <td><input type="button" name="btn5" value="Button5"></td>
        <td><input type="button" name="btn6" value="Button6"></td>
      </tr>
    </table>
  </form>
</body>
</html>
```

saved it as **'GUIV5.htm'** and opened up the program in my Internet Browser. The following screenshot was displayed on the classroom projector.

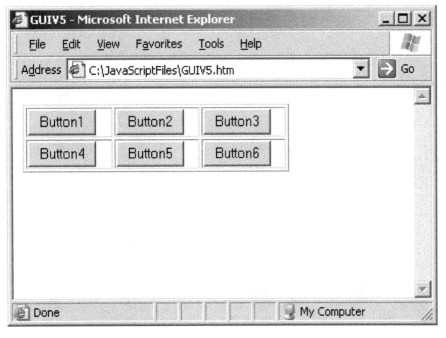

"It's not obvious," I said, "but the table is now being displayed as 70% of the browser window. Watch what happens if we now 'widen' the size of the window---the size of the table will be adjusted accordingly."

I did exactly that--widened my Browser Window. The following screenshot was displayed on the classroom projector.

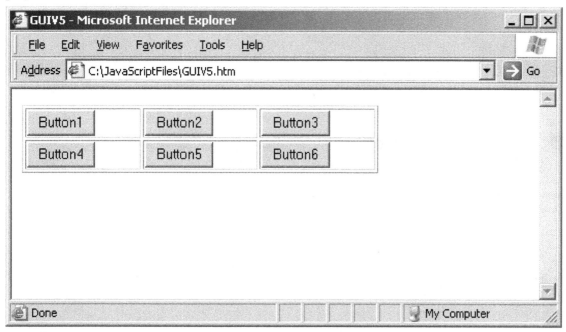

"Does everyone see how the table size has been adjusted to 70% of the screen?" I asked. "All we needed to do was specify a width parameter within the <table> tag.."

<table border="1" width="70%">

"I see," Mary said, but all of the cell widths are equal--I presume that's because our Browser has calculated that the size of each one of the buttons is identical."

"That's right Mary," I said, "if the caption for one of the buttons was larger, the cell width--and therefore the column width---would expand."

"Is there a way to exercise a bit more control over the layout?" Ward asked. "I'm not sure I like the way our GUI elements are moving all over the place."

"Automatic repositioning," I said, "is considered a benefit of Browsers--but yes, you can exercise more control over the layout of your GUI by using the width parameter when you define the cells in your table. For instance, suppose we decided that we wanted the column width of column 1 to be about 10% of the screen size, column 2 to be about 20% of the screen, and column 3 to be about 40% of the screen. Here's the code to do that--by specifying the width parameter of the Table Cell tag as a percentage."

I then modified the code from the **GUIV5** example to look like this...

```
<! GUIV6 -- >
<html>
<head>
<title>GUIV6</title>
</head>

</head>

<body>
  <form name="myForm">
    <table border="1" width="70%">
      <tr>
        <td  width="10%"><input type="button" name="btn1" value="Button1"></td>
        <td  width="20%"><input type="button" name="btn2" value="Button2"></td>
        <td  width="40%"><input type="button" name="btn3" value="Button3"></td>
      </tr>
```

```
    <tr>
      <td width="10%"><input type="button" name="btn4" value="Button4"></td>
      <td width="20%"><input type="button" name="btn5" value="Button5"></td>
      <td width="40%"><input type="button" name="btn6" value="Button6"></td>
    </tr>
  </table>
</form>
</body>
</html>
```

saved it as '**GUIV6.htm**" and opened up the program in my Internet Browser. The following screenshot was displayed on the classroom projector.

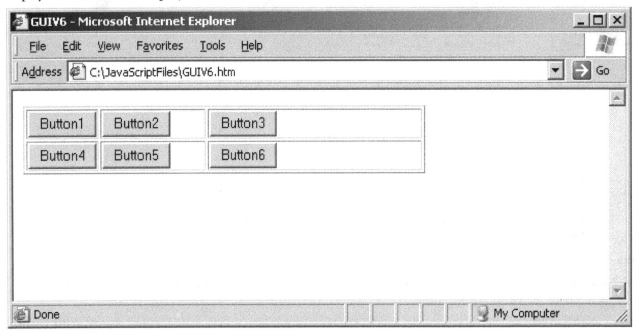

"Let's take a quick look at the code," I said. "This line of code tells our Browser that our first column is to be 10% of the screen size..."

<td width="10%"><input type="button" name="btn1" value="Button1"></td>

"...this line of code tells our Browser that the second column is to be 20% of the screen size..."

<td width="20%"><input type="button" name="btn2" value="Button2"></td>

"...and finally this line of code tells our Browser that this column is to be 40% of the screen size..."

<td width="40%"><input type="button" name="btn3" value="Button3"></td>

"So those percentages are a percentage of the screen, and not a percentage of the table?" Ward asked.

"That's right Ward," I said, "for that reason, if you are going to use width parameter with a percentage, make sure that the individual cells add up to the percentage specified for the table."

"I'm not sure we got exactly what we wanted," Rhonda interjected. "Shouldn't the second column be twice the width of the first column, and the third column twice the width of the second column. That's not what is being displayed."

"You're absolutely right Rhonda," I said, "we didn't get exactly the result we were looking for. The reason for that is our Browser is still intent on adjusting the column sizes based on the data that it is being asked to display. If the captions for Buttons 1 and 4 were null, the results would be much closer to what we want."

"So how do we get our GUI to look exactly the way we want it?" Linda asked.

"We can specify pixels for the width of the Table and the cells," I said, "but I want to emphasize that the way the Browser window behaves and readjusts is the way the designers intended. When we specify pixel widths for Tables and cells, we're doing so based on the way the GUI looks on the computer monitor we are using---not the monitors that the users of our program will be using. Pixel widths aren't automatically adjusted by the Browser---the Browser simply displays what we tell it."

"In other words," Dave said, "by using percentages for our width parameters, we're ensuring that our display looks 'OK' on any computer monitor that displays our program."

"Absolutely right Dave," I said. "Using pixels for our width may result in a perfect GUI on our computer monitor-- but if a user of our program runs the program, the GUI could look pretty bad. By using a percentage for the width parameter, we ensure that the GUI is at least 'OK'.

"I think I see now," Rhonda said, "but could you show us what this GUI would look like used pixels for the width parameter?"

"I can do that," I said.

I then modified the code from the **GUIV6** example to look like this...

```
<! GUIV7 -- >
<html>
<head>
<title>GUIV7</title>
</head>

</head>

<body>
  <form name="myForm">
    <table border="1" width="350">
      <tr>
        <td width="50"><input type="button" name="btn1" value="Button1"></td>
        <td width="100"><input type="button" name="btn2" value="Button2"></td>
        <td width="200"><input type="button" name="btn3" value="Button3"></td>
      </tr>
      <tr>
        <td width="50"><input type="button" name="btn4" value="Button4"></td>
        <td width="100"><input type="button" name="btn5" value="Button5"></td>
        <td width="200"><input type="button" name="btn6" value="Button6"></td>
      </tr>
    </table>
  </form>
</body>
</html>
```

saved it as **'GUIV7.htm"** and opened up the program in my Internet Browser. The following screenshot was displayed on the classroom projector.

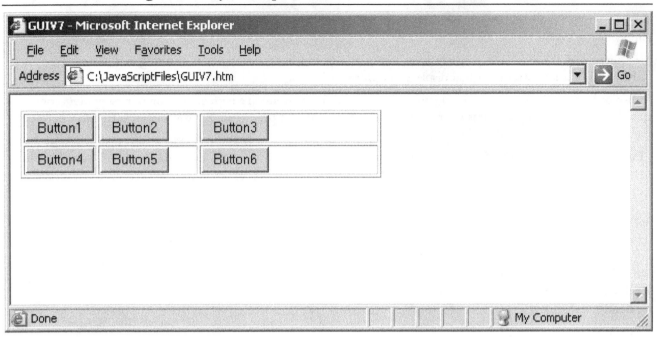

"That's better," Ward said. "That's exactly what we wanted. The second column is twice that of the first, and the third column is twice that of the second column."

"You're right Ward," I said, "by specifying all of our widths in pixels, we got exactly what we wanted..."

```
<table border="1" width="350">
  <tr>
    <td  width="50"><input type="button" name="btn1" value="Button1"></td>
    <td  width="100"><input type="button" name="btn2" value="Button2"></td>
    <td  width="200"><input type="button" name="btn3" value="Button3"></td>
```

"....but take note that if we expand the size of our Browser window, the size of the table never changes. The table--and its cells--are now fixed. By the way, notice how the width of the three table cells is exactly equal to the width of the table..."

"Will we be specifying the dimensions of the Grades calculation program in percentage of pixels?" Dave asked.

"That's a good question Dave," I said. "Why don't I leave that up to the class---think about it over our break, and we'll take a vote on it just before we start working on the GUI for the project."

We had been working for some time, and so I suggested we take a quick break before completing our discussion of the remainder of the HTML GUI Elements we would be using in the Grades Calculation Project.

"When we return from break," I said, "we'll see how we add Text Fields to a Form."

Text Fields

"We use the input type 'text' to add Text Fields to a form," I said, resuming class after break. "Text Fields permit the user to interact with our program by entering text into a Text input area. Let's modify the code from GUIV7 to add two TextFields to the Form..."

I then displayed this code on the classroom projector.

```
<! GUIV8 -- >
<html>
<head>
<title>GUIV8</title>
</head>

<body>
  <form name="myForm">
    <table border="1">
      <tr>
```

```
      <td>Name:</td>
      <td><input type="text" name="txt1"></td>
    </tr>
    <tr>
      <td>Email:</td>
      <td><input type="text" name="txt2"></td>
    </tr>
  </table>
</form>
</body>
</html>
```

I then saved the program as '**GUIV8.htm**" and opened up the program in my Internet Browser. The following screenshot was displayed on the classroom projector.

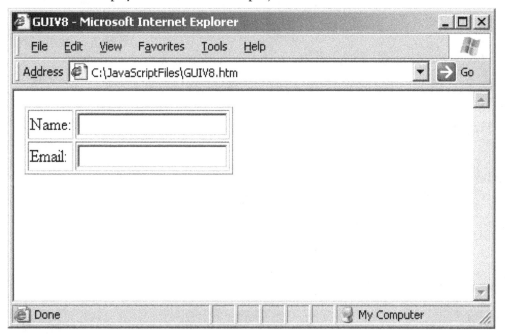

"Do you see the two Text Fields?" I asked, as I entered text into them.

"As was the case with the buttons we added to our Form," I said, "all we really needed to do was to specify an <input> tag with a type parameter equal to 'text'. As was the case with our buttons, we specified a name parameter for the Text Fields."

```
<tr>
  <td>Name:</td>
  <td><input type="text" name="txt1"></td>
</tr>
<tr>
  <td>Email:</td>
  <td><input type="text" name="txt2"></td>
</tr>
```

"I notice," Peter said, "that there's no value parameter for the Text Field like there was for a button."

"That's right Peter," I said, "the value parameter for the button GUI element is used to give the button a caption. Text Fields don't have captions of their own--it's up to us to create an identifying caption which we did by simply typing it into an adjacent Table Cell, which is what we did with this line of code..."

```
<td>Name:</td>
```

"...and this one..."

```
<td>Email:</td>
```

"The Text Field width for both the name and email address seem a bit small to me," Dave said, "is there any way to widen them?

"Dave," I answered, "you must be reading my mind, I was about to say that it's possible to specify a width for our Text fields by including a value---in pixels---for the size parameter. Take a look at this code..."

I then modified the code from the GUIV8 example to look like this...

```
<! GUIV9 -- >
<html>
<head>
<title>GUIV9</title>
</head>

<body>
  <form name="myForm">
    <table border="1">
      <tr>
        <td>Name:</td>
        <td><input type="text" name="txt1" size="25"></td>
      </tr>
      <tr>
        <td>Email:</td>
        <td><input type="text" name="txt2" size="40"></td>
      </tr>
    </table>
  </form>
</body>
</html>
```

I then saved the program as '**GUIV9.htm**" and opened up the program in my Internet Browser. The following screenshot was displayed on the classroom projector.

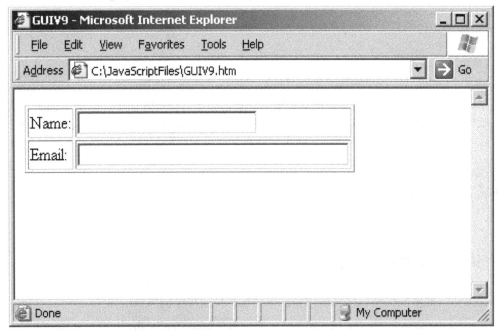

"That's better," Dave said. "That's exactly what I wanted.

No one seemed to have any problems understanding what we had done with the Text Field GUI element--now it was time to move onto the Radio Button object.

Radio Buttonss

"The last GUI element that we'll be discussing today is the Radio Button." I said. "The Radio Button is the most complicated of the GUI elements we'll learn about today."

"Why is that?" Rhonda asked.

"Because of the unique nature of the Radio Button," I said, "Do you remember earlier today I mentioned that only one Radio Button can be selected at one time? I'm afraid I simplified things just a bit. In actuality, more than one Radio Button object can be selected at a given time, provided they both are not a member of the same Radio Button group."

"A Radio Button group?" Mary asked. "What's that? I'm afraid I don't understand."

"A Radio Button group is a logical grouping of Radio Buttons," I said. "For instance, suppose we need to create a GUI in which we ask the user two distinct questions, each of which requires a Yes/No answer. Radio Buttons are ideal to represent the Yes/No answers for each question, but if we have two questions, that means that two of the four Radio Buttons will need to be selected by the user to represent the two answers. Now this is where a Radio Button group comes into play. We can tell our Frame that a pair of the Yes/No Radio Buttons belong to a group, and the other pair belong to another."

"So that would permit one button in each Radio Button group to be selected?" Dave asked.

"Exactly Dave," I said.

"Can you illustrate this for us?" Kate asked.

"Sure thing Kate," I said. I then took a moment to create and display this illustration on the classroom projector.

Are you married?   **Do you play golf?**

● Yes   ○ Yes

○ No   ● No

Radio Button   **Radio Button**
Group #1   **Group #2**

"Ordinarily," I said, "with four Radio Buttons on a Frame, only one of the Radio Buttons can be selected at one time. However, if we tell Javascript that the two left most Radio Buttons belong to Radio Button Group #1, and the two right most Radio Buttons belong to Radio Button Group #2, it's possible for the user to select a Radio Button from each one of the groups."

Everyone seemed content with this explanation--although I suspected they really wanted to see it in action.

"Let's add four Radio Buttons and two Radio Button Groups to a Form," I said, "and associate two of the Radio Buttons with one group, and two with the other."

I then displayed this code on the classroom projector.

```
<! GUIV10 -- >
<html>
<head>
<title>GUIV10</title>
</head>

<body>
 <form name="myForm">
```

```
<table border="1">
  <tr>
    <td>Are you married?</td>
    <td>Do you play golf</td>
  </tr>
  <tr>
    <td><input type="radio" name="radMarried" value="Yes" checked>Yes</td>
    <td><input type="radio" name="radGolf" value="Yes" checked>No</td>
  </tr>
  <tr>
    <td><input type="radio" name="radMarried" value=No>No</td>
    <td><input type="radio" name="radGolf" value="No">No</td>
  </tr>
</table>
</form>
</body>
</html>
```

...saved the program as **'GUIV10.htm**" and opened up the program in my Internet Browser. The following screenshot was displayed on the classroom projector.

"Do you see how we have two Radio Buttons selected simultaneously," I said, "one from each group?"

I then demonstrated how it was possible to select just one of the Radio Buttons on the left, and just one of the Radio Buttons on the right side of the Frame--but not two from Radio Button Group 1 or two from Radio Button Group 2 simultaneously.

"Let's take a look at the code in GUIV10 now," I said, "We needed to 'polish' this GUI quite a bit, and so we added two identifying captions to describe each of the two Radio Button group. These appear in a row above the rows containing the Radio Buttons..."

```
<tr>
  <td>Are you married?</td>
  <td>Do you play golf</td>
</tr>
```

"...here's the code to create four Radio Button objects---notice that Radio Buttons are created by specifying an input type parameter of 'radio'. We specify the Radio Button group name by specifying a value for the name parameter, and we specify a caption for the Radio Button itself by specifying the value parameter. Furthermore, by specifying 'checked', we tell JavaScript to display a particular Radio Button as 'selected' when the Browser first displays our form..."

```
<tr>
  <td><input type="radio" name="radMarried" value="Yes" checked>Yes</td>
  <td><input type="radio" name="radGolf" value="Yes" checked>No</td>
</tr>
<tr>
  <td><input type="radio" name="radMarried" value="No">No</td>
  <td><input type="radio" name="radGolf" value="No">No</td>
</tr>
```

I realized I had given them a lot to think about.

"I think I see what's going on here," Rhonda said. "We have two Radio Buttons whose name argument is 'radMarried'. That's how JavaScript knows that those two Radio Buttons are a member of the same Radio Button group."

"That's right Rhonda," I answered, "specifically, a Radio Button group named 'radMarried. In the same way, we have two Radio Buttons whose name argument is 'radGolf'. Those two Radio Buttons are members of a Radio Button group named 'golf'. Remember, only one Radio Button in a Radio Button group can be selected at one time. By specifying two Radio Button groups, we therefore can have two Radio Buttons in our Form selected at once."

"I presume," Ward said, "that next week we'll learn how to work with these Radio Buttons in code? I mean, right now, they look very pretty, but they don't do anything."

"Indeed we will Ward," I said,

I waited to see if there were any more questions. I could see that many of my students had been following along with my series of demonstrations, and at this moment, were happily executing various versions of their own GUI Forms. No one seemed to have any questions, and so it was time to move onto implementing our design for the Grades Calculation GUI. I then distributed this exercise for the class to complete.

Create the GUI for the Grades Calculation Project

Exercise 11-1 Create the GradesGUI program for the Grades Calculation Project

In this exercise, you'll create the GradesGUI.htm program for the Grades Calculation project. This program will be used to display the Graphical User Interface version of the Grades Calculation project.

1. Use Notepad (if you are using Windows) and enter the following code.

```
<! GradesGUI -->
<html>
<head>

<title>Grades Calculator</title>

</head>
<body>
<form name="Grades">
<table border="1">
 <tr>
  <td><b><u>Student Types</b></u></td>
  <td><b><u>Grades</b></u></td>
  <td><input type="text" name="txtStudentType" value="English" disabled="true"></td>
  <td></td>
 </tr>
 <tr>
  <td><input type="radio" name="radStudentType" value="English" checked>English Student</td>
  <td>Midterm:</td>
  <td><input type="text" name="txtMidterm"></td>
  <td></td>
 </tr>
```

```html
<tr>
 <td><input type="radio" name="radStudentType" value="Math">Math Student</td>
 <td>Final Exam:</td>
 <td><input type="text" name="txtFinalExam"></td>
 <td></td>
</tr>
<tr>
 <td><input type="radio" name="radStudentType" value="Science">Science Student</td>
 <td>Research Paper:</td>
 <td><input type="text" name="txtResearch"></td>
 <td></td>
</tr>
<tr>
 <td></td>
 <td> Presentation:</td>
 <td><input type="text" name="txtPresentation"></td>
 <td></td>
</tr>
<tr>
 <td><input type="button" name="btnCalculate" value="Calculate Grade"></td>
 <td>Numeric Grade</td>
 <td><input type="text" name="txtNumericGrade" value="Not Yet" disabled="true"></td>
 <td></td>
</tr>
<tr>
 <td><input type="button" name="btnReset" onclick="ResetAll()" value="Reset"></td>
 <td>Letter Grade</td>
 <td><input type="text" name="txtLetterGrade" value = "Not Yet" disabled="true"></td>
 <td></td>
</tr>
</table>
</form>
</body>
</html>
```

2. Save your source file as **'GradesGui.htm'** in the \JavaScriptFiles\Grades folder (select File-Save As from Notepad's Menu Bar). Be sure to save your source file with the file name extension 'htm'.

3. Open your source file within your Internet Browser, and observe its behavior. You should see a GUI that looks like this.

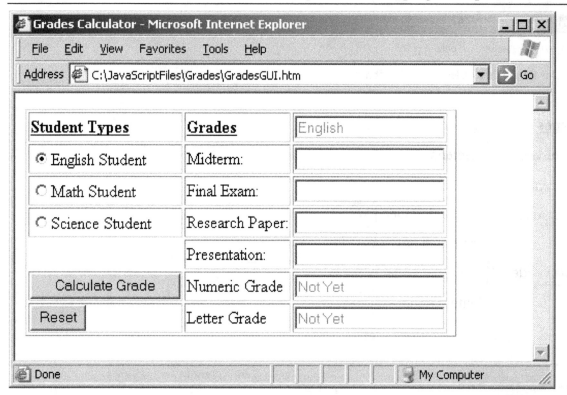

4. Unfortunately, until we write code for our GUI Element's event handlers, the program won't perform any calculations.

Discussion

No one in the class had a great deal of trouble completing the exercise---although the exercise was pretty long and tedious, everything in the exercise was something we had discussed earlier in the class.

"Wow, that is really something," Ward said. "I'm really impressed with this. A real working GUI."

"It is impressive Ward," I said. "but at this point, what we have is a pretty Graphical User Interface with very little functionality. In other words, the GUI looks good--but it doesn't do much of anything. You'll notice that if you click on the Radio Buttons, each one displays a certain amount of default behavior in that each Radio Button is selected, and the others unselected. You can enter text into the TextFields, and also click on each one of the two buttons. All of these actions produce behavior of some kind--but right now, none of this behavior is contributing toward calculating the student's grade. That's what we'll work on next week."

No one had any questions about what we had done. Still, I decided it would be a good idea to go over the code line by line.

"Let's take a look at the code now," I said. "As we've seen during today's class, we begin the process of creating our GUI by first creating a form, in this case, a Form called 'Grades'..."

```
<form name="Grades">
```

"...within the Form, we'll create a table, without a predefined size, consisting of *seven* rows and *four* columns..."

```
<table border="1">
```

"...I noticed that several students, while completing the exercise, experimented creating a table without a border by specifying a border value of 0. I think this is a great idea. If you do so, this is what your GUI will look like..."

"I'll leave it up to you to determine your personal preference," I said.

I waited for a moment before continuing.

"Let's take a look at the *first* row of data in the Table," I said. "This row is essentially just a heading for the other rows, with Student Types and Grades appearing as ordinary text. However, we do need a Text Field called txtStudentType. As we'll see next week, when the user makes a selection of one of the Radio Buttons, we'll place code in an event handler which will change the value of txtStudentType accordingly. We'll eventually use that value to determine the type of student we are calculating. Since we don't want the user to type into this Text Field, we've assigned a value of true to the disabled property of the Text Field."

```
<tr>
<td>Student Types</td>
<td>Grades</td>
<td><input type="text" name="txtStudentType" value="English" disabled="true"></td>
<td></td>
</tr>
```

"With the disabled property set to true, the user won't be able to make an entry in the Text Field?" Kate asked.

"That's right Kate," I said, "in effect, we've created what amounts to a display label, but it's one that we will be able to access in our code since it has a name."

I waited for a moment to make sure everyone was OK.

"The second row in the Table" I said, "contains one Radio Button, one identifying caption, and one Text Field. Notice that the name argument of the Radio Button---radStudentType--designates the one and only Radio Button Group in our GUI. Notice also, that by default, the English Student Radio button is checked.."

```
<tr>
 <td><input type="radio" name="radStudentType"  value="English" checked>English Student</td>
 <td>Midterm:</td>
 <td><input type="text" name="txtMidterm"></td>
 <td></td>
</tr>
```

"In a similar way," I said, "the third row in the Table contains one Radio Button, one identifying caption, and one Text Field. Notice that the name argument of the Radio Button---radStudentType--is the same name as designated for the Radio Button on the second row...."

```
<tr>
 <td><input type="radio" name="radStudentType" value="Math">Math Student</td>
 <td>Final Exam:</td>
 <td><input type="text" name="txtFinal"></td>
 <td></td>
</tr>
```

"...the fourth row in the Table contains one Radio Button, one identifying caption, and one Text Field. Again, notice that the name argument of the Radio Button---radStudentType--is the same name as designated for the other Radio Button GUI elements..."

```
<tr>
 <td><input type="radio" name="radStudentType" value="Science">Science Student</td>
 <td>Research Paper:</td>
 <td><input type="text" name="txtResearch"></td>
 <td></td>
</tr>
```

"...the fifth row in the Table contains just one identifying caption, and one Text Field..."

```
<tr>
 <td></td>
 <td> Presentation:</td>
 <td><input type="text" name="txtParticipation"></td>
 <td></td>
</tr>
```

"...We're nearly done creating our GUI now," I said, "The sixth row contains the Calculate button, one identifying caption and one Text Field named txtNumericGrade. The Text Field will be used to display the value of the calculated numeric grade for the student---but you'll need to wait until next week to find out how we do that. Notice how we pre-set the value of the Text Field to 'N/A' to alert the user that a calculation has yet to be performed. Also, since we don't want the user typing into this Text Field, we set the disabled property to true...."

```
<tr>
<td><input type="button" name="btnCalculate" value="Calculate Grade"></td>
<td>Numeric Grade</td>
<td><input type="text" name="txtNumericGrade" value="N/A" disabled="true"></td>
<td></td>
</tr>
```

"...Finally, this is the last row of the table consisting of a button, the Reset Button, an identifying caption and a Text Field named txtLetterGrade that will be used to display the value of the calculated letter grade for the student. Once again, we set the value of the TextField to 'N/A' and disable it to prevent the user from typing into it..."

```
<tr>
<td><input type="button" name="btnReset" onclick="ResetAll()" value="Reset"></td>
<td>Letter Grade</td>
<td><input type="text" name="txtLetterGrade" value = "N/A" disabled="true"></td>
<td></td>
</tr>
```

"...followed by closing table, form and body tags..."

```
   </table>
  </form>
</body>
```

"What's the function of the Reset button?" Chuck asked.

"The Reset button," I answered, "will be used to 'reset' the GUI to its initial state."

"What does that mean?" Rhonda asked.

"When the Reset button is clicked by the user," I said, "we'll clear all entries in the Text Fields---including the disabled Text Fields---and 'check' the English Student Radio Button to on."

I asked if anyone had any questions. No one did--It had been a long and fulfilling class. I dismissed class for the day.

Summary

In this chapter, you learned how to create a Javascript Graphical User Interface. You saw that developing a GUI is a matter of creating a form, and with the form created, adding other HTML objects--objects like Buttons, Radio Buttons, Labels and TextFields.

These objects, when placed on a Form, exhibit default behavior when a form containing them is created. Despite their default behavior, these objects do little else--it won't be until our final week of class that we learn to initiate some kind of behavior when the user interacts with the object.

Chapter 12---Event Handling In JavaScript

In this, our final chapter, we'll follow my Introduction to JavaScript class as we take the Graphical User Interface for the Grades Calculation Project that we developed last week, and create and associate 'Event Procedures' with the objects on our Form to give our GUI intelligence.

JavaScript Event Handling

I began the final class of my Introduction to JavaScript course by saying that in our final meeting together, we would complete the Grades Calculation Project by finishing up with the GUI we began last week, and delivering and installing it on a PC in the English Department.

"So we'll actually be delivering the program today? Ward asked.

"That's right Ward," I said, "we'll be installing our program at the end of today's class. Earlier in the week, Frank Olley called me to find out if we were on target to complete the project today, and when I told him we were, he asked if it would be possible to deliver and install the program as part of today's class. I told him that would be fine with me. When Frank heard that, he was elated, and he told me that he would arrange to have his two work study students come in today to get acquainted with our program. This might mean that today's class goes a little bit longer than usual---I do hope you can all hang in there and help me deliver and install our program in the English Department."

> **Note: In addition to installing our program on a Desktop PC, we could install it on a Web Server, such as http://www.johnsmiley.com/LTPJavaScript/GradesGUI.htm**

"I wouldn't miss it for anything," Linda said.

"Me neither," Steve said. "I think it will be exciting to see how the work study students like the program."

From the looks on the faces of the rest of my students, I had a feeling that all of them felt the same way, and would be paying a visit to the English Department as well.

"It's a shame," Mary said suddenly, "but it doesn't look like Rose and Jack will make it to our final class. Has anyone heard from them? Are they still in Liverpool?"

"I've heard from them," I said, excitedly "On Thursday evening, I spoke with both of them, and at the time, they were aboard their ship somewhere in the North Atlantic. They said the weather was unusually frigid for April, and when asked whether they would be making it back on time for today's class, they told me they had spoken to the ship's Captain who assured them they'd be arriving in New York harbor early this morning--a few hours head of schedule. I expect both of them to be here before the end of today's class."

"That's great news," Rhonda said, "it will be great to see them again."

"Will our delivery and installation of the Grades Calculation program on a PC in the English Department wrap up the SDLC?" Valerie asked.

"Just about," I replied. "Phase 5 of the Systems Development Life Cycle, which is the Implementation phase, will begin today with the delivery and installation of our program, and conclude over the course of the next week or so as I---and hopefully some student volunteers---train work study students in the English, Math and Science departments to use the program. Phase 6 of the SDLC, which is the Audit and Maintenance phase, will begin today as well as we observe and study how well the program performs."

What's an Event?

"So what exactly do we have left to complete with the Grades Calculation project?" Rhonda asked. "Aren't we nearly done with it?"

"Almost," I said, "Last week we created a program called DrawGUI, which displays the Graphical User Interface, or GUI, for the Grades Calculation project. As it stands right now, the GUI looks great, but it's basically an empty shell---it doesn't react to any 'events' that the user of our program will trigger while working with it---and as a result, at this moment, it's incapable of calculating the grade for a student."

"What exactly is an event?" Bob asked. "Is that something that a programmer causes to happen when he writes code?"

"No Bob," I said, "an event is something that is triggered by the user of our GUI when he or she interacts with it."

"What do you mean by triggered?" Rhonda asked.

"For instance," I said, "the GUI we created last week consists of a Form, two Buttons, three Radio Buttons, and seven Text Fields---four of which the user can type values into. Ultimately, when the user runs our program, the GUI will be displayed, and the user will then use his or her mouse to select a type of student by clicking on one of the three Radio Buttons. Depending upon the type of student the user selects, two, three or four updateable Text Fields will be enabled. The user will then enter appropriate grades into these Text Fields using their keyboard, and when he or she is finished, the user will then click on the Calculate button, resulting in the display of a final numeric and letter grade in two 'display only ' Text Fields on the Form. At that point, if the user has more grades to calculate, he or she will then click on the Reset button, and start the process all over again---otherwise they will simply close the window within their Internet Browser."

"Were each one of those user actions you mentioned an event?" Kate asked. "In the scenario you presented, I counted three mouse clicks---one when the user clicks on a Student Type Radio Button, one when the user clicks on the Calculate Button, and one when the user clicks on the Reset Button---plus an unknown number of keystrokes when the user enters the composite student grades into the enabled Text Fields. Is each one of these actions an event?"

"Not quite Kate," I said, "but you're close. Each one of those actions isn't an event, but each one of those actions triggers an event. One way to conceptualize an event is to picture an event as a ripple in a pond, caused by the action of someone tossing in a stone or a pebble. The action--the stone toss--isn't the event---the event is the ripple generated by the action. Furthermore, each interaction of the user with an object on the GUI generates one of these ripples. We'll see shortly that our program can react to these ripples, provided we write something called an Event Procedure. As the name implies, Event Procedures are code that react to events or ripples."

"I think I understand what you are saying," Mary said. "You're saying that when the user clicks on a Radio Button, for instance, that an event--or one of these ripples as you called it--is generated. Do we need to program that behavior into the Radio Button?"

"That's a good question Mary," I said. "Fortunately, the behavior to generate the event is 'built into' the Radio Button itself. There's nothing we need to do to generate the event. What we must do is create the Event Procedure with code to react to the event when it occurs, and that's what we'll be learning in the next few minutes."

What's an Event Procedure?

"I understand that an Event Procedure is code that can detect and react to events?" Lou said. "Is an Event Procedure a function that we write in the program that displays the GUI?"

"That's right Lou," I said, "When we define our GUI object, using the HTML Input statement, we can optionally name an event name that we wish to detect, and then specify the name of a function containing our event procedure. We then write the code for the Event Procedure and then placed it in that function. The function can either reside in the same program that displays the GUI, or it can be place in an external JavaScript file, like we did with some of the functions earlier in the class."

"We haven't specified an event name in any of our Input statement yet, have we?" Rhonda asked.

"Not yet Rhonda," I said, "we'll be doing that shortly."

"Will our program have more than one Event Procedure?" Peter asked.

"Each one of our GUI objects can have its own event procedure," I said, "and that makes sense since the actions we wish to perform when the user clicks on the Radio Button is different from the actions we wish to perform when the user clicks on a command button---although as you'll see, instead of coding distinct event procedures for each of our three Radio Buttons, we'll write a single event procedure to handle all of three of them."

"Can an object generate more than one event?" Mary asked.

"Good question Mary," I said, "and the answer is 'yes'----GUI objects are capable of generating multiple events. For instance, if the user clicks their mouse on a Button object, a click event is generated. Likewise, if the user double clicks their mouse on a Button object, a double click event is generated."

Note: For a list of events that HTML GUI objects can generate, follow this link

http://www.w3schools.com/htmldom/dom_reference.asp

"What about the Text Fields on the Form?" Barbara said. "Will we be creating an Event Procedure for those objects?"

"At this point," I said, "I don't think we're interested in reacting to any keystroke events the user may trigger, although it may be something we add to the project if we enhance it in our JavaScript Intermediate Programming class."

Implementing Event Procedures in your code

"I'm still having trouble visualizing how this works," Rhonda said.

"I think I can help with an example," I said. "Here's a program that displays a simple GUI that displays a form with two Buttons and two Radio Buttons...."

I then displayed this code on the classroom projector.

```
<! Example12-1 -- >
<html>
<head>
<title>GUI Demo with NO Event Procedures</title>
</head>

<body>
<form name="myForm">
<table border="1" width="143">
 <tr>
  <td width="59"><input type="radio" name="radQuestion" value="Yes">Yes</td>
  <td width="68"><input type="button" name="btn1" value="Button1"></td>
 </tr>
 <tr>
  <td width="59"><input type="radio" name="radQuestion" value="No">No</td>
  <td width="68"><input type="button" name="btn2" value="Button2"></td>
 </tr>
</table>
</form>
</body>

</html>
```

"There's really nothing new happening here," I said, "when we load this code into our Internet Browser, it will display a Form with two Buttons and two Radio Buttons."

I then saved this code as 'Example12-1.htm' and opened it up within my Internet Browser. The following screenshot was displayed on the classroom projector...

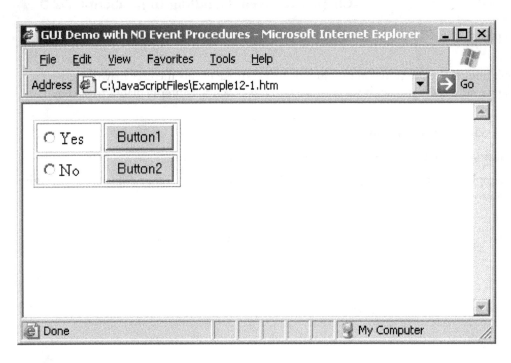

Our First Event Procedure

"Now," I said, "let's create Event Procedure functions to react to the events the Radio objects trigger--we'll save the button objects for later."

"So we'll create two event procedure functions, one for each of the Radio Button objects?" Steve asked.

"That's how we'll start out Steve," I said, "We could actually create just one event procedure function, and 'pass' information to the function to let us know what Radio Button object generated the event. But that's a bit more complex--let's start with a basic event procedure first."

"I know you mentioned this," Rhonda said, "but I'm afraid I didn't totally understand. Where will be placing these event procedure functions?"

"Functions can be placed in the <head> section of our HTML," I said, "but I think you know me well enough by now to realize that I don't like cluttered code---I prefer to place my functions in an external JavaScript file. For that reason, I prefer to create a file called events.js, and place my event procedure functions in there. Right now, we'll be writing two event procedure functions in all---and each one will simply display the name of the Radio Button object that the user has clicked."

I then displayed this code on the classroom projector and placed it in a file called **'events.js'**.

```
//events.js
function YesButton_Click() {
   alert("Yes Radio Button has been clicked")
}
function NoButton_Click() {
   alert("No Radio Button has been clicked")
}
```

"Wow, there's not much code in those Event Procedure functions, is there?" Valerie said

"That's right Valerie," I answered. "Event Procedure functions don't have to be lengthy. Really, all we're doing here is displaying an alert box that let's the user know what Radio Button object has been clicked."

"How do these event procedure functions get triggered?" Blaine asked. "Is there something magical about their name?"

"No Blaine, it's not the name" I answered, "We tell our GUI objects what function to execute when a given event occurs. That way, when the event occurs, JavaScript knows what function to execute."

"That sounds complicated," Rhonda said.

"Actually," I said reassuringly, "once we have the functions written, letting our GUI objects know what function to execute is surprisingly easy to do. As they say, a picture is worth a thousand words."

I then displayed this code on the classroom projector.

Don't Forget: If typing these examples and exercises isn't something you want to do, feel free to follow this link to find and download the completed solutions for all of the examples and exercises in the book. Just click on the JavaScript book, then follow the link entitled exercises ☺

http://www.johnsmiley.com/main/books.htm

```html
<! Example12-2 -- >
<html>
<head>
<script src='events.js'></script>
<title>GUI Demo with Event Procedures</title>
</head>

<body>
<form name="myForm">
<table border="1" width="143">
 <tr>
  <td width="59"><input type="radio" name="radQuestion" value="Yes"
                  onclick="YesButton_Click()">Yes</td>
  <td width="68"><input type="button" name="btn1" value="Button1">/td>
 </tr>
 <tr>
  <td width="59"><input type="radio" name="radQuestion" value="No"
                  onclick="NoButton_Click()" >No</td>
  <td width="68"><input type="button" name="btn2" value="Button2"></td>
 </tr>
</table>
</form>
</body>
</html>
```

I then saved the program as '**Example12-2.htm**' and opened it up within my Internet Browser. When I clicked on the Radio Button captioned 'Yes', the following screenshot was displayed.

Sometimes my students are skeptical, and so I clicked on the Radio Button captioned 'No'---the following screenshot was displayed.

"I see," Rhonda said excitedly, "when you clicked on the 'No' Radio Button, the word 'No' was displayed in an Alert Box and when you clicked on the 'Yes' Radio Button, the word 'Yes' was displayed in an Alert box. That's really impressive."

"I don't know whether you noticed the slight changes we made," I said, noticing that everyone in the class shared Rhonda's excitement, "so let me go over them. The first thing we did was to add a reference to our external JavaScript file in the <head> section..."

```
<script src='events.js'></script>
```

"...then, we registered the YesButton_Click() function to be triggered when the radQuestion Radio Button's Click event is triggered. We do that by coding an 'onclick' parameter..."

```
<td width="59"><input type="radio" name="radQuestion" value="Yes"
        onclick="YesButton_Click()">Yes</td>
```

"I get it," Peter said. "onclick is the name of the Radio Button *event* that is triggered when the user clicks on the Radio Button, and 'YesButton_Click() is the name of the function to execute when that happens."

"Excellent Peter," I said, "that's exactly right."

"How do we know what the name of the event is?" Rhonda asked. "I would never know that I needed to code 'onclick'. Are there any other events that a Radio Button can generate?"

"There are many Rhonda," I said, "this is where JavaScript documentation comes in handy. Actually, GUI Objects are part of the HTML Document Object Model, or DOM for short, and you can find information about the various GUI objects, their event names, and their properties and methods here..."

http://www.w3schools.com/htmldom/dom_reference.asp

I paused before continuing.

"As you can see," I said, "we've coded an *onclick* statement for both of our Radio Buttons..."

```
<td width="59"><input type="radio" name="radQuestion" value="No"
        onclick="NoButton_Click()" >No</td>
```

I waited a moment before continuing. "We've just implemented our first Event Procedure to 'react' to events on our GUI," I said, "and I think you'll agree that it wasn't all that bad."

"No it wasn't bad at all," Kate said, "I think I understand what's going on---but what about the Buttons on the Form. Do we need to create a separate Event Procedure for those as well---or can we use the Event Procedure we coded for the Radio Buttons?"

"In theory," I said, "we could use the same Event Procedure to react to events triggered by both objects. However, it's my personal preference to create distinct Event Procedures for the various types of objects on a Form. For now, let's create two Event Procedures for the Button objects called btn1_Click and btn2_Click."

I then added the two event procedures for the button objects to the existing code in events.js, and displayed the file on the classroom projector.

```
//events.js
function YesButton_Click() {
  alert("Yes Radio Button has been clicked")
}

function NoButton_Click() {
  alert("No Radio Button has been clicked")
}

function btn1_Click() {
  alert("Button1 has been clicked")
}

function btn2_Click() {
  alert("Button2 has been clicked")
}
```

"Now," I said, "we need to add an 'onclick' statement to each of the button definitions..."

```
<! Example12-3 -- >
<html>
<head>
<script src='events.js'></script>
<title>GUI Demo with Event Procedures</title>
</head>

<body>
<form name="myForm">
<table border="1" width="143">
 <tr>
  <td width="59"><input type="radio" name="radQuestion" value="Yes"
                  onclick="YesButton_Click()">Yes</td>
  <td width="68"><input type="button" name="btn1" value="Button1"
                  onclick="btn1_Click()"></td>
 </tr>
 <tr>
  <td width="59"><input type="radio" name="radQuestion" value="No"
                  onclick="NoButton_Click()" >No</td>
  <td width="68"><input type="button" name="btn2" value="Button2"
                  onclick="btn2_Click()"></td>
 </tr>
</table>
</form>
</body>
</html>
```

I then saved the program as '**Example12-3.htm**' and opened it up within my Internet Browser. When I clicked on the Button captioned 'Button1', the following screenshot was displayed.

"...and when I clicked on the Button captioned 'Button2', the following screenshot was displayed.

"That's cool," Linda said, "our program now has intelligence--it knows what GUI object has been clicked."

"I've been following along with this example," Rhonda said, "but I'm not getting any Alert messages. I wonder what I've done wrong. Is it because my function names don't match yours exactly."

I took a quick trip to Rhonda's workstation. Her error was very subtle.

"I see the problem Rhonda," I said, "and it's not your naming convention. As long as the function name you reference via the onclick statement matches the name of the function event procedure you coded, you're fine. Your name matches--the problem is that you didn't include an empty set of parentheses after the name of your function. Without it, your function is not executed when the event is triggered."

Rhonda made the change and was obviously pleased when her program ran properly.

Dave had a question.

'I think you mentioned earlier," he said, "that it's possible to 'pass' information to the event procedure functions. Would that be a way to streamline the four event procedure functions we have into two, or possible just one function?"

"Excellent question Dave," I said, "you must be a mind-reader. That's exactly what I'd like to do next. Let's code only one event procedure function for the Radio Button objects, and one event procedure function for the Button objects. However, in order to determine exactly which Radio Button or Button object has been clicked, we'll need to modify the event procedure functions to accept an argument that passes the name of the object that has been clicked. Let me show you."

I then modified the code in the 'events.js' to look like this....

```
//events.js
function radQuestion_Click(ButtonName) {
  if (ButtonName == "Yes") {
    alert("Yes Radio Button has been clicked")
  }
  if (ButtonName == "No") {
    alert("No Radio Button has been clicked")
  }
}
function Button_Click(ButtonName) {
  if (ButtonName == "Button1") {
    alert("Button1 has been clicked")
  }
  if (ButtonName == "Button2") {
    alert("Button2 has been clicked")
  }
}
```

"Notice," I said, "that we now have just two functions. The first, radQuestion_Click(), accepts a single argument called ButtonName, which will contain a value indicating which one of the two Radio Button objects has been clicked. The second function, Button_Click(), also accepts a single argument called ButtonName to do the same thing. Let's modify Example12-3.htm to call these event procedures."

I then displayed this code on the classroom projector.

```
<! Example12-4 -- >
<html>
<head>
<script src='events.js'></script>
<title>GUI Demo with Event Procedures</title>
</head>
<body>
<form name="myForm">
<table border="1" width="143">
  <tr>
    <td width="59"><input type="radio" name="radQuestion" value="Yes"
                  onclick="radQuestion_Click(value)">Yes</td>
    <td width="68"><input type="button" name="btn1" value="Button1"
                  onclick="Button_Click(value)"></td>
  </tr>
  <tr>
    <td width="59"><input type="radio" name="radQuestion" value="No"
                  onclick="radQuestion_Click(value)" >No</td>
    <td width="68"><input type="button" name="btn2" value="Button2"
                  onclick="Button_Click(value)"></td>
  </tr>
```

```
</table>
</form>
</body>

</html>
```

I then saved the program as 'Example12-4.htm' and opened it up within my Internet Browser. When I clicked on each of the individual GUI objects, an alert box displayed a message indicating which one had been clicked.

"Now our GUI is really intelligent," I said. "And best of all, we reduced the number of event procedures from four to two. In fact, it wouldn't take much work to reduce the code in 'events.js' to just a single event procedure. Let's take a look at the code that lets our Radio Button objects know what event procedure function to execute when the user clicks on them. Notice that this code is a little different from the previous version, in that it is passing an argument to the function..."

```
<td width="59"><input type="radio" name="radQuestion" value="Yes"
   onclick="radQuestion_Click(value)">Yes
</td>
```

"What does the *value* argument mean?" Ward asked.

"value," I said, "is the parameter we used to designate the caption for the Radio Button when we defined it. We initialized it to 'Yes', and we then use this argument in the radQuestion_Click event procedure to determine which of the two Radio Buttons has been clicked...."

```
function radQuestion_Click(ButtonName) {
  if (ButtonName == "Yes") {
    alert("Yes Radio Button has been clicked")
  }
  if (ButtonName == "No") {
    alert("No Radio Button has been clicked")
  }
}
```

"ButtonName," I said, "is the name of the argument in the radQuestion_Click function. When this function is called from our GUI program, the caption of the Radio Button is passed to it, and used within the if statement."

"So value," Linda said, "really just refers to the caption of the Radio Button object that's being clicked."

"Exactly Linda," I said. "Both Radio Button click events trigger the same event procedure function. In a similar way, a click of the Button object triggers the Button_Click event procedure, which is also expecting a single argument representing the caption of the Button. Here's the coding for the Button object in our GUI..."

```
<td width="68"><input type="button" name="btn1" value="Button1"
   onclick="Button_Click(value)">
</td>
```

"...and here's the function Button_Click..."

```
function Button_Click(ButtonName) {
if (ButtonName == "Button1") {
alert("Button1 has been clicked")
}
if (ButtonName == "Button2") {
alert("Button2 has been clicked")
}
}
```

I paused to see if I had lost anyone---it looked like everyone understood what was going on.

"If we wanted to," I continued, "we could write a single event procedure function and have each one of our four GUI objects execute that function when they are clicked. Since each one of them has a unique value parameter, we could then use that as a passed argument to display a unique message. Here's what that function might look like..."

```
//events.js
```

```
function Button_Click(ButtonName) {
   alert(ButtonName + " Button1 has been clicked")
}
```

"Wow, that's streamlined," Mary said.

"Of course, if we did that," I added, "we would need to execute the same event procedure for each of our two Radio Buttons and Button objects, like this..."

```
<! Example12-5 -- >
<html>
<head>
<script src='events.js'></script>
<title>GUI Demo with Event Procedures</title>
</head>
<body>
<form name="myForm">
<table border="1" width="143">
 <tr>
  <td width="59"><input type="radio" name="radQuestion" value="Yes"
                  onclick="Button_Click(value)">Yes</td>
  <td width="68"><input type="button" name="btn1" value="Button1"
                  onclick="Button_Click(value)"></td>
 </tr>
 <tr>
  <td width="59"><input type="radio" name="radQuestion" value="No"
                  onclick="Button_Click(value)" >No</td>
  <td width="68"><input type="button" name="btn2" value="Button2"
                  onclick="Button_Click(value)"></td>
 </tr>
</table>
</form>
</body>
</html>
```

I then saved both the new version of '**events.js**' and '**Example12-5.htm**', and opened Example12-5.htm in my Internet Browser. As promised, when I clicked on each one of the GUI objects, a unique message was displayed informing me as to which object had been clicked.

My students were obviously impressed.

"I can see that the ability to pass information onto an event procedure in this way can be extremely useful," Barbara said.

"Absolutely right Barbara," I agreed, "Information like this gives our Event Procedures intelligence as to what GUI objects triggered the event, and allows us to 'fine tune' our reaction to the event based on the object that triggers it. As I mentioned earlier, however, I try not to get too fancy when I write event procedure functions. There's certainly nothing wrong with writing separate event procedure functions for each GUI object on your form."

I glanced the computer lab, and could see a number of students coding up their own versions of GUI and Event Procedures--obviously fascinated with this newfound ability.

Passing your Event Procedure a reference to your GUI object

"Is there anyway to manipulate the object that triggers an event from its Event Procedure?" Dave asked.

"What do you mean Dave," Linda asked.

"For instance," he said, "could you change the Caption of a button when the user clicks on it?"

"Interesting that you should ask that question Dave," I said. "I was about to ask the class the same thing."

"Is there ever a need to do such as thing?" Mary asked.

"Yes there is," I said. "In fact, we'll need to update the GUI in the Grades Calculation program in order to display the calculated numeric and letter grade. Remember, we designed the GUI with two Text Fields that we can display those values in."

"That's right," Linda said, "I had forgotten about that."

"Is that going to be a problem?" Kate asked. "Can't we refer to or update an object on our Form from within the Event Procedure function?"

"It's not a problem Kate," I said, "we just need to be sure we refer to the form using the proper syntax. As you'll see in a moment, that's where the name of the form comes in. Let's modify the function we just wrote to change the caption of btn1, if that's the button that's been clicked, so that it displays our favorite programming language."

```
//events.js
function Button_Click(ButtonName) {
  alert(ButtonName + " Button has been clicked")
  if (ButtonName == "Button1") {
    document.myForm.btn1.value = "I Love JavaScript"
  }
}
```

"As you can see," I said, "I added an If statement to the Button_Click function. It checks to see if the object that has been clicked is btn1. If it is, then we set the value property of btn1 to 'I Love JavaScript. Notice that we need to tell JavaScript the name of our form, in this case myForm. The form is part of the hierarchy within the HTML Document Object Model, which is why we need to preface the name of our form with the word 'document...'"

document.myForm.btn1.value = "I Love JavaScript"

"That makes sense," Ward said. "It really seems easy to work with objects on the form from within our function."

"It really is," I said, "and it will be crucial when we finish up the code in the Grades Calculation project in a few moments."

"Do we need to change any of our code in Example12-5.htm?" Rhonda asked.

"No, not at all," I said, "all we had to do was change the code in our Button_Click() function. Let's load up Example12-5.htm again, and see what happens when we click on Button1."

I did exactly that. When I clicked on the Button captioned 'Button1', the following screenshot was displayed.

"...and then the caption of Button1 was changed..."

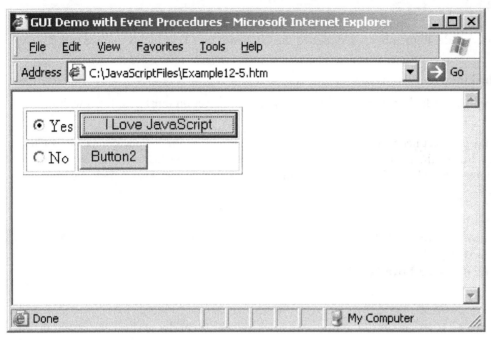

"Wow, the caption of the button changed!" Rhonda said.

"Aren't Event Procedures great!" I said. "The code in the Button_Click() function was triggered when we clicked on Button1, and used an If statement to determine if the event was triggered by Button1. It was, and so it changed the caption of Button1 by modifying the value property of the btn1 object…"

```
if (ButtonName == "Button1") {
    document.myForm.btn1.value = "I Love JavaScript"
}
```

"Extremely powerful," Ward said, "I can see a lot of application for code like this back at work. Is it time to modify the Grades Calculation project now? I can't wait to see what we do with it?"

Implementing Event Procedures in the Grades Calculation Project

Fifteen minutes later I was about to begin discussing the Grades Calculation Project modifications we were about to make when I noticed two people approach our classroom door. It was Rose and Jack--back from their long journey!

"Rose and Jack," I said, "Welcome back. It's great to see you! I was getting a little worried that you might not make it back in time for our final class."

"Professor Smiley has been keeping us apprised of the development with the Grades Calculation Project," Rose explained to the class. "And of course, we took our laptops along with us. We're right on pace…well, just about on pace, to complete the course, and the project, with all of you. I don't think we've missed a beat."

"I'm glad that you both were able to be with us today," I said. "Your attendance will help put a nice close to the project we all started together so many weeks ago. Let's start making those changes to the Grades Calculation project now. The first thing we need to do is modify each one of the Student classes."

"Why is that?" Rhonda asked. "I thought they were working perfectly fine."

"We'll be using the Student classes in interaction with our GUI to calculate the student's grade," I said, "and as part of that, we'll need to execute the calculate() method of each one of those classes. But there's a problem."

I saw quite a few puzzled looks on the faces of my students.

"Right now," I said, "when we execute the calculate() methods of the student classes, the code in each displays Prompt boxes for the input of the student grade components, and then displays the result in an alert box."

"We don't need to do that," Kate said, "our GUI takes care of the input of the component grades via our four Text Fields, and takes care of the display of the final letter and numeric grade on the form in the captions of our display only Text Fields."

"Absolutely right Kate," I said, "the calculate() methods of those classes simply won't work with our GUI. We need a calculate() method that uses the values the user enters into the Text Fields."

"Does that mean we need to modify the way the Calculate() methods work in those classes?" Kate asked.

"If we do that," Ward chimed in, "then we won't be able to use the non-GUI version of the project we've written."

"Ward's right," I said, "if we modify the way the existing calculate() methods work, the version of the Grades Calculation project that doesn't use the GUI will no longer work."

"Is that a problem?" Linda asked. "Is anyone likely to use that version?"

"That's a good question Linda," I said, "In general, in the programming world, it's a good idea to avoid 'breaking' or disable the functionality of existing code. Even though it's not likely anyone will ever use that version of the program, we can't be absolutely sure. For that reason, we'll create another method, called calculateGUI() designed to calculate grades---but specifically NOT to generate any display of the final letter or numeric grade. Instead, those properties will be updated, and our GradesGUI.htm program will be modified to update our GUI with the values of those properties."

"Will we need to make this modification for all our Student classes?" Valerie asked.

"Absolutely correct, Valerie," I said. "For each one of the Student classes, we'll create a calculateGUI() method."

I waited to see if there were any questions before distributing this exercise for the class to complete.

Exercise 12-1 Modify the EnglishStudent Class to include the calculateGUI() method

In this exercise, you'll modify the EnglishStudent class to include a calculateGUI() method.

1. Using Notepad (if you are using Windows) locate and open the EnglishStudent.js source file you worked on last week. (It should be in the \JavaScriptFiles\Grades folder)
2. Modify your code so that it looks like this.

```
//EnglishStudent Class

function EnglishStudent() {

var ENGLISH_MIDTERM_PERCENTAGE = .25
var ENGLISH_FINALEXAM_PERCENTAGE = .25
var ENGLISH_RESEARCH_PERCENTAGE = .30
var ENGLISH_PRESENTATION_PERCENTAGE = .20
var midterm = 0
var finalExamGrade = 0
var research = 0
var presentation = 0
var finalNumericGrade = 0
var finalLetterGrade = ""

this.calculate=calculate
this.calculateGUI=calculateGUI
this.displayGrade=displayGrade
this.getFinalNumericGrade=getFinalNumericGrade
this.getFinalLetterGrade=getFinalLetterGrade
this.setMidterm=setMidterm
this.setFinalExamGrade=setFinalExamGrade
this.setResearch=setResearch
this.setPresentation=setPresentation

function setMidterm(temp) {
  if (parseInt(temp) < 0 | parseInt(temp) > 100) {
    alert("Invalid Midterm Grade (" + temp + ") Program Terminating")
    exit
  }
  else
    midterm = temp
}

function setFinalExamGrade(temp) {
  if (parseInt(temp) < 0 | parseInt(temp) > 100) {
```

```
      alert("Invalid Final Exam Grade (" + temp + ") Program Terminating")
      exit
    }
    else
      finalExamGrade= temp
    }
function setResearch(temp) {
  if (temp < 0 | temp > 100) {
    alert("Invalid Research Grade (" + temp + ") Program Terminating")
    exit
  }
  else
    research = temp
  }
function setPresentation(temp) {
  if (temp < 0 | temp > 100) {
    alert("Invalid Presentation Grade (" + temp + ") Program Terminating")
    exit
  }
  else
    presentation = temp
}

function getFinalNumericGrade() {
  return finalNumericGrade
}

function getFinalLetterGrade() {
  return finalLetterGrade
}

function calculate() {
  setMidterm(parseInt(prompt("Enter the Midterm Grade","")))
  setFinalExamGrade(parseInt(prompt("Enter the Final Examination Grade","" )))
  setResearch(parseInt(prompt("Enter the Research Grade","")))
  setPresentation(parseInt(prompt("Enter the Presentation Grade","")))
  finalNumericGrade =
    (midterm * ENGLISH_MIDTERM_PERCENTAGE) +
    (finalExamGrade * ENGLISH_FINALEXAM_PERCENTAGE) +
    (research * ENGLISH_RESEARCH_PERCENTAGE) +
    (presentation * ENGLISH_PRESENTATION_PERCENTAGE)
  if (finalNumericGrade >= 93)
    finalLetterGrade = "A"
  else
  if ((finalNumericGrade >= 85) & (finalNumericGrade < 93))
    finalLetterGrade = "B"
  else
  if ((finalNumericGrade >= 78) & (finalNumericGrade < 85))
    finalLetterGrade = "C"
  else
  if ((finalNumericGrade >= 70) & (finalNumericGrade < 78))
    finalLetterGrade = "D"
  else
  if (finalNumericGrade < 70)
    finalLetterGrade = "F"
}

function calculateGUI() {
  finalNumericGrade =
```

```
      (midterm * ENGLISH_MIDTERM_PERCENTAGE) +
      (finalExamGrade * ENGLISH_FINALEXAM_PERCENTAGE) +
      (research * ENGLISH_RESEARCH_PERCENTAGE) +
      (presentation * ENGLISH_PRESENTATION_PERCENTAGE)
    if (finalNumericGrade >= 93)
      finalLetterGrade = "A"
    else
    if ((finalNumericGrade >= 85) & (finalNumericGrade < 93))
      finalLetterGrade = "B"
    else
    if ((finalNumericGrade >= 78) & (finalNumericGrade < 85))
      finalLetterGrade = "C"
    else
    if ((finalNumericGrade >= 70) & (finalNumericGrade < 78))
      finalLetterGrade = "D"
    else
    if (finalNumericGrade < 70)
      finalLetterGrade = "F"
}
function displayGrade() {
  alert("*** ENGLISH STUDENT ***\n\n" +
  "Midterm grade is: " + midterm + "\n" +
  "Final Exam is: " + finalExamGrade + "\n" +
  "Research grade is: " + research + "\n" +
  "Presentation grade is: " + presentation + "\n\n" +
  "Final Numeric Grade is: " + finalNumericGrade + "\n" +
  "Final Letter Grade is: " + finalLetterGrade)
}
}
```

3. Save your source file as '**EnglishStudent.js**' in the \JavaScriptFiles\Grades folder (select File-Save As from Notepad's Menu Bar). Be sure to save your source file with the file name extension 'js'.

4. You won't be testing your modified EnglishStudent class until we have completed the work on the other classes in the project.

Discussion

"It looks like all we've done is add another calculate() method to the EnglishStudent class," Rhonda said.

"That's close Rhonda," I said. "We've added a method to our class called calculateGUI() which is similar to the already existing calculate() method. The calculate() method we wrote a few weeks ago prompts the user for the component grade pieces by executing the Prompt() method. The calculateGUI() method that we just added to the EnglishStudent uses four properties---midterm, finalExamGrade, research and presentation---to perform its calculation.

```
midterm * ENGLISH_MIDTERM_PERCENTAGE) +
  (finalExamGrade * ENGLISH_FINALEXAM_PERCENTAGE) +
  (research * ENGLISH_RESEARCH_PERCENTAGE) +
  (presentation * ENGLISH_PRESENTATION_PERCENTAGE)
```

"It then updates the finalNumericGrade and finalLetterGrade properties accordingly..."

```
if (finalNumericGrade >= 93)
    finalLetterGrade = "A"
  else
  if ((finalNumericGrade >= 85) & (finalNumericGrade < 93))
    finalLetterGrade = "B"
  else
  if ((finalNumericGrade >= 78) & (finalNumericGrade < 85))
    finalLetterGrade = "C"
```

```
    else
    if ((finalNumericGrade >= 70) & (finalNumericGrade < 78))
      finalLetterGrade = "D"
    else
    if (finalNumericGrade < 70)
      finalLetterGrade = "F"
}
```

"By the way," I said, "don't forget this crucial line of code..."

this.calculateGUI=calculateGUI

"...this 'registers' our calculateGUI() method with JavaScript. Without it, no instance of our EnglishStudent class could execute the method."

"How will those four properties be updated?" Dave asked. "In the current version of the program, the calculate() method property the user to enter the component grade pieces. I presume the EnglishStudent Properties will be updated via the Text Fields on our GUI?"

"That's right Dave," I said. "When the user clicks on the Calculate button, based on the type of student he or she is calculating, an appropriate Student object will be instantiated, and the component grade values from the GUI will then update the objects properties. Most of this work will take place in the modified GradesGUI.htm program we'll work on at the end of this class."

I waited to see if there were more questions--there were none. I then distributed this exercise for the class to complete.

Exercise 12-2 Modify the MathStudent Class to include the calculateGUI() method

In this exercise, you'll modify the EnglishStudent class to include a calculateGUI() method.

1. Using Notepad (if you are using Windows) locate and open the MathStudent.js source file you worked on last week. (It should be in the \JavaScriptFiles\Grades folder)
2. Modify your code so that it looks like this. (Modified code is in green)

```
//MathStudent Class
function MathStudent() {

var MATH_MIDTERM_PERCENTAGE = .50
var MATH_FINALEXAM_PERCENTAGE = .50
var midterm = 0
var finalExamGrade = 0
var finalNumericGrade = 0
var finalLetterGrade = ""

this.calculate=calculate
this.calculateGUI=calculateGUI
this.displayGrade=displayGrade
this.getFinalNumericGrade=getFinalNumericGrade
this.getFinalLetterGrade=getFinalLetterGrade
this.setMidterm=setMidterm
this.setFinalExamGrade=setFinalExamGrade

function setMidterm(temp) {
  if (parseInt(temp) < 0 | parseInt(temp) > 100) {
    alert("Invalid Midterm Grade (" + temp + ") Program Terminating")
    exit
  }
  else
    midterm = temp
}
function setFinalExamGrade(temp) {
  if (parseInt(temp) < 0 | parseInt(temp) > 100) {
    alert("Invalid Final Exam Grade (" + temp + ") Program Terminating")
```

```
      exit
    }
    else
      finalExamGrade= temp
    }
function getFinalNumericGrade() {
  return finalNumericGrade
}
function getFinalLetterGrade() {
  return finalLetterGrade
}
function calculate() {
  setMidterm(parseInt(prompt("Enter the Midterm Grade","")))
  setFinalExamGrade(parseInt(prompt("Enter the Final Examination Grade","" )))
  finalNumericGrade =
    (midterm * MATH_MIDTERM_PERCENTAGE) +
    (finalExamGrade * MATH_FINALEXAM_PERCENTAGE)
  if (finalNumericGrade >= 90)
    finalLetterGrade = "A"
  else
  if ((finalNumericGrade >= 83) & (finalNumericGrade < 90))
    finalLetterGrade = "B"
  else
  if ((finalNumericGrade >= 76) & (finalNumericGrade < 83))
    finalLetterGrade = "C"
  else
  if ((finalNumericGrade >= 65) & (finalNumericGrade < 76))
    finalLetterGrade = "D"
  else
  if (finalNumericGrade < 65)
    finalLetterGrade = "F"
}
function calculateGUI() {
  finalNumericGrade =
    (midterm * MATH_MIDTERM_PERCENTAGE) +
    (finalExamGrade * MATH_FINALEXAM_PERCENTAGE)
  if (finalNumericGrade >= 90)
    finalLetterGrade = "A"
  else
  if ((finalNumericGrade >= 83) & (finalNumericGrade < 90))
    finalLetterGrade = "B"
  else
  if ((finalNumericGrade >= 76) & (finalNumericGrade < 83))
    finalLetterGrade = "C"
  else
  if ((finalNumericGrade >= 65) & (finalNumericGrade < 76))
    finalLetterGrade = "D"
  else
  if (finalNumericGrade < 65)
    finalLetterGrade = "F"
}
function displayGrade() {
  alert("*** MATH STUDENT ***\n\n" +
  "Midterm grade is: " + midterm + "\n" +
  "Final Exam is: " + finalExamGrade + "\n\n" +
```

```
      "Final Numeric Grade is: " + finalNumericGrade + "\n" +
      "Final Letter Grade is: " + finalLetterGrade)
}

}
```

3. Save your source file as '**MathStudent.js**' in the \JavaScriptFiles\Grades folder (select File-Save As from Notepad's Menu Bar). Be sure to save your source file with the file name extension 'js'.

4. You won't be testing your modified MathStudent class until we have completed the work on the other classes in the project.

Discussion

No one had any major problems completing the exercise, although several students did make the typical case sensitivity typos, and one student forgot to 'register' the calculateGUI() method

"It's extremely important to be sure that the method names are spelled correctly," I said, "and that the names match the 'registration' information in the top of the class."

Fortunately, I discovered these errors as I strode around the classroom. I wanted to be sure that all of my students had a good, working program by the end of today's class."

"As was the case in the EnglishStudent class," I said, "what we've done here is to add a calculateGUI() method to the MathStudent class. As you would expect, since the calculation for a Math student is not the same as a calculation for an English student, the code is a bit different."

Everyone (especially Rose and Jack) seemed anxious to continue coding, and so I distributed this exercise to the class to complete.

Exercise 12-3 Modify the ScienceStudent Class to include the calculateGUI() method

In this exercise, you'll modify the ScienceStudent class to include a calculateGUI() method.

1. Using Notepad (if you are using Windows) locate and open the ScienceStudent.js source file you worked on last week. (It should be in the \JavaScriptFiles\Grades folder)

2. Modify your code so that it looks like this. (Modified code is in green)

```
//ScienceStudent Class

function ScienceStudent() {

var SCIENCE_MIDTERM_PERCENTAGE = .40
var SCIENCE_FINALEXAM_PERCENTAGE = .40
var SCIENCE_RESEARCH_PERCENTAGE = .20

var midterm = 0
var finalExamGrade = 0
var research = 0
var finalNumericGrade = 0
var finalLetterGrade = ""

this.calculate=calculate
this.calculateGUI=calculateGUI
this.displayGrade=displayGrade
this.getFinalNumericGrade=getFinalNumericGrade
this.getFinalLetterGrade=getFinalLetterGrade
this.setMidterm=setMidterm
this.setFinalExamGrade=setFinalExamGrade
this.setResearch=setResearch

function setMidterm(temp) {
  if (parseInt(temp) < 0 | parseInt(temp) > 100) {
    alert("Invalid Midterm Grade (" + temp + ") Program Terminating")
    exit
  }
  else
```

```javascript
    midterm = temp
}
function setFinalExamGrade(temp) {
  if (parseInt(temp) < 0 | parseInt(temp) > 100) {
    alert("Invalid Final Exam Grade (" + temp + ") Program Terminating")
    exit
  }
  else
    finalExamGrade= temp
}
function setResearch(temp) {
  if (temp < 0 | temp > 100) {
    alert("Invalid Research Grade (" + temp + ") Program Terminating")
    exit
  }
  else
    research = temp
}
function getFinalNumericGrade() {
  return finalNumericGrade
}
function getFinalLetterGrade() {
  return finalLetterGrade
}
function calculate() {
  setMidterm(parseInt(prompt("Enter the Midterm Grade","")))
  setFinalExamGrade(parseInt(prompt("Enter the Final Examination Grade","" )))
  setResearch(parseInt(prompt("Enter the Research Grade","")))
  finalNumericGrade =
    (midterm * SCIENCE_MIDTERM_PERCENTAGE) +
    (finalExamGrade * SCIENCE_FINALEXAM_PERCENTAGE) +
    (research * SCIENCE_RESEARCH_PERCENTAGE)
  if (finalNumericGrade >= 90)
    finalLetterGrade = "A"
  else
  if ((finalNumericGrade >= 80) & (finalNumericGrade < 90))
    finalLetterGrade = "B"
  else
  if ((finalNumericGrade >= 70) & (finalNumericGrade < 80))
    finalLetterGrade = "C"
  else
  if ((finalNumericGrade >= 60) & (finalNumericGrade < 70))
    finalLetterGrade = "D"
  else
  if (finalNumericGrade < 60)
    finalLetterGrade = "F"
}
function calculateGUI() {
  finalNumericGrade =
    (midterm * SCIENCE_MIDTERM_PERCENTAGE) +
    (finalExamGrade * SCIENCE_FINALEXAM_PERCENTAGE) +
    (research * SCIENCE_RESEARCH_PERCENTAGE)
  if (finalNumericGrade >= 90)
    finalLetterGrade = "A"
```

```
  else
  if ((finalNumericGrade >= 80) & (finalNumericGrade < 90))
    finalLetterGrade = "B"
  else
  if ((finalNumericGrade >= 70) & (finalNumericGrade < 80))
    finalLetterGrade = "C"
  else
  if ((finalNumericGrade >= 60) & (finalNumericGrade < 70))
    finalLetterGrade = "D"
  else
  if (finalNumericGrade < 60)
    finalLetterGrade = "F"
}

function displayGrade() {
  alert("*** SCIENCE STUDENT ***\n\n" +
  "Midterm grade is: " + midterm + "\n" +
  "Final Exam is: " + finalExamGrade + "\n" +
  "Research grade is: " + research + "\n\n" +
  "Final Numeric Grade is: " + finalNumericGrade + "\n" +
  "Final Letter Grade is: " + finalLetterGrade)
}

}
```

3. Save your source file as '**ScienceStudent.js**' in the \JavaScriptFiles\Grades folder (select File-Save As from Notepad's Menu Bar). Be sure to save your source file with the file name extension 'js'.

4. You won't be testing your modified ScienceStudent class until we have completed some more work--so be patient!

Discussion

Again, no one had any major problems completing this exercise---everyone properly coded the modifications to the ScienceStudent class.

"What's our next step now?" Rose asked.

"Well," I said, "with the modifications to all three Student classes completed, it's time to turn our attention to creating the three Event Procedure functions we'll be creating for our GUI?"

"Three Event Procedure functions?" Jack asked.

"That's right Jack," I said. "We'll be creating an Event Procedure that will be shared by all three of our Radio Buttons, one Event Procedure for our Calculate button and one Event Procedure for our Reset button."

"That should be a piece of cake if they're similar to the ones you showed us this morning," Kate said.

"They will be similar," I answered. "We start with the Event Procedure for our three Radio Buttons, and we'll call it the radStudentType_Click Event Procedure, and place it a special JavaScript file you create just for your event procedures called events.js file. The main feature of radStudentType_Click()will be to determine which one of the three Radio Buttons representing a Student Type has been clicked, and to then hide or display the appropriate Text Field objects for that Student Type. The Event Procedure will also display, as a caption in a display only Text Field, the Student Type---you'll see that we'll use this as a 'signal' to our Calculate button Event Procedure as to the type of Student object to create."

I then distributed this exercise for the class to complete.

Exercise 12-4 Create the radStudentType_Click() Event Procedure in the events.js file

In this exercise, you'll create a special JavaScript file called events.js, to hold the Event Procedure functions you create today. Then you'll code and place the radStudentType_Click() function in this file.

1. Using Notepad (if you are using Windows) create a new file, and place the following code in it.

```
//events.js

function radStudentType_Click(StudentType) {
  if (StudentType == 'English' ) {
```

```
      document.Grades.txtStudentType.value = 'English'
      document.Grades.txtMidterm.disabled = false
      document.Grades.txtMidterm.value = ''
      document.Grades.txtFinal.disabled = false
      document.Grades.txtFinal.value = ''
      document.Grades.txtResearch.disabled = false
      document.Grades.txtResearch.value = ''
      document.Grades.txtResearch.size = 20
      document.Grades.txtPresentation.disabled = false
      document.Grades.txtPresentation.value = ''
      document.Grades.txtPresentation.size = 20
      document.Grades.txtNumericGrade.value = 'Not yet'
      document.Grades.txtLetterGrade.value = 'Not yet'
      document.Grades.txtMidterm.focus()
   }

   if (StudentType == 'Math' ) {
      document.Grades.txtStudentType.value = 'Math'
      document.Grades.txtMidterm.disabled = false
      document.Grades.txtMidterm.value = ''
      document.Grades.txtFinal.disabled = false
      document.Grades.txtFinal.value = ''
      document.Grades.txtResearch.disabled = true
      document.Grades.txtResearch.visible = false
      document.Grades.txtResearch.value = 'N/A'
      document.Grades.txtResearch.size = 1
      document.Grades.txtPresentation.disabled = true
      document.Grades.txtPresentation.value = 'N/A'
      document.Grades.txtPresentation.size = 1
      document.Grades.txtNumericGrade.value = 'Not yet'
      document.Grades.txtLetterGrade.value = 'Not yet'
      document.Grades.txtMidterm.focus()
   }
}

   if (StudentType == 'Science' ) {
      document.Grades.txtStudentType.value= 'Science'
      document.Grades.txtMidterm.disabled = false
      document.Grades.txtMidterm.value = ''
      document.Grades.txtFinal.disabled = false
      document.Grades.txtFinal.value = ''
      document.Grades.txtResearch.disabled = false
      document.Grades.txtResearch.value = ''
      document.Grades.txtResearch.size = 20
      document.Grades.txtPresentation.disabled = true
      document.Grades.txtPresentation.value = 'N/A'
      document.Grades.txtPresentation.size = 1
      document.Grades.txtNumericGrade.value = 'Not yet'
      document.Grades.txtLetterGrade.value = 'Not yet'
      document.Grades.txtMidterm.focus()
   }

}
```

2. Save your source file as **'events.js'** in the \JaveScriptFiles\Grades folder (select File-Save As from Notepad's Menu Bar). Be sure to save your source file with the file name extension 'js'.

3. You won't be testing the radStudentType_Click() Event Procedure until you complete your work on GradesGUI.htm in Exercise 12-7.

Discussion

No one seemed to have any problems completing the exercise.

"Let's take a look at the code in our radStudentType_Click() Event Procedure function," I said. "This code may look confusing---but I think as soon as I explain it, you'll see what's going on."

I paused before continuing.

"The function header," I said, "reflects the fact that we'll be passing a single argument to our Event Procedure..."

function radStudentType_Click(StudentType) {

"What we'll be doing," I said, "is calling our Event Procedure, and passing a value equal to the caption of the Radio Button that has been clicked. In this way, our Event Procedure will know what Radio Button has been clicked."

"Where's the calculation taking place?" Rhonda asked.

"The radStudentType_Click() event procedure isn't responsible for the calculation," I said. "It's responsible for 'setting up' the GUI to accept the appropriate grade component pieces. For instance, if the user clicks on the English Student Radio Button..."

if (StudentType == 'English') {

"...this is the code we execute, first setting the caption of the txtStudentType Text field to 'English'..."

document.Grades.txtStudentType.value = 'English'

"...then we set the disabled Property of the txtMidterm Text Field to false, in effect enabling it..."

document.Grades.txtMidterm.disabled = false

"...then we 'null' out whatever value is currently stored in the Text Field..."

document.Grades.txtMidterm.value = ''

"...Since the English Student calculation requires values for all four component pieces grades, we do the same thing for the txtFinal, txtResearch, and txtPresentation Text Fields as well..."

```
document.Grades.txtFinal.disabled = false
document.Grades.txtFinal.value = ''
document.Grades.txtResearch.disabled = false
document.Grades.txtResearch.value = ''
document.Grades.txtResearch.size = 20
document.Grades.txtPresentation.disabled = false
document.Grades.txtPresentation.value = ''
document.Grades.txtPresentation.size = 20
```

"Why are we setting the size property of txtResearch and txtPresentation to 20?" Dave asked.

"Good question Dave," I said, "I almost forgot. If the Student Type selected by the user DOES NOT require the entry of a component grade piece, we disable that Text Field and also set its size to 1--making it obvious that no entry should be made in it. Because there's the possibility that the Text Field may have been re-sized to 1, when the user selects a Student Type of 'English', it's important to set the Text Field to its original size--which is 20."

I waited for more questions before continuing.

"Finally," I said, "we place 'Not yet' into the txtNumericGrade and txtLetterGrade Text Fields, and execute the focus() method on the txtMidterm Textfield. Placing 'Not yet' into these two Text Fields let's the user know that the student's grade has not yet been calculated.

```
document.Grades.txtNumericGrade.value = 'Not yet'
document.Grades.txtLetterGrade.value = 'Not yet'
document.Grades.txtMidterm.focus()
}
```

"What's the function of executing the focus() method?" Ward asked.

"The focus() method," I set, "places the cursor in the txtMidterm Text Field."

"That makes sense," Rose said, "since the Midterm Grade should probably be the first entry the user makes."

"Absolutely Rose, " I said. "This process is then repeated, checking for the other two Student types. Notice that for a Math student, we set the disabled properties of two Text Fields---txtResearch and txtPresentation---to true, and also set their sizes to 1, along with placing 'N/A' in the Text Field..."

```
if (StudentType == 'Math' ) {
  document.Grades.txtStudentType.value = 'Math'
  document.Grades.txtMidterm.disabled = false
  document.Grades.txtMidterm.value = ''
  document.Grades.txtFinal.disabled = false
  document.Grades.txtFinal.value = ''
  document.Grades.txtResearch.disabled = true
  document.Grades.txtResearch.visible = false
  document.Grades.txtResearch.value = 'N/A'
  document.Grades.txtResearch.size = 1
  document.Grades.txtPresentation.disabled = true
  document.Grades.txtPresentation.value = 'N/A'
  document.Grades.txtPresentation.size = 1
  document.Grades.txtNumericGrade.value = 'Not yet'
  document.Grades.txtLetterGrade.value = 'Not yet'
  document.Grades.txtMidterm.focus()
}
```

"...setting their size property to 1 will make the Text Field very 'narrow', which you will see when we execute GradesGUI in a few minutes. In conjunction to placing 'N/A' into the Text Field, this will provide a valuable visual cue that nothing is to be entered into the Text Field...."

"Cool, very cool," I heard Jack say.

"For a Science Student," I said, "the code is very similar--except that only the Presentation Text Field is disabled..."

```
if (StudentType == 'Science' ) {
  document.Grades.txtStudentType.value= 'Science'
  document.Grades.txtMidterm.disabled = false
  document.Grades.txtMidterm.value = ''
  document.Grades.txtFinal.disabled = false
  document.Grades.txtFinal.value = ''
  document.Grades.txtResearch.disabled = false
  document.Grades.txtResearch.value = ''
  document.Grades.txtResearch.size = 20
  document.Grades.txtPresentation.disabled = true
  document.Grades.txtPresentation.value = 'N/A'
  document.Grades.txtPresentation.size = 1
  document.Grades.txtNumericGrade.value = 'Not yet'
  document.Grades.txtLetterGrade.value = 'Not yet'
  document.Grades.txtMidterm.focus()
}
```

"What do you think folks?" I said, "are you confused?"

"On the contrary," Rhonda said excitedly, "I can't wait to see this code execute. Disabling and narrowing Text Fields--sounds like magic."

"Unfortunately," I said, "we won't be able to test the radStudentType_Click Event Procedure until we're done with the rest of our exercises."

No one had any questions, and so it was time to move onto coding the CalculateButtonEvent Procedure class.

"The btnCalculate_Click() Event Procedure," I said, "is probably the most complex of the Event Procedures we'll write today. There will be no need to determine which of the two Buttons have been clicked, as this Event Procedure will only be executed when the Calculate Button is clicked. However, we will need to determine the caption for the txtStudentType Text Field object, and depending upon its value, instantiate either an EnglishStudent, MathStudent or ScienceStudent object, set its Grade Component Properties, and execute its calculateGUI() method.

Once that's done, the btnCalculate_Click() Event Procedure will display the student's final numeric and letter grades on the GUI."

I then distributed this exercise for the class to complete.

Exercise 12-5 Create the CalculateGrade() Event Procedure in the events.js file

In this exercise, you'll create the btnCalculateGrade_Click() Event Procedure for the Grades Calculation project.

1. Using Notepad (if you are using Windows) place the following code in the events.js file you created in Exercise 12-5. You already have one function in there called radStudentType_Click. Add this one after it.

```
function btnCalculateGrade_Click(StudentType) {
 if (StudentType == 'English' ) {
  var x = new EnglishStudent()
  x.setMidterm(document.Grades.txtMidterm.value)
  x.setFinalExamGrade(document.Grades.txtFinal.value)
  x.setResearch(document.Grades.txtResearch.value)
  x.setPresentation(document.Grades.txtPresentation.value)
  x.calculateGUI()
  document.Grades.txtNumericGrade.value = x.getFinalNumericGrade()
  document.Grades.txtLetterGrade.value= x.getFinalLetterGrade()
 }


 if (StudentType == 'Math' ) {
  var y = new MathStudent()
  y.setMidterm(document.Grades.txtMidterm.value)
  y.setFinalExamGrade(document.Grades.txtFinal.value)
  y.calculateGUI()
  document.Grades.txtNumericGrade.value = y.getFinalNumericGrade()
  document.Grades.txtLetterGrade.value= y.getFinalLetterGrade()
 }

 if (StudentType == 'Science' ) {
  var z = new ScienceStudent()
  z.setMidterm(document.Grades.txtMidterm.value)
  z.setFinalExamGrade(document.Grades.txtFinal.value)
  z.setResearch(document.Grades.txtResearch.value)
  z.calculateGUI()
  document.Grades.txtNumericGrade.value = z.getFinalNumericGrade()
  document.Grades.txtLetterGrade.value= z.getFinalLetterGrade()
 }
}
```

2. Save your source file as **'events.js'** in the \JaveScriptFiles\Grades folder (select File-Save As from Notepad's Menu Bar). Be sure to save your source file with the file name extension 'js'.
3. You won't be testing the btnCalculateGrade_Click() Event Procedure until you complete your work on GradesGUI.htm in Exercise 12-7.

Discussion

Again, no one seemed to have any problem completing the exercise.

"Let's take a look at the code in our btnCalculateGrade_Click() Event Procedure class," I said. "As you saw while coding this Event Procedure, it's logic is dependent upon knowing what kind of student type the user wants to calculate. What will happen is this--when the user clicks on the Calculate Button, we'll pass the Event Procedure the value of txtStudentType which will then be used by the Event Procedure to create an appropriate object type. That's why the event procedure function header contains a single argument called StudentType..."

```
function btnCalculateGrade_Click(StudentType) {
```

"If the StudentType is equal to 'English'..."

```
if (StudentType == 'English' ) {
```

"...then we create an instance of an EnglishStudent object..."

```
var x = new EnglishStudent()
```

"...set the Midterm Property of the object equal to the value of the txtMidterm Text Field. by executing the setMidterm() method of the EnglishStudent object. Notice how we use the document object, the name of our Form--Grades---and the name of the Text Field to retrieve that value, and pass it as an argument to setMidterm().."

```
x.setMidterm(document.Grades.txtMidterm.value)
```

"...in the same way, we update the FinalExamGrade, Research and Presentation properties of the English Student object..."

```
x.setFinalExamGrade(document.Grades.txtFinal.value)
x.setResearch(document.Grades.txtResearch.value)
x.setPresentation(document.Grades.txtPresentation.value)
```

"...then we execute the calculateGUI() method of the English Student object. Doing so, calculate the English Student object FinalNumericGrade and FinalLetterGrade properties..."

```
x.calculateGUI()
```

"...then we execute the getFinalNumericGrade() and getFinalLetterGrade() methods of the English Student Object to update the txtNumericGrade and txtLetterGrade Text Fields..."

```
document.Grades.txtNumericGrade.value = x.getFinalNumericGrade()
document.Grades.txtLetterGrade.value= x.getFinalLetterGrade()
}
```

"…we also have If statements to determine if the Event Procedure has been passed an argument equal to 'Math' or 'Science', and appropriate code to instantiate both the MathStudent and ScienceStudent objects."

```
if (StudentType == 'Math' ) {
  var y = new MathStudent()
  y.setMidterm(document.Grades.txtMidterm.value)
  y.setFinalExamGrade(document.Grades.txtFinal.value)
  y.calculateGUI()
  document.Grades.txtNumericGrade.value = y.getFinalNumericGrade()
  document.Grades.txtLetterGrade.value= y.getFinalLetterGrade()
}
if (StudentType == 'Science' ) {
  var z = new ScienceStudent()
  z.setMidterm(document.Grades.txtMidterm.value)
  z.setFinalExamGrade(document.Grades.txtFinal.value)
  z.setResearch(document.Grades.txtResearch.value)
  z.calculateGUI()
  document.Grades.txtNumericGrade.value = z.getFinalNumericGrade()
  document.Grades.txtLetterGrade.value= z.getFinalLetterGrade()
}
```

"Wow, I can't wait to see how this works," Ward said. "This is getting really exciting."

"We'll be able to see this in action in a few minutes," I said. "but first we need to code one more Event Procedure function."

"What's next?" Linda asked.

"The btnReset_Click Event Procedure," I said, "Using this Event Procedure, we'll reset our GUI to the way it looks when our Form is first displayed by making all four of our Text Field enabled, clearing their contents, selecting the English Student Radio Button, and displaying 'English' as the caption of the txtStudentType Text Field Object.."

I then distributed this exercise for the class to complete.

Exercise 12-6 Create the btnReset_Click Event Procedure in the events.js file

In this exercise, you'll create the btnReset_Click() Event Procedure for the Grades Calculation project.

1. Using Notepad (if you are using Windows) place the following code in the events.js file you created in Exercise 12-5. You already have two functions in there called radStudentType_Click and btnCalculateGrade_Click. Add this one after it.

```
function btnReset_Clickl() {
  document.Grades.txtStudentType.value = 'English'
  document.Grades.txtMidterm.disabled = false
  document.Grades.txtMidterm.value = ''
  document.Grades.txtFinal.disabled = false
  document.Grades.txtFinal.value = ''
  document.Grades.txtResearch.disabled = false
  document.Grades.txtResearch.value = ''
  document.Grades.txtResearch.size = 20
  document.Grades.txtPresentation.disabled = false
  document.Grades.txtPresentation.value = ''
  document.Grades.txtPresentation.size = 20
  document.Grades.txtNumericGrade.value = ''
  document.Grades.txtLetterGrade.value = ''
  document.Grades.txtMidterm.focus()
  document.Grades.radStudentType[0].checked = true
}
```

2. Save your source file as **'events.js'** in the \JavaScriptFiles\Grades folder (select File-Save As from Notepad's Menu Bar). Be sure to save your source file with the file name extension 'js'.

3. You won't be testing the btnReset_Click() Event Procedure until you complete your work on GradesGUI.htm in Exercise 12-7.

Discussion

"Let's take a look at the code in our btnReset_Click Event Procedure," I said. "Some of this code you may recognize from the radStudentType_Click event procedure. First, we set the caption of the txtStudentType Text Field to 'English', since that's the Radio Button that we'll be selecting--or checking..."

```
document.Grades.txtStudentType.value = 'English'
```

"...We enable each one of our Text Fields, 'nulling' out whatever values are contained in them, and also setting the size Properties of the txtResearch and txtPresentation Text Fields to 20..."

```
document.Grades.txtMidterm.disabled = false
document.Grades.txtMidterm.value = ''
document.Grades.txtFinal.disabled = false
document.Grades.txtFinal.value = ''
document.Grades.txtResearch.disabled = false
document.Grades.txtResearch.value = ''
document.Grades.txtResearch.size = 20
document.Grades.txtPresentation.disabled = false
document.Grades.txtPresentation.value = ''
document.Grades.txtPresentation.size = 20
```

"...We also 'null' the captions of the txtNumericGrade and txtLetter Text Fields..."

```
document.Grades.txtNumericGrade.value = ''
document.Grades.txtLetterGrade.value = ''
```

"...then we execute the focus() method for the txtMidterm Text Field to place the cursor in it..."

```
document.Grades.txtMidterm.focus()
```

"...finally, we set the checked property of our first Radio Button---the English Student Radio Button---to true.

document.Grades.radStudentType[0].checked = true

"...because our Radio Buttons are a member of a single Radio Button group---and therefore all have the same name---we can't refer to them individually by name, we need to refer to them as if they are members of an array, which they really are."

"This is really interesting code," Jack said. "I find the ability of our Event Procedure to work with objects on the GUI really awesome---I know I'll have a lot of application for this."

I paused for questions before continuing.

"That's it for our Event Procedure classes," I said.

"Are we done now?" Rhonda asked.

"Not quite yet Rhonda," I said. "We have just one more exercise to complete, and that's to modify our DrawGUI program."

"What changes do we have to make to the DrawGUI program?" Lou asked.

"We need to include references to the Event Procedures we just coded," I said, "After that, we'll be ready to fully test the GUI for the Grades Calculation project!"

I then distributed this final exercise for the class to complete.

Exercise 12-7 Modify the GradesGUI project to execute the Event Procedures

In this exercise, you'll modify the GradesGUI.htm program you wrote last week to execute the Event Procedures you just coded.

1. Using Notepad (if you are using Windows) locate and open the GradesGUI.htm source file you worked on last week. (It should be in the \JavaScriptfiles\Grades folder)
2. Modify your code so that it looks like this.

```html
<! GradesGUI -->
<html>
<head>

<script src='events.js'></script>
<script src='functions.js'></script>
<script src='Englishstudent.js'></script>
<script src='MathStudent.js'></script>
<script src='ScienceStudent.js'></script>

<title>Grades Calculator</title>

</head>
<body>

<form name="Grades">
<table border="0">
<tr>
<td><b><u>Student Types</b><u></td>
<td><b><u>Grades</b></u></td>
<td><input type="text" name="txtStudentType" value="English" disabled="true"></td>
<td></td>
</tr>
<tr>
<td><input type="radio" name="radStudentType" onclick="radStudentType_Click(this.value)"
value="English" checked>English Student</td>
<td>Midterm:</td>
<td><input type="text" name="txtMidterm"></td>
<td></td>
</tr>
<tr>
<td><input type="radio" name="radStudentType" onclick="radStudentType_Click(this.value)"
value="Math">Math Student</td>
<td>Final Exam:</td>
```

```
<td><input type="text" name="txtFinal"></td>
<td></td>
</tr>
<tr>
<td><input type="radio" name="radStudentType" onclick="radStudentType_Click(this.value)"
value="Science">Science Student</td>
<td>Research Paper:</td>
<td><input type="text" name="txtResearch"></td>
<td></td>
</tr>
<tr>
<td></td>
<td> Presentation:</td>
<td><input type="text" name="txtPresentation"></td>
<td></td>
</tr>
<tr>
<td><input type="button" name="btnCalculate" onclick="btnCalculate_Click(txtStudentType.value)"
value="Calculate Grade"></td>
<td>Numeric Grade</td>
<td><input type="text" name="txtNumericGrade" value="N/A" disabled="true"></td>
<td></td>
</tr>
<tr>
<td><input type="button" name="btnReset" onclick="btnReset_Clickl()" value="Reset"></td>
<td>Letter Grade</td>
<td><input type="text" name="txtLetterGrade" value = "N/A" disabled="true"></td>
<td></td>
</tr>
</table>
</form>
</body>
</html>
```

2. Save your source file as **'Grades.htm**' in the \JaveScriptFiles\Grades folder (select File-Save As from Notepad's
Menu Bar). Be sure to save your source file with the file name extension 'htm'.

3. Use Internet Explorer to Open your Source File.

4. Your Form should appear. You should notice that the English Student Radio Button is already selected for you,
and that the word 'English' appear as the caption for the txtStudentType Text Field (the Text Field is located in the
upper right hand portion of the Form).

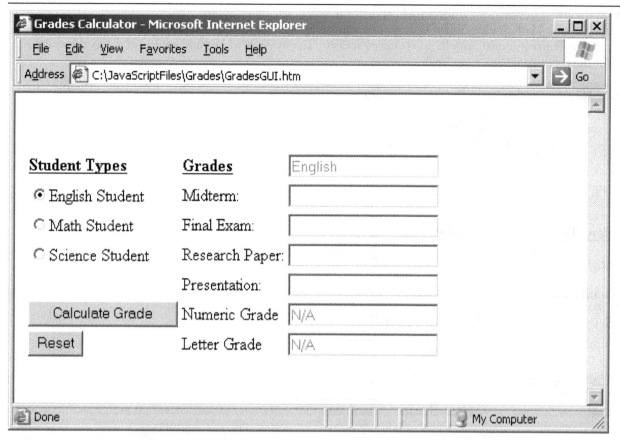

5. We want to calculate the grade for an English Student. When the Form is first displayed, the English Student Radio Button is already selected, so we don't need to select it. Enter 70 into the Midterm Text Field, 80 into the Final Exam Text Field, 90 into the Research Paper Text Field and 100 into the Presentation Text Field. Now click on the Calculate Button. A final numeric grade of 84.5 should be displayed--with a letter grade of 'C', as the captions for the txtNumericGrade and txtLetterGrade Text Field objects.

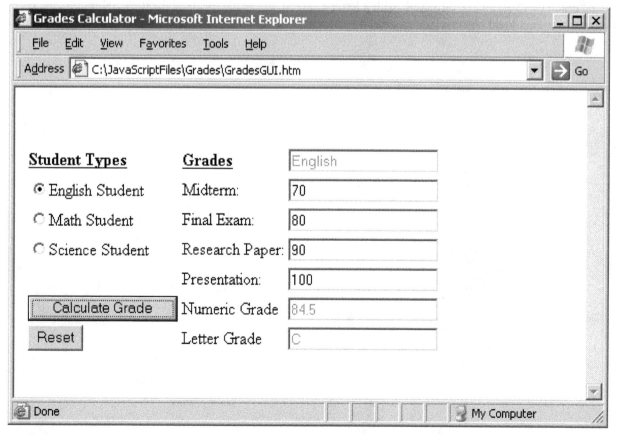

6. Click on the Reset button---the Form should appear the way it was first displayed.
7. Now click on the Math Student Radio Button. The Research Paper and Presentation Text Fields should become disabled, and their size minimal, with 'N/A' as their captions. The word 'Math' should appear in the as the as the caption for the txtStudentType Text Field.

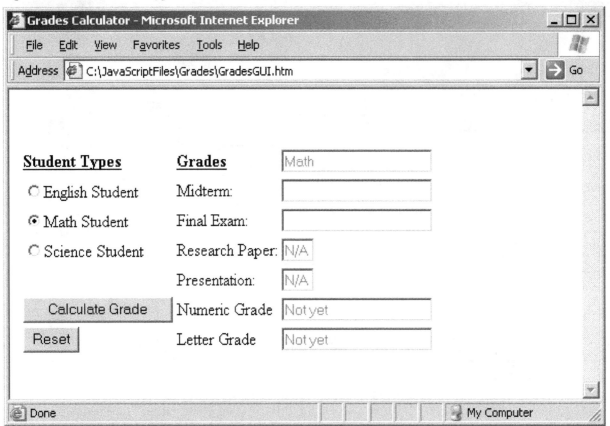

8. Enter 70 into the Midterm Text Field and 80 into the Final Exam Text Field. Click on the Calculate button. A final numeric grade of 75 should be displayed--with a letter grade of 'D', as the captions for the txtNumericGrade and txtLetterGrade Text Field objects.

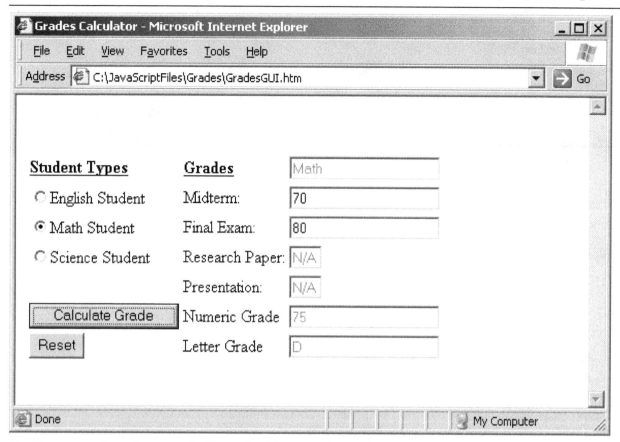

10. Click on the Reset button---the Form should appear the way it did when it was first displayed.

11. Now click on the Science Student Radio Button. The Presentation Text Field should become disabled, and its size minimal, with 'N/A' as its caption. The word 'Science' should appear as the caption for the txtStudentType Text Field.

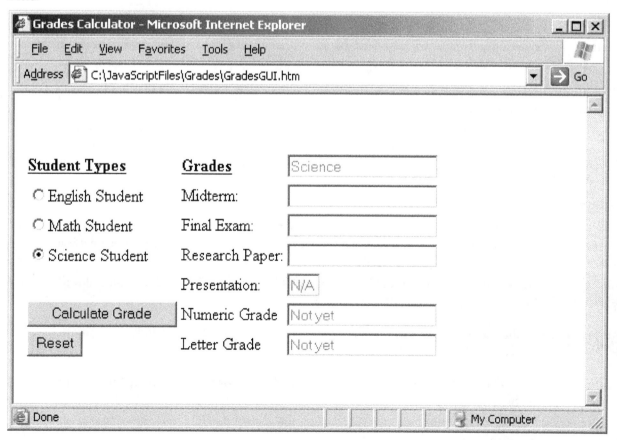

12. Enter 70 into the Midterm Text Field, 80 into the Final Exam Text Field, and 90 into the Research Text Field. A final numeric grade of 78 should be displayed--with a letter grade of 'C', as the captions for the txtNumericGrade and txtLetterGrade Text Field objects.

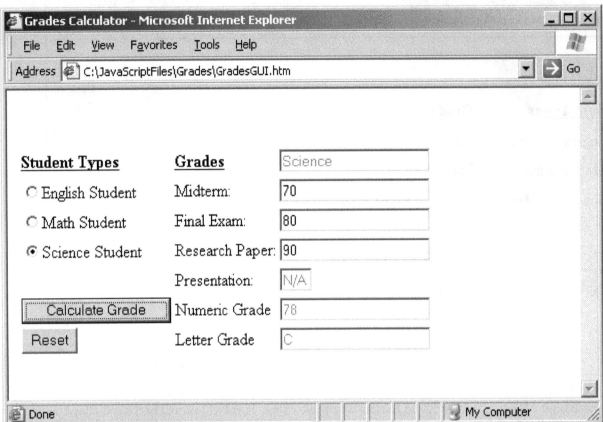

13. Close your program. It is FINISHED!!!

Discussion

"Wow, I'm nearly speechless, and you know how hard that is," Rhonda said. "Those Event Procedures really work great!"

"Yes they do," I agreed.

I could tell that Rhonda wasn't the only one who was impressed.

"Let's take a look at the code that produced this magic," I said. "In actuality, we didn't need to do all that much to achieve it---all we really needed to do was tell JavaScript what functions to execute when our various GUI objects were clicked--and that was pretty easy. The first thing we needed to do was to include a reference to our newly created events.js file..."

```
<script src='events.js'></script>
```

"...then we needed to add code for the click events of the Radio Buttons, and for the Calculate and Reset buttons. In the case of the Radio Buttons, the same event procedure was executed for each one, and we designate it using the onclick tag of the input statement.."

```
<td><input type="radio" name="radStudentType" onclick="radStudentType_Click(this.value)"
value="English" checked>English Student</td>
...
<td><input type="radio" name="radStudentType" onclick="radStudentType_Click(this.value)"
value="Math">Math Student</td>
...
<td><input type="radio" name="radStudentType" onclick="radStudentType_Click(this.value)"
value="Science">Science Student</td>
```

"...notice that we are passing, as an argument to the radStudentType_Click() function, the value of 'this', where this is the Radio Button that's being clicked."

"That's pretty clever," Rhonda said. "JavaScript knows which one of the three buttons has been clicked, and passes the caption, or value, as an argument to the function."

"Exactly Rhonda," I said, who was obviously proud of her understanding of the process.

I paused for a moment before continuing.

"Next up was to code the Click event for the Calculate button," I said. "Once again, we code on the onclick tag of the input statement. As was the case with the Click event for the Radio Button, we are also passing an argument to btnCalculate_Click, in this case, the caption, or value, of the txtStudentType Text Field, which will be used to determine the type of student grade to calculate..."

```
<td><input type="button" name="btnCalculate" onclick="btnCalculate_Click(txtStudentType.value)" value="Calculate Grade"></td>
```

"It really is amazing to see this in action," Ward said, "I can't wait to get back to work and develop some robust GUI's and event procedures."

I had a feeling Ward wasn't the only one in the class looking forward to that prospect.

"Finally," I said, "here's the code for the Reset button. Nothing fancy here, we just execute the btnReset_Click() event procedure---with no arguments necessary. Clicking on the Reset button restores our form to way it was when we first opened our program."

```
<td><input type="button" name="btnReset" onclick="btnReset_Clickl()" value="Reset"></td>
```

"As you can see," I concluded, "with the event procedures written, it's just a matter of telling our program which event procedure to execute when a given event occurs, and letting the event procedures do their work."

"And that they did," Ward said. "So we're done?"

Testing the Program

"That's right Ward," I said, "we're now done with the Grades Calculation Project."

"When do we deliver it?" Mary asked.

"And what version do we deliver?" Linda asked. "Will you be installing your version of the project?"

"When I spoke to Frank Olley earlier in the week," I said, "I explained to him that, excluding my version of the program, we had 18 different versions of the program---and that since this was a student project, I'd rather have him use one of yours, not mine."

I could see some excitement building among the students in the class.

"I invited Frank to visit us today to select the 'winning' project," I said, "but in Frank's mind, you're all winners--and I have to agree. It's going to be hard to select one project to install in the English Department."

"So what are we going to do?" Ward asked.

"Frank had a good suggestion," I said, "and here it is. He suggested that prior to showing up in his department at the end of today's class, that we all pick one version of the program as the one we wish to install in the English Department. So here's what I'm going to ask you to do. I would like everyone to take a few moments to test his or her own version of the program to verify that it's working properly, then come up to the front of the classroom and pick up a voting ballot that I've prepared. Take the ballot, walk around the classroom and observe everyone's project, and then record your vote for what you consider the best project you see. The project that receives the most votes will be the one that we install in the English Department. Again, I'm removing my project from consideration--so please don't vote for mine! This is your project and one of you deserves to have the place of honor in Frank Olley's English Department."

"Can you give us some guidelines on testing our programs?" Linda asked, after a moment or two.

"That's a good question," I said. "Obviously, at a minimum, the program must work---that is, it needs to properly calculate the grade for each one of the three types of students. You should also make sure that the version of the Graphical User Interface you designed is attractive and easy to use."

"I would think that most of the bugs have been discovered by now," Valerie comments.

"I'm not sure we can say that with 100% certainty," I said, "There's always the possibility that something has slipped through our fingers. But I would say that I'm fairly confident that our programs are bug free. Obviously, the more complicated the programs we write, the less certain you can feel, and the more thorough your testing needs to be."

"Is it possible to test each and every combination of grades and student types?" Rhonda asked.

"You're right Rhonda," I said. "There are quite a few possible combinations of different student types and grades, and testing every one of them would be next to impossible We've been testing our programs all along with a scenario for each type of student---and we should take this testing one step further. For instance, test scenarios where each component grade is zero, where one or more component grades, but not all, are zero, where all component grades are 100%, where some are 100%. Above all, make sure you calculate the grades manually first so that you know what the correct answer should be."

"In other words," Dave said, "test the extreme limits of each component."

"That's right Dave," I said. "We saw a few weeks ago how the introduction of a zero into a program can produce errors. Try to 'break' your program now, before you give it to the user to work with."

"I did something similar to what you suggested," Chuck said, "except that I used Excel to develop a worksheet of possible scenarios, with the correct answers, and then ran my program to test as many as I could and verify the correct answer."

"That's a great idea Chuck," I said.

I then gave the class fifteen minutes to test their projects one last time, and then asked them to review and evaluate their fellow students' projects and vote for the project they thought was 'best'. As I collected their ballots and tallied the results, I asked everyone to give me a diskette with a copy of their project on it as well.

"Class is officially dismissed for today," I said. "I hope to see you all in the English Department in a few minutes!"

I called Dave aside. Dave had volunteered to coordinate the installation of the 'winning' program. I handed Dave a diskette containing the project that had received the most votes.

"Dave, would you mind installing this program?" I asked him, "I have a few things to wrap up here."

"Not at all," Dave said, as he glanced at the student's name on the disk and smiled. "That project really was great---I guess it pays to ask a lot of questions! I'll take care of this."

Delivering and Implementing the Grades Calculation Project in the English Department

No sooner had I packed up my things and was preparing to make my way out the door of the classroom than a former student of mine approached me with a problem. Half an hour later, I finally arrived in the English Department.

As I entered, I could hear quite a bit of excited talk and conversation taking place. I could see an incredible amount of activity taking place. The area was packed with students---my students, plus two students whom I recognized as work-study students---plus Frank Olley, David Burton and Robin Aronstrom were there."

Frank Olley caught sight of me.

"John, this program is absolutely great," he said excitedly. "I can't believe what a great job your students did with this. I, David and Robin really love it--plus the two people who really count, the work-study students who will be using it."

Amidst the hullabaloo, I glanced towards the middle of the open space in the English department, and noticed a small table with a computer sitting on it. Seated at the table were the two work-study students, and there was Rhonda, standing in front of the computer, training the two work-study students who would be using her version of the program to calculate grades for the English, Math and Science Departments!.

"Rhonda's been proudly demonstrating her program to our work-study students for the last fifteen minutes," Frank explained. "She's obviously very proud of it, and they love it also--they haven't gotten up from their chairs yet. Rhonda really did a great job with it."

I wandered over to them and caught Rhonda's eye.

"I'm flabbergasted that the class voted for my version of the project," Rhonda said. "To say that this has made my week in an understatement--more like my year. I'm just so honored that someone like me, with absolutely no programming background, could actually write a program like this. I felt like I asked so many stupid questions during the course.."

"Rhonda," I interrupted, "you know what I always say, the only stupid question is the question you don't ask. Your questions were always good ones, plus I know they were questions that some of the other students in the class were dying to ask. By the way, when I put this JavaScript course together, I had someone just like you in mind---an inquisitive person, anxious to learn, but with no programming background. You did a great job."

"Really?" she said, "You know I really enjoyed the course very much. You should consider taking those notes of yours and writing a JavaScript book."

"Maybe I'll do that someday," I told her.

I spent the next few minutes observing the two work-study students---Rita and Gil--work with the program. They had no problem whatsoever with it---Rhonda's GUI was nicely designed, and both of them really seemed to be enjoying working with it.

"Believe me," Rita said, "this is a lot better than the method we had to use before"

"You can say that again," Gil said, "calculating these grades using a calculator was a real pain in the neck."

"From what I can see," I told the assembled class as they gathered around us, "the system works as designed. The ultimate users of the project---Rita and Gil--have been using the program for the last few minutes to calculate grades, and as you've all probably seen, they're extremely pleased with it. I want to thank Dave for installing Rhonda's version of the project on this PC. By installing it, we have begun phase 5 of the SDLC, the Implementation phase. Installation, fine tuning, and training are all part of this phase."

Frank Olley came over and stood right next to me, obviously pleased at the time savings and accuracy the program would achieve. I turned to him and told him that this phase of the SDLC would last for at least the next week.

"Pairs of students have volunteered to be 'on site' during the week to make observations and assist with any problems that might come up," I explained.

"It's comforting to know they'll be here," he said. "What are those notes that I've seen you taking."

"Even though we're now in the midst of phase 5 of the SDLC," I replied, "we can proceed concurrently with phase 6 which is Feedback and Maintenance."

"Feedback and maintenance?" Frank asked.

"We want to make sure that the program is behaving according to the Requirements Statement you and I agreed upon when we agreed to write the program for you," I explained. "A big part of this phase is just observing the system to see how it's being used."

"And how it's being admired," Frank Olley added.

"Positive feedback is a wonderful thing," I said smiling.

"What about program maintenance?" Frank asked.

"The maintenance phase handles any changes to the program that are necessitated by governmental regulations, changes in business rules, or changes that you decide you want to make to the program," I replied.

"After seeing the great work you've done on the project," he said, "I'm sure I'll have more work for your class."

"Sadly though," I said, "this is the end of our introductory JavaScript course. But many, if not all of these students, will be signed up for my Intermediate JavaScript programming course starting in five weeks. Maybe we can work on any enhancements you have then."

Frank Olley seemed happy with that idea, and left me to chat with the two work-study students. Linda, meanwhile, stopped by to see me, and asked to see the notes I had taken..

"Interesting observations," Linda said, "I can see we still have some work to do."

"One thing I think we'll need to work on immediately," I said to her, "is to change the font size of the text on our Form. I can barely see what's going on from here."

"Maybe we can tackle that in the Intermediate class," she said.

"Frank," I said as I approached him, Rhonda and the work-study students, "on behalf of the class, I want to thank you for a wonderful learning experience. I'm sure we'll be in touch."

I shouted across the room to the rest of my students, "I've got to take off now. Everyone please be mindful of your coverage schedules, and if you have any problems at all, you all know where to find me--remember, my email address is johnsmiley@johnsmiley.com. I hope to see you all in five weeks."

Summary

Congratulations! You've finished the Introductory JavaScript class, and completed and implemented the Grades Calculation Project. I hope you felt the excitement of completing, delivering and installing the Grades Calculation project as much as the students in my class did, because you were a big part of it.

What's next? At this point, you should feel confident enough to tackle a variety of JavaScript programs. I hope that by following my introductory computer programming class, you've seen how real-world applications are developed. The step-by-step methodology that we followed to complete the program should be one that you follow in your own programming work.

That's not to say that all projects go as smoothly as this one did. You can expect your share of mistakes, misinterpretations, and misunderstandings along the way. Nonetheless, developing a computer program is always exciting, and if you love it as I do, it's always fun.

As I close, I just want to give you a few words of advice.

First, remember that in programming, there's rarely a single 'correct' solution. Ultimately, if your program achieves the desires of the person who needs to use it, you've developed the 'correct' solution. In the beginning of your programming experience, don't waste your time trying to achieve the best solution. Move onto other projects to broaden your experience.

Second, always be your own best friend. Inevitably, while trying to work through a solution, there will be frustrating moments. Never doubt yourself, and never get 'down' on yourself.

Finally, remember that there is always more to learn. The world of programming is an endless series of free learning seminars. All you need to do is open up a manual, read a Help file, surf the Internet, or pick up a copy of a good book, and you are well on your way. You can never know it all, let along master it all. But always move in that direction. Good luck, and I hope to see you in another JavaScript class some day!

Index